terra australis 25

Terra Australis reports the results of archaeological and related research within the south and east of Asia, though mainly Australia, New Guinea and island Melanesia — lands that remained *terra australis incognita* to generations of prehistorians. Its subject is the settlement of the diverse environments in this isolated quarter of the globe by peoples who have maintained their discrete and traditional ways of life into the recent recorded or remembered past and at times into the observable present.

Since the beginning of the series, the basic colour on the spine and cover has distinguished the regional distribution of topics as follows: ochre for Australia, green for New Guinea, red for South-East Asia and blue for the Pacific Islands. From 2001, issues with a gold spine will include conference proceedings, edited papers and monographs which in topic or desired format do not fit easily within the original arrangements. All volumes are numbered within the same series.

List of volumes in *Terra Australis*

Volume 1: Burrill Lake and Currarong: Coastal Sites in Southern New South Wales. R.J. Lampert (1971)

Volume 2: Ol Tumbuna: Archaeological Excavations in the Eastern Central Highlands, Papua New Guinea. J.P. White (1972)

Volume 3: New Guinea Stone Age Trade: The Geography and Ecology of Traffic in the Interior. I. Hughes (1977)

Volume 4: Recent Prehistory in Southeast Papua. B. Egloff (1979)

Volume 5: The Great Kartan Mystery. R. Lampert (1981)

Volume 6: Early Man in North Queensland: Art and Archaeology in the Laura Area. A. Rosenfeld, D. Horton and J. Winter (1981)

Volume 7: The Alligator Rivers: Prehistory and Ecology in Western Arnhem Land. C. Schrire (1982)

Volume 8: Hunter Hill, Hunter Island: Archaeological Investigations of a Prehistoric Tasmanian Site. S. Bowdler (1984)

Volume 9: Coastal South-West Tasmania: The Prehistory of Louisa Bay and Maatsuyker Island. R. Vanderwal and D. Horton (1984)

Volume 10: The Emergence of Mailu. G. Irwin (1985)

Volume 11: Archaeology in Eastern Timor, 1966–67. I. Glover (1986)

Volume 12: Early Tongan Prehistory: The Lapita Period on Tongatapu and its Relationships. J. Poulsen (1987)

Volume 13: Coobool Creek. P. Brown (1989)

Volume 14: 30,000 Years of Aboriginal Occupation: Kimberley, North-West Australia. S. O'Connor (1999)

Volume 15: Lapita Interaction. G. Summerhayes (2000)

Volume 16: The Prehistory of Buka: A Stepping Stone Island in the Northern Solomons. S. Wickler (2001)

Volume 17: The Archaeology of Lapita Dispersal in Oceania. G.R. Clark, A.J. Anderson and T. Vunidilo (2001)

Volume 18: An Archaeology of West Polynesian Prehistory. A. Smith (2002)

Volume 19: Phytolith and Starch Research in the Australian-Pacific-Asian Regions: The State of the Art. D. Hart and L. Wallis (2003)

Volume 20: The Sea People: Late-Holocene Maritime Specialisation in the Whitsunday Islands, Central Queensland. B. Barker (2004)

Volume 21: What's Changing: Population Size or Land-Use Patterns? The Archaeology of Upper Mangrove Creek, Sydney Basin. V. Attenbrow (2004)

Volume 22: The Archaeology of the Aru Islands, Eastern Indonesia. S. O'Connor, M. Spriggs and P. Veth (2005)

Volume 23: Pieces of the Vanuatu Puzzle: Archaeology of the North, South and Centre. S. Bedford (2006)

Volume 24: Coastal Themes: An Archaeology of the Southern Curtis Coast, Quuensland. S. Ulm (2006)

Volume 25: Lithics in the Land of the Lightning Brothers: The Archaeology of Wardaman Country, Northern Territory. C. Clarkson (2007)

terra australis 25

Lithics in the Land of the Lightning Brothers: The Archaeology of Wardaman Country, Northern Territory

Chris Clarkson

ANU
THE AUSTRALIAN NATIONAL UNIVERSITY

E PRESS

ANU
E PRESS

© 2007 ANU E Press

Published by ANU E Press
The Australian National University
Canberra ACT 0200 Australia
Email: anuepress@anu.edu.au
Web: http://epress.anu.edu.au

National Library of Australia Cataloguing-in-Publication entry

Clarkson, Chris.
Lithics in the land of the lightning brothers : the
archaeology of Wardaman Country, Northern Territory.

Bibliography.
ISBN 9781921313288 (pbk.).
ISBN 9781921313295.(online)

1. Wardaman (Australian people) - Victoria River Region
(N.T.) - Antiquities. 2. Social archaeology - Victoria
River Region (N.T.). 3. Cave dwellings - Victoria River
Region (N.T.). 4. Victoria River Region (N.T.) -
Antiquities. I. Title.

930.1099429

Series Editor: Sue O'Connor

Typesetting and design: ANU E Press

Cover: A pair of large striped anthropomorphs from a rockshelter site known as Murduya near the Yingalarri waterhole in Wardaman Country. The image
was photographed with the permission of senior Wardaman Traditional Owners present at the time. Photo taken by the author and reproduced with the
permission of the Wardaman Aboriginal Corporation.
Back cover map: *Hollandia Nova*. Thevenot 1663 by courtesy of the National Library of Australia.
Reprinted with permission of the National Library of Australia.

Table of Contents

List of Figures

List of Tables

Appendix D. Descriptions of excavated materials from Jagoliya

Appendix E. Descriptions of excavated materials from Gordolya

Foreword

Although Chris Clarkson journeyed to the remote Victoria River region of the Northern Territory to investigate the prehistoric past, it is not the exotic location of the study that makes this an important work. Rather, it is the new intellectual landscape in which he has situated this project that created the praiseworthy volume you hold. Developing the already distinctively Australian approach to flaking technology, Clarkson presents quantified analyses of the ways artefact attributes changed during manufacture and varied through time and space. While his results are congruent with earlier generations of typological research, Clarkson has gone far beyond the constraints of arbitrary shape classifications to explore the nature of variation in artefact form, measuring shifts in tool character, standardisation and diversity. His discussion of chronological change and continuity in technological practices is powered by not only the original depiction of tools and tool production, but also his embedding of those practices in interpretations of altered land use and mobility to create an understanding of continuous, long-term adaptations.

The connecting of foraging theory and lithic interpretation has been rarely attempted in Australia, but in this work Clarkson succeeds in magnifying the interpretative power of each through identifying the significant connections between them. Regional studies of alterations in archaeological debris of tool use have formed the basis for scientific examinations of prehistoric life and cultural change for nearly a century. During much of that time descriptions of the archaeological materials remained similar, and those descriptions continued to be abstracted from interpretations of the subsistence practices of prehistoric foragers. Ultimately, those historical typological characterisations of 'traditions' and 'cultures' did not yield coherent or potent understandings of past life ways, and it is only in recent years, with the quantified expressions of reduction and reference to the articulation of technology to foraging strategies and risk, that the field has been revitalised.

This volume presents a novel and forceful model of the technological responses to past subsistence activities, a model which not only enhances our understanding of ancient life in Australia but also offers a research direction to be explored by others. Such a monograph establishes Chris Clarkson as one of the foremost figures in a new and exciting generation of Australian archaeologists who are seeking to embed technically sophisticated analyses in broad and theoretically robust explanations of Australia's human past.

Peter Hiscock

Preface

This monograph reports on 15,000 years of technological and social change in a region of northern Australia located on the edge of the semi-arid zone amidst mesas, deep gorges and dry basalt plains. It is a region best known for its spectacular rock art, and more particularly the striped anthropomorphic figures known as the 'Lightning Brothers' which decorate the walls of some rockshelters in the south of the traditional lands of the Wardaman people. The region is also known for its rich archaeological record, and has been the subject of intensive archaeological study since Davidson's research there in the 1930s.

This monograph is based on a PhD thesis submitted at The Australian National University in 2004. It employs foraging theory and recent thinking about the strategic organisation of lithic technology to explore changing settlement and subsistence practices in this region since the end of the Last Glacial Maximum. Applying this approach to the explanation of assemblage variability in Wardaman Country offers new insights into the possible reasons for technological and social change in this region over the last 15,000 years. Two chapters that originally appeared in the PhD Thesis, one expounding the role of modern Darwinian theory in the explanation of cultural change and the other exploring technological provisioning across space in Wardaman Country, do not appear in this monograph. The latter has since been published elsewhere (Clarkson 2006).

The ideas about technological responses to different foraging practices developed in this monograph are tested against assemblage data from four rockshelters located in different parts of Wardaman Country. The results suggest that major changes in lithic technology and land use took place in reaction to increased subsistence risk brought on by declines in the abundance and predictability of resources. These declines may have been triggered by the onset of ENSO-driven climatic variability after 5,000 BP, which appears to have reached its greatest severity in northern Australia between c. 3,500 and 2,000 BP.

This study has important implications for our understanding of northern Australian prehistory, including the potential causes of broadly similar technological changes across large parts of the top end and the timing of increased inter-regional contact and the spread of new technologies. It also illustrates the importance of tracking continuity in manufacturing traditions as a means of understanding the kinds of social processes that underlie regional technological changes.

Acknowledgements

Many people have helped in the production of this monograph and I would like to thank all those who have assisted in various ways over the years. Some people deserve special mention. My sincerest thanks must first go to Peter Hiscock without whose insight and energy Australian archaeology would be a much less rewarding subject. Peter's commitment to understanding the past through stone artefacts has had a profound and enduring influence on myself, and no doubt on the entire Australian academy.

Bruno David and Josephine Flood introduced me to the archaeology of Wardaman Country and helped me gain access to many collections. I hope this book makes a valuable contribution to their research in this region.

This study could not have been undertaken without the financial support of two generous funding organizations: the Institute of Aboriginal and Torres Strait Islander Studies (AIATSIS) and the Wenner Gren Foundation for Anthropological Research. AIATSIS funded two field seasons as well as a large number of radiocarbon dates, while Wenner Gren helped fund my second field season. The Centre for Archaeological Research made large numbers of radiocarbon dates available, and funded pilot studies of the phytolith records from Jagoliya, Nimji and Gordolya. Lynley Wallis and Doreen Bowdery carried out the phytolith studies for little financial reward, for which I am very grateful. Thanks also to Glenn Summerhayes who generously conducted PIXE/PIGME analysis on a large number of chert samples. My gratitude also goes to the Australian Nuclear Science and Technology Organisation (ANSTO) for funding the AMS dates for Garnawala 2.

My friends and fellow students at The Australian National University contributed greatly to this work with their enthusiasm and advice. I would especially like to thank Alex Mackay, Brit Asmussen, Boone Law, Oliver Macgregor and Sophie Collins for making my time at the ANU a pleasurable and memorable one. Ben Jeffares offered stimulating discussions about all things evolutionary.

The Wardaman Aboriginal community made fieldwork enjoyable amidst wilting heat and continuous clouds of flies. My special thanks to Bill Harney, July Blootcher, Lilly Gin.ginna, and Oliver Raymond for introducing me to their country and providing every opportunity to pursue my research. Mick Pearson's advice and logistical help is also gratefully acknowledged. All original photographs of rock art and archaeological sites were taken and published with the permission of traditional owners and the Wardaman Aboriginal Corporation.

This work simply could not have been accomplished without the help of Alex Mackay, Kelvin Hawke, Garry Estcourt, Darren Rousel and Catriona Murray who gave up months of their lives to carry out fieldwork. I am immensely grateful for their friendship, good humour and unwavering attention to detail in what were very difficult conditions at times.

The staff of the School of Archaeology and Anthropology at ANU - Sue Fraser, David MacGregor, Marian Robson and Paul Johns – worked tirelessly in the background to allow us all to get on with our research. Dave Macgregor deserves special thanks for tolerating my disproportionate use of space and for producing all manner of equipment at a moment's notice.

The University of Queensland School of Social Science provided me with a postdoctoral fellowship that gave me the time to revise my thesis into a Terra Australis monograph. I am grateful to their help and support in producing this work, and for help in funding production costs.

Finally, I would like to thank Rachel Bekessy for her love and support throughout the light and dark days of this work, and my family for understanding my pursuit of a stimulating if impoverishing career in archaeology.

1. Defining Research Questions in Northern Australian Lithic Studies

Archaeologists have long sought the meaning of variation and patterning in the stone artefact assemblages strewn across the landscape and buried in the ground. Foraging theory and theory stipulating the strategic role of lithic technology in hunter-gatherer societies suggests that much of this variation could reflect responses to different settlement and subsistence practices as well as responses to varying levels of risk and uncertainty. This monograph explores whether temporal variation in stone artefact assemblages from four rockshelters in one region of the Northern Territory could reflect changes in such factors over the last 15,000 years. The study provides a detailed exploration of changing stone implement manufacture as well as alterations to technological provisioning strategies – or the strategic organisation of stone artefact manufacture, transport, use-life and discard – as climate and resource structure fluctuated in this region since the end of the Last Glacial Maximum.

The study is set within Wardaman Country, a region located around 120km southwest of Katherine in the eastern Victoria River region (Figure 1.1). It is neatly positioned between the semi-arid zone to the south and the wet tropics to the north, and is therefore well located to explore the effects of climate change on past human land use practices. Wardaman Country is also an ideal setting for a study of long-term technological and social change because it has been a focus of archaeological research since the 1930s. Wardaman Country has also played an important role in defining key research questions in northern Australian prehistory, beginning with Davidson's (1935) seminal work on the origins and spread of cultural practices across northern Australia. This was followed by Mulvaney's (1969) definition of the northern Australian industrial sequence at Ingaladdi, and then by Cundy's (1990) doctoral thesis on technological change at Ingaladdi. Flood, David and others have more recently investigated the antiquity of Wardaman rock art, and this has resulted in a number of excavations at impressive rock art sites throughout the region (Attenbrow *et al.* 1995; David 1991; David *et al.* 1992; David *et al.* 1990; David *et al.* 1994; McNiven 1992). A number of other theses concerned with industrial change and typological variability have also demonstrated the suitability of these sites and assemblages to addressing detailed questions about landuse and industrial variability (Gregory 1998; Sanders 1975). This research history, and the recovery of many thousands of stone artefacts from well-dated sites spanning the last 15,000 years, makes this area particularly attractive for investigating long-term cultural and technological changes in northern Australia.

Problems in North Australian Prehistory

Stone artefacts and rock art have taken centre stage in past constructions of northern Australian prehistory. Whereas rock art studies have tended to emphasize the dynamics of inter-regional connections, rapid and major change and social differentiation over time (Chippindale and Taçon 2000; David and Lourandos 1998; David *et al.* 1994; Morwood 2002; Mulvaney and Kamminga 1999), interpretations of stone artefacts are usually conservative and emphasize stasis over long periods (Holdaway 1995:787). Examples of the view that stone artefacts offer only limited information about the past are not difficult to find in the recent literature. For instance, Chippendale and Taçon (2000:90) comment: "the long-term archaeological record... is overwhelmingly a story of lithics, which is not easy to interpret in human terms. It is not unfair to say that in Arnhem Land, the archaeology tends to offer 'chronology without information'". Similarly, Morwood (2002:xi) writes "in the past, archaeologists have generally relied on 'hard' evidence, such as stone artefacts... in their reconstructions of the past. However, these do not tell us much – if anything – about many important developments in Aboriginal ideology, territoriality, resource use and social organization". Mulvaney and Kamminga (1999:39) also comment on the diminishing importance of stone in comparison to rock art: "there is now better understanding of other material remains, including the remarkable chronological, pictorial and cognitive record provided by rock art, so that stone artefacts play a less significant role in current interpretations of prehistoric chronology".

Figure 1.1. The location of the study region in relation to major physiographic features and the edge of the semi-arid zone.

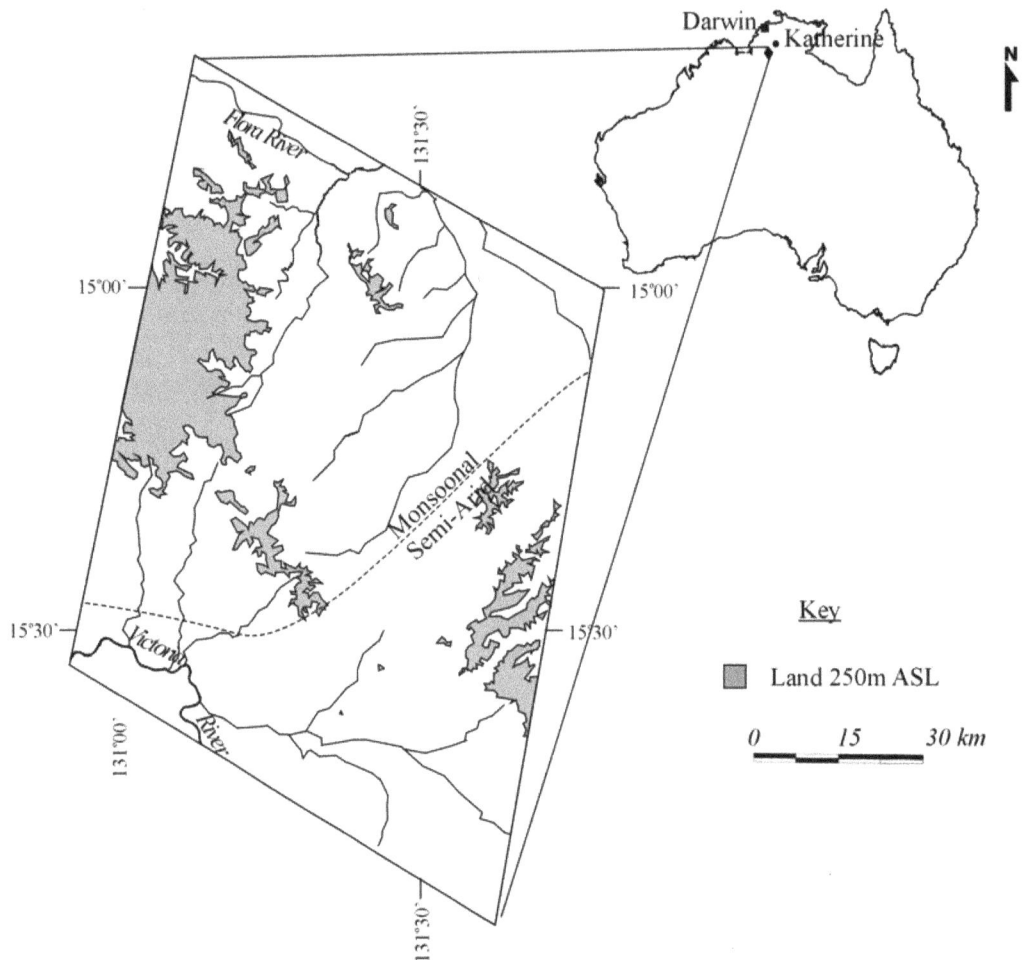

While these assessments are undoubtedly overly negative, it must nevertheless be conceded that most archaeologists recognise only a single technological change taking place somewhere between 6,000 and 3,000 years ago in the northern Australian archaeological record (Bowdler and O'Conner 1991; Holdaway 1995). This single division hardly contributes to a sense of dynamism in Australian stone artefact studies. This change involved the superposition of a later industry, in which a suite of new and morphologically regular implements including tulas, bifacial points, unifacial points, burins and burrens appear for the first time (Figure 1.2), over an earlier industry in which core and flake production was dominant and relatively few typologically regular retouched flakes are to be found. Against this single sudden change, there is often seen to be an element of technological continuity involving the continued production of edge ground axes, 'scrapers' and 'core tools' from Pleistocene times (Jones and Johnson 1985; Morwood and Hobbs 1995a; Mulvaney 1969; Schrire 1982).

It now seems apparent that the timing of this major industrial change is not coeval across the continent, nor even throughout northern Australia, and temporal lags of up to several millennia clearly preceded the appearance of the new types in different regions (Attenbrow et al. 1995; Bowdler and O'Conner 1991; Clarkson and David 1995; Flood 1995; Hiscock 1993b; Smith and Cundy 1985). Despite a common understanding that these changes were sudden, there is also mounting evidence that aspects of this transition were gradual and took place over several thousand years. Yet archaeologists have rarely examined the nature of this transition in detail, and this has greatly diminished our ability to understand the mechanisms driving such changes.

Figure 1.2. Common implement types discussed in the text (backed artefact reproduced from Hiscock and Attenbrow (2005a) with permission).

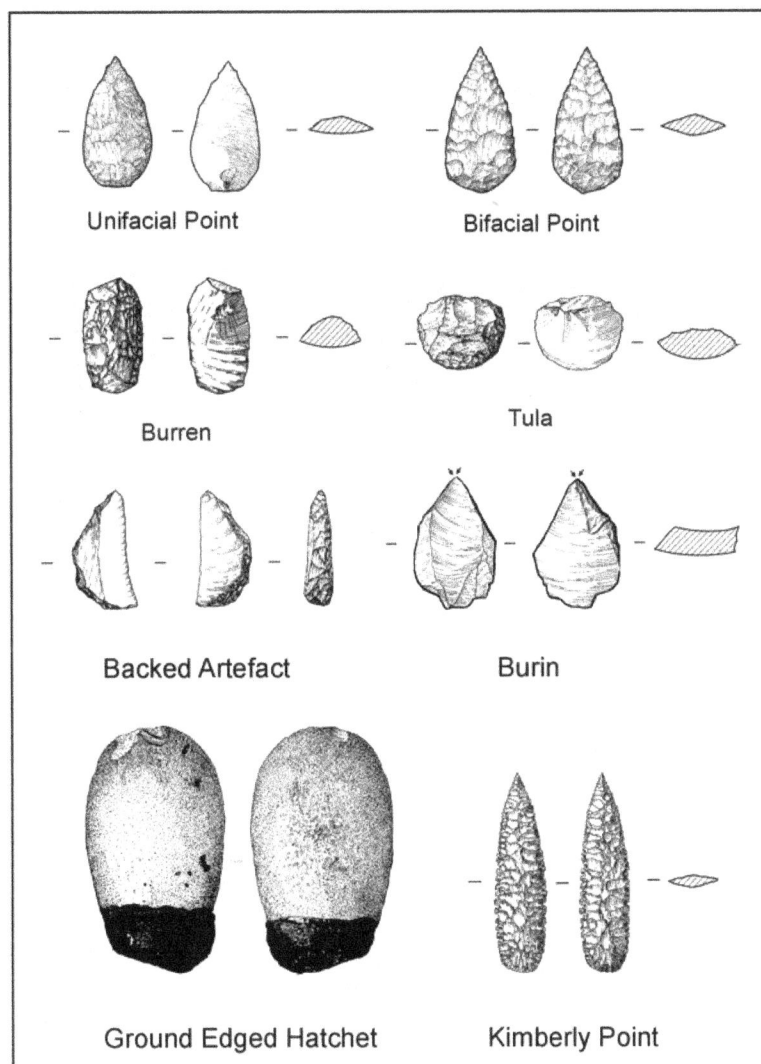

The problem of the classification of Australian retouched implement forms has been a focus of archaeological inquiry since archaeology began in this country, and this is no less the case in northern Australia. For instance, the relationship of unifacial and bifacial points to one another has occupied much attention in the literature with various archaeologists arguing for or against a continuum in these implement forms (Allen and Barton n.d.; Flood 1970; Hiscock 1994a; Jones and Johnson 1985; Roddam 1997; Schrire 1982). Their relationship to the pressure flaked Kimberley points of northwestern Australia and to the pressure and percussion flaked 'pirri' points of South Australia has also remained ambiguous (Akerman and Bindon 1995; Elkin 1948; Tindale 1985). The relationships of retouched flakes such as 'scrapers', 'burrens', 'burins' and other miscellaneous 'adze-like' flakes to similar forms found in other regions also remains unresolved. Indeed, it is difficult to see how these problems can be adequately resolved without first undertaking detailed studies of artefact production and the effects of raw material availability and resharpening on implement morphology in a number of key regions.

Another important problem in northern Australian lithic studies is the explanation of distinct geographic boundaries in the distribution of each implement type. For instance, an intriguing question for many Australian archaeologists is the apparent division between the distributions of bifacial points and backed artefacts. Bifacial points are found only in the central northern tip of the continent while backed artefacts are found only in the southern two thirds (Figure 1.3), with little geographic overlap between the two types. Interestingly, Dortch (1977) and O'Connor (1999) have suggested that a distinctive form of 'backed point' found in the Pilbara region is evidence of an overlap between these northern and southern industries, but few other such potential overlaps are documented (Dortch 1977; Hiscock 1988; Hiscock and Hughes 1980; O'Connor 1999; Smith and Cundy 1985).

Figure 1.3. Distribution map of common retouched implement forms in Australia (modified from Hiscock 1994b).

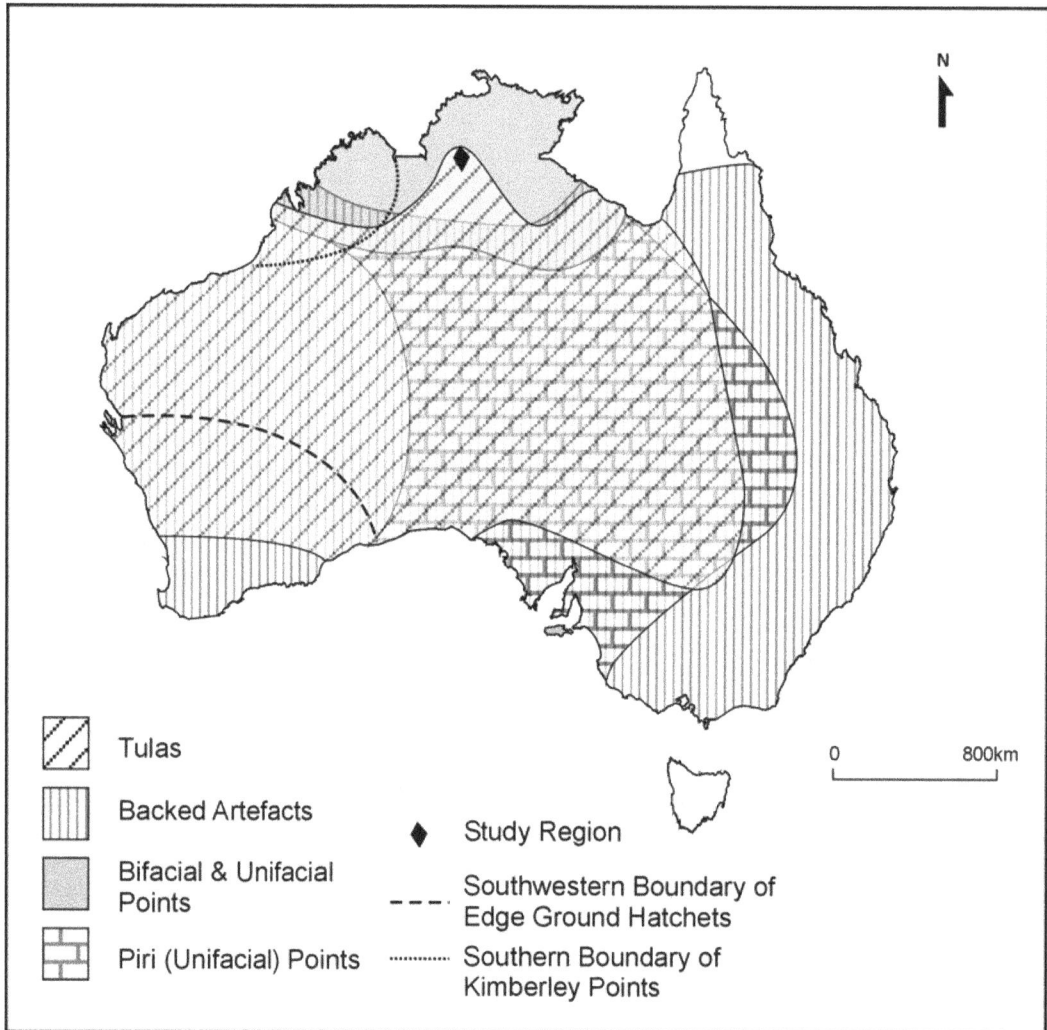

Some archaeologists have seen such discontinuities in the geographic and temporal occurrence of stone technologies as indicating an incursion of new populations into Australia, equipped with new technologies and perhaps even responsible for the introduction of the dingo (Dortch 1977; Glover 1973; Mulvaney 1969). Others have treated geographic boundaries in stone artefact types as a convenient framework on which to pin models of socio-linguistic and/or internal demographic readjustment in the mid- to late Holocene. For example, McConvell (1990; 1996) sees this north-south technological discontinuity as likely linked to the spread of a set of very homogeneous and therefore quite recent Pama-Nyungan (PN) languages across most of southern Australia, leaving an isolated pocket of more diverse and therefore possibly much older non-Pama-Nyungan (NPN) languages in the northwestern third of the continent. It is often noted that the distribution of this NPN grouping corresponds very well with the distribution of bifacial points (Clendon 2006; Evans and Jones 1997; McConvell 1990, 1996). The PN language spread is attributed by McConvell to the migration of peoples outward from a homeland somewhere near the Gulf of Carpentaria where the greatest diversity in PN languages occurs (McConvell 1990, 1996). Likewise, Evans and Jones (1997) support a socio-linguistic model of technological diffusion, but believe such a spread could have taken place without migration through the diffusion of socio-cultural practices and ethnic affiliations. In their view, this would have involved the spread of a package of new cultural practices that presented opportunities for new connubial alliances and included a suite of new technologies. Clearly, the issue of origins, language and technology of northern Aboriginal Australians remains at the heart of current archaeological debate, and there is much room for new models and reappraisals of the evidence at this time.

The problem with these techno-linguistic models stems from the common typo-genetic view that specific implement morphologies are linked to discrete groups of people, such that the appearance of new forms must necessarily imply the arrival or spread of new people or new ethnic identities. It is difficult to see, however, how the complex distributional configuration of technologies shown in Figure 1.3 in any way supports such models. For instance, the distribution of tulas does not conform to a single spread zone, nor does that of unifacial piri points or bifacial points. A model that advanced multiple, but not necessarily simultaneous diffusions of new technologies might go further toward explaining such a pattern, but no such model has been proposed in recent years.

Growing dissatisfaction with diffusionist/techno-linguistic explanations has given rise to a third theory concerning the origins and emergence of new lithic technologies in northern Australia. This model views the complex and overlapping distribution of retouched technologies as representing independent emergence and spread of curated implement forms in multiple locations that formed part of a broader technological response to increased economic risk in the mid-Holocene as climatic variability increased and effective precipitation decreased. The new technologies are argued to have provided a solution to the increasing problem of maintaining a supply of tools in the face of increased mobility and/or unpredictable access to raw materials (Clarkson 2002a; Clarkson and Wallis 2003; Hiscock 1994b, 2002, 2005). These new standardized retouched 'toolkits' are seen to have increased economic success in times of greater hardship in three ways: first, by extending the use-life of stone tools so that reprovisioning need not interfere with critical and time-stressed activities such as procuring food and water in highly variable environments; second, by serving as light-weight multifunctional tools that could be easily interchanged and replaced without requiring regular and time-consuming reworking of the haft; and third, by enhancing the performance characteristics of tools by standardizing those features that are most important for tool function (i.e. tulas are highly effective tools for adzing hard woods, points increase penetration power, backed artefacts likely increase killing power and effectiveness by adding multiple barbs to a spear, etc.). It should be stated, however, that the functional properties so often attributed to these Australian stone artefact types are highly conjectural, and few if any studies have conclusively demonstrated any link between particular forms and enhanced performance.

This last explanation for the appearance of new stone artefact types begins to incorporate explicit modelling of the ways in which technology might articulate with broader economic systems and constraints. This approach reflects the fact that archaeologists are increasingly looking to human behavioural ecology as a theoretical umbrella under which to unite propositions about the organizational and functional roles of technology with ideas about appropriate human responses to foraging in different contexts, as modelled from optimal foraging theory.

While behavioural ecology has sometimes been treated with suspicion in anthropology for its use of simple mathematical models formulated from observations of non-human organisms, as well as its reliance on optimization theory, it nevertheless serves a useful purpose in providing testable hypotheses that make the operation of complex systems such as human culture more accessible or tractable (Winterhalder 2002). It is therefore their simplicity and elegance that makes formal models attractive to archaeologists trying to understand the causes of behavioural and material patterning. Of course, optimality studies have been around for a long time, and have formed a major if implicit component of behavioural and processual explanation. Unlike those employed in human behavioural ecology, however, earlier optimality models lacked formal expression and sometimes left open the definition of actors, constraints and currencies. This monograph aims to further develop and test ecological models that relate technological strategies to changing economic circumstances in later northern Australian prehistory.

Defining the Aims of the Research

Australian prehistory has been largely built on the record of lithic industrial change, but has made interpretive use of stone artefacts in unsophisticated ways that fail to incorporate an understanding of the factors giving rise to assemblage variability. Consequently, northern Australian prehistory is filled with theoretical, methodological and empirical problems of the sort that may only be effectively bridged by detailed regional studies of stone technology from multiple sites spanning comparable time periods. At present, very few studies of this sort exist.

From this brief overview it is possible to identify several important shortcomings in northern Australian Prehistory. These are:

- a poor grasp of temporal changes in stone artefact production systems, leading to overly static impressions of long-term change;
- poor understanding of the manufacture and transformation of stone artefacts, and hence systemic problems encountered when interpreting typological variation;
- failure to explore the nature of transitions between apparently distinctive phenomena, forcing gradual changes into the background, while bringing sudden transformational change to the foreground; and
- the use of underdeveloped models specifying the interaction of key economic, environmental and technological variables and their likely effects on assemblage variation.

Redressing these problems will be a major long-term undertaking in Australian archaeology, but this monograph takes one small step in this direction by exploring four interconnected issues that may potentially be addressed through the study of assemblage variation in Wardaman Country.

The Nature of Technological Change in Wardaman Country over the last 15,000 years

If we are to look to the stone artefactual record for evidence of the ways in which the lives of people occupying Wardaman Country have changed over time, it is essential that an accurate description of technological change is developed. As argued above, this requires greater attention to the temporal and spatial distributions of major stone reduction technologies, and closer examination of the nature of the transition between earlier and later assemblages to see whether this is sudden or gradual. To meet this objective, a detailed analysis of the stone artefacts from four rockshelters located throughout Wardaman Country will be undertaken, focussing on describing the timing, nature and tempo of changes in lithic technology.

Typological Variation, Implement Manufacture and Morphological Continuums

North Australian prehistory is largely built on stone typologies, yet the relationships between the various implement forms is poorly understood, as is the sequence of manufacturing actions involved in their production or the changes in morphology they undergo throughout their use-life. Studying past manufacturing systems requires an understanding of the technological features preserved on artefacts that are indicative of specific knapping behaviour. It also requires that the sequence of knapping actions be time-ordered, such that each artefact can be ranked in order of reduction so that transformations in the technological and morphological features of artefacts can be tracked as reduction intensity varies. Ranking reduction in this way also can help determine discard thresholds by identifying combinations of characteristics that led to the discontinuation of use. Addressing this issue involves formulating *reduction sequence models* that track morphological changes in stone artefact morphology from initial production through to final discard, and in so doing, identifies the morphological continuums that underlie conventional type boundaries. Common northern Australian typologies are employed here as a preliminary basis from which to explore implement manufacture, although this is not meant to support the notion that types represent real and discrete kinds. In fact, many of the analyses presented will expose the non-reality of discrete types and lend support to recent suggestions that new classifications are needed to better link individual artefacts to the technological processes that created them (Hiscock 2001a; Hiscock and Clarkson 2000).

Technological Change and Landuse

A primary goal of lithic analysis is to develop an understanding of the causal factors that brought about technological change. This issue involves developing an understanding of the relationships between various models of land use and the sorts of technological responses we might expect in certain circumstances. By approaching assemblage variability in terms of the ordering and location of stone procurement, tool design, raw material reduction, and discard in the landscape, and matching these observations to ideas about the various advantages offered by different design alternatives in different contexts, I seek to explore the ways in which people organized their use of the landscape in terms of frequency of use, levels of mobility, the size of foraging territories, the levels of uncertainty in resource acquisition, and the degree of forward planning exercised in exploiting various areas. Addressing this question involves developing a set of predictions derived from optimal foraging theory (particularly patch choice, settlement and mobility patterns and time allocation) that relate the changing availability of critical resources to optimal modes of land use through time. These predictions will then be tested against changing assemblage composition through time. The aim is to identify patterned behaviour in the way sites are provisioned with raw materials and different kinds of toolkits through time. This will include a study of the distances traveled, the form and quantity of materials imported, the degree to which they are reduced and conserved, and the diversity of manufacturing and other tasks performed through time. Changes in provisioning and landuse can be inferred from these results with implications for the way societies were structured at the time.

Wardaman Country in Broader Context

While gaining an understanding of changing patterns of stone artefact manufacture is interesting and rewarding in itself, the ultimate value of regional studies of this kind lies in their contribution to answering the 'big questions' in Australian archaeology. A further objective of this study therefore is to consider how changes in one region may help interpret similar changes in other nearby regions, and what these may mean for socio-demographic change in northern Australia more generally. This last issue therefore involves consideration of multiple lines of evidence, including archaeological, linguistic, environmental, skeletal and genetic data at regional and continental scales to build an interpretive model of later prehistoric changes in Aboriginal society.

There are a number of reasons for drawing together so many lines of evidence. The first is a matter of strengthening the argument. By drawing together multiple supporting interpretive strands, it is possible to build a stronger and more interconnected argument (Wylie 1989). Secondly, taking a broad view of long-term socio-demographic processes at regional and continental scales makes it possible to examine key elements of the social and environmental context in which long-term technological changes took place in any specific region. In this way, the study of stone artefact assemblages has the potential to contribute a vital and unique perspective on the past, because it provides a tangible record of human behaviour intimately linked to the means by which people extracted a living from their environment.

Chapter Outline

Naturally, the themes discussed in this book develop as a series of chapters, and it is usually helpful to signpost at the outset where the various kinds of information to be presented can be found.

Chapter 2 examines a number of optimal foraging models and develops predictions about the kinds of technological strategies that should be appropriate in particular foraging contexts. This chapter also examines the role of risk in hunter-gatherer economies and technologies as a constraint on human action and a potential catalyst for technological innovation. Chapter 3 details the various techniques employed to reconstruct stone artefact production patterns and to describe change and variation in stone artefact manufacture. A review of the physiography of the area is presented in Chapter 4, along with predictions about the effects that climate change should have on technological provisioning strategies over time. Chapter 5 provides summaries of the excavation procedures, stratigraphy, dating and cultural materials recovered from each of the four rockshelters. Chapter 6 constructs reduction sequences for cores, flakes and the various retouched implement forms found in Wardaman Country. Documenting reduction sequences allows reconsideration of typological diversity and evaluation of the use-lives of various implement forms helpful in identifying the changing performance characteristics of toolkits over time. Chapter 7 presents data on the sequence of technological changes in the region over the last 15,000 years, and determines whether technological changes are consistent with those predicted in Chapter 4. Chapter 8 draws together each of the analyses presented to build a picture of major changes in Aboriginal society since the end of the LGM. The chapter concludes with a discussion of the implications of broad economic and technological changes for our understanding of social processes, ontology and inter-regional connections.

2. Modelling Optimality in Subsistence and Technology

Like many aspects of life, successful foraging depends on continuous monitoring and optimization of subsistence related behaviours to suit changing circumstances, so that returns in critical resources such as food, water, raw materials, etc. match or exceed the effort expended in procuring them. There are various ways in which people might improve their subsistence strategies in response to changing conditions. These include modifying techniques of locating, capturing and processing resources, as well as modifying the efficiency or other properties of the technologies that are vital to making a living.

We can better understand how people might optimize their subsistence and technological strategies to suit particular circumstances by considering various bodies of theory dedicated to understanding human-land interactions. The first is optimal foraging theory (OFT), which was developed within evolutionary ecology to understand which foraging behaviours work best given different situations and constraints. The second body of theory is derived from processual and behavioural archaeology and attempts to specify the best ways to organize technology given different foraging practices. The third is design theory, which attempts to determine how much energy should be invested in technology and which designs should work the best in any given situation.

Mithen has argued that attempts to improve foraging returns might aim at doing two things. The first is to try and increase returns in food, energy etc. in terms of the quantity of a resource harvested for a given amount of time. Mithen (1990) calls this strategy *utility increase*. Another is to try to reduce the risk of failure to harvest or process resources so as to avoid critical shortfalls. Mithen (1990) calls this second strategy *risk reduction*. Both of these strategies can be thought of as *meliorizing* strategies (Dawkins 1982) - that is, ways of 'doing better' in social and physical interactions so that the chances of success are increased, whether this is thought of in terms of social prestige, individual wellbeing or reproductive success (Smith 1983).

Optimal Foraging Theory

Four optimal foraging models are relevant to the problem of utility increase and risk reduction and these are briefly presented so as to later develop predictions about how technology and landuse might be expected to respond to different circumstances. OFT models are typically written out as formal mathematical models, but such descriptions are not required to understand the basic principles.

OFT and Utility Increase

Diet Breadth. The diet breadth model is designed to predict the food items a forager should attempt to 'handle' (i.e. pursue, capture, process, and consume), and those they should overlook in order to continue searching for something else that will provide greater returns (Hawkes and O'Connell 1992; Kaplan and Hill 1992:63; MacArthur and Pianka 1966). The model states that once resources are ranked in terms of their profitability after search and handling time are factored in, foragers should always choose to pursue resources that yield the highest rate of return upon encounter, irrespective of the encounter rate of each prey item. Lower ranked resources will be pursued in order of diminishing returns only when higher ranked resources are unavailable (Gremillion 2002). A drop in the density of higher ranked prey should result in foragers broadening the diet to include lower ranked resources.

Patch Choice and Time Allocation. The patch choice model specifies which areas a forager should choose to search in order to obtain the maximum return when resources are unequally distributed (i.e. patchy) (MacArthur and Pianka 1966). This model is similar to the diet breadth model in postulating that foragers should search higher ranked patches first (those yielding the highest returns after search and handling time are factored in), and should search lower ranked patches as higher ranked ones become depleted (Smith 1983).

Central Place Foraging and Field Processing. This model attempts to solve problems stemming from situations in which resources are located in a different place to where they will be consumed (Orians and Pearson 1979). This model examines the cost of bringing people and resources together once round-trip time from the patch to the place of resource consumption is factored in. The general rule is that larger load sizes and greater pre-processing will be more profitable the further one must transport the resource (Beck *et al.* 2002; Bettinger *et al.* 1997; Jones and Madsen 1989; Metcalfe and Barlow 1992; Rhode 1990).

Resource Depression and Patch Choice. Resource depression is defined as declines in the encounter rates for prey species in a given patch. It often results from over-exploitation, prey relocation, changes in prey behaviour that make capture more difficult, and microhabitat change through climate change or human land use (Broughton 2003; Broughton and O'Connell 1999; Charnov *et al.* 1976; Nagooka 2002). The central place foraging model suggests a strategy that might help foragers cope with resource depression. This predicts that more use should be made of less-depleted patches further out from the central place once closer patches become depleted. This is because more distant and previously under-utilised patches should contain higher densities of high-ranked prey. This makes longer-distance travel more worthwhile so long as the return rate is above that of nearer patches once travel costs are factored in (Broughton 2003:63). Foragers should relocate the central place (typically a residential base) when foraging returns fall below those that can be obtained elsewhere once relocation costs are factored in (Hayden 1981; Kelly 1992:46; Sahlins 1972:33).

Mobility and Settlement Pattern. A fourth popular component of OFT specifies which settlement and mobility patterns will be optimal in fine-grained or patchy environments. The *geometric model of optimal dispersion* divides environments into two polar extremes – those with stable/evenly dispersed resources and those with mobile/clumped resources (Horn 1968). To minimize round trip time while foraging in each of these environment types, foragers should choose an optimal settlement location that also maximizes the probability of locating any resource clump. Travel costs increase as resources become more mobile or more clumped.

In stable/evenly dispersed environments a variety of resources will be within foraging distance of any camp, and hence foragers should choose to exploit resources in small dispersed social units, moving the residential camp frequently over short distances as needed in a more or less 'random walk' pattern (Figure 2.1) (Cashdan 1992; Smith 1983). Aggregation at a central location, on the other hand, is an optimal response to mobile/clumped resources, as moving closer to one resource would simply move the camp further from others (Figure 2.1) (Cashdan 1992; Smith 1983). Intermediate resource distribution patterns should favour a similarly intermediate settlement pattern (Smith 1983:634).

This OFT model (see Figure 2.1) is consistent with a range of predictions made by other researchers interested in the same question. For instance, Harpending and Davis (1977) found that people should aggregate in large groups when the amount of variance in total calories between patches is large, and that people should distribute themselves more uniformly in smaller groups if variance is small.

The mobility and settlement pattern model also corresponds closely to Binford's (1980) forager/collector continuum. In stable/evenly dispersed environments, Binford states that 'foragers' should make frequent residential moves over typically short distances, acquiring resources on an 'encounter' basis and 'mapping onto' the resources in the landscape. Binford (1980:7) suggests that the size of foraging units might also reduce in accordance with scarcity and dispersal of resources. In mobile/clumped environments, 'collectors' locate the camp at one resource and send out small foraging parties ranging over long distances and targeting specific clumps of resources in 'logistically organised' foraging trips.

Figure 2.1. The Horn (1968) geometric model of optimal dispersion. Optimal settlement locations (triangles) are predicted for stable/evenly dispersed environments (solid circles), and for mobile/clumped environments (open circles). The mean round-trip travel cost from settlement to resource locations, weighted by the probability of locating the resource, is given by *d*.

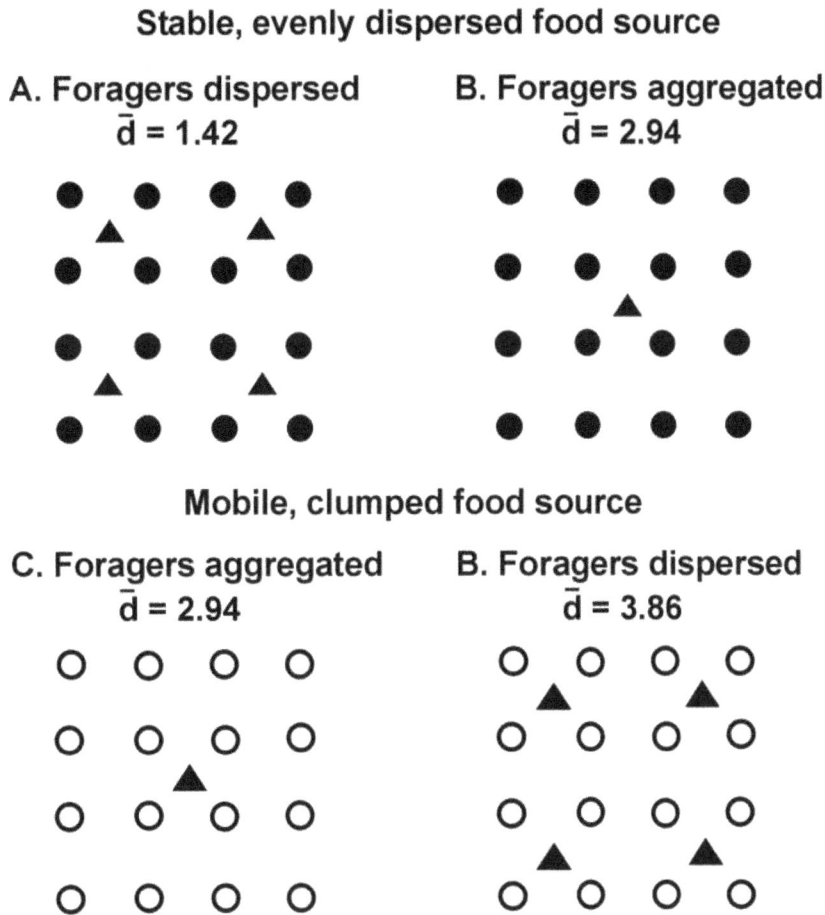

Stable, evenly dispersed food source

A. Foragers dispersed
$\bar{d} = 1.42$

B. Foragers aggregated
$\bar{d} = 2.94$

Mobile, clumped food source

C. Foragers aggregated
$\bar{d} = 2.94$

B. Foragers dispersed
$\bar{d} = 3.86$

OFT and Risk Reduction

A second strategy for optimizing foraging returns is to find ways of reducing the risk of failing to obtain critical resources, as this can be a serious problem due to the highly variable (stochastic) nature of foraging environments. Stochastic variation presents two distinct problems: *uncertainty* due to imperfect information, and *risk*, or the consequences of unavoidable variation (Christenson 1982; Smith 1983; Winterhalder 1986; Winterhalder *et al.* 1999). In the case of uncertainty, foragers have incomplete information about their environment, making correct predictions about optimal foraging conditions more difficult.

Risk, or the *effect* of variation on foraging returns over a given period, may mean that people employ coping strategies that minimize variance rather than strictly following a utility increase strategy, especially if food storage is ineffective or costly and temporal variation in resources is substantial (Colson 1979; Minc and Smith 1989; Smith 1983). Risk can result from stochastic variation in such variables as the frequency, predictability or duration of resource availability (and can be associated with severe resource depression and climatic variability), or the spatial extent or spatial homogeneity of resources (Halstead and O'Shea 1989:2.3).

Populations affected by stochastic variation are said to be 'risk sensitive', and may either act in a manner that is 'risk averse', if attempting to reduce variation, or 'risk prone', if attempting to benefit from it. Attempts have been made to incorporate risk as an explicit component of many OFT models, including prey choice, patch use, group size and time allocation (Caraco 1979a, b; Caraco *et al.* 1980; Green 1980; McNamara 1982; Smith 1983; Stephens and Charnov 1982; Thompson *et al.* 1974). A major finding of this research is that risk-sensitive strategies can be predicted from the relationship between the minimum dietary needs of a forager and the expected benefits accruing from alternative strategies (Smith 1983). Stephens and Charnov (1982) have formalised this observation in the 'extreme variance rule', which simply states that foragers seeking to minimise the chance of falling critically short of resources should always choose the strategy that yields expected returns above requirements and with the *least variance*. However, if the mean expected returns for all strategies falls critically below the threshold for meeting basic requirements, then foragers should choose the strategy with the *most variance*. Although this last strategy is counter-intuitive, it simply means that under conditions of shortage, foragers should take greater risks in the hope of obtaining a return above minimum requirements. Cashdan (1985) makes the additional observation that the amount of effort foragers should invest in risk reduction strategies will depend on the cost of loosing the resource.

Five coping strategies for risk averse populations have gained attention. These are mobility, intensification, storage, diversification, group foraging, and exchange. Some of these strategies will be better suited to local conditions than others. Halstead and O'Shea (1989) also argue that their use may be employed in a hierarchical fashion, such that short-term, low-level risks may be locally addressed through the use of such strategies as mobility, diversification and local exchange. At much greater severity, however (i.e. where shortfalls are beyond the local capacity to absorb), high-level strategies may be employed, such as inter-regional exchange and intensification that could potentially lead to subsistence transitions (see also Hawkes and O'Connell 1992; Larson *et al.* 1996; Leonard 1989). Unfortunately, with the exception of group foraging, few of these models have received formal mathematical modelling and hence theoretical and empirical investigation of these concepts remains largely qualitative.

Mobility. Mobility can offset spatial variability in resource abundance by spatially redistributing people and food, either by moving people to food (residential mobility), or by moving food to people (logistical mobility) (Cashdan 1985, 1992; Sobel and Bettles 2000). Increasing mobility in situations of high variance in the distribution of resources may reduce risk by increasing the resource encounter-rate within and between patches. It may also help reduce uncertainty by enabling sampling of a much broader range of patches to obtain up-to-date information about fluctuating resource abundance.

Storage. The physical storage of resources can counter periodic shortages in availability by laying aside surplus in anticipation of later shortfalls. Storage typically involves large investments of time and effort in advance of need, and this added cost may reduce overall returns. People should therefore only invest in storage in times of surplus if resource abundance fluctuates severely, and if the production rate remains above minimum requirements after the preparation of foodstuffs and the manufacture of storage facilities is factored in. Transport costs entailed in moving surplus into storage, or accessing it later on, also decrease as mobility decreases, and hence storage should be more common among relatively sedentary peoples (Cashdan 1985). In some regions of the world (especially tropical regions), storage is difficult due to the rapid rate at which food stuffs spoil in hot and humid conditions, and foragers may be forced to look to other solutions to critical fluctuations in resource abundance.

Intensification. Another strategy for dealing with shortages is to intensify harvesting, processing, and/or food storage – in short, increasing the total time and effort spent foraging in order to reduce variance in supply. The term intensification is usually used in Australia to signify a broad suite of changes in subsistence, demography and social organisation and the rise of cultural complexity (Bender 1981; Lourandos 1985), but is taken here simply to mean greater investment of time and labour in foraging, or specialisation on a few key resources that yield the highest returns under sustained exploitation. Such a strategy is likely to be short-sighted, however, unless the productivity of the resource is resistant to intensive exploitation, or unless resource productivity can be enhanced, such as through water control or the creation or regeneration of habitats (Bird *et al.* 2005; Jones 1969; Larson *et al.* 1996; Leonard 1989; Richerson *et al.* 2001; Winterhalder 1986). Intensification can therefore be thought of as a means of reducing risk through increasing the productivity of a given unit of land, rather than increasing the amount of land as might be attempted when reducing risk through increased mobility. Intensification may serve as a risk reduction strategy if the resources chosen for exploitation are hardy and resistant to the fluctuations causing shortage in other resources.

Diversification. Diversification is essentially identical to increasing diet breadth, except that it might mean regularly allocating more time to capturing and handling resources of lower-value if this reduces variance in returns while still meeting minimum requirements. Populations acting in a risk prone manner might be expected to continue targeting high-ranked, but highly unpredictable prey. The sexual division of labour in hunter-gatherer societies is sometimes seen as a means of incorporating both of these strategies into subsistence routines, where women typically target low-risk, low-ranked resources, and men target high-ranked prey with unpredictable returns (Hawkes 1990, 1991; Hawkes and Bliege Bird 2002; Hawkes and O'Connell 1992).

Group Foraging. Group living/foraging may also offer advantages to risk sensitive populations. Sharing information about environmental conditions, for instance, can help reduce uncertainty in prey location, while information can also be acquired from older people to help dampen the effects of temporal variation (Sobel and Bettles 2000). Secondly, cooperation in subsistence tasks may enhance efficiency through the division of labour, increasing the chances of locating prey, or by reducing foraging-area overlap. Thirdly, group living/foraging may help reduce variance in resource capture rates if yields are shared among group members. Different sharing rules can provide quite different predictions for optimal group size, including whether game is shared only between the foraging party itself (and their various dependants) or whether it is centrally pooled with other such parties and redistributed within a larger settlement.

Exchange. Reducing risk by way of exchange can extend beyond the foraging group to regional networks. These networks can act as a kind of 'social storage' by setting up mutual obligations between people that can provide assistance in times of shortage (Weissner 1982). This may take the form of *balanced reciprocity*, otherwise known as 'trade', where goods assessed to be of equivalent value by both parties are exchanged to obtain vital resources. In ethnographic cases, these systems often involve the transformation of surpluses into non-perishable goods for exchange during bad times (Sobel and Bettles 2000). Reciprocity can also take the form of *generalised exchange*, where an extensive network of partners agree to aid one another in times of shortage, thereby pooling risk so that variance is minimized by spreading losses over a much larger unit than the individual or local group (Cashdan 1985; Weissner 1982). Reciprocal exchange systems often operate by individuals making small, regular and predictable losses or contributions in return for larger, uncertain payoffs later on. Non-reciprocal exchange, otherwise known as theft or raiding, can also be a risk reduction strategy (Sobel and Bettles 2000). Such a strategy should be considered 'risk prone' in the sense that payoffs can be large, but the consequences can also be severe.

Predicted Foraging Responses to Changing Resource Structure and Abundance

The OFT models reviewed above make a number of useful predictions about possible human responses to changing resource abundance and spatial and temporal variability in resource availability. Together, they predict that as high-ranked prey become scarce through resource depression, or as conditions become more variable, foragers pursuing a goal of utility increase and/or risk reduction should:

- broaden the diet to include lower-ranked prey, or, specialise on a few sustainable resources
- include a wider range of patches in the itinerary, including closer, lower-ranked patches and more distant, higher-ranked ones
- intensify production where possible, such as by creating suitable habitats for high-ranked or dependable resources

- as foraging range increases, spend more time field processing resources found at greater distance to the central place
- form larger social groups that enhance energetic efficiency through cooperative foraging, allowing the pooling of information and a reduction in variance through sharing
- invest in physical food storage, or if impractical, invest in mechanisms of social storage such as reciprocal exchange (if risk averse) or theft and raiding (if risk prone)

If environments within the foraging range are patchy, or become patchier as a result of climate change or human alteration of the landscape, we should expect to see a greater tendency toward aggregation at a central location and logistical forays mounted to exploit surrounding patches. Over time, aggregation at a central place will likely result in resource depression in the surrounding area (Hames 1980), resulting in the same set of alterations to pursuit, processing and patch selection noted above. Alternatively, if there is no change in patchiness, but a reduction in overall prey density, people may be forced to spend more time overall engaged in the food quest. In the context of stable/evenly distributed resources where people essentially employ a 'random walk' encounter pattern (Brautingham 2003), this may simply involve higher mobility aimed at covering more ground, and an increase in total foraging range. In the case of logistical mobility, resource depression will probably involve travelling further to more productive patches.

Alterations to foraging patterns that result from resource depression and microhabitat change may also be reflected in changes to the organisation of technology. Broadening the diet (i.e. increasing handling time) and exploiting more distant patches (i.e. increasing travel time), for instance, could place greater demands on technology and may lead people to invest more time in improving the energetic efficiency of subsistence-related technologies (Jeske 1992). Likewise, large amounts of time spent travelling to and from distant, higher-ranked patches will reduce time and energy budgets left for foraging (Torrence 1983, 1989). Hence designing technologies that increase prey capture rates, reduce travel, handling or other costs, or altering the organisation of technology in ways that reduce opportunity and subsistence costs may all be beneficial strategies.

The Organisation of Technology

A second body of theory derived from processual and behavioural archaeology explores ways in which people can modify the spatial and temporal organisation of technology to improve foraging returns in different contexts. These strategies are centred on hunter-gatherer technologies in which human labour forms the bulk of the energy inputs, and the harnessing of external energy sources such as solar, water, wind or fossil fuels is largely unpracticed (Torrence 1989).

Utility Increase and the Organisation of Technology

Much of the theorizing about the organisation of technology has built on a dichotomy between 'curated' and 'expedient' technologies. These terms are typically used to distinguish between organised, planned, and carefully designed, executed and husbanded technologies in the former case and technologies that lack these properties in the latter (Bamforth 1986; Parry and Kelly 1987). In reality though, all subsistence technologies are likely to incorporate a degree of planning and design, with much of the variability between systems likely to reflect emphasis on different performance characteristics that enhance utility increase in specific contexts. Only in extremely rare cases where raw materials are truly ubiquitous, there are no constraints on time, and almost any tool will do the job, would we expect to find a total lack of planning and design in hunter-gatherer technologies.

The use of these terms also often seems contradictory in the literature and hence some debates can become confusing. For instance, Nelson (1991:63) suggests that transporting prepared cores to a workplace can comprise a 'curation' strategy by mitigating the "incongruity between availability of tools or raw material and the location of tool-using activities". She then states that the subsequent use of these stockpiled materials as needed constitutes an 'expedient' strategy. This example is typical of the kind of confusion that has plagued debates about the organisation of technology.

Because of this confusion, the following sections attempt to break down the concepts of curation and expedience into their various components, which are here termed performance characteristics after Schiffer and Skibo (1987; 1997). They are recombined later using the concept of technological provisioning as discussed by Kuhn (1995).

Organising Technologies Through Time Budgeting. The time-budgeting model developed by Torrence (1983) states that by scheduling activities such as raw material procurement, implement manufacture and tool maintenance in such a way that they do not interfere with food-getting or other important activities, opportunity costs (that is, lost opportunities to pursue subsistence activities) can be minimized without compromising tool functionality or availability. In essence, all foraging activity is time-limited, as overall utility gain is partly defined by time spent searching for and harvesting resources. Hence, foragers should seek to minimise the time spent making the necessary technologies ready for use when subsistence opportunities present themselves.

Binford (1977; 1979) found that the arctic Nunamiut foragers could reduce opportunity costs and/or increase energetic efficiency by 'embedding' various technological activities within more important subsistence tasks, thereby reducing costs associated with travel, or by restricting technological activities to periods of 'down-time' (such as during lean seasons, while waiting for game, or after dark while in camp). This allowed the Nunamiut to manufacture tools long in advance of use so as not to detract from pursuit or handling time. However, the time saved in travel by embedding procurement will be offset by the limited quantity of material that may be transported if foraging has already resulted in obtaining a full load (Myers 1989:85). In the absence of substantial transport technology, group foraging might assist in this situation if unsuccessful foragers within the group are available to carry raw materials or other processed resources back to camp.

Organizing technological activities so as not to compete with important subsistence tasks, and to reduce overall energy expenditure through embedding, should have specific consequences for assemblage variability. These are:

1. the types of raw materials present in assemblages should reflect patch visitation, as procurement should be embedded within foraging trips
2. there should be higher levels of anticipatory manufacture, maintenance, and reworking of toolkits at locations where more downtime is expected to occur. This should lead to more complex assemblages accumulating at these locations

Organising Technologies under Mobility Constraints. The OFT models presented above predicted that increasing mobility will enhance returns in situations where resources are mobile/unstable, or where higher returns can be obtained from more distant patches. However, increasing mobility comes at a cost. An individual encumbered by too much equipment may experience reduced success in searching for and capturing prey as well as incurring greater travel costs due to excessive weight or the awkwardness of the load. As most hunter-gatherer groups are mobile (because 'naturally' occurring crucial resources are often unevenly distributed in time and space) and typically make little use of transport technology, carrying costs are expected to be quite high and to limit the number of specialised tools that can be deployed (Kuhn 1995; Shott 1989:19; Torrence 1983:13).

Ethnographic research has demonstrated that in situations of frequent residential mobility (as typically occurs in fine-grained/stable environments), foragers typically reduce the number of transported items in the toolkit, and make use of a more limited number of multipurpose tools (Ebert 1979; Kelly 1988, 1992; Shott 1989; Torrence 1983). Binford (1979) calls these transported toolkits *personal gear*. Shott regressed toolkit diversity and mobility data for contemporary hunter-gatherer populations and found a highly significant inverse relationship between mobility frequency and toolkit diversity. However, Shott also found mobility to be multidimensional (Kelly 1992), as is predicted by the settlement and mobility models presented above. In contrast to this first pattern, Shott found that toolkit diversity showed a different pattern among groups that carried out long-range logistical forays from a central place in order to exploit clumped/mobile resources. The toolkits employed by these groups showed increased diversity, presumably because logistical forays tended to target specific resources that were better handled using specialised tools.

The central place foraging model presented above also predicts that as the magnitude of mobility increases (i.e. distance out from a central place), foragers should process more resources at the source rather than transport them unprocessed. Such long distance transportation is more likely to characterise logistical forays. Foragers intent on field processing distant resources must carry with them not only those technologies that aid capture, but also those needed to process the resource. An increase in tool complexity might therefore be expected when foragers aim to process resources far from the residential base, as the transported toolkit is expected to perform both capture and handling related functions. This is exactly what Shott found when he plotted the range of foraging trips against the complexity of toolkits.

Alternatively, foragers may occasionally choose to transport bulkier tools to frequently used processing sites. Binford (1979) calls these items *site furniture*. Infrequent high cost exercises like the establishment of site furniture can be thought of as 'investment now for higher payoff later'. When mobility magnitude is low, foragers should simply transport the resource back to the residential camp for processing, and hence no additional technologies need be transported. Alternatively, residentially mobile foragers can simply transport themselves to the resource and thereby circumvent all additional transport costs. The use of site furniture may be profitable in any situation (i.e. either high or low mobility - logistical or residential) where people regularly return to a processing site.

Binford also suggests that mobile foragers will often make use of *situational gear*, or technological items procured from local contexts, retrieved from caches or recycled from existing personal gear, as situation dictates, and without considerable forward planning. Such a strategy is likely to occur most frequently among foragers engaged in high residential mobility, where toolkit diversity is low, and hence the necessary tools must be cobbled together from available materials.

A number of predictions can be made from this discussion of strategies for utility increase under highly mobile conditions. These include:

1. reduced toolkit diversity and complexity as residential mobility increases
2. greater toolkit diversity and complexity as logistical mobility increases
3. greater processing of resources at procurement locations as logistical mobility increases
4. greater use of site furniture if site revisitation is frequent or predictable
5. increased local procurement, opportunistic scavenging and recycling of technological gear as mobility increases

Risk Reduction and the Organisation of Technology

The following set of organisational strategies play a direct role in dampening the effects of variation on subsistence returns, mostly by planning for periods of time-limited foraging and unpredictable shortfall by ensuring that technologies are functional where and when they are needed (Torrence 1989). Torrence (1989) argues that unlike risk reduction in the subsistence strategies described above, which typically involve long-term investments aimed at spreading losses over many months or years, technological risk reduction (among hunter-gatherers at least) typically alleviates risk over very short periods (i.e. minutes to days).

Scheduling and Risk Reduction. Torrence (1983; 1989) argues that temporal constraints can create 'time-stress' if foragers are caught unprepared for urgent tasks (such as capturing seasonal or mobile prey whose availability is extremely limited or whose location is difficult to predict) or if competing activities (such as manufacturing tools or harvesting prey) are poorly managed. She argues that foragers can reduce the risk of failure to capture resources in such situations by planning for future time-limited opportunities and scheduling technological activities so that they do not interfere or compete with other important tasks at crucial times. This goal can be achieved by dividing technological activities such as procurement, maintenance and discard into small time parcels and 'juggling' these to meet the range of needs at the appropriate times. The archaeological signature for this strategy should be essentially the same as that for time-budgeting above.

Retooling and Raw Material Procurement. In times and places where the availability of resources is highly variable, foragers may be uncertain about when the next opportunity for raw material procurement and retooling will present itself. Foragers faced with such uncertainty about future movements and opportunities should procure materials whenever they are encountered if there is room in the toolkit for new material. Such a practice would help reduce the risk of being caught without tools and tool-making potential at times of critical need. Frequent retooling would also help ensure tools are always at their most functional.

Brantingham's (2003) 'neutral procurement' model, although designed for other purposes, helps explore the effects of such a procurement strategy in fine-grained environments where foragers follow a random walk model and raw materials are distributed randomly throughout the landscape. Brantingham makes four assumptions for this model: 1) that there are limits on what foragers can carry and that new material will be procured only when the transported supply needs replenishing (the zero-sum game), 2) that raw materials are consumed at a constant rate over time, and 3) that all raw materials will be procured on encounter if toolkit supply is below the maximum irrespective of abundance or quality, and 4) that enough stone will be procured to refill the toolkit to maximum capacity.

The applicability of these assumptions in real world situations is obviously questionable in some cases. For instance, we should expect foragers to meliorate their behaviour in response to changing circumstances, such as when transported stone supply is low. Such responses might include slowing the rate of material consumption if a certain amount of time has elapsed and no new source has been encountered (presumably at the expense of tool performance), or moving purposefully to the closest source rather than continuing a random walk pattern that might take them further from a source and allow stone supply to 'clear' entirely. However, it is necessary to make assumptions of this kind if models are to retain generality, and these assumptions are not unreasonable.

Brantingham's simulation of 5000 time-steps indicates that raw material richness does not vary by much in a fine-grained environment (that is, when raw material diversity is calculated as a ratio to sample size), but the proportions of different materials in the toolkit does show pronounced distance decay relationships as time since procurement increases. Unfortunately, Brantingham does not model situations where raw materials are unevenly distributed, which is likely to be the case for most environments. However, we can predict that in such cases the rate of material consumption should be curvilinear, with foragers slowing the rate of consumption as they move further from a source to ensure that the toolkit is not entirely cleared before more stone can be procured. Torrence also argues that to increase overall toolkit performance in risky situations, foragers should select higher quality materials wherever possible. Risk reduction may therefore sometimes result in foregoing local raw materials (and perhaps slowing the rate of raw material consumption) and holding out until higher quality materials can be procured. In this way, Bamforth (1986) is right to argue that raw material procurement has its own costs, even if it is embedded in other activities.

We can therefore modify earlier predictions about the meaning of raw material variability to include the following:

1. in fine grained/stable environments the proportions of raw materials in an assemblage will reflect time since last procurement
2. under risky conditions, the rate of raw material consumption will vary according to uncertainty over supply
3. under risky conditions, raw material proportions may be out of phase with patch use history

Design Theory

A third set of theory helpful in understanding ways in which foragers can optimize subsistence returns draws on the design theory that is deeply embedded in Schiffer's behavioural archaeology. Modifying the design of technologies can enhance certain performance characteristics to solve different technological problems (Fitzhugh 2001; Hayden *et al*. 1996).

Like time-budgeting and the particular solutions to mobility constraints, modifications to toolkit design should also leave identifiable traces in the archaeological record. For instance, as costs associated with search and capture of prey go up as encounter rates with high-ranking prey decrease, evolutionary ecologists predict that foragers should invest in improving the design of technologies that reduce costs upon encounter (Broughton and O'Connell 1999:155). This is because energy returns are largely intrinsic to resources, and the best way to increase returns as diet breadth increases is to increase the efficiency with which resources are handled by making better designed tools (Bright *et al*. 2002; Ugan *et al*. 2003).

A number of studies have examined performance characteristics under the control of the manufacturer that might be emphasized for tools designed to perform specific functions. For instance, penetration might be enhanced in projectile point design by reducing tip thickness, increasing leading edge sharpness, and decreasing cross-sectional area and the angle of intersection of the distal margins (Ahler and Geib 2000; Guthrie 1983). Killing power might be enhanced by increasing the depth of projectile penetration, and this can be achieved by designing the projectile to cut a wide enough hole that 'haft drag' created by binding and haft elements is reduced (Friis-Hansen 1990; Frison 1989). Symmetry and weight will also affect the balance and stability of the projectile (Beck 1998). However, these performance characteristics come at a cost. Wider points increase penetration depth, for instance, but also reduce ease of penetration. Tip thinness increases ease of penetration, but at the cost of higher breakage rates. Sharper tips mean more frequent sharpening etc. Thus the user will be forced to balance a number of trade-offs between ease and depth of penetration and resistance to breakage (see also Schiffer and Skibo 1997:31-32). Other performance characteristics will be emphasized in other contexts: high edge angles for scraping tasks, edge length and low edge angle for cutting tasks, a stout point for drilling etc.

Improvements in the regularity and processing efficiency of millstones in central Australia (Gorecki *et al*. 1997; Smith 1985) serves as a good example of how people might have invested in technology to obtain higher returns from low ranked resources. Indeed, improvements in grindstone design could have been a major factor associated with colonisation of truly arid 'barrier deserts' out of better-watered Pleistocene and early Holocene 'refuges' (Veth 1993a, b; but see David 2002 for an argument for a late-Holocene advent of seed grinding millstones). First colonisation of these environments would likely have resulted in rapid depression of higher-ranked prey that are extremely sensitive to over-predation, and the concomitant use of more labour intensive resources such as starchy seeds from trees and grasses (Cane 1984; Devitt 1988; O'Connell and Hawkes 1984). Investing more effort in procurement, design and processing efficiency of millstones would likely have made these food items more attractive as dietary staples, and probably greatly facilitated the occupation of these arid regions.

The assumption of design theory in the context of optimising subsistence strategies is that people should invest more effort in designing and manufacturing tools if doing so helps achieve returns above minimum requirements. Ugan *et al*. (2003) and Bright *et al*. (2002) have found that for a sample of common hunter-gatherer technologies, greater investments of 'techtime' are typically associated with higher rates of return.

Utility Increase and Tool Design

The following observations about technological design criteria could result in utility increase in specific situations, although it is difficult to know which ones in particular since empirical studies of this sort have not been undertaken.

Standardisation. One way in which to reduce time spent manufacturing and maintaining tool components and thereby obtain higher returns in resource handling may be to employ standardised components so that the costs incurred in manufacturing one component of a technology need not be incurred again in order to accommodate new components when old ones need replacing. An example would be the standardisation of stone projectile tips used within composite technologies such as spears, arrows or darts, where the haft typically takes much longer to manufacture than the point (Hayden 1979; Keeley 1982; Odell 1994; Torrence 1989). Reducing variation in the size and shape of the inserts would minimise additional expenditure on modifying the haft to accommodate the new tip.

Another case in which standardisation may result in utility increase is in minimising wastage of time and materials in procuring and manufacturing tools. A common assertion in lithic studies, for instance, is that technologies that produce flakes of equal size and shape in sequence from a block of stone with little waste or failure between blows (as in formal blade technologies or recurrent Levallois production), can maximise cutting edge for raw material usage, thereby increasing efficiency in tool manufacture and reducing procurement costs (Nelson 1991). Standardisation may also assist in regularising tool performance and in making estimates of probable tool use-life (Hiscock 2005).

Hafting. Hafting is a clear example of a way in which tool design can result in utility increase. Keeley (1982) explains that hafting can achieve this in a number of ways, including 1) by making particular tool forms functional in ways that they otherwise would not be (e.g. projectile points, or tools with small cutting edges), 2) by increasing the force that may be exerted during work by increasing leverage, 3) by enhancing the efficiency or precision of work (e.g. drill bits, gravers), 4) by conserving lithic material by exposing only small portions of the edge to use-damage, and 5) by decreasing the likelihood of loss.

Portability. Shott (1989) reasons that higher mobility will not only reduce toolkit diversity and tend to increase toolkit complexity, but will likely also result in a reduction in the size of the mobile toolkit if travel costs are severe. This might mean transporting a small number of larger tools if toolkit diversity is low (as in the case of high residential mobility), or a number of smaller ones if toolkit diversity is advantageous (as in cases of higher logistical mobility).

Versatility. Assuming that the number of tasks performed by foraging groups remains much the same, Shott's (1989) analysis indicates that changes in mobility should generally result in changes in toolkit diversity, with high mobility frequency leading to low toolkit diversity, and high mobility magnitude leading to high toolkit complexity. Essentially, what is implied in this argument is that logistical forays tend to target specific resources, and that the use of specialized tools that are more efficient at performing certain tasks will result in greater returns than could be achieved with more generalised tools. This relationship between number of tools and number of functions is termed *versatility*, and higher versatility is expected when toolkit diversity is low.

Flexibility. In contrast to versatility, flexibility refers to the potential for a tool or raw materials to be recycled for use in some other task (Nelson 1991; Shott 1986). As residential mobility increases and toolkit diversity decreases, foragers might be more inclined to make greater use of situational gear. An additional design element for low diversity toolkits then may be to build in flexibility in such a way that toolkits can be opportunistically recycled to perform a range of unscheduled tasks. In contexts of low mobility, and of predictable requirements for tools in particular locations, it is often suggested that foragers should stock-pile raw materials at the central place or locations of anticipated use (Kuhn 1992, 1995; Nelson 1991). The central place foraging model, however, suggests cases in which this pattern might not hold - principally where raw materials are being transported over long distances. In contexts of low residential mobility, or where logistical forays are also relatively short, there may be little need to pre-process materials, and stockpiling at the residential base would be the optimal strategy for providing maximum flexibility.

Use-Life. One insight gained from modelling optimal technological investment concerns the period of tool use required to recoup and build on the costs in time and energy incurred in raw material procurement and tool manufacture. In the case of complex technologies, for instance, outlays of time and energy may be substantial even before a tool is used. However, in cases where greater initial investment results in utility increase, this initial outlay is cost-effective so long as the artefact survives long-enough to repay investment and reap the long-term benefits of improved performance (Ugan *et al.* 2003).

In the context of stone artefact technologies, use-life can be extended by designing implements with the potential to undergo more resharpening/recycling events per unit weight, a concept Hiscock (2005) and Macgregor (2005) call *extendibility*. They argue that certain classes of artefacts, generalised retouched flakes ('scrapers') and bifacial points for instance, are likely to be quite different in the degree to which use-life can be extended. Scrapers are typically retouched in a single plane, and increasingly encounter step terminations and high edge angles as reduction continues, such that each retouching event reduces the potential for another. Bifacial technologies, on the other hand, facilitate longer use-lives by allowing step terminations to be removed from the opposite edge, are more successful at maintaining edge angles, and benefit from the establishment of scar patterns on both faces that help flake detachments run to the centre-line without terminating abruptly (Kelly 1988; Kelly and Todd 1988; Macgregor 2005; Whittaker 1994). Bifacially flaked ground edge axes probably represent the quintessential extendable technology, as they possess many of the advantageous characteristics of bifaces (in terms of their potential to overcome flaking errors and maintain required geometry), but have the added advantage of additional size and weight (which enables many more rejuvenation events before exhaustion) and a ground edge that can be easily rejuvenated to provide a highly functional edge in chopping tasks for long periods (Hiscock 2005).

Similarly, Beck (1995; 1998) has explored the issue of use-life for projectile points in terms of the costs of manufacture and repair. She examined failures in side and corner-notched Great Basin points, and found that side-notching tended to weaken points at their centre, making them more likely to break in half. A central break means that less of the original tool is left for re-tooling. A way of minimizing the costs of breakage then is to encourage points to break as near to the tip or as near to the base as possible, an explanation she adopts for the rise of corner-notching as the dominant strategy in Great Basin point manufacture after c. 5,000 BP.

Embedding points deep within the haft or resin so that only the tip is exposed might constitute an additional strategy for minimizing loss through breakage (Ahler and Geib 2000). Mulvaney (1969) and Akerman (1981) have made similar observations regarding the use of an extensive resin casing to protect the fragile edges of Kimberley points. Akerman (1981:488) also suggested that affixing points to a slotted haft rather than a split haft, and using a large piece of resin rather than bindings and notches, might help reduce breakage rates by allowing points to break free of the haft when excessive lateral force is applied. Lashing and notching would make the point too rigid, and may result in snapping the tip and the foreshaft (if used). The use of large amounts of resin adhesive also allows the mounting of extremely small points, aiding penetration, although at the expense of cutting potential. As small points might often be expected to result from extensive reworking and resharpening, such a strategy might enable the use of these points to be extended until replacement points were available.

An advantageous spin-off of long use-life implements that are resharpened many times is that many flakes are produced from their edges that are often well-suited to fine cutting tasks such as skinning and butchering (Kelly 1988; Kelly and Todd 1988). The selection of high quality raw materials may also extend the use-life of tools as high quality cryptocrystalline rocks are generally better suited to the fine retouching that characterizes most resharpening events (Goodyear 1989; Gould and Saggers 1985).

Increasing the use-life of tools therefore increases the long-term payoff when manufacturing costs are high, and should be detectable in stone artefact assemblages as attempts to increase the extendibility of implements through retouching, improved geometry and the selection of high quality raw materials.

Tool Design and Risk Reduction

Certain technical performance characteristics can also serve to reduce risk. In one sense all of the technical strategies described so far may help reduce risk, if by increasing capture rates and processing efficiency foragers can ensure production remains above minimum requirements despite the effects of stochastic variation. Foragers should therefore invest more heavily in technology when risk is a significant factor. However, the design criteria reviewed so far do not specifically target the reduction (or harnessing) of variance in foraging returns. Three aspects of tool design in particular are likely to aid in risk reduction.

Reliability and Maintainability. Foraging time will be limited by the functionally effective life of the tools on which successful capture depends (Ugan *et al.* 2003). In time-limited situations that result from fleeting encounters with mobile game or reductions in search time due to longer travel times to and from a patch, foragers may benefit from increasing the length of time for which a technology is functional before repairs are needed. For example, Binford (1979) found that there was little time for the Nunamiut to undertake tool maintenance during the thirty days or so in which caribou are available, and hence they invested a great deal of energy in advance of use in ensuring their tools would perform reliably for the required duration.

Bleed (1986) has examined the design principles that help ensure technological reliability, and has contrasted these with maintainability. Tools designed to be reliable will tend to be sturdy and over-designed to withstand more than the range of stresses they are expected to have to endure during use. This might entail increasing the size of a tool if this adds strength, or it might involve added attention to joints or fitting, or the use of redundant or standby components that ensure continued functioning if one or more components fail.

Because reliable technologies are designed not to breakdown, their repair often requires longer maintenance periods using specialised repair kits capable of fixing any damaged component. Reliable technologies therefore also tend to be maintained by specialists and in contexts where a range of maintenance tools are available. The repetitive tasks to which reliable technologies are best suited will also mean they are not as versatile as maintainable ones, and truly reliable technologies might therefore be expected to accompany higher toolkit diversity.

In contrast, Bleed (1986) sees maintainable technologies as likely to be simpler than those designed for reliability. They may also tend to have a series design in which each component performs a distinct task, but with the disadvantage that if one component fails, the entire system fails. Consequently, maintainable systems must be designed to be easily repaired and brought quickly back into service. The simpler nature of maintainable technologies also means that the user should be capable of fixing damaged components easily and quickly with available tools.

Bleed illustrates his arguments by contrasting the simple portable toolkit carried by !Kung San men and designed to make unscheduled repairs quick and easy, with the reliable technologies of arctic foragers that emphasize reliability due to the restricted time available for seasonal hunting. To increase reliability, the Nunamiut, for instance, rely on redundancy, and transport many well-crafted, specialised tools to the location of intended use, including multiple tools of the same kind. They also cache tools and components at locations around the landscape to reduce the risk of being caught without necessary technologies at critical times.

Bleed further argues that a way to improve the performance of critically important technologies is to add some features of maintainability to reliable technologies, so that "if the worst happens and the system fails when it is needed, it can be rapidly repaired for continued use" (Bleed 1986:740). Torrence (1989) points out that this is exactly what arctic foragers do by incorporating simple and maintainable 'series designed' elements into their tools. Myers (1989:87) also offers the example of the Mesolithic composite weapons comprised of multiple backed artefact components that bring features of both reliability (i.e. redundancy in backed artefact assemblies that enhance performance and mitigate against partial loss or breakage) and maintainability (use of standardised components that can be easily replaced) to the tool, an argument others have also run to explain the adoption of backed technologies in other parts of the world (Bleed 2001; Hiscock 2002; Neeley and Barton 1994).

Technological Investment and Tool Performance. Torrence (1989) argues that risk prone populations should invest heavily in toolkit design and manufacture if this helps dampen the effects of variability and time-stress. Torrence suggests tool specialisation and complexity are the two most obvious signatures of increased investment. The degree to which foragers invest in technology should also be dependent on the costs of failure. Using the same data presented in her earlier paper (Torrence 1983),

Torrence sees a dependence on highly mobile game as a big factor creating the type of short-term risk that foraging technologies can help overcome, and that high latitude foragers that predominantly pursue mobile game are therefore more likely to invest heavily in specialised tools including tended and untended facilities. While the association between latitude and dependence on mobile game (and hence risk) is real, many other populations also experience high levels of stochastic variation and time-limited resource availability, such as foragers in mid-latitude arid environments or those dependant on a highly variable monsoon in tropical regions. Furthermore, any population can be become risk prone if variability is heightened or introduced into the system, such as might result from increased climatic variability.

In risk averse populations, technologies can therefore be expected to be:

1. better designed for high performance and a limited range of functions, as indicated by higher toolkit diversity and complexity
2. made from higher quality raw materials where possible

Innovation and Variation. Following Stephens and Charnov (1982), Fitzhugh proposes that as risk sensitive populations begin to experience mean yields below minimum requirements, they should switch from a risk-averse to a risk prone attitude to technological innovation – or the process of constructing and testing new technologies that *might* give higher payoffs than existing ones. Fitzhugh's model is presented in Figure 2.2. In the top graph (A), productivity from foraging is shown over time. In the bottom graph (B), the dynamic feedback between resource productivity and proclivity for risk-taking behaviour is shown as a sigmoidal curve (utility/time). The model predicts that foragers will switch to a risk-prone strategy of technological innovation in the hope of higher payoffs when returns are below the dashed line in A, and return rate falls into the shaded area in B. This model accounts for the way in which new variation may be stimulated once people are able to perceive changes in conditions. Under periods of extreme shortfall then, we might expect to find evidence for experimentation and variation in technologies in the hope that foragers might secure higher returns that at present. Fitzhugh (2001:144) argues that invention and experimentation is most likely to focus first on technologies that may enhance capture rate of larger, high-ranked prey, but as these are driven to decline, inventiveness should gradually turn to hardier, and more reproductively stable r-selected species. Finally, Fitzhugh makes a number of predictions about the circumstances likely to increase risk and lead to greater technological innovation:

1. movement into unfamiliar environments
2. rapid climatic change
3. depletion of high–ranked prey
4. heightened competition between groups

Toward a Synthesis

So far a great many subsistence and technological strategies have been listed that foragers could employ to increase energetic efficiency, reduce risk and thereby increase the chances of success in subsistence and other aspects of life. Combining these individual strategies into a synthetic model that places causal factors in their proper order (i.e. resource availability and structure, then subsistence organisation and then technology) is not easy, especially if we are to heed Torrence's warning about the hopeless inadequacy of rigid settlement/subsistence typologies. Most formulations appear to begin with a series of propositions about technological problems that need solving, without stipulating the conditions giving rise to these problems (e.g. Hayden *et al*. 1996). No simplified model is ever completely satisfactory, and there are many points of potential overlap and ambiguity in any system. For instance, similar aspects of technological organisation (such as embedded procurement and advance manufacture) could equally stem from changing levels of mobility or the need for risk reduction, even though in one context the goal is to reduce travel costs and in the other it is to buffer against future uncertainty by ensuring tools are made well in advance of need.

Figure 2.2. Illustration of the relationship between stochastic variation and risk sensitivity, after Fitzhugh (2001). A: hypothetical return rate from foraging over time, B: sigmoid curve representing utility / time (gain rate) for foraging.

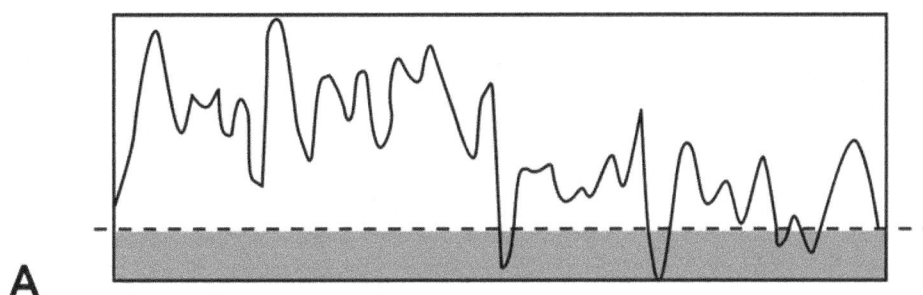

A

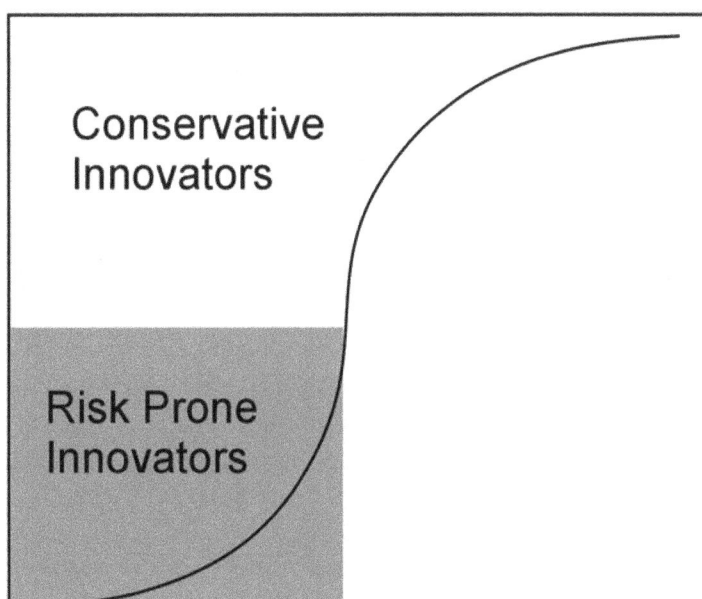

Conservative
Innovators

Risk Prone
Innovators

B

One model that has made significant progress in uniting the various themes in technology and subsistence touched upon in this chapter is Kuhn's (1995) system of technological provisioning. With some additional specification for the situations in which different provisioning strategies are likely to obtain, this model would seem to be a convenient and powerful tool for studying subsistence and technological change in the archaeological record.

Kuhn's Provisioning Model

Kuhn has portrayed the strategies employed to balance subsistence against technological costs as a range of alternatives involving planning for the nature, timing and location of use. To be most successful, technological planning must take into account temporal and spatial fluctuations in the frequency, predictability and range of residential moves, functional requirements for exploiting different kinds of resources, time-stress and urgency of use, opportunities for maintenance, the richness and diversity of foraging opportunities and the availability of replacement raw materials; in other words, the range of factors outlined above. As we have seen, different variable states, as well as variation in these over time, should elicit different responses in terms of the way raw materials are provisioned and the specific design of the toolkits themselves. Kuhn describes two provisioning strategies that represent solutions to the problem of maintaining a constant supply of effective tools under conditions where mobility, and access to and predictability of resources varies. These strategies are called the *provisioning of individuals*, and the *provisioning of places* and subsume the more common and problematic concepts of 'curated' and 'expedient' technologies (Kuhn 1995:22).

Individual Provisioning

Individual provisioning represents a response to situations where future contingencies must be planned long in advance with little certainty over where or when extractive and maintenance tasks will take place (Binford and Binford 1966). This strategy can be linked to situations of high logistical mobility in variable/patchy environments, to high residential mobility where foraging opportunities may not coincide well with opportunities to reprovision with raw materials, and where down-time cannot be scheduled with any certainty. Individual provisioning might be expected to arise as a result of increasing resource depression leading to longer travel times to more distant patches, fewer and more time-limited encounters with high-ranked mobile prey, and increased climatic variability creating greater stochastic variation in resource availability. Longer travel times should also give rise to greater pre-processing of resources to increase utility per unit load (Beck *et al.* 2002; Bettinger *et al.* 1997; Jones and Madsen 1989; Metcalfe and Barlow 1992).

Individual provisioning cross-cuts the categories of mobility, risk reduction, and time-stress discussed above. In keeping with the principles of optimal design for each of these situations, toolkits designed for individual provisioning will tend to be portable, versatile, flexible, maintainable and reliable (i.e. with features of both), and will be made well in advance of use, and hence, be on-hand when and where they are needed.

Kuhn argues that this strategy has direct consequences for the production and design of toolkits. For instance, the significant transport costs entailed in high mobility are likely to select for light-weight stone tools of smallish size (Shott 1989). Frequency of mobility is also likely to constrict the diversity of tool-kits, with a focus on versatile, multi-functional tools, as opposed to a number of tools each designed for specific tasks (Shott, 1986). High logistical mobility should create a trend toward the opposite extreme - that of specialised and diverse toolkit manufacture - with each tool better suited to a limited range of functions. Because access to replacement material may be unpredictable, tool use-life should be extended (Hiscock 2005; Macgregor 2005), or tools should have the capacity for recycling so that unscheduled tasks can be performed (Dibble 1995; Kuhn 1995). Because they are small, these portable toolkits are also more likely to be employed as components in composite, hafted tools (Keeley 1982; Odell 1989). To meet the requirements of maintainability they may be designed as interchangeable tool bits to fit pre-fabricated hafts, thus requiring a degree of standardization in their morphology. To offset the risk of breakage at times of critical need they may also be manufactured from higher quality raw materials (Goodyear 1989), or form one of a number of multiple redundant components (Bleed 1986; Myers 1989).

This set of features is not exhaustive and additional designs are conceivable. The point is that the provisioning of individuals should have predictable archaeological correlates.

Place Provisioning

The provisioning of places is a more favourable strategy when the location and timing of activities to be performed in the future is predictable and mobility is low. This strategy would tend to be employed at locations where the diversity or richness of subsistence opportunities is greater, such as when high-ranked or stable resources are abundant and close by, variance in foraging returns is low, and resources are patchy and suited to exploitation from a central place of low residential mobility. Provisioning of places promotes the transport of raw material, or 'tool making potential' in Kuhn's words, to a site of relatively longer-term residence, where the type of equipment needed can be predicted and where the range and quantity of extractive tasks may be greater, and hence greater flexibility in tool form may be desirable. Since this provisioning strategy is best adopted under conditions of low mobility and relatively short range logistical foraging, material can be expected to be transported to the central place over relatively short distances, and therefore not to have been pre-processed to any significant degree. Raw material stockpiling should therefore be a common feature of place provisioning (Parry and Kelly 1987), and might include such strategies as the provisioning of large blocks and cores that offer maximum flexibility in terms of the creation of fresh sharp edges of a range of shapes and sizes with minimal processing required. The supply of raw material to provisioned sites need not digress completely from broad patterns of raw material supply, however, and distance decay relationships should still be expected. This is because procurement will still reflect patch use, while the degree and rate of consumption will reflect time since procurement and the anticipated time until the next procurement.

While each of these strategies is portrayed as an alternative to a given set of economic and/or ecological constraints, in reality both forms may co-exist to differing degrees within different segments of the total land use system. It should be possible therefore to find elements of individual provisioning within a predominantly place provisioned landscape, and vice versa, depending on the levels of mobility required to exploit resources in each patch and the levels of variance experienced in each.

Kuhn's model is elegant and contains most of the ingredients required to deduce changing patterns of land use, mobility and risk, and from these infer likely changes in resource availability and subsistence organisation. As a useful heuristic, it can also be broken apart more easily than the highly ambiguous and often confused concepts of curation and expedience.

Conclusion

Human foragers must make complex decisions about the world in order to survive, reproduce and compete with their conspecifics. Optimality models help us understand the sorts of decision foragers *should* make in given situations and their likely effects on fitness differentials, even if no one ever really acts like this all of the time or even cognizes problems in this way. That these models appear to explain even some human behaviour, let alone accounting for many situations with pleasing accuracy (Smith 1983), attests to their utility in anthropology and their ongoing importance in helping explain human evolution and cultural variability. The focus on two kinds of models – utility increase and risk reduction – allows many of the day-to-day decisions facing foragers to be modelled and particular responses and coping strategies predicted. Placing subsistence concerns first, rather than relegating them to a shadowy background as many technological models have done, provides us with a set of statements about the likely factors giving rise to particular technological problem solving strategies. For the most part these seem to be aimed either at maximising energetic efficiency under different constraints or maximising or minimising variation in returns when environmental conditions are variable and minimal requirements are at stake. The various models presented form a complex set of entangled problems and solutions that are not easily synthesized into a single interpretive scheme. Kuhn's provisioning model, however, takes us at least some way toward that goal by providing a coherent account of the likely relationship between subsistence concerns and technological problem solving strategies. With this interpretive scheme in place, it is now possible to explore in more detail the methods by which we can detect changes in provisioning in the archaeological record.

3. Procedures for Lithic Analysis

Understanding and depicting all aspects of a technological system should properly begin with the methods of manufacture themselves. Perhaps the best way to examine the manufacturing process is to understand the various procedures and strategies knappers employed to gain control over the material being worked and determine their frequency in archaeological assemblages. From this we may determine their significance in relation to other features of the assemblage (such as the geographic location of the assemblage relative to the occurrence of raw materials, the type and quality of raw materials, etc.). By briefly reviewing the methods of stone fracture and its many intertwined variables and problems, a list of important technological features and their likely strategic significance can be generated. These can be later used to reconstruct the manufacturing system, explore changes in raw material useage and provisioning strategies. I will then detail methods that are useful for understanding, depicting and measuring stone artefact reduction, as this will form the basis for many of the analyses presented later in this monograph.

Stone Fracture, Knapping Strategies and Morphological Attributes

The process of fracture propagation that underlies flaked stone artefact manufacture is complex, and the effects of various core morphologies on the fracture path are not well understood. Yet it is the fracture path that ultimately determines the morphology of flakes and cores, and archaeologists have therefore begun to try and understand this process and the means by which people may alter and control it. Without delving too far into the details, it is possible to briefly describe some of the main principles and the most common fracture features that result.

In most forms of flaking, force is directed into the *platform* (i.e. any surface receiving force) of a nucleus with an indentor (any object imparting force to a nucleus) using one of three techniques: striking the nucleus at high velocity with either a hard indentor such as a hammerstone (hard hammer percussion) or a soft indentor such as a piece of wood, bone or antler (soft hammer percussion), slowly applying pressure through a process called *dynamic loading* (pressure flaking), striking a positioned punch (indirect percussion), or applying compressive force by placing the nucleus on an anvil and striking it from above (bipolar technique) (Cotterell and Kamminga 1987; Kooyman 2000).

Skilled flintknappers observe that in most flaking force is directed into the nucleus using both an inward and outward motion (Crabtree 1972; Whittaker 1994), creating both 'opening' and 'shearing' stresses in the nucleus (Figure 3.1a) (Macgregor 2001). Fracture occurs when stresses within the nucleus reach a critical threshold and break the molecular bonds holding the nucleus together.

The most common form of fracture is known as *conchoidal fracture*, which begins from pre-existing flaws in the surface of the nucleus close to the point of impact and creates what is known as a *Hertzian cone*, as illustrated in Figure 3.1b. The Hertzian cone propagates in a circle around the contact area and expands down into the nucleus in a cone shape at an angle partly dependant on the angle of applied force. If the nucleus is struck close to the edge, only a partial cone will be visible on the flake (Figure 3.1b). Whether or not a fracture will continue to propagate through the core once a cone is formed (i.e. and not just leave an incipient cone in the nucleus), depends on whether the force of the blow is sufficient to accelerate and overcome the inertia of the material that is to be removed. Once fracture is initiated, a number of counteracting stresses created by the magnitude and direction of force (tensile, bending and compressive stresses) will influence the path it then takes through the core. In conchoidal fracture, the path will typically first head into the core before diving back toward the free face, creating the *bulb of force*, and then stabilizing on a path that is more or less parallel to the free surface (Macgregor 2001).

Figure 3.1. Types and features of fracture initiation and termination (after Andrefsky 1998; Cotterell and Kamminga 1987). A: fracture variables, B: formation of a hertzian cone, C: fracture initiations, and D: fracture terminations.

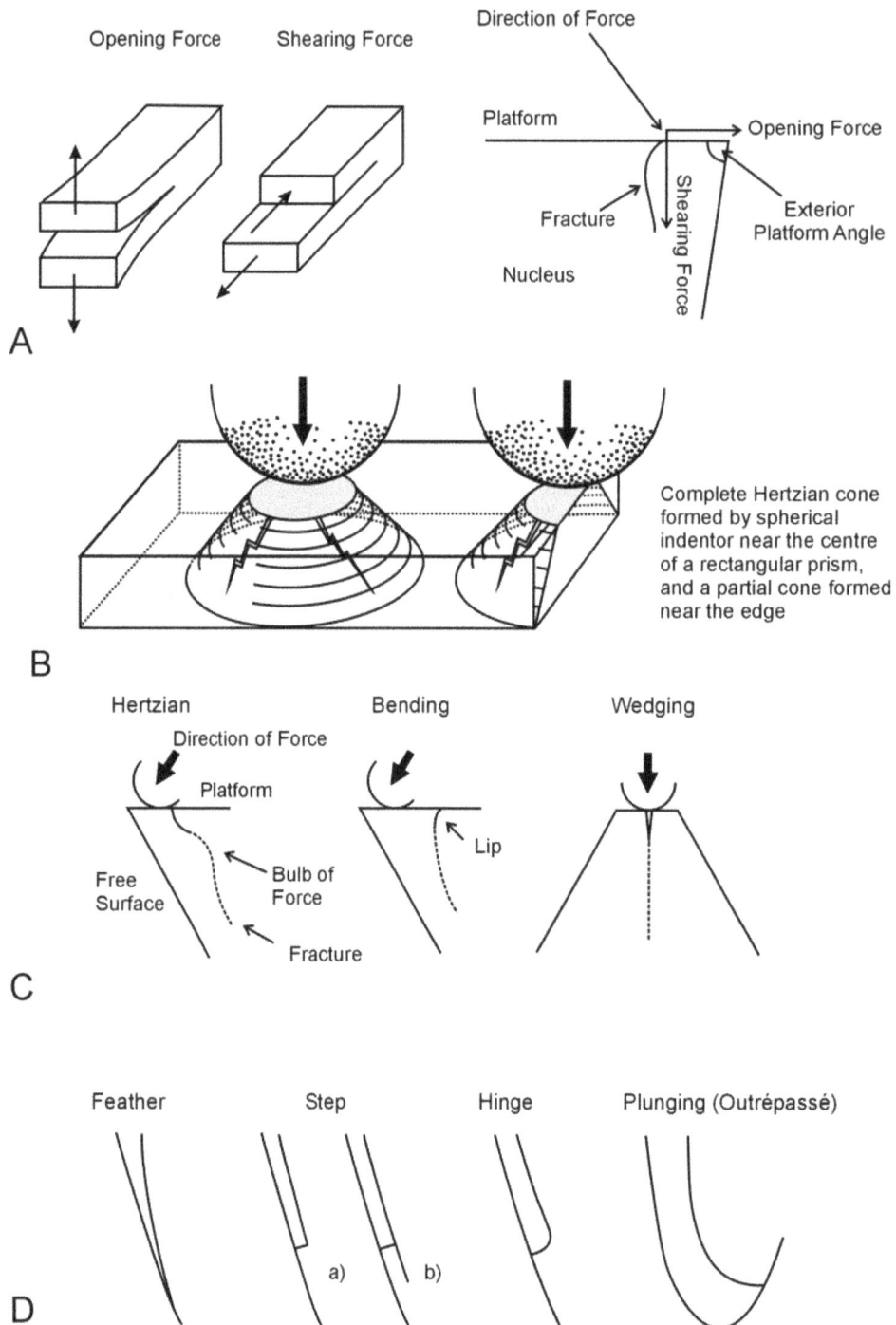

Opening Force   Shearing Force   Direction of Force

Platform   Opening Force

Fracture   Shearing Force   Exterior Platform Angle

Nucleus

A

Complete Hertzian cone formed by spherical indentor near the centre of a rectangular prism, and a partial cone formed near the edge

B

Hertzian   Bending   Wedging

Direction of Force

Platform

Free Surface   Bulb of Force   Lip

Fracture

C

Feather   Step   Hinge   Plunging (Outrépassé)

a)   b)

D

Conchoidal flakes (i.e. those with Hertzian initiations) often retain a ring crack at the *point of force application* (PFA), and an *eraillure scar* just below the point of percussion on the bulb of force (Figure 3.2). Undulations in the fracture path also often leave *compression waves* on the ventral surface of flakes. Fissures radiating out from the point of percussion are also often found on the ventral surfaces of flakes, but are most often seen on fine grained materials.

Figure 3.2. Fracture features often found on the ventral and dorsal faces of a conchoidal flake (reproduction is by courtesy of the Trustees of the British Museum).

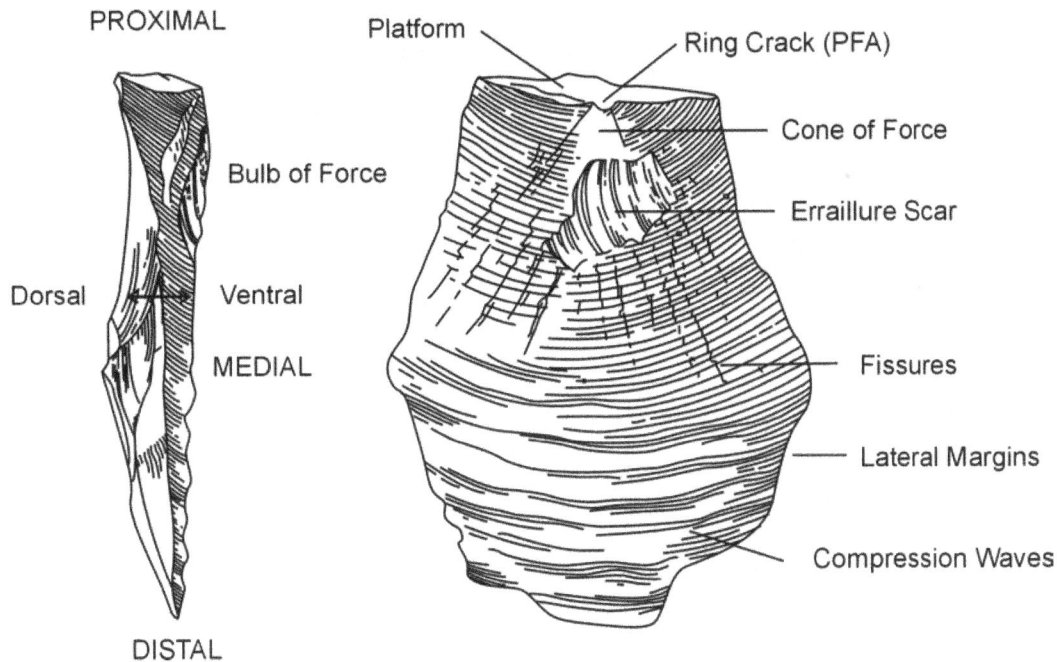

Force eventually exits the nucleus either gradually and at a low angle, creating a *feather termination*, or more rapidly and at around 90 degrees, creating a *step* or *hinge termination* (Figure 3.1d). Not all fractures follow this path, however, and the fracture path sometimes travels away from the free surface and exits on the other side of the nucleus, creating a *plunging* or *outrépassé termination* (Figure 3.1d). Pelcin's (1997c:1111) controlled experiments have shown that when all other variables are held constant, increasing platform thickness will produce regular changes in termination type from feather through to hinge terminations, as the force becomes insufficient to run the length of the free face. The direction of force is also often implicated as a determinant of either hinge or step terminations, but this proposition has not been tested under controlled circumstances. Others have suggested that thick platforms and inward-directed force are more likely to produce outrépassé terminations given sufficient force to initiate a fracture (Crabtree 1968; Faulkner 1972:110-115; Hiscock 1988; Phagan 1985:237, 243).

Less commonly, fracture will initiate behind the point of percussion, creating a *bending initiation*, which dives rapidly toward the free face without forming a Hertzian cone, and leaves a pronounced 'lip' on the ventral edge of the platform (Figure 3.1c). Bending initiations are most commonly formed on nuclei with low angled platforms and have a fracture surface that often resembles a diffuse bulb, even though no bulb is present (Cotterell and Kamminga 1987:689). Although it has long been thought that bending initiations are typically produced by soft hammer and pressure flaking, Pelcin (1997c:1111) found that bending initiations were repeatedly created on cores with low platform angles when blows were placed relatively far in from the edge, suggesting that their frequent association with soft hammer and pressure flaking is more likely a factor of the common use of these techniques in knapping cores with low platform angles (e.g. bifaces) than it is of either force or indentor type (see also Patterson and Sollberger 1978). Pelcin (1997b) was also able to show that soft hammer flakes were on average longer and thinner than hard hammer flakes, and that this technique was therefore better suited to bifacial thinning than hard hammer percussion. Hence the association between soft hammer/pressure and bending initiations is likely to be coincidental rather than causal.

Compression fractures created by bidirectional forces produce a *wedging* initiation that results in flattish fracture surfaces without a bulb of force (Figure 3.1c) (Cotterell and Kamminga 1987). Because compression fractures are typically initiated by particles driven into existing percussion cracks, flakes created through this process often exhibit battered or crushed platforms with cascading step scars on the platform edge (Cotterell and Kamminga 1987). Bipolar cores and flakes that have been rested on an anvil most commonly display this form of initiation. Because the anvil on which the nucleus is supported can also act like a hammerstone, bipolar flakes can at times exhibit platform and initiation features at both ends, such as crushing, dual bulbs of force and bi-directional compression waves. When nuclei are stabilised on an anvil, problems of inertia – or the probability of a blow moving the core rather than detaching a flake - can be dramatically reduced. This technique is therefore ideally suited to working very small cores (Hiscock 1982b, 1988:18).

Recent controlled fracture experiments have revealed that the closer the Hertzian cone is to the edge of the nucleus, and the lower the external platform angle (EPA), the less material needs to be accelerated away from the core, and hence the less force will be required to initiate a fracture (Dibble and Pelcin 1995; Dibble and Whittaker 1981; Macgregor 2001:46; Pelcin 1997a, b, c; Speth 1974, 1975, 1981). The more these variables are reduced, however, the smaller also the resulting flake will be. This relationship is illustrated in Figure 3.3a, and can be seen to be a simple result of changing core geometry. Alternatively, increasing platform angle and striking further from the edge requires greater force input to initiate a fracture, but also results in larger flakes (Figure 3.3b). Increasing force input by too much can result in longitudinal splitting of the flake or crushing of the platform edge. At some point, increasing EPA and/or platform angle will reach a threshold at which the amount of force required to detach a flake will exceed the inertia of the nucleus itself, and will result in moving the nucleus rather than detaching a flake (Phagan 1985:247). At this point, force requirements can be reduced by decreasing EPA, platform thickness or both, or by stabilising the core on an anvil.

Figure 3.3. The effects of increasing or decreasing platform angle and platform thickness on flake size.

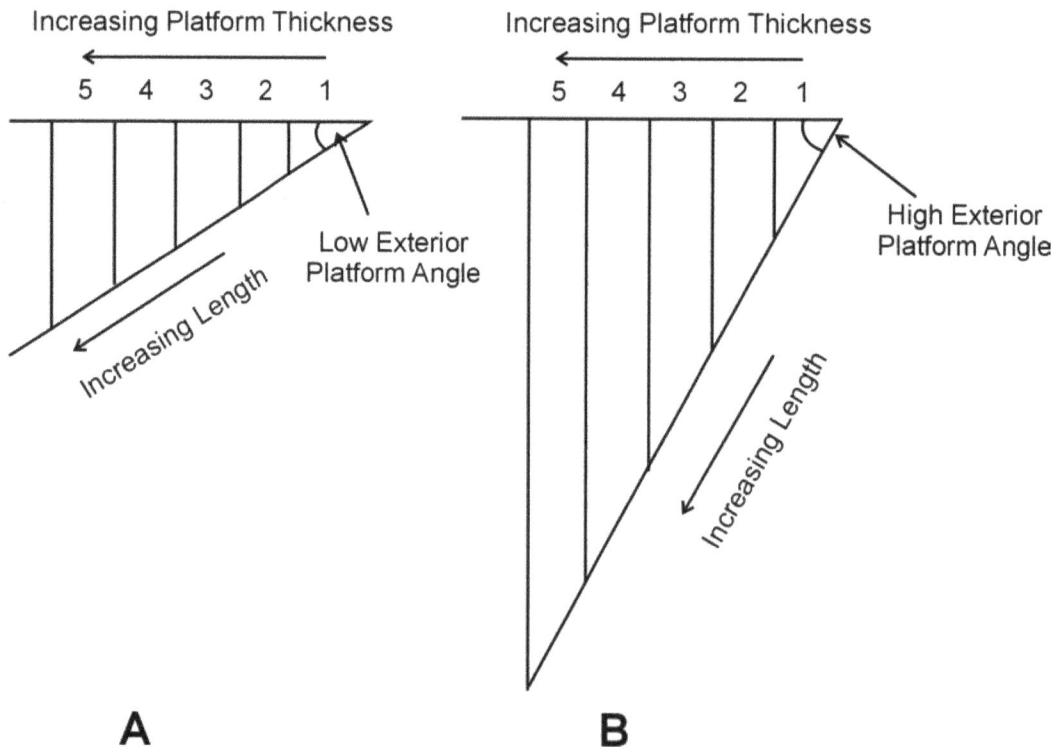

Most recently, Macgregor's (2001, 2005) experiments have demonstrated that removing some of the mass of the free face (such as might occur through overhang removal for instance) allows a blow to be placed further from the platform edge (given the same amount of force) than would have been possible were it not removed (thereby detaching a larger flake). Furthermore, Macgregor found that the morphology of the free face directly affected the morphology of the resulting flakes. His experiments demonstrated that features such as large pre-existing step or hinge terminations on the free face will decrease the viable platform area at which fractures can be successfully initiated. In the case of pre-existing step and hinge fractures, more force and the placement of blows further into the nucleus was required to successfully remove a pre-existing step or hinge termination without adding another one. It can be expected then that as more step and hinge terminations build up on the dorsal surface it will become increasingly difficult to remove them from the free face, as the viable platform area will become too small and the amount of force required too excessive to strike off a flake without shattering the platform, adding new step terminations, splitting the flake longitudinally, creating an outrépassé termination, or failing to initiate a flake altogether. A study by Pelcin (1997a) also demonstrated that varying the shape of the free face morphology affected the dimensions of the resulting flakes by changing the distribution of mass over the resulting flake. Flat-faced cores with no longitudinal ridges (*arrises*) on the free face produced shorter flakes with expanding margins and bigger bulbs of force, while cores with two longitudinal ridges on the face produced flakes that were longer and more parallel-sided with smaller bulbs of force. Pelcin's findings confirm the observations of flintknappers that setting up ridges running the length of the core face aids the production of longer, thinner, and more parallel-sided flakes (Crabtree 1972:31; Whittaker 1994:106).

The study of fracture mechanics has progressed a great deal in a very short time, but many questions are still unanswered, such as the effects of different raw materials, hammerstone size and velocity, direction of force and more complex core morphologies on the fracture path. It is also uncertain how well (or at least how directly) principles distilled from controlled experiments can be applied to archaeological assemblages. Nevertheless, studies of fracture mechanics continue to dispel myths about the causes of certain fracture features, and serve as a source of hypotheses about why particular knapping strategies might have been applied in the past. As these processes operate today in exactly the same way they did in antiquity, they offer a rare and invaluable link between the 'static' artefacts found in the archaeological record and the 'dynamics' of past human behaviour.

We can therefore identify a number of trade-offs between the interdependent variables of platform size, platform angle, core inertia, force input and nucleus morphology that knappers must manipulate to gain control over the fracture path and to extend the reduction of raw materials. A large number of strategies were employed in the past to modify force variables, rectify problematic morphologies and prevent prematurely damaging the nucleus.[1] These focus on variables that are under the direct control of the knapper and tend to be visible archaeologically. In exploring the type and frequency of various fracture features and deducing the significance of the reduction techniques employed in the past, the analyst must be aware of the pre-eminent role that fracture mechanics plays in shaping each individual artefact. Much of the behaviour associated with working stone likely revolves around gaining and maintaining control over the fracture path so as to remove flakes of desirable shape and size while avoiding premature damage to the nucleus. Studying the interactive effects of core morphology and force variables, and the point in the reduction sequence at which certain techniques are employed (such as platform preparation, core rotation, etc) therefore allows us to piece together the strategies people used to gain control over the fracture process, to shape cores and flakes in different ways, to recover from certain problems, and the point at which cores were deemed to contain no further reduction potential for the task at hand.

Capturing the complexity of the reduction process can be achieved by recording many variables on cores and flakes that reflect these processes and decisions. These include:

---

[1] see Table 1 of Clarkson and O'Connor 2005 for a list of common strategies for overcoming problems in core geometry and inertia.

- the number of scars found on cores as a measure of overall reduction intensity as well as the success in maintaining suitable core geometry
- the number of platforms on cores as a measure of attempts to overcome problems in the geometry of cores and prolong reduction
- the nature, complexity and circumference of the platform surface that was flaked as measures of the constriction of available platform area
- platform angles and size as a measure of likely force inputs and platform constriction
- the presence of overhang removal and faceting as an indication of the desire to strengthen platforms, increase the size of flakes and control platform angles
- the types of terminations found on cores and flakes as an indication of how successfully force variables and core geometry were controlled
- rates of longitudinal splitting as a measure of force control
- the type of fracture initiations as a rough guide to the techniques of force application used
- the size and shape of the cores as an indication of reduction thresholds and problems in core geometry that led to strategy switching or discard
- the shape and size of flakes as a measure of consistency in the products of flaking

Many of these attributes are used to infer changing core reduction practices over time in the study region, and the results will be presented later in this monograph.

Understanding the combination of reduction techniques and strategies employed in space and time is also vital to understanding the technological solutions people adopted to changing foraging and land use conditions. Documenting changes in the frequency of various alternative reduction strategies also requires that we have a system for placing these techniques in their proper position within the reduction sequence. This means finding ways of time-ordering the various manufacturing products produced over the reduction sequence. Such a system can be established by hypothesising the sorts of changes in core and flake morphology that should accompany continued reduction, and using combinations of these attributes to place each specimen into an appropriate time-slice within the reduction continuum. The following sections explore ways that this can be achieved for cores, flakes and retouched flakes.

Depicting the Core and Flake Reduction Process

As stone-working is a reductive technology, the measurement of the degree to which this process has progressed often forms the basis of many modern analyses. Quantifying extent of reduction allows estimations to be made of the amount of time and energy invested in the production of an artefact, the level of departure of the observed form from its original form, the amount of material likely to have been created as a product of the process, the position in the sequence at which changes in manufacturing strategies took place, and their likely effects on artefact morphology. At a higher interpretive level, many archaeologists see measures of reduction as critical to testing of behavioural models that hypothesize the place of stone artefacts in broader systems of time budgeting and land use. Consequently, measures of reduction have come to be associated, at least implicitly, with discussions of risk (Bamforth 1986; Bamforth and Bleed 1997; Myers 1989; Torrence 1989), cost (Bleed 1996), and efficiency (Jeske 1992) in past technological systems. These discussions build on the assumption that the differential distribution of sequential steps and stages through space and time will reflect aspects of planning, land use, ecology and settlement and subsistence patterns effecting people's daily lives (Kuhn 1995; Nelson 1991). Measures of reduction are consequently fast becoming a central component of lithic analysis, and underlie an important component of technological analysis – reduction sequence models.

Measures of reduction are also a particularly important means of detecting the sorts of changes in technological organisation and toolkit design outlined in the previous chapter. It was argued for instance that foragers may choose to extend the life of their toolkits when the chances of being caught without tools or tool making potential creates subsistence risk, or when greater initial investment requires a longer use-life to recoup the costs of manufacture. One way that this may be achieved is to take the reduction of stone into later stages, by rotating cores more heavily, adopting stone-working strategies that prolong reduction and provide greater utility per unit weight of stone removed, and by resharpening and recycling tools rather than discarding them and making new ones.

Reduction Sequence Models

Sequence models are theoretical constructs that attempt to time-order phenomena by positioning them at points along a temporal continuum. In lithic studies, sequence models are typically used to determine the ordering of technical actions and outcomes involved in the reduction of stone materials. Models of this sort often use measures of reduction intensity to track changes in artefact morphology throughout the reduction process, enabling the identification of common forms and the use of particular techniques at different points along the way. Sequence models have proved particularly useful in understanding and graphically depicting the various steps and transformations that characterise a wide range of lithic reduction strategies across space and time. While all reduction events form a continuum, reduction sequence models also allow us to envisage the process of reduction as either continuous in its spatio-temporal or physical arrangement (that is, the entire process takes place in one place and in a continuous sequence, or forms are gradually reduced through use and resharpening), or staged, such that various components of the process (such as procurement, initial shaping, resharpening, recycling and discard) all take place in different places at different times, with one kind of action often taking place in anticipation of another kind of future action (Bleed 2002). The notion of staging is also useful in conceptualising the way implements might be designed and transformed, with toolmakers sometimes making decisions to radically change the way a piece was to be used and shaped.

As Bleed (2001) and Dibble (1995) have pointed out, not all sequence models share the same research goals or even the same philosophical underpinning. Some approaches promote a normative view of reduction that focuses on revealing the predetermined stages prehistoric artisans went through to produce specific 'end-products' in accordance with a mental template – a charge Dibble (1995), Bleed (2001) and Shott (2003) have levelled at the *chaîne opératoire* school. Others seek to draw out the contingent nature of technological responses to changing options and circumstances by examining the nature and frequency of artefacts at different stages of reduction across space and time. This view sees production strategies as rarely involving a simple linear sequence of activities with predictable results, but rather an "expanding array of alternatives defined by intervening options and outcomes" (Bleed 1991:20). Others still have used sequence models to expose the non-reality of essentialist typologies by demonstrating the existence of underlying morphological continuums (Clarkson 2002a, 2005; Hiscock and Attenbrow 2002, 2003; Morrow 1997).

Bleed (2001) sees different approaches to sequence modelling as falling into one of two categories, which he calls 'teleological' and 'evolutionary'. Teleological models treat sequences as "a set of internally determined actions that follow one from another and lead to a predetermined goal", whereas evolutionary models describe results that are produced "by selected interaction between conditions and variables" (Bleed 2001:121). Evolutionary models therefore attempt to express the variation within a particular reduction system as much as the central tendency. Thus, while reduction sequences provide a useful means of ordering different assemblage components into reduction stages, they should not be taken to demonstrate normative modes of behaviour or the existence of 'mental templates' for stone artefact production.

The following sections identify ways in which reduction sequences can be modelled for cores, flakes and retouched implements. As variation in reduction pathways is of as much interest as central tendency, techniques for depicting variation in these reduction processes are also considered.

Modelling Core Reduction

Both fracture mechanics and basic engineering principles would suggest that striking more and more mass from a core will affect its size and geometry, which will have direct consequences for the nature of force input, the viability of different reduction strategies and the size and morphology of the flakes produced over the sequence.

We can speculate for instance that the gradual reduction of cores will result in more flake scars and less cortex, that continued use of a platform will result in a decrease in platform size, and that as more mass is struck from a core the size of the core and resulting flakes might also decrease. If cores are rotated during this process to create fresh platforms once old ones become damaged or unproductive, they should begin to preserve signs of former flaking on the platform surfaces as well as indications of the existence of old platforms. Morphological changes in core form and in the strategies used to prolong core reduction can be tracked as the number of rotations increases.

Another way to show variation in the reduction pathways and use of different techniques is to assign frequencies to various stages of sequential or dendritic reduction flow charts, or what Bleed (1991, 2001, 2002) calls 'event trees', as shown in Figure 3.4. Event trees summarize overall production systems by identifying their steps (events) and showing how they relate to one another, thereby helping clarify the dynamic relationships between static and formally diverse remains (Bleed 1996). Event trees accommodate the possibility that reduction sequences may not form a straight-line, and also add the potential for quantification of the level of variation in the system by attaching frequencies to various steps. They may also help determine the probability of failure associated with each step by examining the proportions of failed pieces belonging to each stage (Bleed 1996).

Figure 3.4. An 'event tree' describing the sequence of manufacturing actions and the frequencies attached to each conceptual stage of the process. Reproduced from Bleed (2001).

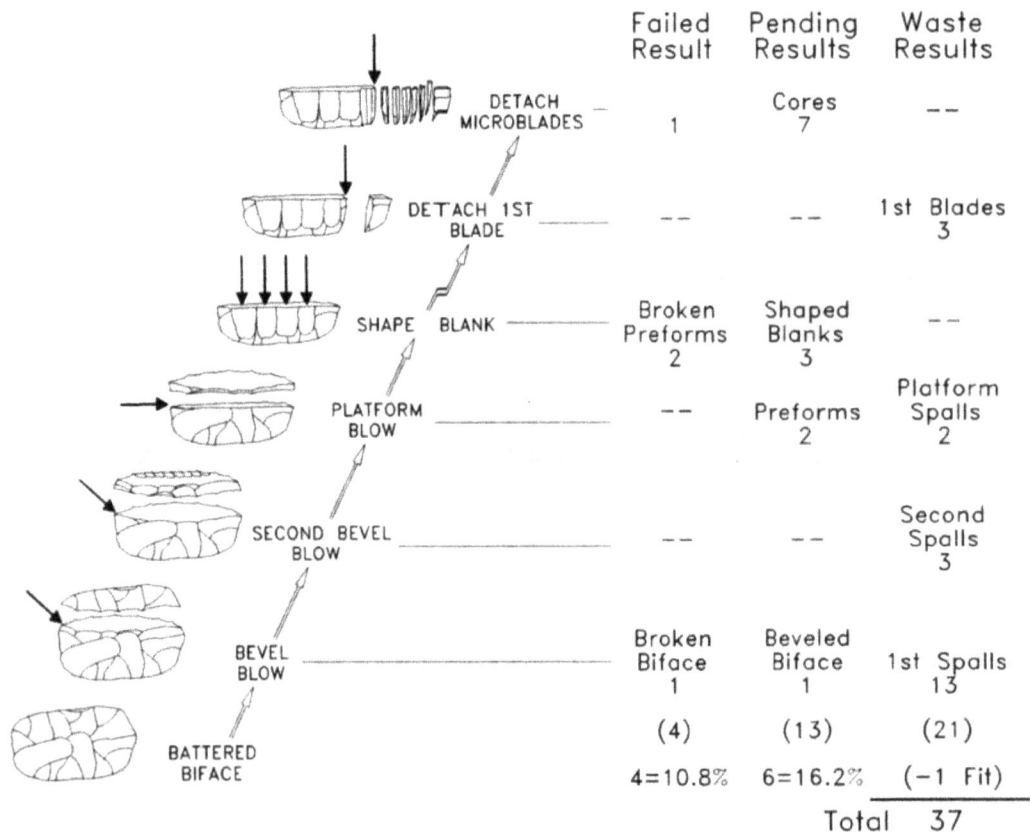

Modelling Flake Reduction

Lithic analysts have devised numerous means of assigning flakes from archaeological assemblages into reduction stages, and thereby measuring reduction intensity. This has typically involved experimental production and description of debitage from each stage of a hypothesized reduction sequence, or resulting from different reduction techniques, in the hope of comparing the characteristics of the experimental debitage (such as platform and dorsal attributes, weight or breakage patterns) to archaeological materials such that each artefact in an assemblage can be assigned its likely position in the reduction sequence or its likely manufacturing technique (e.g. Ahler 1989; Austin 1997; Bradbury and Carr 1999; e.g. Bradley 1975; Flenniken 1981; Newcomer 1971; Odell 1989; Patterson 1982, 1990; Patterson and Sollberger 1978; Shott 1996; Stahle and Dunn 1984; Steffen *et al*. 1998; Baulmer and Downum 1989; Bradbury 1998; Bradbury and Carr 1999; Morrow 1997; Prentiss 1998; Prentiss and Romanski 1989; Root 1997; Shott 1994; Sullivan and Rozen 1985). Unfortunately, these analyses generally fail to demonstrate that the stages followed experimentally were those followed in the creation of the archaeological assemblage (as might be demonstrated through refitting for example) (Hiscock 1988; Newcomer 1975:98; Schindler *et al*. 1984), or that the debitage resulting from each step can be reliably identified in archaeological contexts.

To avoid this analogical approach, flake reduction is instead approached in terms of simple and universal changes in flake morphology that are deduced from the analysis of changing core morphology, as reflected in dorsal and platform scar morphology. This type of analysis is called *diacritical analysis* (Sellet 1993), and aids in the construction of hypothetical reduction models.

The reduction process can be modelled by examining stages in flake scar superimposition on the platform and dorsal surfaces of flakes and the stages of decortication present. For example, the first flakes struck from cores are expected to preserve cortex on all exterior surfaces. Middle stages will preserve scars from prior removals on the dorsal surface, less cortex, and may begin to show scarring on the platform that results from rotation of the core and the use of an old core face as a platform once flaking resumes. Late stage flakes should show no cortex, complex platform morphologies and a number of other features such as greater elongation, more dorsal scarring, higher incidence of non-feather terminations, etc.

Modelling Retouched Flake Reduction

Retouched flakes are most commonly the subject of detailed lithic analysis, but until recently few techniques existed to measure the amount of time and labour invested in their production. A number of procedures have been proposed and tested in recent years that offer a means of measuring reduction for different forms of retouching (Clarkson 2002b; Hiscock and Clarkson 2005a, b; Kuhn 1990).

Elsewhere I have published a procedure for assessing scar abundance using estimation of retouch scar coverage (Clarkson 2002b). This 'Index of Invasiveness' calculates intensity of retouch by estimating the extent of retouching around the perimeter of a flake as well as the degree to which it encroaches onto the dorsal and ventral surfaces. The index is calculated by conceptually dividing an artefact into eight segments on each face. Each segment is then further divided into an inner 'invasive' zone, ascribed a score of 1, and an outer 'marginal' zone, ascribed a score of 0.5. Scores of 0 (no retouch), 0.5 (marginal) or 1 (invasive) are allocated to each segment according to the maximum encroachment of scars into one or other of these zones (Figure 3.5). The segment scores are then totaled and divided by 16 to give an index between 0 and 1. Experimental evidence for a strong and significant positive relationship between the index and the number of retouch blows and demonstrates the percentage of original weight lost from each specimen that is linear when log transformed (Clarkson 2002b). Little variation is evident in the rates of index increase between raw materials of varying fracture quality. The Index of Invasiveness has the advantage of being fast to calculate and versatile, and is well suited to the measurement of both unifacial and bifacial retouch with minimal inter-observer error (Clarkson 2002b:71).

A limitation of measuring surface coverage of retouch scars is that it is less suited to assemblages in which artefacts exhibit predominantly steep and marginal unifacial retouch, as might commonly occur on backed artefacts or steeply retouched scrapers. For instance, the Index of Invasiveness would not readily increase above 0.25 in such cases, no matter how much reduction takes place. In assemblages with non-invasive marginal retouch, alternative measures of reduction may be more appropriate, such as Kuhn's index of reduction.

Figure 3.5. The Index of Invasiveness (from Clarkson 2002b).

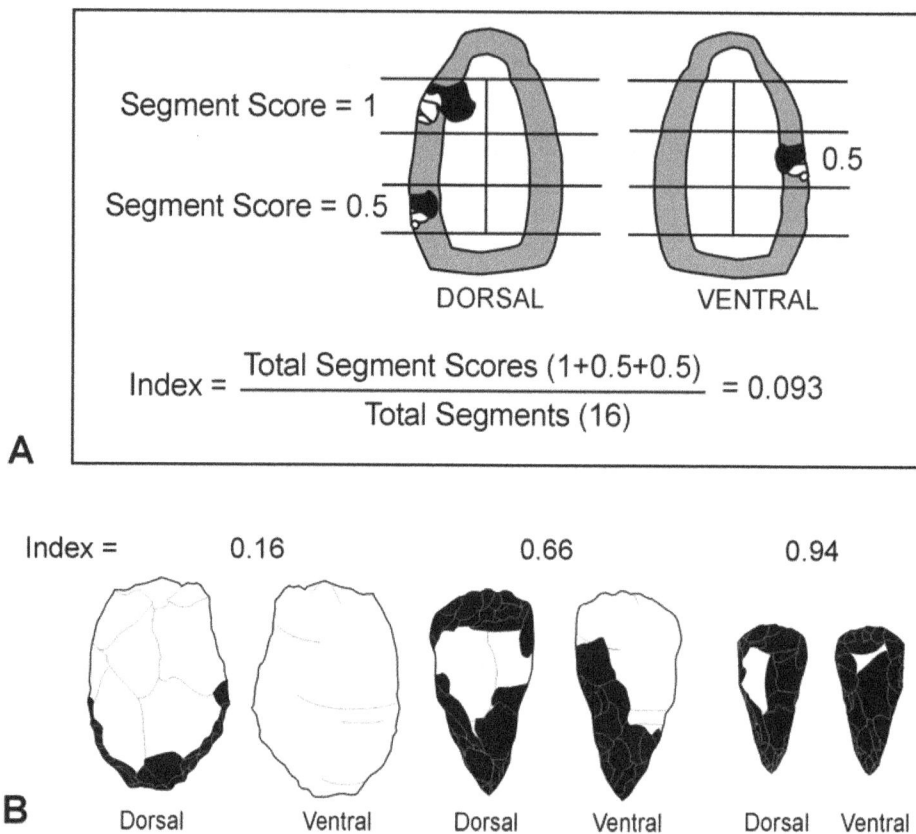

Segment Score = 1

Segment Score = 0.5

0.5

DORSAL   VENTRAL

$$\text{Index} = \frac{\text{Total Segment Scores } (1+0.5+0.5)}{\text{Total Segments } (16)} = 0.093$$

A

Index =   0.16   0.66   0.94

B   Dorsal   Ventral   Dorsal   Ventral   Dorsal   Ventral

Figure 3.6. The geometric index of unifacial reduction (GIUR).

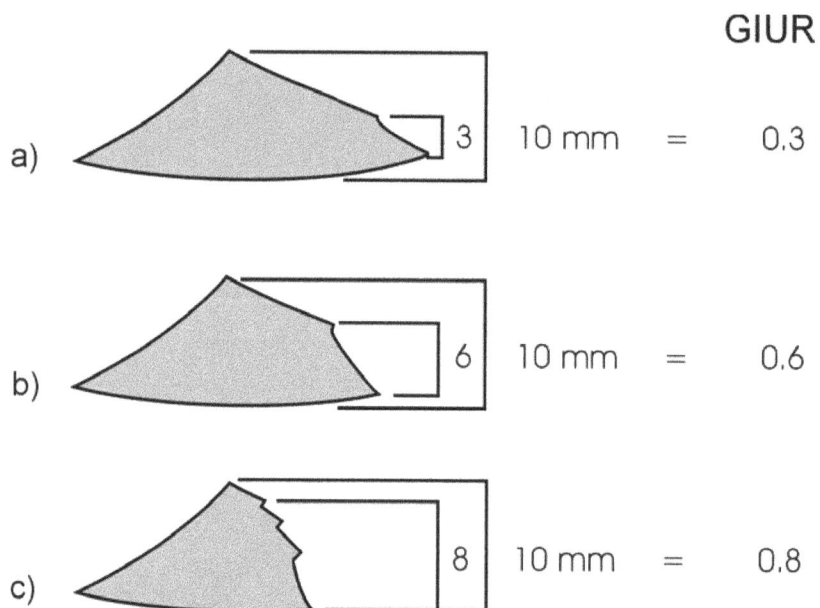

GIUR

a)   3 10 mm = 0.3

b)   6 10 mm = 0.6

c)   8 10 mm = 0.8

Kuhn's (1990, 1995) Geometric Index of Unifacial Reduction (GIUR) is a fast and sophisticated quantitative measure of flake margin attrition. The GIUR calculates the ratio between retouch height and flake thickness, expressed as a figure between 0 and 1 (Figure 3.6). Although theoretically sensitive to variation in the cross-sectional shape of flakes (and particularly 'flat flakes' – see Dibble [1995]), recent independent experimental testing has revealed that Kuhn's Index is a robust and reliable measure of dorsal unifacial reduction that is linear when the percentage of original weight lost from specimens is log transformed (Hiscock and Clarkson 2005a, b). The GIUR also out-performs many other measures of unifacial reduction against which it has been compared.

In this study, the Index of Invasiveness will be measured on all retouched flakes (i.e. those with unifacial and bifacial retouch), while the GIUR will also be used to measure unifacial dorsal retouch. Together, these techniques form a powerful and generic means of ordering any retouched specimen into its position within a reduction sequence. Understanding these continuums also allows us to partition variation in meaningful ways and offers us an alternative to traditional classifications that often employed analytical units that masked and obscured the underlying reduction processes creating much of the observed variation in retouched flake characteristics.

Like core reduction sequences, understanding the system of retouching and implement production helps us test predictions about toolkit design and technological investment decisions. These include the overall degree to which different forms are reduced as a reflection of increased use-life, the suitability of different forms to multiple resharpening events as might be predicted for maintainable tools, the level of variation in implement form as a reflection of transportability, and likelihood of use in composite technologies.

Analysing Artefact Form

Reduction sequences provide a fundamental means of describing the various reduction pathways through which artefacts move in response to the contingencies of functional demand and raw material availability. They also help determine the temporal ordering of technical actions and changes to the form of artefacts. Also of great interest in exploring technological variation and in testing predictions of provisioning models, however, is documenting changes in the morphological properties of artefacts (often called formal variation) that take place as reduction continues. For retouched flakes this might involve changes in such attributes as edge curvature, edge shape, edge angle, the location of retouch and the frequency of notching. For cores it might involve changes in the shape and size, the numbers of scars and core rotations. This section therefore describes a number of techniques used to document formal variation in stone artefacts as reduction continues.

Measures of Core Size and Shape

The principle measures of core size and shape used in this study involve changes to the shape of the core face and platform, often plotted in relation to measures of size such as weight or length. The shape of the core can also be calculated as the ratio between platform width and distal width, or length:width. Coupled with a knowledge of core reduction technique (i.e. bipolar reduction vs. single platform core reduction), these measures can be extremely useful tools for exploring the effects of changing morphology on the size and shape of flakes produced at each stage of reduction as well as inferring which techniques best suite certain core shapes and the production of certain implement forms.

Measures of Flake Size and Shape

Flake size can be measured as surface area (length x width), by weight, or by any other axial measure such as length, thickness, width or maximum dimension. Shape can also be measured in a number of ways. For instance, the expansion or contraction of the lateral margins can be calculated as the *marginal angle*, or the angle of convergence of the lateral margins toward the distal margin. This is calculated using the following formula:

$$\tan\frac{\theta}{2} = \frac{\left(\dfrac{\text{proximal width - distal width}}{2}\right)}{\text{length}}$$

And hence angle of the lateral margins (θ) = $2\tan^{-1}\dfrac{\text{proximal width - distal width}}{2 \times \text{length}}$

The measurement procedure for this index is shown in Figure 3.7a. Expanding margins return negative angles, while margins that contract along their length have positive angles. Parallel sided artefacts have an angle of 0. Other ways of measuring flake shape are also possible, such as the angle between the proximal end and medial width, the angle between the medial width and the distal end, or some other combination of these.

Shape can also be measured for retouched edges using a number of indices. One is the angle of the retouched edge, and this can be calculated as the mean of several edge angle measurements taken at regular intervals along the retouched edge (3 intervals are used here). Another is the index of edge curvature, measured by dividing the maximum diameter of retouch by the total depth of retouch (Figure 3.7b) (Clarkson 2002a; Hiscock and Attenbrow 2002, 2003). Negative results indicate concave edges, while positive ones indicate convex edges. Curvature can be used to measure overall edge shape as well as more minor features, such as concavities and notches.

Blank Selection

Archaeologists are often interested in the process of blank selection, or the selection of a sub-set of flakes for further use, retouching and/or transport away from the site. Blank selection is of interest as it has the potential to inform us about design considerations (such as tool performance, reliability/maintainability, suitability to prehension and hafting and multifunctionality), a range of environmental and cultural constraints (functional, material, technological, socioeconomic and ideological) (Hayden et al. 1996). It can also tell us about the level of standardisation in the production system, both in terms of overall flake production and selection from the larger pool of flake variation. The approach adopted here to determining the relationship of selected blanks to the overall pool of variation is to plot flakes at early stages of retouching against the larger pool of variation in size and shape. Graphical techniques will be used, as well as statistical measures of variance and central tendency to compare and contrast the size, shape, and standardisation of blanks.

Conclusion

This chapter has drawn together various approaches to the description of assemblage variation that are of analytical importance in the analysis of technological change. The review of stone artefact manufacturing strategies and approaches to building reduction sequences serves as the basis from which to explore changes in the organisation and design of lithic technologies in later chapters and to detect broad changes in technological provisioning and land use.

Figure 3.7. Measurement procedures for describing flake shape. A: angle of the lateral margins, and B: curvature of the retouched edge.

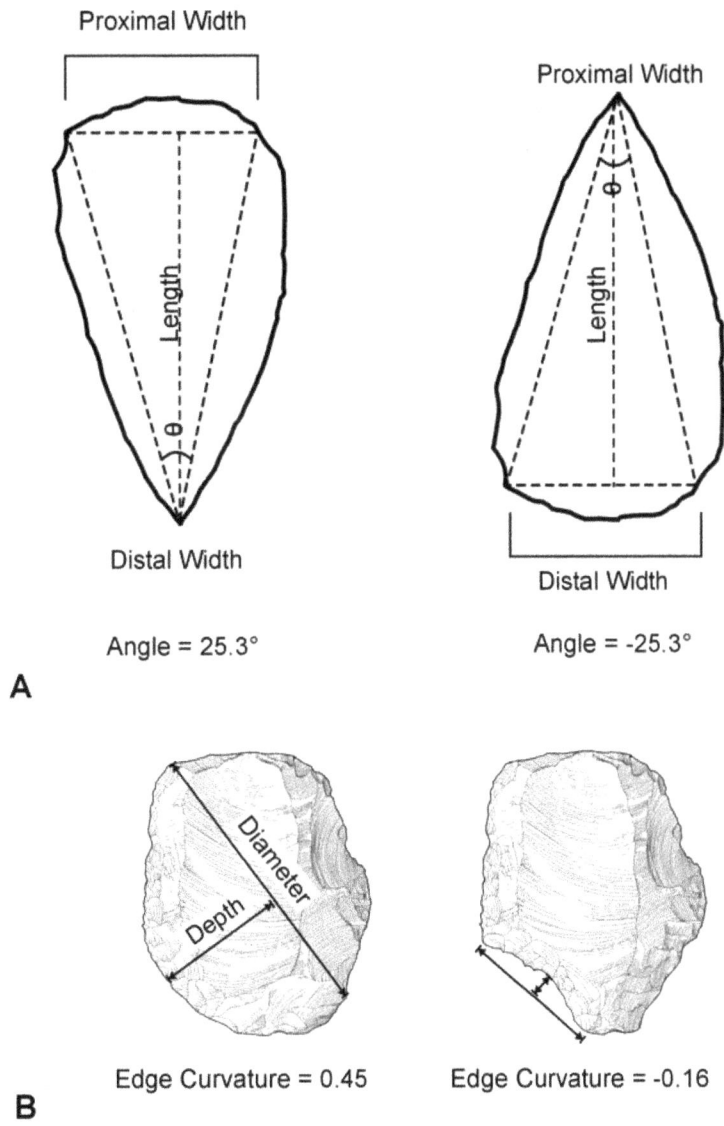

4. Wardaman Country: Physiography and Climate Change

Wardaman Country is a region of spectacular mesas, deep and unscalable gorges, broad black soil plains and gently rolling hills and woodlands. Standing above the plains in places are red sandstone outliers, deeply weathered by time and the ravages of the tropical climate. These outcrops provide numerous overhangs, crevices and declivities that have offered shelter to people and preserved their artistic activities over thousands of years. In places among the rocky hills and gorges, and on the flood plains, water holes dot the landscape and act as loci for human and animal habitation alike in what is otherwise a hot, brown region for most of the year, and an often flooded and verdant one for the remaining few months.

This chapter presents an overview of the physiography and record of climate changes for the study region. From this a number of predictions are developed about the likely responses of human foragers to the opportunities and constraints offered by the nature and structuring of resources in the region over the last 15,000 years. These predictions are based on the principles of optimization in settlement, subsistence and technology presented in Chapter 2.

Overview of the Region

Wardaman Country is roughly 8,932km^2 in area and is located ~120 km southwest of Katherine. It is bordered by the Victoria River in the southwest, which drains the southern half of the region, the Flora River to the north, draining the northern and eastern areas into the Daly River, and is bordered on the eastern edge by the Sturt Plateau. This is roughly the country claimed by Wardaman Aboriginal people today as defined by Merlan (1989), and loosely represents the distribution of Wardaman speakers and the outer boundary of clan estates as it probably existed around the time of European contact in the late 19th Century (Figure 4.1).

The main access to the region today is via the Victoria River Highway, which cuts the study area approximately in half. There are no towns in this area and the closest are Katherine to the northeast and Timber Creek to west; both of which are roughly 60km from the edge of Wardaman Country.

Climate

Wardaman Country has a warm dry monsoonal climate, receiving almost all of its rainfall between November and March, most of which falls in January and February. The region receives 900mm annual rainfall in the northwest and around 650mm in the southeast where rainfall becomes less intense and reliable (Sweet 1972:3), and vegetation and soils become increasingly typical of semi-arid to arid lands (Slayter 1970). Temperatures range from a mean of around 29°C in June and July, to about 38°C in November and December. Minimum temperatures range from 10°-13°C in winter to between 21°-24°C in summer. Rainfall is the primary factor effecting vegetation growth, which is generally restricted to the short wet season.

Hydrology

A dry monsoonal climate means that Wardaman Country is a parched place for most the year, but is very wet during the monsoon season, when low lying country is often inundated and waterholes and ephemeral creeks fill and overflow. During the dry season, waterholes and creeks dry up, and permanent water is generally scarce with only a few exceptions. The Flora River and northern reaches of Hayward Creek in the north, for instance, are spring fed and maintain at least a weak flow throughout the year (Figure 4.2) (Pontifex and Mendum 1972:23), while the Victoria River, although stagnant during the dry season, maintains good water supplies in long reaches throughout the driest seasons (Sweet 1972:16) (Figure 4.3). Away from major rivers, most permanent waterholes are small and are found predominantly in the western and northern portions of the region as isolated pools amongst sandstone gorges, in creek beds in rocky areas and cut into the limestone along drainage lines. Apart from these sources, only eight large permanent waterholes exist in Wardaman Country. These are the Yingalarri (Ingaladdi), Jinginya (Johnston Waterhole), Geberung, Wynbarr (Wynbara), as well as the Hayward Hole, Geleji and two other waterholes on Hayward Creek, all of which occur at least 10km apart in sandstone country. Wardaman country is today situated in a region of very high inter-annual variability in rainfall (Dewar 2003), and one in which the predictability of rainfall may have been low for a very long time.

Figure 4.1. Location of Wardaman Country, the survey region and sites discussed in the text.

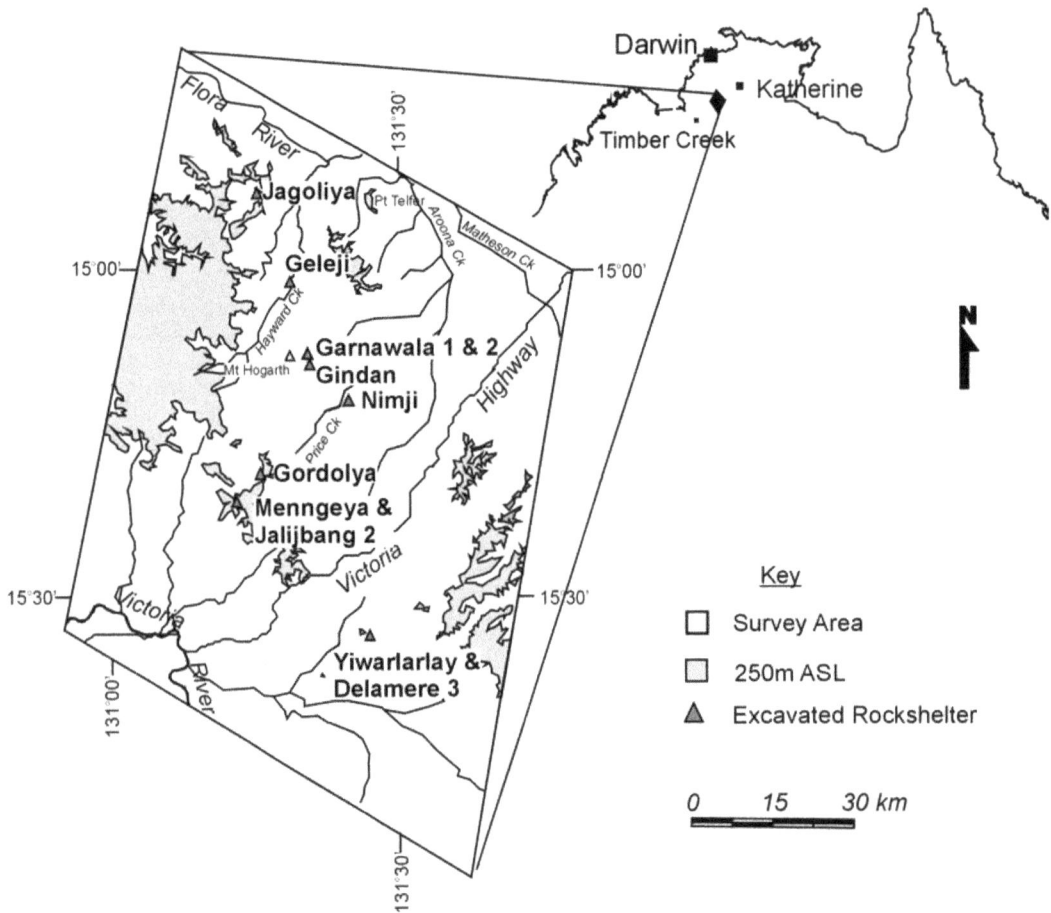

Physiography

Wardaman Country is made up of four main physiographic units that broadly characterize the geology and geomorphology of the region (Figure 4.4). These are the *Victoria River Plateau, Delamere Plains and Benches, Sturt Plateau* and the *Daly River Basin*.

Victoria River Plateau. This unit occurs as tablelands, inland plains and gently sloping plateau primarily along the western edge of Wardaman Country. The tablelands are 150 to 250m high and are capped by resistant Jasper Gorge Sandstone (Figure 4.5). The Victoria River and some of its tributaries are deeply incised into the tablelands in the southwest of the region and form spectacular gorges with walls up to 150m high (Sweet 1972:7). A gently sloping plateau occurs on the extreme central western margin of the region and forms an irregularly dissected scarp. Inland plains are found in the extreme southwestern corner of Wardaman Country in the Victoria River valley itself.

Figure 4.2. Permanent waterhole on the Flora River.

Figure 4.3. Large permanent waterhole along the Victoria River.

Figure 4.4. Location of the major physiographic units in Wardaman Country.

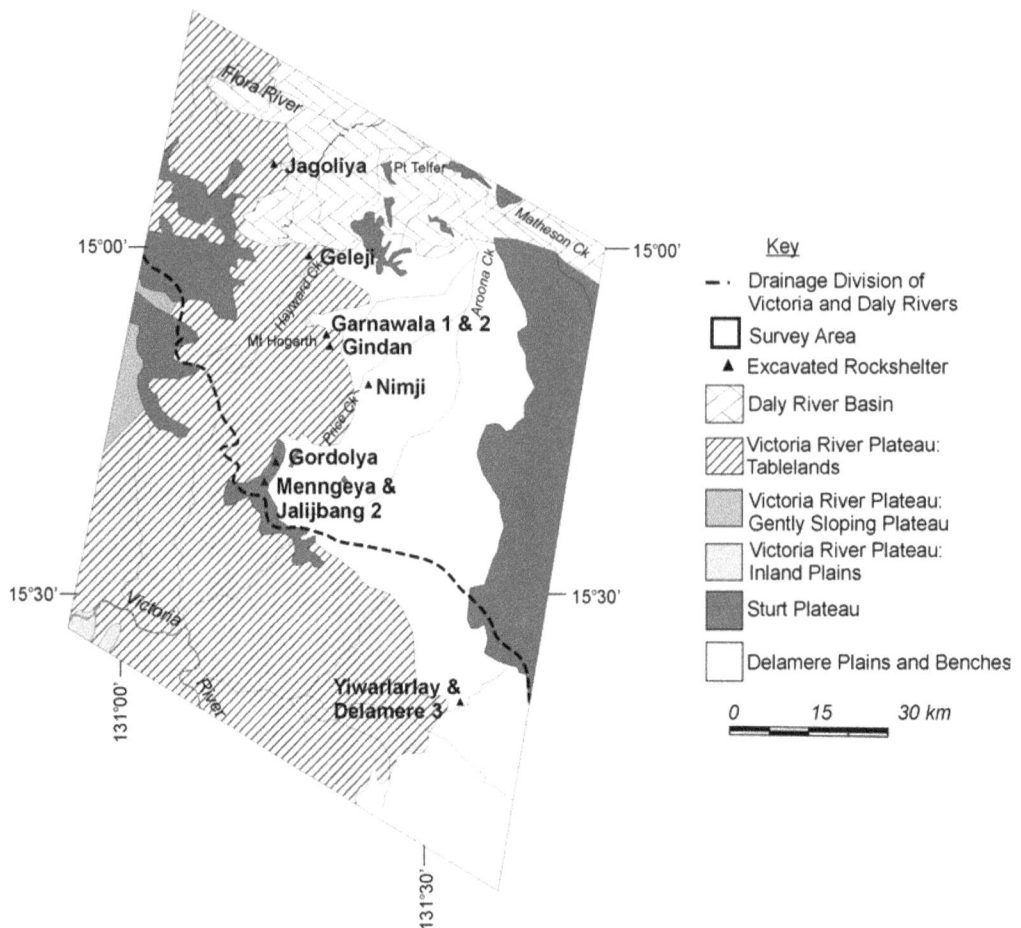

Delamere Plains and Benches. This unit is made up of plains with rounded and terraced low hills underlain by the Antrim Plateau Volcanics. This unit occurs primarily in a central band through Wardaman Country. The terraces are formed by resistant basalt and chert bands within the volcanics. Northwesterly trending ridges of aeolian origin are also formed by sandstone interbedded with the volcanics (Figure 4.6), and these are often cavernously weathered to form deep rockshelters and overhangs ideal for human habitation and the survival of rock art panels (Sweet 1972:7). Bands of quartzite often run alongside these sandstone ridges and result from contact with basalt lava flows. The weathering and disintegration of these sandstone outliers has also resulted in the formation of extensive sand sheets in some places.

Sturt Plateau. This is a laterite-covered plateau that represents the remnants of a very extensive weathered peneplain (Figure 4.7). It is preserved largely on the eastern boundary of Wardaman Country, although remnants also occur as mesas in the centre and northwest of the region.

The *Daly River Basin* is a sub-mature basin in the northern part of the region, which has been retarded by a barrier of resistant sandstone at its north-western edge, beyond Wardaman Country. Soil and alluvial sand have developed over much of the basin, and stone outcrop is scarce (Figure 4.8) (Pontifex and Mendum 1972:6).

Figure 4.5. Remnant of the Victoria River Plateau.

Figure 4.6. Northwest trending sandstone ridges of the Antrim Plateau Volcanics within the Delamere Plains and Benches.

Figure 4.7. Edge of the Sturt Plateau.

Figure 4.8. View over the Daly River Basin toward the distant hills of the Victoria River Plateau.

The Distribution and Quality of Raw Materials

It has become axiomatic in studies of lithic technology to consider the effects that raw material distribution may have on the level of planning, transport and curation involved in maintaining a supply of stone tools where and when they are needed. In considering the human selection, transport and use of stone suited to implement manufacture, five variables are considered potentially significant. These are the location of flakable stone, nodule size, overall abundance, ease of extraction, and suitability to various forms of reduction. This section examines the 'lithic landscape' as it exists in the study region to help identify possible discontinuities between the distribution of flakable stone and certain other critical resources.

The major forms of raw material found in Wardaman Country are quartzites from two geological formations, cherts from five limestone formations (only three of which actually outcrop in Wardaman Country), hydrothermal jasper and chalcedony, and silcrete from lateritic duricrusts.

Of these, a brown to grey coloured quartzite from the Antrim Plateau Volcanics is by far the most abundant raw material in Wardaman Country, and commonly occurs as ridges and gibbers throughout the region, particularly in association with the northwest trending sandstone formations that were likely metamorphosed into quartzite through contact with basalt flows (Figure 4.9). Bands and ridges of hydrothermal jasper and clear to milky white and yellow chalcedony sometimes occur alongside these quartzite outcrops. With the possible exception of the hydrothermal jasper, which tends to be of poor quality and small size, these sources generally provide abundant nodules, sometimes up to very large size, exhibit extremely good conchoidal fracture and are suited to most forms of reduction.

Figure 4.9. Location of the Antrim Plateau Volcanics and encapsulated sandstone ridges that are frequently associated with quartzite outcrops and gibbers.

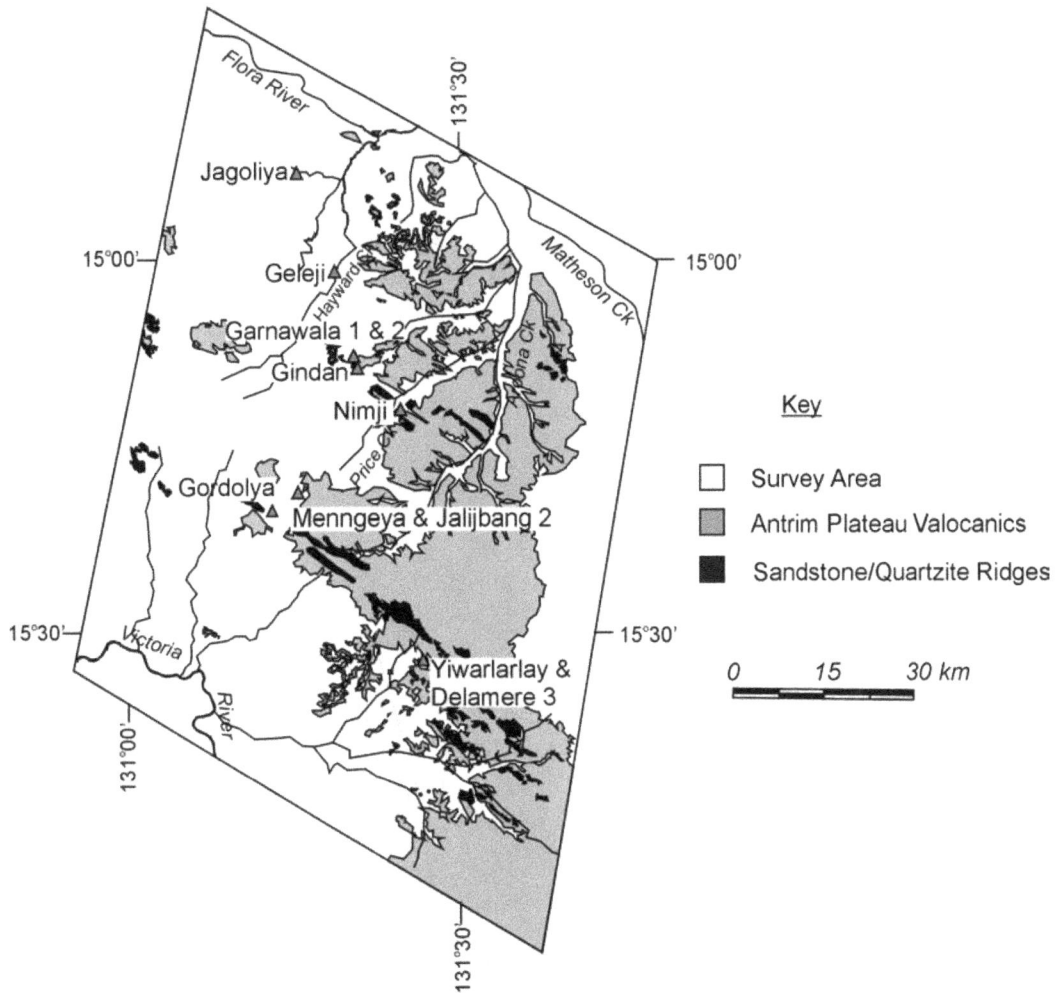

In addition to the numerous quartzite outcrops within the Antrim Plateau Volcanics, a particularly large and intensively quarried source of quartzite was located within the Jasper Gorge formation above a series of rockshelters at a place known to Wardaman people as Gongonmaya, 3.6 km southwest of Mt Hogarth. This consisted of a distinctive white quartzite with yellow and red mottles, with nodules of large size and excellent conchoidal fracture. Other sources of white quartzite likely exist in the Jasper Gorge formation, but these have not been located. The rarity of white quartzite in sites in Wardaman Country suggests that few sources of this material exist.

A number of small silcrete sources were located on the tops of laterite capped tablelands and mesas, but these do not appear to be particularly abundant. One source examined atop remnants of the Sturt Plateau in the western part of Wardaman Country revealed small amounts of a workable fine red silcrete of medium size, but requiring extensive preparation to remove a thick cortex.

Chert is particularly abundant in the Daly River Basin in terms of both the number of sources and the quantity of usable nodules that are usually of high quality and large size. Chert outcrops within the Banyan, Tindall, and Jinduckin limestones, and sometimes forms huge ridges standing tens of metres above the floodplains and stretching for several kilometers in length (Figure 4.10). A wide range of colours and cortex types are found in these chert formations, however, two distinctive and archaeologically visible forms of high quality exist. The first is a deep maroon chert, sometimes with purple or caramel veins, present in the Banyan Chert Member and outcropping as huge ridges at various points along Hayward Creek in the north of the study area. The second is a distinctive bright yellow chert from the Tindall Limestone that outcrops along Matheson Creek near the eastern edge of Wardaman Country. The differential occurrence of these materials in archaeological sites therefore acts as a guide to both the direction of travel and the relative importance of each of these sources in the past.

Figure 4.10. Map showing the location of different chert sources in Wardaman Country.

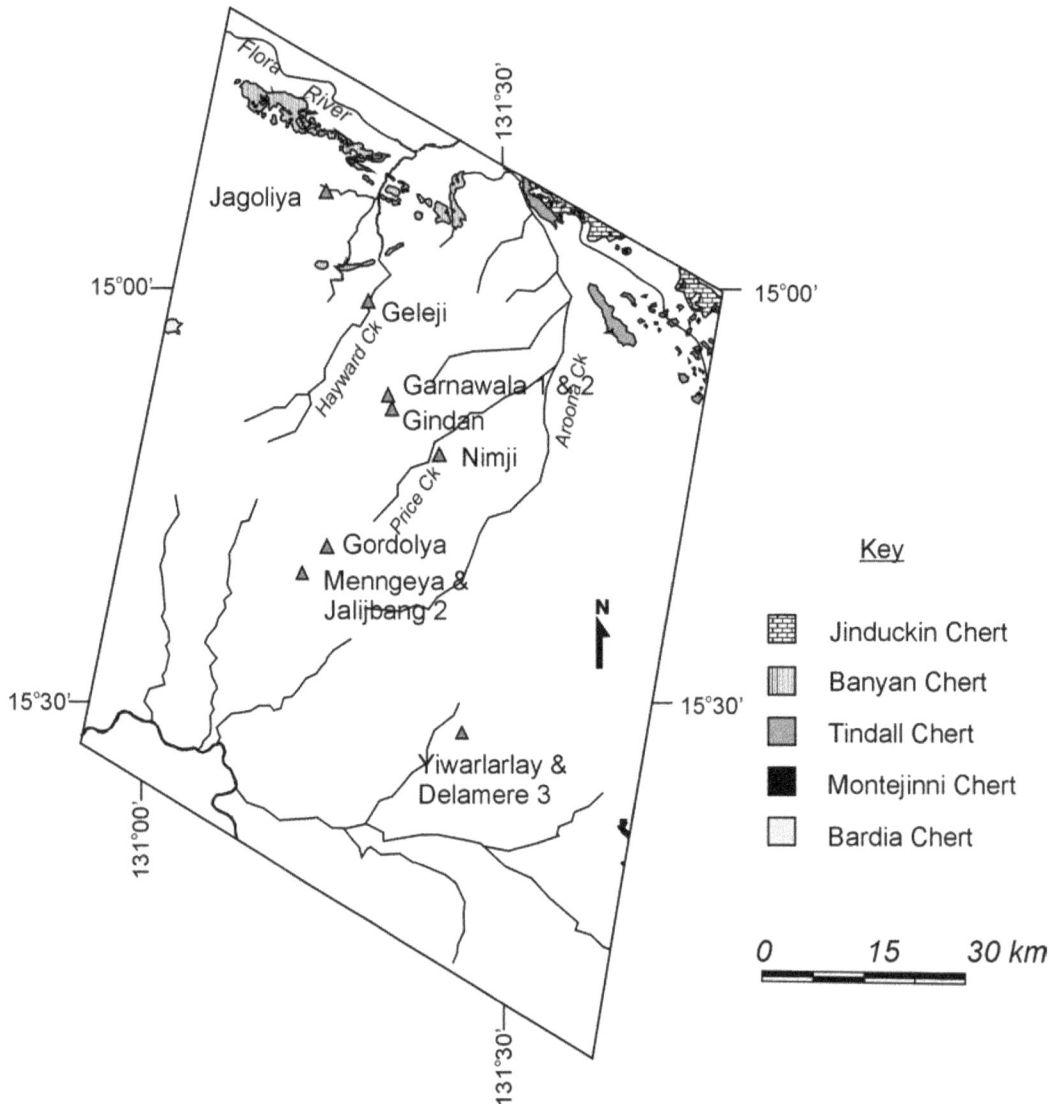

While it is ideal in a study of technological provisioning and land use for raw materials to be isolated, discrete and to some degree distant from one another, this is not always the case in Wardaman country, as many suitable raw materials co-occur in some places (e.g. chalcedony, hydrothermal jasper and quartzite). While this complicates the study of raw material rationing and technological responses to changing raw material supply, it nevertheless provides a common and complex scenario more typical of many regions in Australia. It also provides an opportunity to examine the interplay between the selection of raw materials given different combinations of the five variables listed above (location, size, abundance, ease of extraction and suitability), under conditions of more or less abundance rather than scarcity.

The Differential Distribution of Resources in the Landscape

It is possible to also briefly consider the overall distribution and co-occurrence of various resources in the landscape. A number of discontinuities and overlaps appear to exist that are likely to have had significant implications for foraging and land use in Wardaman County. The first, and perhaps most significant of these is a general disjunction between the location of large permanent waterholes and that of raw materials. In the southern part of the study region, for example, quartzite usually occurs at least several kilometers from the major waterholes. On the other hand, quartzite, chalcedony and jasper often outcrop where shelter is abundant. This is not so true in the north of the study area where a rich and diverse range of floral, faunal and stone resources co-occurs in the Daly River Basin with large permanent waterholes and springs being particularly common. This is a combination that would likely have favoured human habitation of this region throughout longer, hotter, dry seasons.

Climate Change

The Last Glacial Maximum (c. 22-17 kya) was experienced in Australia as a period of extreme aridity (De Deckker 2001:1), creating hydrological systems, vegetational communities and fluctuating climates with no modern analogue (Horton 1993; Lambeck and Chappell 2001). Aridity extended to the exposed continental shelf, with precipitation at around half that of today. This combination of factors would have created severe drought, cold and winds that led to massive dust storms and encouraged dune expansion while discouraging tree growth in many parts of Australia (Frakes et al. 1987). The draining of the extensive shallow water bodies in the Gulf of Carpentaria would likely have reduced the development and onshore movement of tropical cyclones bringing rain to the continental interior (Webster and Streten 1978). The LGM saw a massive outward expansion of the arid zone, with deserts literally meeting the coast in both northwestern and southern areas of Australia, as well as the northward migration of major vegetation zones in northern Australia during the LGM. Wardaman Country was then probably over 200 km further inland and likely also witnessed conditions much drier than today, with shrublands probably covering much of the landscape. With permanent water scarce in Wardaman Country even today, little water would probably have been available, even in the better watered sandstone gorges. Springs may also have dried up during the extreme aridity of the LGM, and it therefore may not be surprising that no signs of human habitation have been found in the study region during this period.

Immediately following the LGM, glacial melting took place at an irregular rate until around 7000 BP, by which time sea levels had more or less reached their present position (Lambeck and Chappell 2001). During this last marine transgression, sea levels rose very rapidly across the flat exposed continental shelves and probably resulted in drowning landscapes such as the Arafura plain (between northern Australia and New Guinea) at a lateral rate of up to a metre a week (Mulvaney and Kamminga 1999:121).

The late glacial period was one of rapid environmental change, including marked climatic reversals that saw the onset of very tropical conditions in some areas between 15,000 and 11,500 BP, and a rapid swing back toward full glacial conditions during the Younger Dryas between c. 10,800 and 10,200 radiocarbon years ago (centered on around 11,530 Cal BP) (Adams et al. 1999; Kershaw 1995). Although no firm radiocarbon dates are yet available for human occupation in Wardaman Country before c. 10,000 BP, extrapolation of age estimates to basal occupation of some sites suggests that people were moving into the region sometime around c. 15,000 years ago, presumably as the climate ameliorated (Figure 4.11).

Figure 4.11. Calibrated radiocarbon ages (solid line) for each of the excavated sites in the region based on the lowest date, as well as the estimated basal age (dashed line) of each site determined using linear regression.

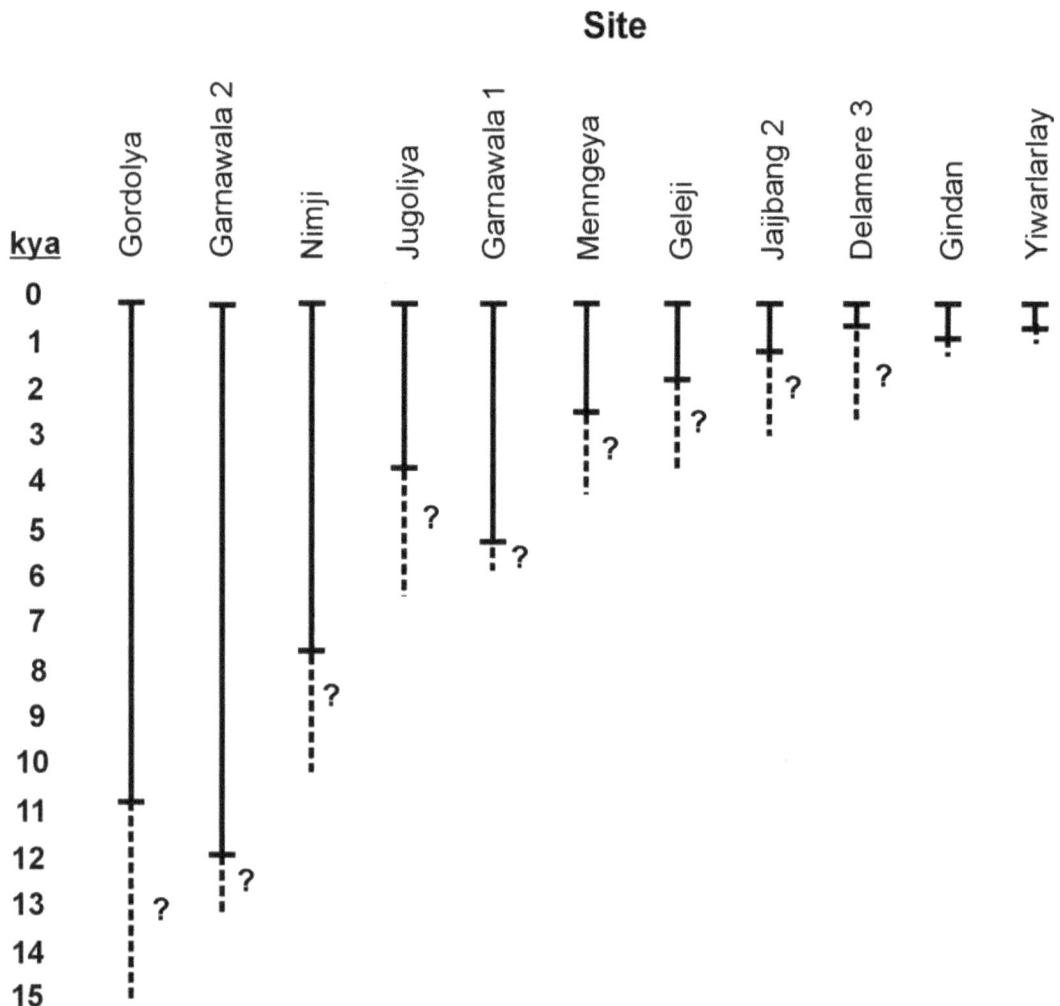

The Pleistocene-Holocene boundary was a time of rapid climatic amelioration marked by an increase in lake water levels in northern Australia and the southward movement of vegetative communities to their present position (Kershaw 1995).

Generally, the early Holocene in Australia is characterized as a period of increased precipitation (i.e. up to 50% wetter in northern Australia than in modern times), with an early to mid-Holocene optimum (that is, somewhere between 8,000 and 5,000 BP depending on exact location) of warmer and wetter conditions (Gagan *et al*. 1994; Kershaw 1983, 1995; Kershaw and Nix 1989; McGlone *et al*. 1992; Nix and Kalma 1972) with reduced interannual variability (Chappell 2001:177).

The middle to late Holocene is thought to have been a period of increasing aridity, although exactly when the onset of increased aridity occurs is not well documented and appears to vary with location. A number of studies point to a later onset of peak Holocene aridity in northern Australia than that found in more southern latitudes (McGlone *et al*. 1992; Schulmeister and Lees 1995) (Figure 4.12). For example, studies of north coastal cheniers are interpreted as indicating decreased wet season precipitation from 2,800 to 1,600 BP (Lees 1992a, b; Lees *et al*. 1990; Lees *et al*. 1992), whereas records of terrestrial floods from waterfalls in three locations in northern Australia spanning the last 30,000 years indicate extreme flood magnitudes between c. 8,000 and ~3,600 years ago, followed by floods of considerably smaller magnitude in the last 2,000 to 3,000 years (more recent deposits exhibited disturbance) (Nott and Price 1999). A pollen record from Groote Eylandt indicates a marked decline in precipitation between 4,000 and 3,500 BP, with increased rainfall during the last thousand years (Schulmeister and Lees 1992).

Figure 4.12. The timing of major wet and dry phases for several regions of Australia and other selected locations during the Holocene (from Schulmeister and Lees 1995).

Comparison of Holocene Wet Phases (Black)

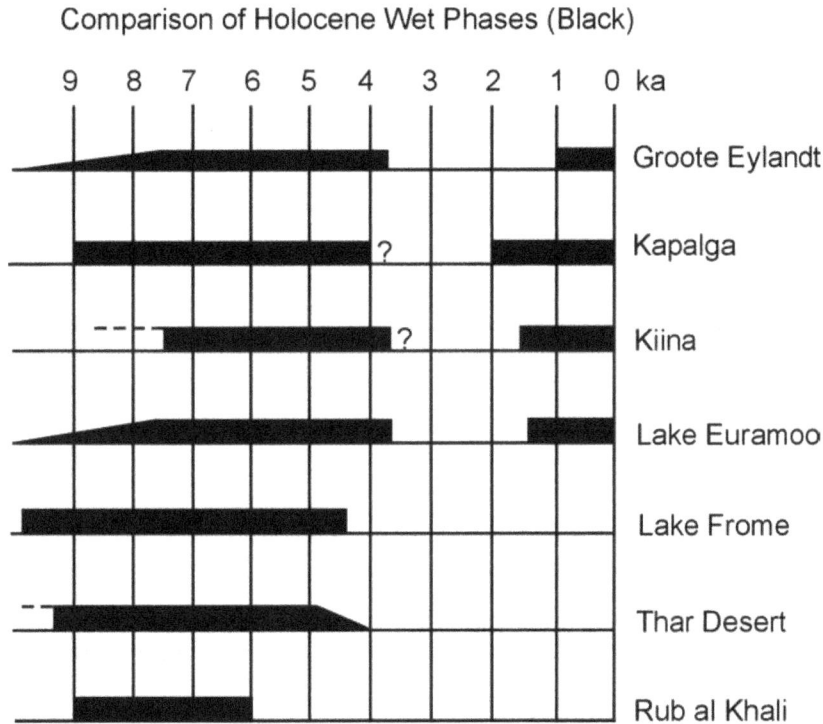

These general trends toward increased aridity in the mid-Holocene are supported by records of flood deposits in the Kimberley (Gillieson *et al.* 1991) and by other indicators such as δ^{18}O records extracted from coral, foraminifera, varve, lake and sea bottom sediments from sites in Australian and the circum-Pacific region (Brookfield and Allan 1989; Hope and Golson 1995; Kershaw 1995; Koutavas *et al.* 2002; McCarthy and Head 2001; McGlone *et al.* 1992; McPhail and Hope 1985; Rodbell *et al.* 1999; Singh and Luly 1991).

Climatic Variability

Within these longer-term trends, the El Niño/Southern Oscillation (ENSO) phenomenon has exerted a strong influence on climatic patterns in tropical and eastern Australia for some time, although exactly how long and to what degree is the subject of ongoing research (Jones *et al.* 1999; McGlone *et al.* 1992; Schulmeister and Lees 1992). Today, ENSO constitutes the largest single source of interannual climatic variability on a global scale, especially within the dynamical core of the Indo-Pacific region (Allan *et al.* 1996; Diaz and Markgraf 1992; Glantz 1991; Glantz *et al.* 1991; Rowland 1999a). In recent times, ENSO events have had wide-ranging and often severe impacts on terrestrial and marine ecosystems. The worst of these (for example the 1957-8, 1972-3, 1982-3, 1987-88 and 1997-8 events) have caused considerable economic hardship and many fatalities through increased periods of drought, frosts, bushfires, cyclones, high temperatures, severe winds and storms (Allan *et al.* 1996; Anderson *et al.* 2006; Bourke 1998; Glantz 1996; Glantz *et al.* 1991).

The term ENSO refers to inter-annual reversals in ocean-atmosphere interactions of the Walker Circulation system that operates in the Indo-Pacific basin (Allan *et al.* 1996; Enfield 1989; Trenberth and Hoar 1996; Webster and Palmer 1997). ENSO embraces two distinct phases that tend to oscillate between two extremes - El Niño and La Niña - and occurs as a consequence of 'see-saw-like' reversals in sea-level pressure, ocean currents, sea surface temperatures and trade winds between the southeastern tropical pacific and the Australian-Indonesian region (Diaz and Markgraf 1992). The state of the system is typically monitored by the Southern Oscillation Index (SOI), which is the ratio of sea-level pressures between Tahiti and Darwin.

During El Niño events there is a weakening of sea-level pressure in the southeastern tropical Pacific, accompanied by a decrease in the strength of trade winds. This results in a weakening of the cool oceanic upwelling along the western coast of South America, in turn causing sea-surface temperatures to rise. Warmer sea surface temperatures give rise to increased evaporation and heating of the troposphere, resulting in increased convection and rainfall over the coast of Ecuador and Peru, over parts of the Andean cordillera, and to a lesser extent, the southern United States and central Chile (Allan *et al*. 1996; Diaz and Markgraf 1992; Enfield 1992). El Niño events result in bringing drought to many parts of Australia, southern Africa, northern India, Sahelian Africa, Indonesia and South-East Asia (Allan *et al*. 1996:22; Enfield 1992:97).

In contrast, La Niña events represent an intensification of the 'normal' ocean-atmosphere circulation pattern, and have impacts that are generally opposite to those of El Niño (Allan *et al*. 1996:22).

The structure and duration of ENSO events are highly variable (and no two events are exactly alike), but El Niño phases typically last between 12-18 months and tend to recur every 3-7 years. Quasi-cyclical changes in intensity at decadal and greater time-scales have also been noted (Anderson 1992; Kerr 1998, 1999; Trenberth and Hoar 1996).

Based on a review of long-term palaeoenvironmental proxy climate indicators, McGlone *et al*. (1992) have suggested that the ENSO phenomenon may have intensified in the last 5,000 years. Shulmeister and Lees (1995) also argue for the onset of Walker Circulation dominated climate with ENSO-scale variability embedded in the system after c. 4,000 BP. Records for variability in $\delta^{18}O$ isotopes linked to ENSO events also come from annually banded corals from Papua New Guinea, and point to greater variance in amplitude and more extreme ENSO events in the modern period and between 2 and 3,000 years ago. Although there are large gaps in this record (with short interannual sequences only available for seven distinct time periods: 130 ka, 112 ka, 85 ka, 38-42 ka, 6.5 ka, 2-3 ka and modern), later events show significantly greater amplitude in ENSO events than those recorded for the short interannual record dating to c. 6,500 years ago (Tudhope *et al*. 2001). In general, the onset of modern ENSO periodicities is identified by palaeo-ENSO recordes throughout the tropical Pacific region 5,000 years ago, with an abrupt increase in ENSO magnitude 3,000 years ago (Gagan *et al*. 2004). Evidence also exists from a number of locations world-wide for increased ENSO driven climatic variability from the mid-Holocene onwards (Andrus *et al*. 2002; Koutavas *et al*. 2002; Rodbell *et al*. 1999), with evidence that impacts of mid- to late Holocene climatic oscillations may have been far greater than any events recorded in the late-historical period (Ely *et al*. 1993; Graumlich 1993; Hughes and Brown 1992; Knox 1993; Rowland 1999a, b). ENSO-related climatic oscillations no doubt had significant impacts on prehistoric human groups through their effects on the long and short-term availability, stability and structuring of economic resources.

Implications of ENSO-Driven Variability for the Study Region

In Wardaman Country, it can be envisaged that the availability and predictability of surface water would have increased considerably during the early Holocene, that fringing communities and vine thickets may have expanded outward from their present refuges in deep gorges and around permanent waterholes, and that aquatic animals and vegetation might have radiated outward from now permanent waterholes to those that are ephemeral today. This may have created a greater diversity of plant and animal communities throughout Wardaman Country than is present in drier areas today, but may also have resulted in the introduction of new taxa, such as monsoon forest communities, into Wardaman Country which are absent today.

Palaeoclimatic reconstructions for this region are extremely rare, as pollen and macrobotanic remains rarely survive in tropical soils. However, phytolith sequences spanning up to the last 15,000 years from three rockshelter located in Wardaman Country (Jagoliya, Gordolya and Nimji) suggest that wet adapted species and palms were common in this location before 3,500 years ago when they disappeared from the record and were replaced by grasses as the dominant local vegetation (Clarkson and Wallis

2003). A distinct wet phase is also registered at c. 5-7,000 BP and again at about 1,500 BP, with a distinct dry phase between these two periods (Bowdery 2005). This sequence lends credence to the argument that Wardaman Country was wetter and supported a more diverse range of taxa in the early and late Holocene than are presently found in the region.

The onset of ENSO driven inter-annual climatic variability at around 3,500 years ago in northern Australia, while not bringing about changes of the same magnitude as those witnessed during the LGM, could still have significantly altered the location and structuring of resources in Wardaman Country, with plants and animals perhaps having to endure severe droughts followed by severe floods in quick succession. The recent Katherine floods in 1996 showed how catastrophic such isolated, super-monsoons can be for the ecology and inhabitants of the region, and there is evidence that floods of this scale have occurred frequently in the past (Nott and Price 1999). This intensified regime, which probably lasted for another two thousand years or so, may well have transformed the region into its present form, and would likely have dramatically reduced the predictability of resource distribution and abundance from year to year, as game followed patchy rainfall and migrated to better watered areas (Ramp and Coulson 2002), waterholes dried up, plant foods failed to produce and aquatic animals perished or retracted to more permanent water sources, only to be reversed several years later. Variation on this scale would likely have triggered significant responses from humans, flora and fauna, with alterations to the range and abundance of plants and animals, and the rapid emergence of risk reduction strategies by people forced to cope with massive uncertainty in both the economic and social spheres of life, as food supplies waxed and waned and demographic adjustments took place. As climatic variability eased back toward that of the modern period, such risk management strategies may also have diminished in importance, or they may have transformed into significantly different socio-demographic entities. These issues will be explored at length later in this work.

Thus humans occupying the study region after 15,000 years ago would have experienced a colder, drier landscape than today, with marked fluctuations between cold and dry and tropical conditions between 15,000 BP and 10,000 BP. By 7,000-5,000 years ago, conditions were markedly improved, and people would have experienced a wet, stable climate that is probably otherwise relatively unparalleled for the duration of human occupation of the continent. Between c. 3,500 and 2,000 BP, conditions appear to have deteriorated again with the onset of intensified ENSO conditions, with pronounced interannual fluctuations in effective precipitation. The period registers as an arid phase overall, but interannual variation is likely to have been higher at this time than any other in the Holocene, with pronounced droughts resulting from failure of the summer monsoon likely followed by severe floods. By c. 1,500 years ago, climatic conditions appear to have relaxed back toward those of the present day, with interannual variation remaining a strong feature, but with much less severe fluctuations than those experienced previously.

Based on this review of climate and geography, it is possible to make a number of predictions about the likely effects of climatic change on human land use and provisioning over this period:

- The late Pleistocene/early Holocene period is likely to have seen low population densities as humans colonized the study region, possibly for the first time. We should expect high residential mobility during this period as people became familiar with local resources and maintained contact with homeland populations as a means of social storage to buffer against risk, and to find mates (MacDonald 1998). Overall environmental productivity is likely to have been lower than today, perhaps encouraging more mobile foraging regimes to counter frequent resource depression. Large oscillations between cold/dry and warm/humid may have introduced significant subsistence risk (although not if these shifts were gradual and stable within given periods). High mobility and less predictable resource availability might be expected to show up as a tendency toward low diversity individual provisioning.

- The mid-Holocene optimum at around 7,000 BP likely increased local productivity above and beyond that experienced at any time previously, and we might expect populations to have increased at this time, with higher encounter rates with high ranked resources and more predictable subsistence schedules. Mobility would also likely have reduced as local patches became more productive and resource locations more stable. Increases in assemblage size and density and a shift toward place provisioning are expected at this time.

- The onset of ENSO conditions after 5,000 BP, and reaching their peak intensity between c. 3,500-2,000 BP, would likely have created a situation of high subsistence risk. Pronounced interannual variation would have increased the patchiness of the environment, caused higher mobility in large, high-ranked prey as water availability fluctuated, and caused resource depression during periods of prolonged drought. A decline in the human population might be expected under such conditions. Increased mobility and decreased predictability in the scheduling of subsistence activities would likely have caused a shift from place provisioning toward high diversity individual provisioning, with emphasis placed on technological strategies aimed at risk reduction and utility increase.

- Improved conditions by c. 1,500 BP would likely have alleviated some of the stress on subsistence, and although high residential mobility and the use of risk reduction strategies would probably have remained in place due to the continuation of climatic variability, conditions may have improved to the extent that populations increased again and subsistence activities could take on semi-predictable schedules.

These predictions can be tested by examining the sequence of technological changes in dated, stratified sites from the region described in the following chapter, and by examining changes in the specific technological correlates of mobility, risk and the degree of predictability in scheduling subsistence activities discussed in Chapter 2. This analysis will be undertaken in Chapter 6.

Conclusion

Wardaman Country is a rugged, hot, dry region with low overall rainfall that is highly seasonal. The structuring of most of its economic resources is strongly controlled by underlying geology and geomorphology. These factors create a range of constraints and opportunities for foragers inhabiting this region in the past. The inferred fluctuations in resource availability since the terminal Pleistocene help identify reasons why Wardaman Country was perhaps left unoccupied before about 15,000 years ago, as well as the constraints and opportunities placed on human occupation since that time. A sequence of changes in technologies is proposed that maps on to fluctuations in climate since the terminal Pleistocene on demography, subsistence and settlement patterns.

5. The Sites: Nimji, Garnawala 2, Gordolya and Jagoliya

This chapter presents descriptions of the four rockshelter sites discussed in detail in this monograph, focussing on the location, environs, excavation, stratigraphy, dating and cultural materials. These sites are known to Wardaman People as Nimji (Ingaladdi), Garnawala 2, Gordolya and Jagoliya. All appear to date to the terminal Pleistocene/early Holocene period and contain a large number and diversity of stone artefacts, and so are well-suited to answering chronological and technological questions. The sites are located in quite different environmental settings (Table 5.1), and yet similar changes in the nature of stone artefact manufacture and discard can be identified in each.

Table 5.1. Location of excavated rockshelters in relation to land systems, permanent waterholes and stone sources.

Rockshelter	Distance to Permanent Water (km)	Distance to Stone Source (km)	Geomorphic Unit
Nimji	1.74	0.38	Sand Plains
Garnawala 2	10.00	1.50	Sand Plains
Jagoliya	0.08	6.00	Gorge
Gordolya	9.20	4.60	Breakaway

Nimji (Ingaladdi)

Nimji is a large, semi-circular rockshelter (153 m²) located within a weathered sandstone outcrop (759,360 E 8317,580 N) (Figure 5.1 and 5.2). The floor is comprised of a soft, dark grey ashy sand, and is littered with stone artefacts, ochre and European materials. The rockshelter is located amidst sandy plains, with gently rolling basalt, sandstone and quartzite hills to the north and south and sits within the Delamere Plains and Benches. The Nimji outcrop is one of a number of cavernously weathered residuals of cross-bedded quartz sandstone that occur in the surrounding area. These outcrop in varying size from a few metres to several stories high, and are formed from elongate sandstone lenses within the Antrim Plateau Volcanics (Sweet 1972). More than 48 rock art sites have been documented in these residuals surrounding the Nimji site, although Nimji is the only site to have been excavated (David *et al.* 1990:443). Nimji is also located close to Yingalarri, one of the largest permanent waterholes in the study region (~1.7 km to the southwest). Yingalarri waterhole is the last of a number of permanent waterholes found in the sandstone gorges along Price Creek before the country opens out into more open, drier, black soil country to the east.

1963 and 1966 Excavations

John Mulvaney first excavated at Nimji (he called it 'Ingaladdi' after the nearby Yingalarri waterhole) in 1963 as part of a broad-based archaeological survey of northern Australia, resulting in the excavation of a number of rockshelters between Wardaman Country and Arnhem Land. Mulvaney's interest was principally in obtaining a northern Australian industrial sequence for comparison with those already obtained from elsewhere in Australia (e.g. Kenniff Cave in Central Queensland, Capertee in New South Wales, Clogg's Cave in the Australian Highlands and Devon Downs on the Murray River in South Australia). The 1963 dig opened out a 8 m by 1.5 m trench divided into 8 squares running roughly north to south from the back wall toward the front of the shelter (Figure 5.3 and 5.4). The pit ranged in depth from 1 m in W1-2 to 1.9 m in W8 and was dug in up to 14 spits, averaging 11cm each in depth. Mulvaney returned to the site in 1966 to enlarge the sample of retouched artefacts, clarify the antiquity of the site and the engravings on the back wall, and provide greater resolution for typological changes through finer excavation of a second trench. This trench was 6.1 m long (20') by 1.4 m (4'6") wide, was oriented roughly east west, and abutted the foot of the eastern wall of the shelter (Figure 5.5). The trench was divided in half along its long axis to create an "A" and a "B" trench. This created 13 pairs of adjacent squares each measuring 0.68 m (2'3") by 0.47 m (1'6"). The AB trench ranged in depth from 95 cm in Squares AB1 to 192 cm in Squares AB6-10, and was excavated in up to twenty-five spits each averaging 7.6 cm (3") deep. All spits were sieved through a 6.6 mm mesh sieve.

Figure 5.1. Nimji at the time of Mulvaney's 1966 excavation (courtesy of John Mulvaney).

Figure 5.2. View of the floor from the brow of the shelter (courtesy of Colin Macdonald).

Figure 5.3. Plan of Nimji rockshelter showing the location of the 1963 and 1966 excavation trenches, the location of the squares analysed by Cundy (1990), and the location of major rock art panels.

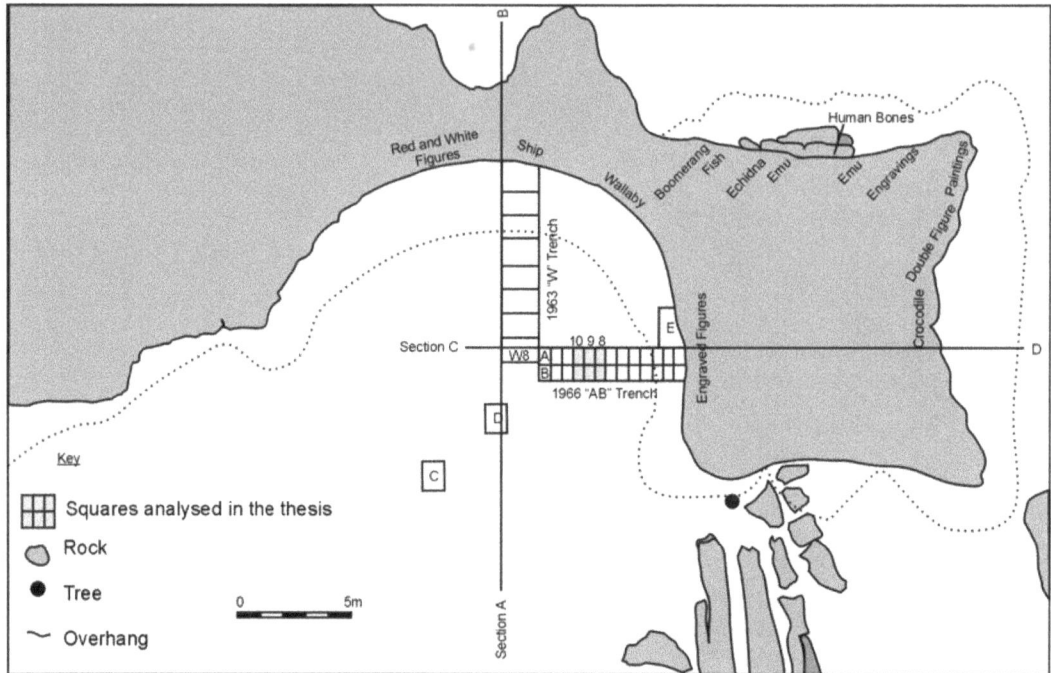

Figure 5.4. North-south and east-west cross-sections of the Nimji sandstone residual, passing through the excavated trenches.

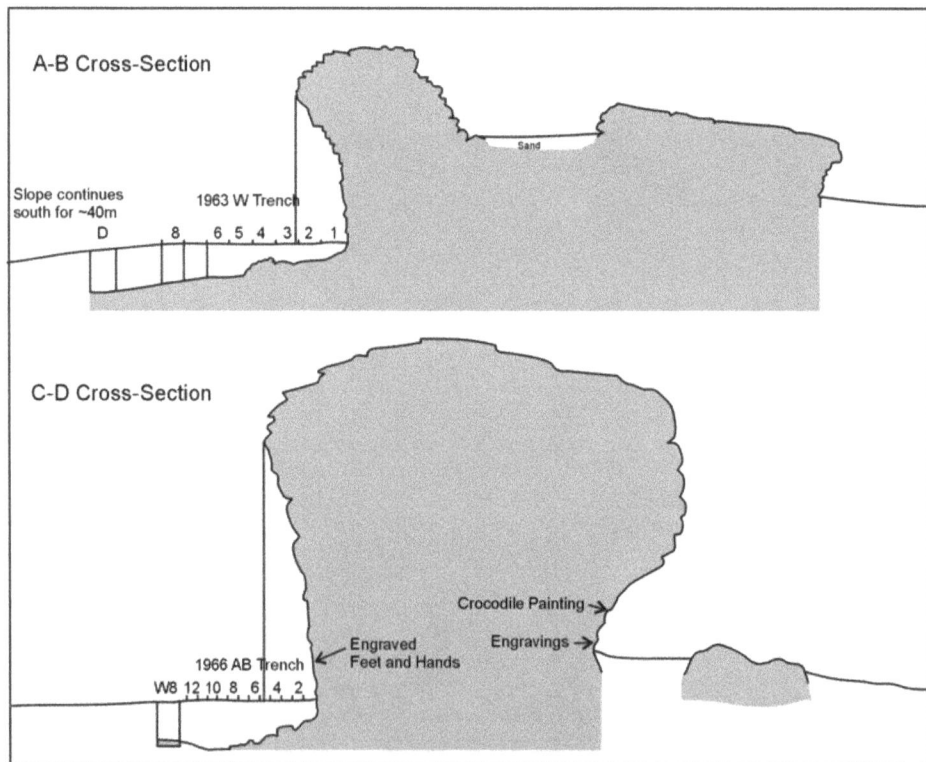

Figure 5.5. The 1966 AB trench at the completion of the excavation (courtesy of John Mulvaney).

Two additional 1.4 x 1.4 m squares were excavated further out from the back wall (Squares C and D) to check the stratigraphy at the front of the shelter. Only 'diagnostic' artefacts conforming to Mulvaney's typology were kept from these squares to enlarge the overall sample of stone implements from the site.

Stratigraphy

The sediments of the Nimji deposit merge continuously into the extensive sand sheet that surrounds the sandstone ridges and outliers in this region (Cundy 1990:92). Stratigraphic profiles redrawn from Mulvaney's and Cundy's (1990) drawings are shown for the 1963 and 1966 trenches in Figures 5.6 and 5.7. A description of the average depth, colour, pH and type of sediments found in each layer for Squares AB8-10 of the 1966 trench, as well as the associated spits, is provided in Appendix B.

From Mulvaney's stratigraphic drawings and notes it appears that finer stratigraphic layering was apparent toward the back of the excavation than at the front in both the 1963 and 1966 trenches. The transition from fine layering to broader and more gradational stratigraphy takes place at around Squares AB5 in the 1966 excavation, and around Squares W3 and W4 in the 1963 trench. As indicated on the section drawings and site profiles, this change appears to correspond with the location of the drip line and the maximum outward extent of the brow of the overhang. It seems that there was also a noticeable darkening of sediments towards the front of the shelter in many cases (i.e. from Squares AB6-13 and W4-8).

Figure 5.6. Section drawings of the 1963 trench, redrawn from Mulvaney's originals.

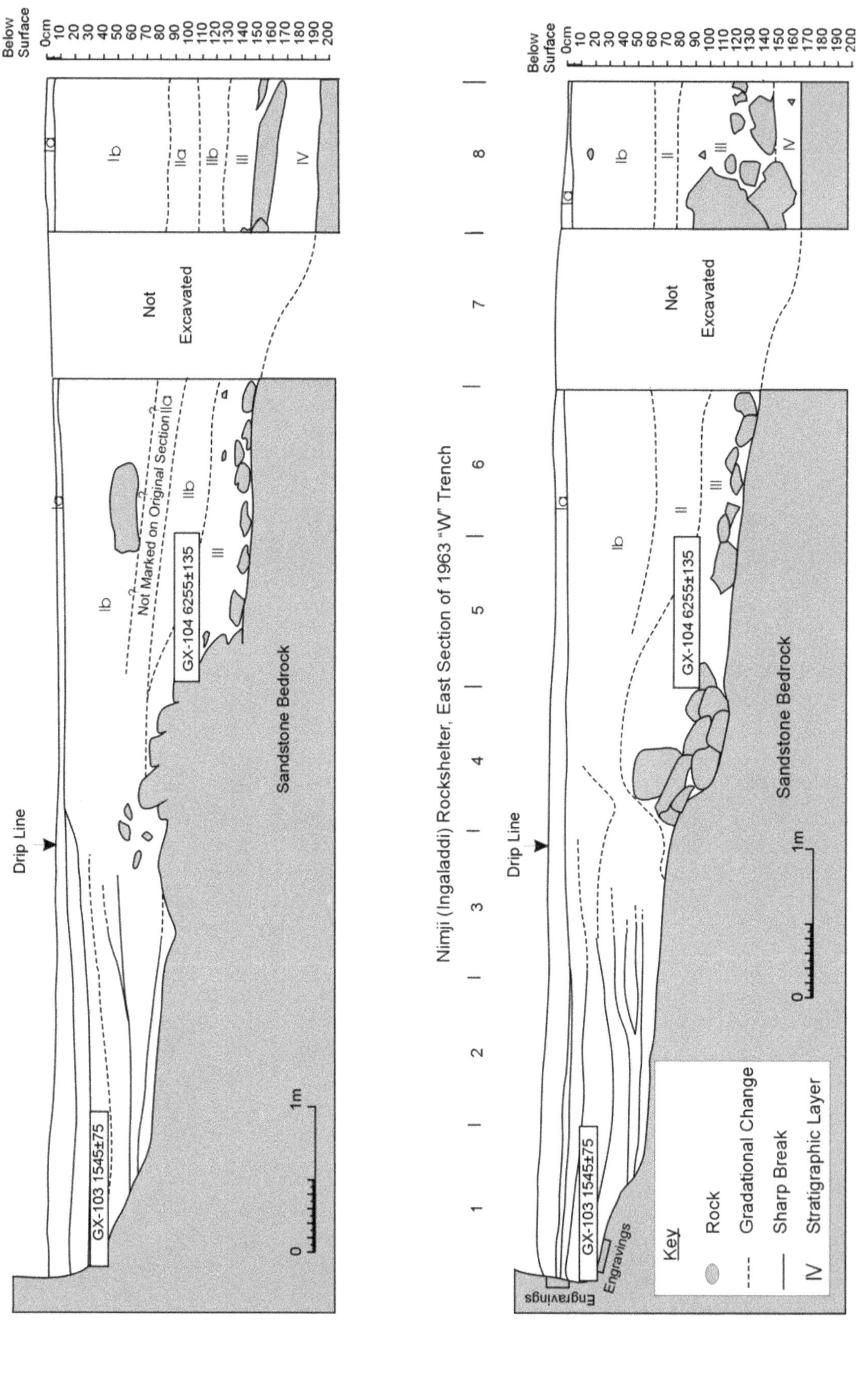

Figure 5.7. Section drawings for the 1966 trench, redrawn from Mulvaney's originals.

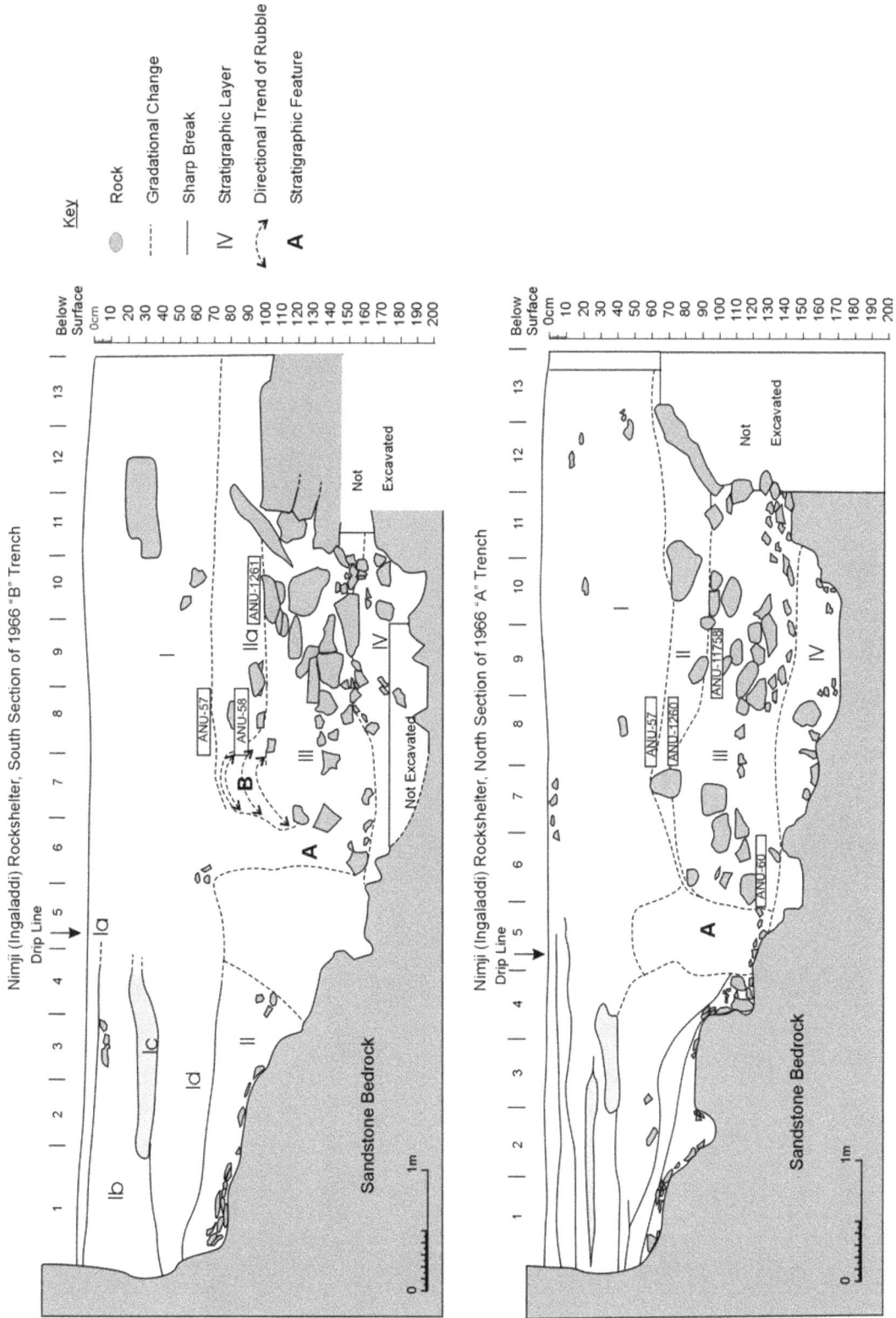

The zone of transition between the front and back of both trenches (Squares A5, B5 & 6 and W3 & 4) shows a break down in finer stratigraphy, an increase in the quantity of roots, darker staining of the sediments and very little rubble. This zone also tends not to preserve the stratigraphic layering present toward the back of both trenches. At the front of the shelter only four distinct stratigraphic layers were found over a maximum depth of around 190cm in the 1966 trench. Rather than forming sharp breaks, these four stratigraphic layers tended to grade into one another. At the top of the profile, Layer I consists of a dark grey ashy sand that is relatively free of rubble, grading into an increasingly rubbly yellow/red sand in Layer II, to a very rubbly orange sand with massive rubble in Layer III, and finally a bright orange sand with finer gravel in Layer IV that appears to derive from the disintegration of the underlying sandstone bedrock. The 1963 trench changes from dark brown sand in Layer I, merging to lighter brown sand with more rock rubble in Layer IIa, a distinctly lighter brown sand in Layer IIb, and finally a very rubbly darker brown sand with a large amount of massive rubble in Layer III. It should be noted that Mulvaney's descriptions of colour change in the 1963 trench appear to be impressionistic and are not based on Munsell colour charts.

Mulvaney saw the change in colour and rock rubble content from Layers I to II as possibly indicating a break in deposition and an apparent change in weathering conditions from those forming the orange rubble in Layer III to that of the dark grey sand in Layer I. Dates returned for each of these layers were also used to support this interpretation (see below). However, Cundy (1990:96) later performed a particle size analysis on bulk sediment samples from the front of the 1966 trench that revealed "no evidence of weathering, sediment sorting or erosional events consistent with a substantial stratigraphic break." Instead, Cundy argued that the stratigraphic changes were best accounted for by two principal factors: the relative size and density of the rock fall and the degree of charcoal content in the fine sediment. While Cundy could find no evidence for a break in deposition, he believed a change in weathering conditions, or a period of catastrophic instability in the structure of the overhang unrelated to environmental changes, could account for the build up of rubble in the lower layers.

Dating

Eleven dates have been obtained for the 1963 and 1966 excavations and these are listed in Table 5.2. For the 1966 trench, one date comes from the base of Layer I (ANU-57, 2890 ± 73), two from the middle of Layer II (ANU-1260, 3,740 ± 80 and ANU-1261, 3,450 ± 110), one from an ambiguous stratigraphic position, but perhaps best ascribed to the transitional zone between Layers II and III (ANU-58, 4,920 ± 100), one from the top of Layer III (ANU-11758, 6,390 ± 80), and one from the base of Layer III (ANU-60, 6,800 ± 270). These dates provide a consistent series of ages that appear to increase with stratigraphic depth. Although ANU-1261 in the A section is lower than ANU-1260 in the B section, this can be explained by the downward tilt in Layer II seen in the A section in Figure 5.7. Both dates therefore likely derive from roughly the same position in the middle to base of Layer II. They also overlap at two standard deviations, and there is therefore no reason to suggest an inversion.

Table 5.2. Radiocarbon dates for the 1966 excavation.

Lab Code	Square	Spit	Layer	Depth (cm)	Radiocarbon Age	Cal BP (2σ range)
ANU-11820	A11	4	I - Top	34.3	810 ± 80	923 (726,719,711) 571
ANU-11821	B9	6	I - Middle	44.5	1220 ± 60	1286 (1171) 973
GX-103	W1	2	I - Middle	40.2	1545 ± 75	1606 (1413) 1294
ANU-57	AB8	10	I - Base	80.0	2890 ± 73	3316 (2996) 2813
ANU-1260	A8	12	II – Middle/Base	92.7	3740 ± 80	4406 (4090) 3868
ANU-1261	B10	14	II – Middle/Base	96.0	3450 ± 110	4055 (3692) 3465
ANU-58	B8	13	II/III - Transition	112.0	4920 ± 100	5908 (5624) 5469
ANU-11819	B9	15	II/III - Transition	113.0	5470 ± 110	6471 (6284) 5954
GX-104	W5?	11?	III - Top	100.0	6255 ± 135	7429 (7184) 6761
ANU-11758	A9	16	III - Top	129.6	6390 ± 80	7432 (7294) 7100
ANU-60	A6	20	III – Base	160.0	6800 ± 270	8168 (7627) 7164

Mulvaney also obtained two dates for the 1963 excavation. These samples come from different stratigraphic positions to those obtained from the 1966 excavation, and date the middle of Layer I

(GX-103, 1,545 ± 75) and the top of Layer III (GX-104, 6,255 ± 135). The GX-103 sample is also from a spit that immediately overlays engravings found on the bedrock at the back of the 1963 excavation trench.

Site Formation

A number of models of site formation have been proposed for Nimji over the years, each involving anthropogenic clearing of rubble from the shelter floor as an agent of disturbance to varying degrees. Mulvaney, for instance, observed at the time of excavation that the feature marked 'B' on the 1966 B section shown in Figure 5.7, resembled a midden-like structure that sloped toward the front and the rear of the excavation, and contained both rock rubble and stone artefacts. Mulvaney suggested that this feature could have been formed through the systematic dumping of rubble and stone artefacts in Square B7 by past occupants of the site. In her M.A. Thesis on the Ingaladdi scrapers, Sanders (1975) took the absence of rubble at the back of the shelter to indicate systematic clearing of rock from the back toward the front of the shelter. Cundy (1990) further developed the idea of anthropogenic disturbance in his PhD Thesis, and argued that the rubbly 'B' feature likely resulted from the digging of an extensive pit into the Level III deposits at the spot marked 'A' in Figure 5.9, and the heaping of the removed material over the existing deposits in Square B7. Cundy argued that the dark brown sand found in feature 'A' in Squares A5 and B6 therefore likely derived from the infilling of the pit with Level I deposits, while the rubble in the "B" feature consisted of heaped up Level III material.

These arguments for digging and/or piling of stone are unconvincing for a number of reasons. A closer examination of the 1963 and 1966 sections (Figure 5.6 and 5.7) reveals that both trenches exhibit almost identical stratigraphic features despite their location in quite different parts of the shelter. For example, as mentioned above, both trenches show the loss of finer stratigraphic layering around half way out from the back wall. This also coincides in both trenches with the beginnings of a darker stained zone that is free from rubble and shows more abundant root activity. Just beyond this point the rubbly III and IV units begin, the Feature B 'rock mound' is found in Square B7, and a darkening of sediments takes place throughout the stratigraphic profile. As noted above, the positioning of these changes in colour, layering and rock content in both excavated trenches closely correspond to the maximum outward extent of the brow of the overhang (Figure 5.5 and 5.6).

These combined features suggest an alternative model of site formation, and one that emphasizes natural processes over anthropogenic ones. It is proposed that the rubbly matrix found in front of Squares W3, A5 and B5 could simply result from the gradual collapse of the overhang, and hence, greater exposure of the outer sediments to the elements, leading to the loss of finer stratigraphic layering through more intense weathering in tropical conditions, darker staining of the sediments through the formation of humic compounds and increased moisture-content from exposure to rain (Bowler 1983). The 'B' feature could then simply represent the last in a series of catastrophic collapses from a disintegrating overhang that resulted in the development of a small mound of exogenous rubble on the surface of Level III deposits directly in front of the present outer limit of the brow of the shelter. The rapid piling up of roof derived material might also explain the 'midden-like' slope in this material toward the front and back of the excavation, as material gradually slid downward on either side of the pile.

An additional line of evidence can be advanced to support this model of natural site formation. If extensive clearing or digging were undertaken toward the back of the shelter in the area of the 1966 trench, and then later infilled with Unit I material, any broad pattern of stone artefact discard evident at the front of the shelter would be unlikely to occur at the back. However, when the combined artefact totals per spit for Squares A5-6 located in the zone of supposed digging (the 'A' feature) are compared with those in the adjoining A7-8 Squares (containing the 'B' feature), a near identical pattern of discard is found, as seen in Figure 5.8. Both samples show bimodal distributions, with peaks located between Spits 5 and 7 and between Spits 14 and 17. It is difficult to believe that this pattern would be replicated in both locations at roughly the same depths had this area been extensively excavated and infilled.

Figure 5.8. Stone artefact numbers from adjacent squares.

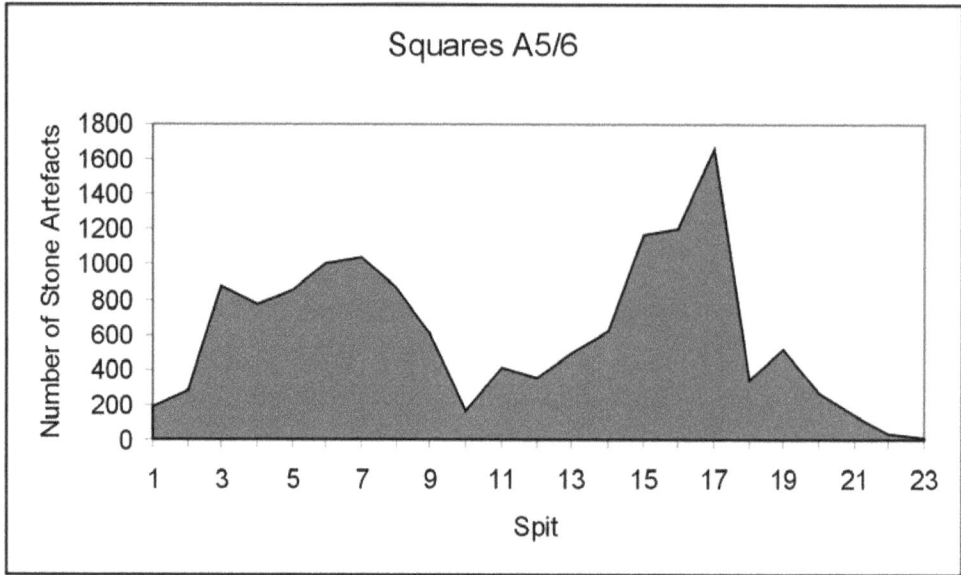

A

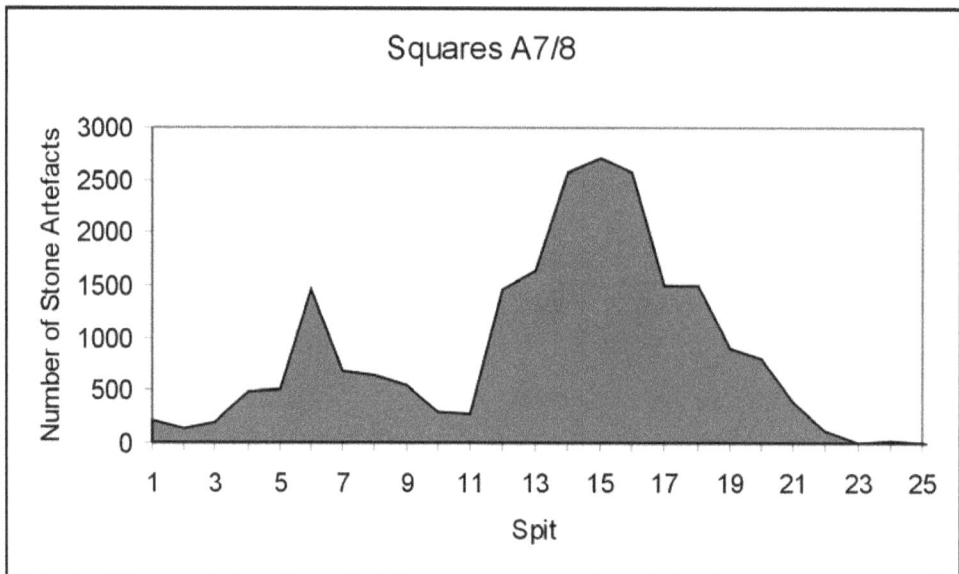

B

Having said this, it does appear that the stratigraphy in Squares AB5-7 of the 1966 trench is more extensively altered, probably due to their location within the present day drip zone, than those squares on either side. Furthermore, as the squares to the font of this zone (Squares AB8-10) are the deepest, and contain the most extensive section of the Level III and IV deposits, these will form the focus for analysis of the stone artefacts from the site. The 1963 trench remains poorly dated and was excavated in spits that are too thick to allow the detection of finer chronological changes. Only Squares AB8-10 from Nimji are therefore discussed in the following chapters.

Sedimentation Rates

Consistent with the model of site formation presented above, examination of the age-depth curve reveals that the Nimji dates for the AB trench Squares 8 through 11 form a coherent sequence of increasing age with depth for both radiocarbon and calibrated ages (Figure 5.9). A linear regression reveals a strong and significant relationship between age and depth (radiocarbon years bp: $r^2 = .978$, p <.0005; Cal BP: $r^2 = .947$, p <.0005), and indicates a deposition rate of around 1cm per 69 years. The tight linear relationship also makes it possible to calculate the first use of the shelter at around 10,000 Cal BP. The only detectable change in sedimentation rate occurs in the top 20cm of the site, which are likely to be of contact age given the presence of European items in the top few spits.

Figure 5.9. Age-depth curve for all dates from the 1966 AB trench.

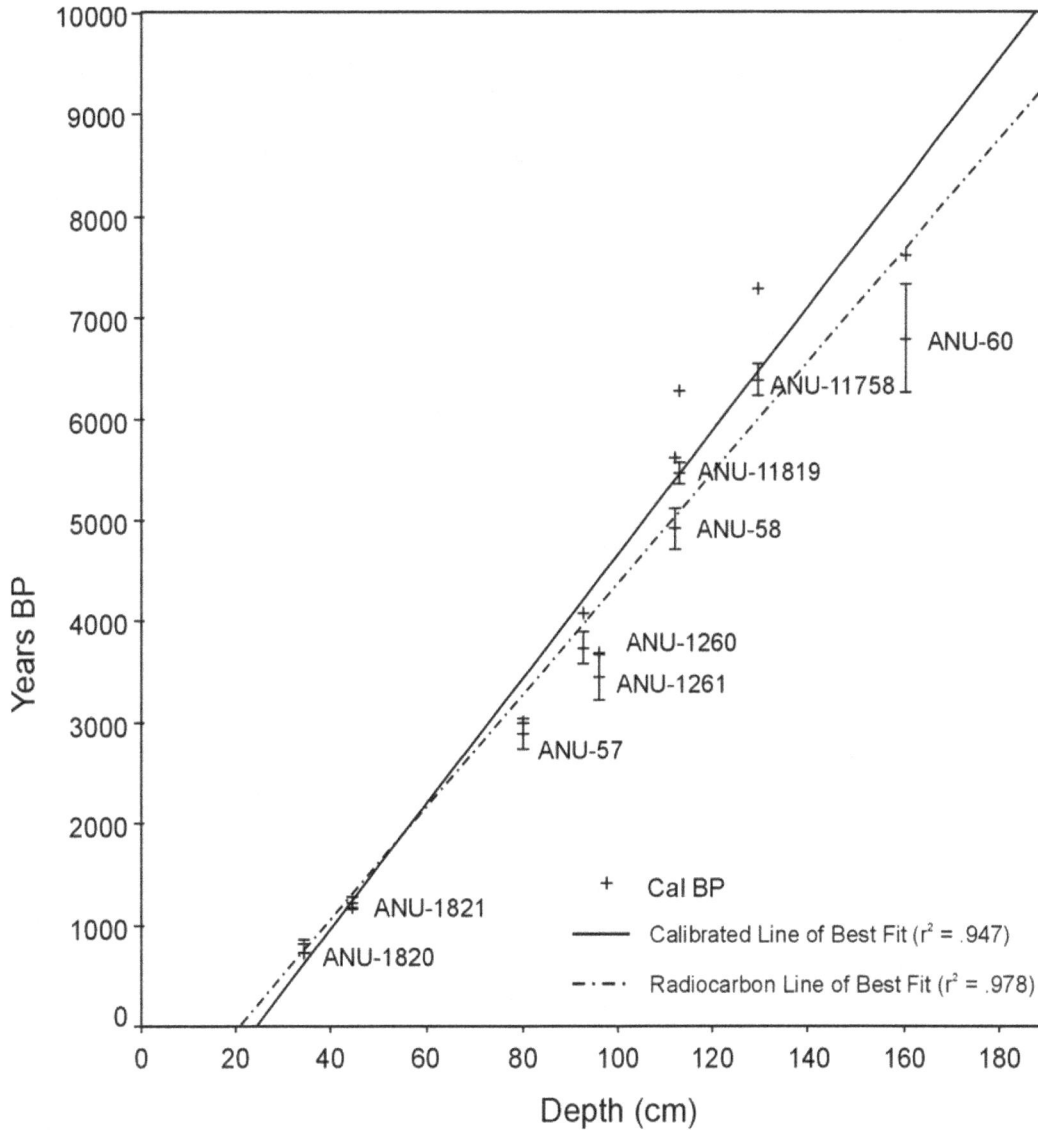

Cultural Materials

Both the 1963 and 1966 excavations recovered massive stone artefact assemblages, rich in retouched artefacts made from a wide variety of raw materials. Mulvaney (1969) divided the assemblage into two cultural units based on stratigraphic and typological changes. The lower industry was comprised of flakes, cores and retouched flakes (scrapers) and was associated with Layers II to IV. The upper industry was present only in Layer I and was characterized by the introduction of pointed blades (hereafter referred to as lancets following Roth [1904] and Cundy [1990]), unifacial and bifacial points, tulas, burrens, burins, stone axes and axe flakes, with large Leilira blades (parallel or pointed elongate flakes (>2:1 length:width) over 10cm in length) appearing toward the very top of the sequence. Scrapers also continued into the upper unit, but cores dropped out almost entirely. Stone artefact deposition formed two distinct peaks of roughly equal size, with the lower one centred on Spits 16 to 18 (c. 6,200-7,200 Cal BP) and the upper one centred on Spits 6 to 8 (c. 1,000-2,000 Cal BP).

Organic remains were extremely rare below the top few spits in both excavations, presumably due to the acid environment of the sandy floor and the ravages of the tropical climate – a situation that is typical of most sites in the study region (see Appendix B for tables of recovered cultural materials). The large size of the sieves has no doubt resulted in the loss of many of the smaller botanic and bone fragments as well as stone artefacts. This is readily apparent when the range and quantity of cultural materials retrieved is compared with those from Garnawala 2, Jagoliya and Gordolya where 3mm sieves were used.

Ochre pieces - some with distinct striations - were also found in large quantities in those squares closest to the back wall. Combined ochre weights for all four squares (AB8-10) show a clear lower peak centred on Spits 13-15 as well as a second though much smaller peak centred on Spits 4 and 5. Burnt earth shows a peak in quantities from Spits 18 to 20, slightly below the lower peak in stone artefact and ochre deposition which should be expected if intense burning during periods of of heightened occupation resulted in baking underlying sediments.

Artefact totals currently exist only for the A trench as well as for other scattered squares, but those for the A trench provide an indication of the likely size of the recovered assemblage. The assemblage from the A trench alone exceeds 61,600 stone artefacts retrieved from the 6.6 mm sieves, but given that this total represents a 1.9% sample of the total area of the site, the total number of artefacts larger than 6.6 mm should exceed three million. Needless to say, the excavated assemblage represents a very large sample, and many of the rarer stone artefact types should therefore be expected to occur in a collection of this size (Hiscock 2001b).

Four local sources of stone (local being defined as less than 10 km from the site), including varieties of chert, chalcedony and quartzite are known to occur within 10 km of Nimji. The closest is an extensive ridge of high quality chocolate brown to grey quartzite over 1 km in length and located ~300 m to the east of site. This quartzite was formed by lava contacting sandstone during formation of the Antrim Plateau Volcanics. This stone tends to outcrop as angular blocks on the ridge top and as rounded and sub-angular nodules on the surrounding black soil plain. Although it is very difficult to differentiate between the many sources of quartzite found within the Antrim Plateau Volcanics, this source was extensively quarried and much of the quartzite found at Nimji and other surrounding sites likely derives from it.

A further two sources of local stone are the hydrothermal pinkish-red cherts and yellow-white chalcedonies that sometimes outcrop as thick veins alongside the quartzite and sandstone ridges of the Antrim Plateau Volcanics. Several sources of hydrothermal chert were inspected in the field, and all were found to be of medium to low quality with abundant internal flaws and weathering plains, with blocks available up to fist size in Aroona Creek around 12 km to the south. The chalcedony, on the other hand, was far less abundant and only one source of good quality stone was located in the field further to the north near Garnawala. Cundy identified a source of agate in the black soil alluvium close to the site, but nodules were of consistently small size and are unlikely to have been intensively exploited. A source of poor quality mottled and brecciated chalcedony was also found to the northwest within one kilometre of the site, and this appears to have been extensively utilized, especially in the early occupation levels at Nimji. This stone is referred to here as local brecciated chalcedony.

Six varieties of non-local stone (defined as derived from greater than 10 km from the site) can also be identified in the Nimji assemblage, with most deriving from sources more than 30 km from the site. These include four distinctive varieties of chert (Banyan Chert, Tindall Chert, Oolitic Chert and Montejinni Chert), a distinctive white, yellow and red quartzite that derives from the Jasper Gorge Sandstone to the west of the site, and silcrete from the lateritic plateaus and mesas to the east and west of the site. Materials that could not be identified were classified as chert, quartzite or other.

Figure 5.10. The Garnawala outcrop with open savanna woodland and sand sheet in the foreground.

Figure 5.11. View of Garnawala 2 rockshelter from the south, showing the rock ledge and the magnificent rock art panels on the back wall.

Garnawala 2

Garnawala 2 is another large rockshelter (676 m^2), also situated within a massive fine aeolian sandstone outcrop with numerous overhangs (Figure 5.10), many of which contain rock art and occupational deposits. The Garnawala ('hawk place') outcrop lies in the central part of the study region (752,000 E 8,325,800 S) at the junction of the Victoria River Plateau and the Delamere Plains and Benches physiographic units. The Garnawala 2 site (Figure 5.11) is located on the northern side of the outcrop and was excavated by Bryce Barker, Bruno David and Josephine Flood in 1990 and 1991 (Clarkson and David 1995; David *et al.* 1994).

Figure 5.12. View from the rock ledge down into the 1990 excavation pit. The analysed squares are the deepest ones furthest from the camera (courtesy of Bryce Barker and Bruno David).

Figure 5.13. Site plan of Garnawala 2 rockshelter showing the location of the analysed squares P27-Q27.

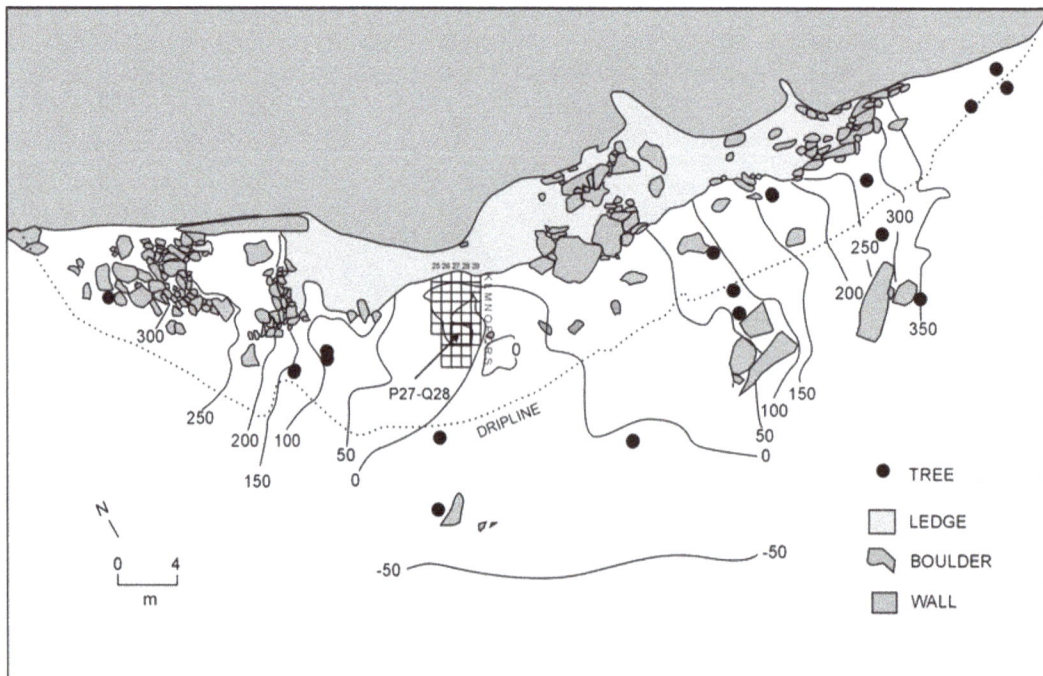

The 1990 and 1991 Excavations

The site was initially excavated as a large grid of 50 x 50 cm squares situated against the rock ledge at the back of the shelter (Figure 5.12 and 5.13). This grid was assigned an alpha-numeric referencing system. Each square was dug in maximum 10-litre 'bucket spits' within stratigraphic layers. All cultural items >2 cm in length were plotted in three dimensions and bagged separately. Sediment samples were collected from each excavation unit of each square. A 3 mm mesh sieve was used to screen the sediments before sorting.

A total of fifteen 50x50 cm squares were fully excavated in 1990 (Squares J26 to N28) and a further 17 peripheral squares were partially excavated to remove loose surface sediments that would otherwise have fallen into the main excavation squares. A small number of abraded grooves were identified on bedrock below the base of Layer II.

In order to follow the bedrock to a greater depth, and thereby obtain a deeper chronological sequence, the original excavations were extended in l991 to include a further six 50 x 50 cm squares, and another seven periphery squares (P26, P29, Q26, R26-R28 and S26-S28). The deepest square was Q28 which reached bedrock at around 1.2 m. No further engravings were uncovered during the 1991 season.

Stratigraphy

The 1990 excavation revealed four well-defined stratigraphic units (Layers I, II, III and V) (Appendix D), with Layers I and II made up of fine ashy sand and containing European and Aboriginal objects, and lower units grading toward a coarse orange sand with pieces of disintegrating sandstone. The excavation proceeded to bedrock, which was only some 30 cm below the surface in the 1990 squares (Figure 5.14). Stratigraphic layers were contiguous between the 1990 and 1991 seasons, however, the 1991 squares closer to the drip line consisted of only three broad stratigraphic units (Layers Ia, III and IV). Layer IV does not occur in the 1990 squares. A maximum of 26 spits were excavated from Square Q28 during the 1991 season and the corresponding stratigraphic layer for each is listed in Appendix D. Squares P27 to Q28 have the deepest deposit and contain a large stone artefact assemblage, and these squares were therefore the focus of the lithic analysis presented later.

Figure 5.14. Section drawing of the 1990 excavation (from Clarkson and David 1995).

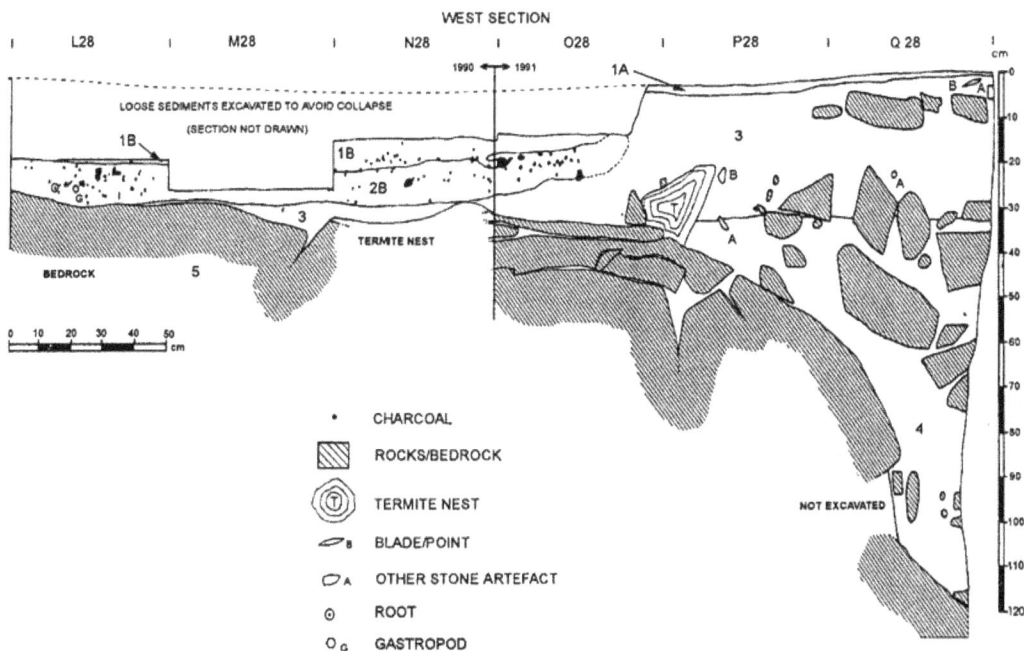

Dating

A total of 21 dates have been obtained for the Garnawala 2 rockshelter (Table 5.3); however, a number of anomalies make interpretation difficult. The greatest difficulty arises from the discrepancy between the age estimates obtained from small pieces of charcoal using AMS dating which are poorly ordered in relation to depth (Spearman's rho = .045, p = .89; ANOVA, F = 172, p = .06), and a series of conventional dates that are strongly ordered (Spearman's rho = .683, p = .04; ANOVA, F = 326, p = .04). The fact that the ordering is significant for conventional dates but not for AMS dates suggests that the mobility of small sized particles of charcoal in the sequence may be to blame for the poor results. The site consists of fairly loose sandy sediments, and there is much potential for movement of materials within such a matrix, as demonstrated by Stockton's (1973) trampling experiments in sandy-floored rockshelters. Termites are also highly active in northern Australian rockshelters (and were observed at Garnawala 2) and constitute another mechanism for the transport of small particles of charcoal upward or downward through the deposit. Larger, combined samples of charcoal are therefore likely to provide more reliable dates than small, individual pieces, and hence only conventional ages will be used to build the chronology of this site.

Table 5.3. Radiocarbon dates from Garnawala 2.

Lab Code	Square	Spit	Layer	Max. Depth (cm)	Radiocarbon Age	Calibrated Age (2δ)	Type
OZD429	Q28	6	III	15.0	2,250 ± 50	2758 (2735) 2468	AMS
OZD430	Q28	9	III	22.6	2,450 ± 50	2736 (2485, 2481, 2469) 2348	AMS
Beta 66434	Q28	12	III	34.7	2,920 ± 120	3380 (3075) 2776	Con.
NZA4626	Q28	13	III/IV	39.3	2,755 ± 67	2998 (2849) 2750	AMS
NZA4627	Q28	17	IV	54.2	10,164 ± 92	12348 (11904, 11820, 11752) 11264	AMS
OZD432	Q28	19	IV	62.5	9,450 ± 110	11160 (10688, 10646, 10644) 10292	AMS
OZD433	Q28	23	IV	89.6	2,610 ± 50	2782 (2748) 2547	AMS
OZD434	Q28	25	IV	106.6	2,080 ± 60	2300 (2040, 2023, 2010) 1896	AMS
Wk-3571	Q28	20	IV	68.5	8,984 ± 98	10360 (10186) 9779	Con.
ANU-11367	Q27	13	IV	46.0	5,670 ± 200	6901 (6445, 6418, 6413) 5993	Con.
ANU-11268	Q28	17/18	IV	55.0	3,850 ± 470	5585 (4244) 3004	Con.
OZD431	Q28	15	IV	48.0	2,180 ± 80	2349 (2291, 2273, 2151) 1951	AMS
Wk-9247	Q27	7	IV	11.4	2,360 ± 50	2705 (2350) 2212	Con.
Wk-9248	Q27	9	IV	19.4	1,640 ± 90	1730 (1533) 1332	Con.
Wk-9249	Q27	11	IV	24.8	1,879 ± 131	2145 (1822) 1524	Con.
Wk-9250	Q27	12	IV	40.7	896 ± 66	947 (790) 673	AMS
Wk-9251	Q28	15	IV	48.0	2,517 ± 68	2660 (2426, 2421, 2360) 2355	AMS
Wk-9252	P27	14	IV	35.0	2,751 ± 60	2997 (2848) 2749	AMS
Wk-9253	P28	13	IV	34.2	5,227 ± 62	6174 (5986, 5970, 5945) 5894	AMS
ANU-11597	Q28	7	IV	17.8	2,160 ± 60	2335 (2148, 2135, 2133) 1954	Con.
ANU-11760	Q28	5	IV	12.8	2,400 ± 670	4091 (2357) 958	Con.

Con. = Conventional

Using only conventional ages as a guide, Layer I and II both appear to have accumulated over the last 200 years, judging by the presence of European artefacts in these layers, while Layer III spans the period >200 BP to c. 2,920 bp (3,075 Cal BP) and is associated with the first appearance of points, tulas and burins. Layer IV spans the period >2,920 to >13,000.

Sedimentation Rates

The depth-age relationship for Square P27-Q28 is shown in Figure 5.15. The age-depth relationship appears to be linear, and shows a strong linear correlation for both the calibrated dates (r^2 = .934, p = <.0005) and uncalibrated dates (r^2 = .943, p = <.0005) with depth. Based on the calibrated line of best fit, 1 cm of deposit accumulated in roughly 138 years. The depth-age curve indicates a likely maximum age for occupation at the site of c. 13,000 Cal BP.

Figure 5.15. Depth-age graph for conventional dates from Garnawala 2, Squares P27-Q28.

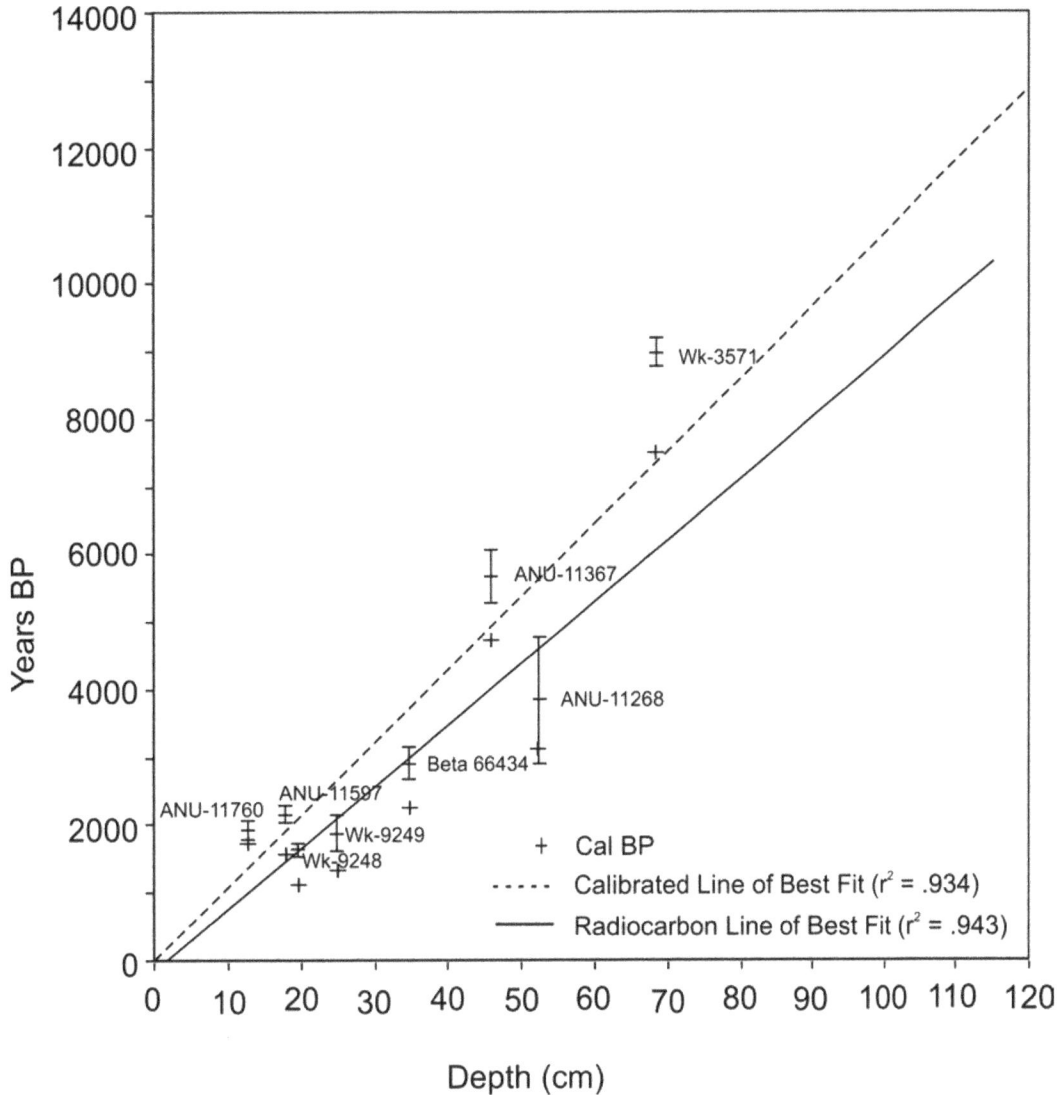

Cultural Materials

Cultural materials were present to bedrock (SU5) in all main squares. Cultural materials were recovered from all spits and appeared in reasonable numbers down to the lowermost levels (Appendix C). Charcoal peaks in Spit 6 and then rapidly decreases in quantity with depth. To some extent this trend is likely to reflect the poor preservation of organic remains at greater depths, and hence it is problematic to interpret this pattern as a reliable signal of the intensity of human burning within the shelter (though the peak in Spit 6 may be significant). Organic matter and bone follow a similar pattern of declining abundance with depth and this is also likely to represent differential preservation.

The same range of stone artefact classes is found at Garnawala 2 as at Nimji, with an apparent transition in typological elements around Spit 12, with the first appearance of the points, burins, tulas, burrens, etc. in large numbers at this time (Appendix C). Two peaks in stone artefact deposition occur over the depth of the site – one in Spit 19 and one in spit 9. The stone artefact assemblage is also very large, with 11,225 artefacts recovered from a single 50 x 50 cm square (Q28), which makes up around 0.05% of the floor area of the site. The total number of artefacts >3 mm within the drip line of the site is therefore likely to be in excess of fifteen million.

Three clearly identifiable local raw materials are present within the assemblage. These are a low-grade white chert, a high grade yellowish chalcedony, and a low-quality pinkish red chert. All three materials are likely of hydrothermal origin and are found in a series of bands around 1.5 km to the south of the site. Another local material is the brown to grey quartzite of the Antrim Plateau Volcanics which outcrops in a wide variety of forms as part of a long NW-SW trending scarp line around 1.5 km to the south. Although local in occurrence, this type of quartzite is common throughout Wardaman country and it is impossible to distinguish it from other sources. The location of all four raw materials follows a characteristic pattern within the Antrim Plateau Volcanics of an elongate ridge of quartzite adjacent to a NW trending sandstone ridge, with various kinds of hydrothermal chert running parallel to the quartzite and sandstone outcrops.

Jagoliya

Jagoliya ('at the black headed python') is a small (~100 m²) sandstone rockshelter and rock art site formed beneath the overhang of a large boulder that has detached and fallen from a cliff immediately to the north of the site (Figure 5.16 and 5.17). The shelter is located at the mouth of a shallow gorge, which forms the junction between a high sandstone escarpment to the west and undulating limestone plains to the east. The site is located close to the northern end of Hayward Creek on Innesvale Station (743,100 E 8,355,100 S) at the junction of the Victoria River Plateau and the Daly River Basin physiographic units. The shelter sits around 80m from a permanent spring-fed waterhole and would have been an attractive location for various activities including fishing, swimming, hunting and gathering bush foods from the plains and the gorge.

The vegetation on the escarpment surrounding the gorge is a low, open, snappy gum woodland with curly spinifex, while a taller woodland and grassland dominates the plains to the east. Spinifex, bloodwood and pandanus occur on the rocky slopes immediately outside the site, but vine thicket, weeping paperbarks and pandanus groves occur deeper within the gorge fringing the narrow permanent waterholes.

The 1998 Excavation

Four 50 x 50 cm squares were excavated in the centre of the sandy shelter floor directly in front of a rock art panel depicting dingoes and anthropomorphs. The site was excavated in up to 37 spits to a total depth of 1.3m, terminating when rock rubble made further progress impossible (Figure 5.18). Two stone artefacts appeared in the last spit at a depth of 1.24 m, and it is therefore possible that cultural material does continue to greater depth, though at extremely low density.

Figure 5.16. View of Jagoliya rockshelter. The opening to the shelter is beneath the two pandanus trees at the base of the rock.

Figure 5.17. View of the shelter floor before excavation. Rock art is visible on the back wall and the excavation squares have been strung out.

Figure 5.18. Jagoliya rockshelter. A: site plan showing excavated squares, and B: cross-section through the site and through the excavated squares.

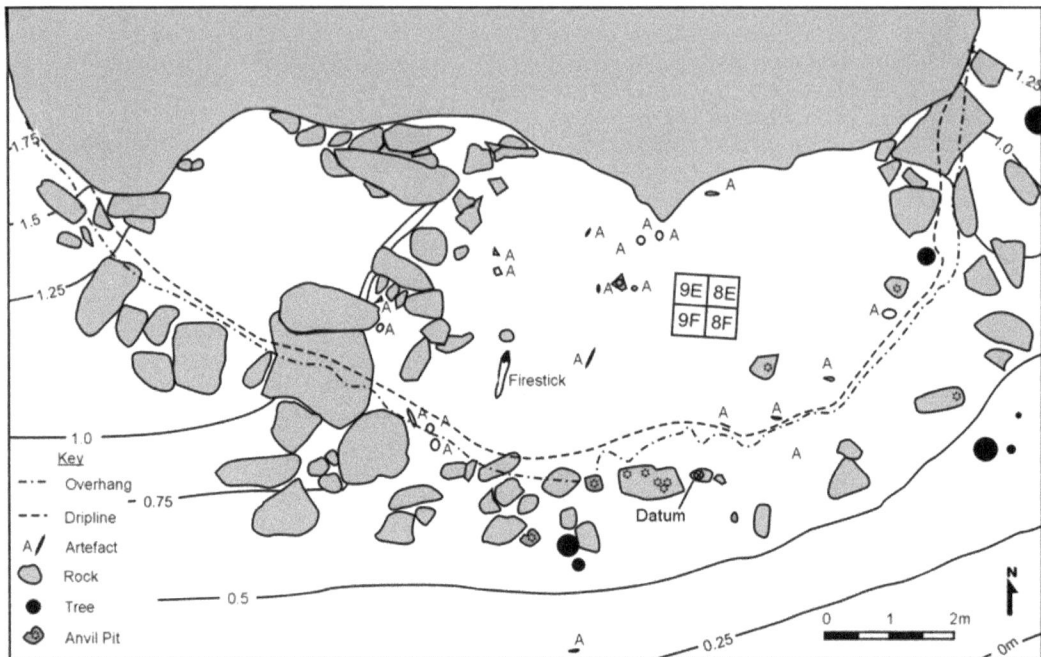

A

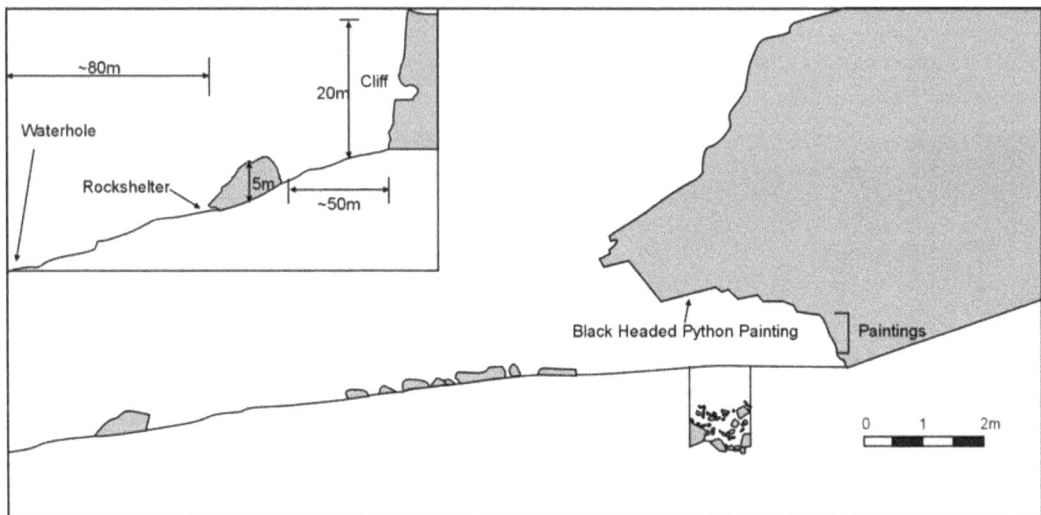

B

Stratigraphy

Excavation revealed a total of seven well-defined stratigraphic units (Figure 5.19). Sediments changed from dark grayish-brown loamy sandy at the top to a reddish-grey clayey sand at the bottom, with the quantity of sandstone rubble and large sandstone blocks increasing with depth (Figure 5.20). A description of each stratigraphic unit and associated spits is provided in Appendix D.

Figure 5.19. Stratigraphic section of Jagoliya rockshelter, Squares 8F-9E.

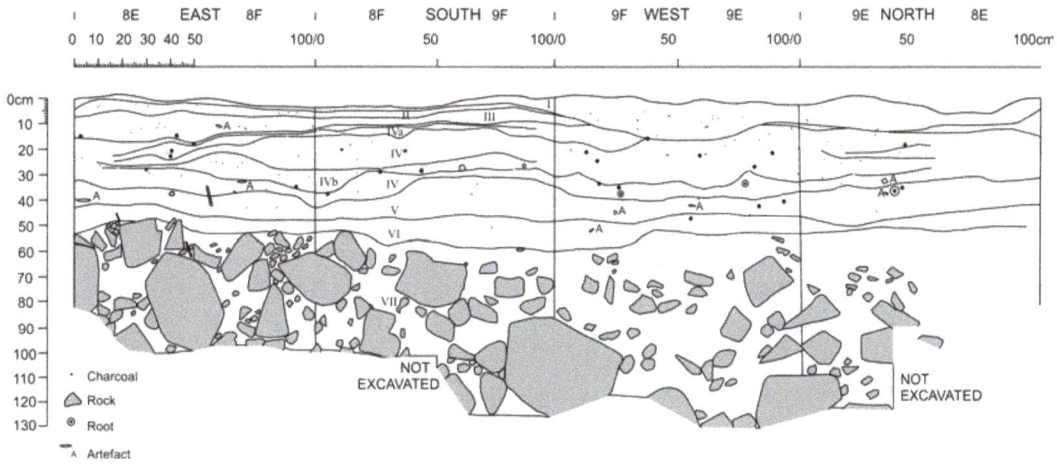

Figure 5.20. View into the completed excavation at Jagoliya. Note the dark band formed by Layer V and the massive rubble at the base of the excavation.

Dating

Four conventional radiocarbon dates have been obtained for the top 55 cm of the site (Table 5.4). The scarcity of charcoal below this depth led to the submission of a further two samples for AMS dating of the lower layers. These samples, however, suffer the same problem as the AMS dates from Garnawala 2 (i.e. temporal inversion) and are therefore rejected. The conventional radiocarbon chronology on the other hand provides a well-ordered series spanning the last 4,000 years.

Table 5.4. Radiocarbon dates obtained for Jagoliya, Squares 8E-9F.

Lab Number	Layer	Square	Spit	Max. Depth (cm)	Radiocarbon Age	Calibrated Age (2δ)	Type
ANU-11266	IVa	8F	9	18.8	270 ± 60	476 (305) 3	Con.
ANU-11267	V	8E	20	44.9	1510 ± 90	1591 (1401)1272	Con.
ANU-11364	VI	9E	22	53.5	2780 ± 200	3385 (2866) 2354	Con.
ANU-11309	VII	9E	23	56.5	3860 ± 230	4861 (4254) 3639	Con.
WK-9246	VII	9E	30	99.8	286 ± 60	497 (309) 4	AMS
WK-9254	VII	9E	33	130.7	982 ± 75	1055 (926) 732	AMS

Con = Conventional

Layers I to III all appear to be of post-contact age (i.e. less than 200 BP) based on the presence of European artefacts such as glass beads and glass flakes. Layer IV appears to be pre-contact, and has an associated date of 270 ± 60. The base of layer V has an associated date of 1,510 ± 90. Points, tulas, burins etc all make their first appearance with the beginning of Layer VI dated to 2,780 ± 200 (2,866 Cal BP). Layer VII begins around 3,860 ± 230 and continues to an unknown depth.

Sedimentation Rates

The age-depth relationship for the site is plotted in Figure 5.21. Much like Nimji and Garnawala 2, sedimentation rates also appear linear over the dated range. The relationship between age and depth is also strong and significant for both uncalibrated (radiocarbon r^2 = .857, p = .02) and calibrated dates (r^2 = .906, p = .01). From the calibrated line of best fit, 1 cm of deposit would appear to have accumulated roughly every 87 years. Extrapolating from this line of best fit, the first occupation of the shelter can be estimated to have taken place around 6,500 years ago Cal BP.

Figure 5.21. Depth-age curve for Jagoliya. Only conventional radiocarbon dates are plotted.

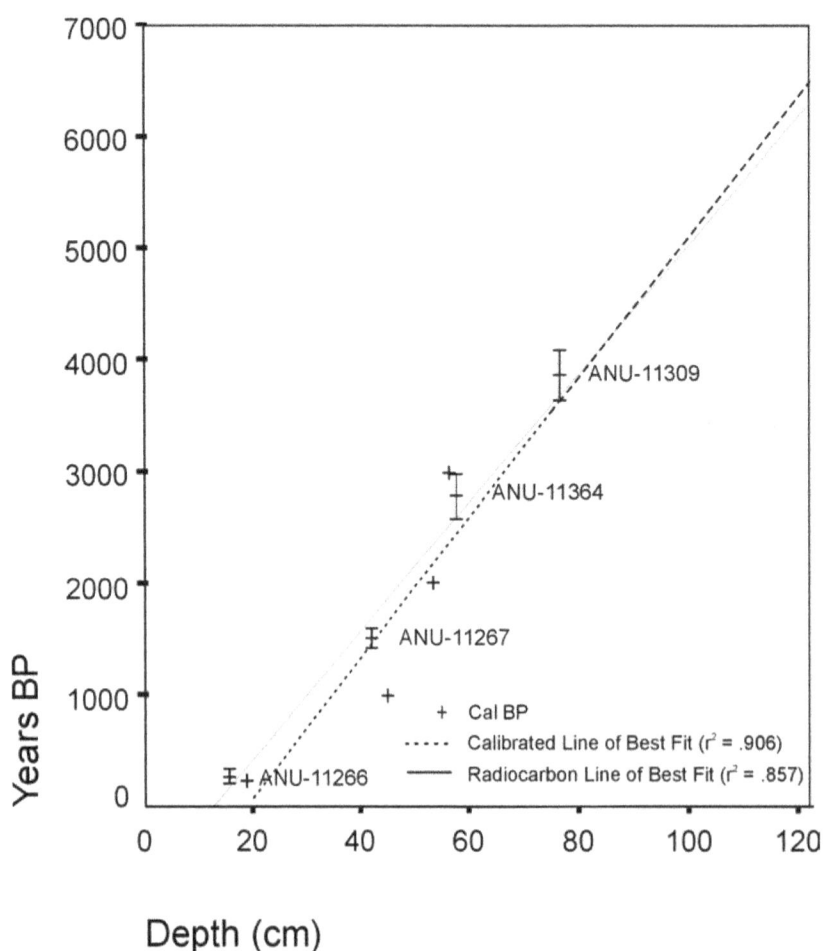

Cultural Materials

Cultural materials occur from the top spit to the base of the excavation. Like the other two shelters, preservation of organic material is poor, and charcoal and other organics (seeds, faecal pellets and bone) reduce in quantity over the depth of the deposit after a peak in Spit 10 (Appendix D). Stone artefacts ochre and burnt earth, on the other hand, all increase between around 55 and 30 cm depth (between c. 3,400-1,200 Cal BP) with a distinct peak at around 40 cm depth (c. 1,500 Cal BP).

The range of stone artefacts is much like that for other sites in the region described above, with Banyan jasper dominating the assemblage. This material is available at its closest around 6km away to the northeast. Other materials including silcrete and Jasper Gorge and Antrim Plateau Volcanics quartzite also appear in the site, but in much lower quantities. These last raw materials are not found locally, and are probably available no closer than around 15km away.

The stone artefact assemblage is small in comparison to Nimji and Garnawala 2, but sizeable enough (n = 8,622) to detect major assemblage changes and conduct detailed technological analysis on complete artefacts. The excavated area amounts to around 1% of the shelter floor area, and the overall site assemblage is therefore estimated to be around 862,200 artefacts larger than 3 mm.

Gordolya

Gordolya ('at the owl') is a medium sized rockshelter (~510 m²), and is the largest shelter in a medium-sized sandstone outcrop known as Jigaigarn (Figure 5.22), situated in the Sturt Plateau physiographic unit. Like the other three sites described so far, Gordolya contains spectacular rock art, with over 147 rock art paintings and 4,556 engravings found on the walls and boulders.

Figure 5.22. View of Gordolya with the excavation in progress in the background (courtesy of Jacqui Collins).

The 1991 Excavation

Gordolya was excavated in 1991 by Jacqui Collins as part of the Lightning Brothers Project (David 1991). As at the other sites, an alphanumeric system was used to divide the shelter floor into 50 x 50 cm squares (Figure 5.23). A 2 x 2 m (16 squares) pit oriented north was excavated immediately adjacent to a large boulder, and directly beneath overhanging painted motifs, with questions concerning the antiquity of rock art and technological change determining the choice of location. The excavation was undertaken in 2 cm bucket spits within stratigraphic layers, and reached bedrock at a maximum depth of around 62.7 cm in Square M24.

Figure 5.23. Site plan of Gordolya rockshelter. A: site plan showing excavated squares, and B: cross-section through the excavated squares.

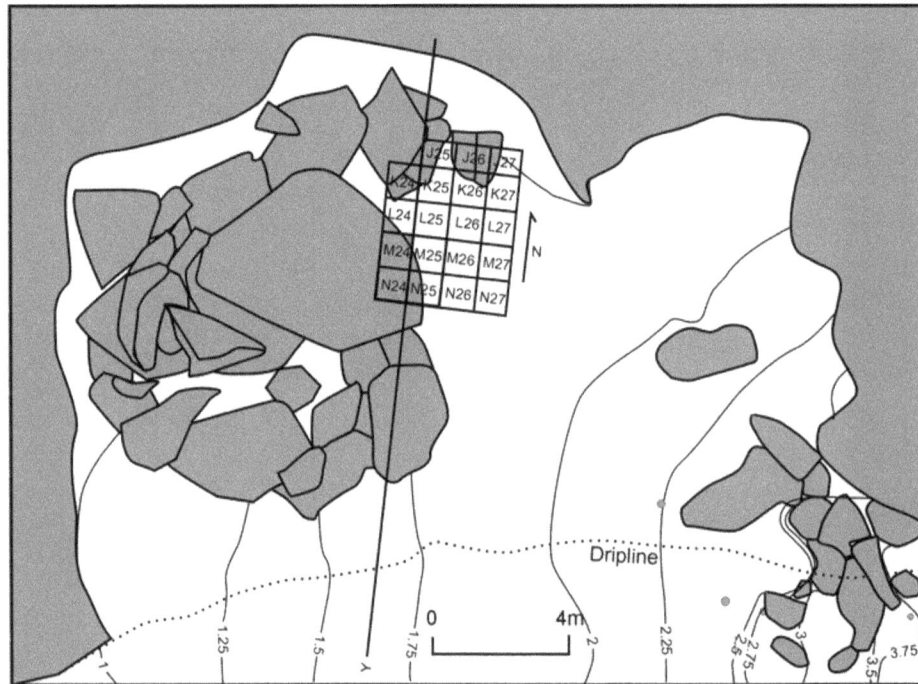

A

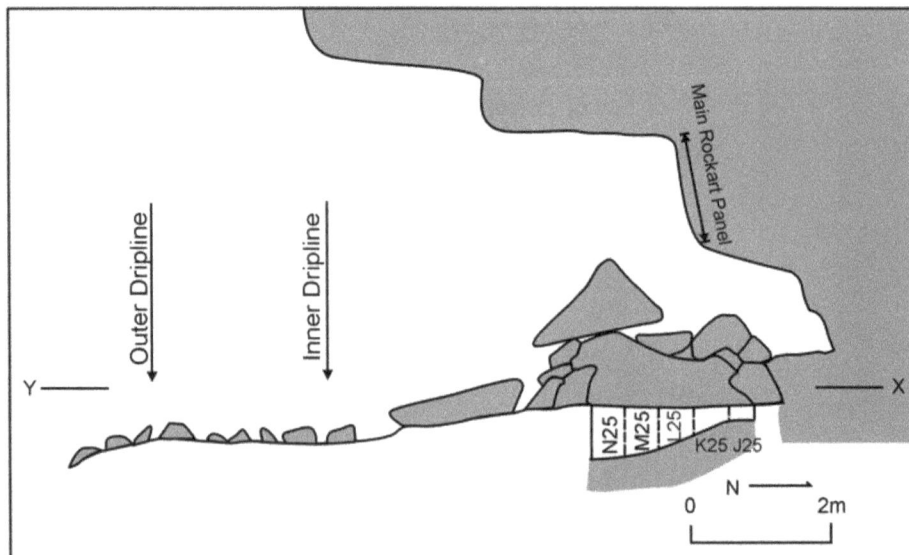

B

Figure 5.24. Section drawings for Gordolya, Squares J27 to N25.

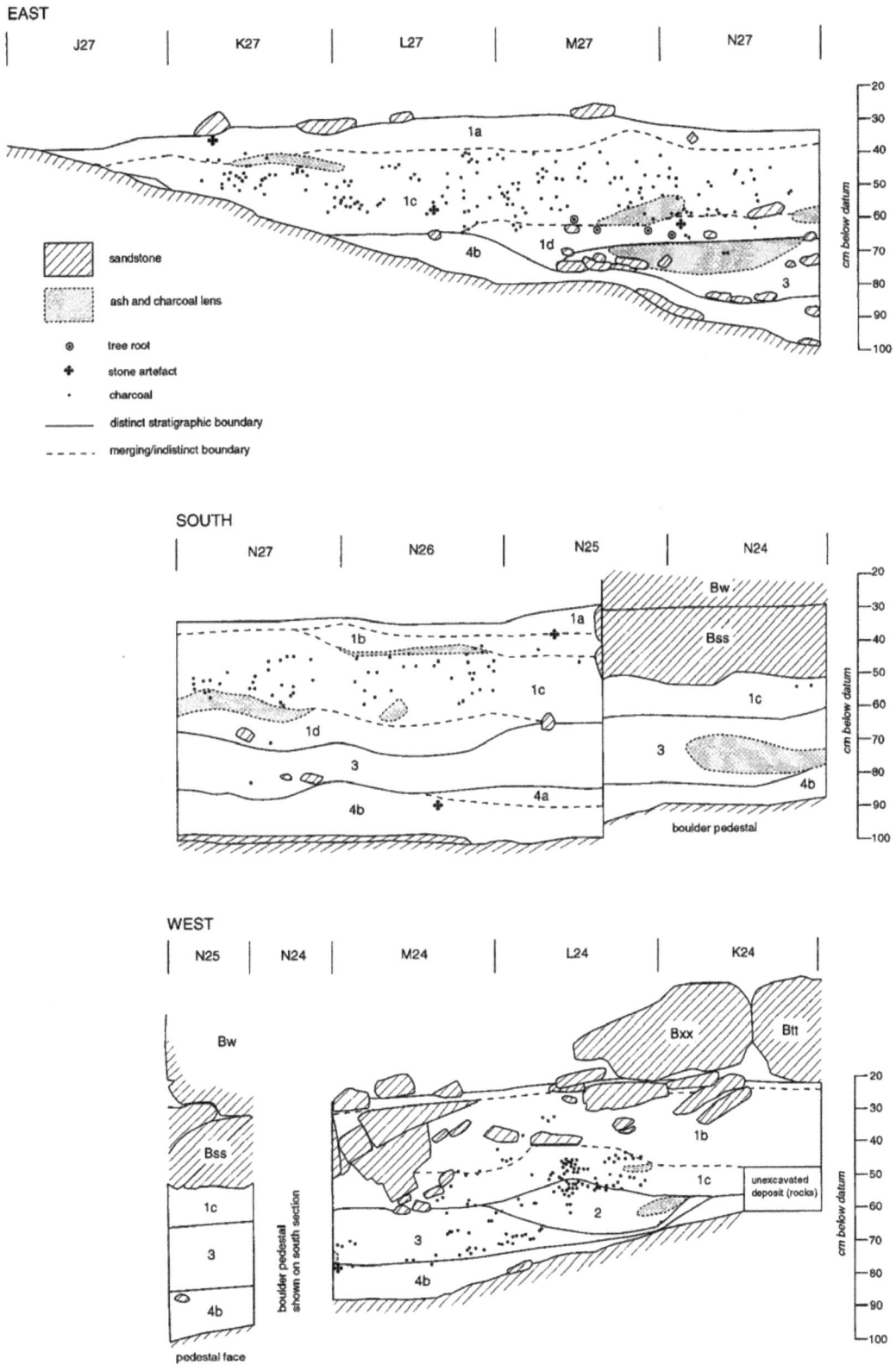

Stratigraphy

David *et al.* (1991:5) describe the stratigraphy of the site in the following way:

> The upper 8-10 cm of the deposits consisted of relatively loose sediments containing leaf matter, small pieces of exfoliated sandstone, stone artefacts, freshwater mussel sells, and red ochre fragments. Underlying sediments rapidly became more compact with depth, and the density of cultural materials dropped significantly until c. 15 cm in depth ...a sterile sandy layer was reached immediately above bedrock.

The stratigraphic profile is provided in Figure 5.24, while the details of each stratigraphic layer (depth, colour, texture, pH) are provided in Appendix E.

Dating

A total of nine dates have been obtained from Gordolya, from Squares M24, M25 and N25, revealing a terminal Pleistocene age for the site. Unlike the other sites described so far, Gordolya has excellent preservation of organic remains, and large amounts of charcoal was present right to the bottom of the cultural layers. Consequently, there was no need for AMS dating, and the set of dates reported in Table 5.5 appears reliable.

Table 5.5. Dates obtained from the Gordolya excavation.

Lab Number	Layer	Square	Spit	Depth (cm)	Radiocarbon Age	Calibrated Age (2δ)
Beta 68162	Ib	M25	7	19.00	340 ± 50	508 (431, 356, 328) 294
ANU-11760	Ic	M25	9	24.20	2070 ± 80	2307 (2036, 2030, 2003) 1833
ANU-11761	III	N25	16	47.6	3840 ± 70	4422 (4240) 3992
ANU-11262	Ic	M25	11	30.00	4700 ± 60	5590 (5462, 5361, 5332) 5307
ANU-11594	III	M24	11	35.10	6010 ± 60	7002 (6853, 6836, 6830, 6822, 6802) 6676
ANU-11763	III	M24	13	43.50	7040 ± 70	7974 (7919, 7901, 7857) 7684
ANU-11759	III - Bottom	N25	18	52.70	7410 ± 100	8394 (8184) 7980
Beta 68163	IV	M25	15	46.00	10110 ± 110	12334 (11689, 11670, 11653) 11232
ANU-11595	IV	M24	17	57.00	10530 ± 90	12929 (12631, 12455, 12429) 11967

Layer I appears to have begun accumulating around 5,300 calendar years ago, and ended in the present period. Layer II is absent from Squares M24-N25. Layer III began accumulating around 8,000 calendar years ago and Layer IV sometime before 12,500 calendar years ago.

Sedimentation Rates

The dates for the M squares form a consistent relationship with depth that is strong and significant for both the calibrated (r^2 = .941, p = <.0005) and uncalibrated (r2 = .937, p = <.0005) dates. This age-depth relationship is plotted in Figure 5.25. The N25 dates apparently have a different slope to the M Squares, reflecting the slight E-W tilt in the stratigraphy of these squares. The nature of this slope is difficult to define, however, since only two dates have been obtained for the N squares. Figure 5.25 indicates that sediments likely began accumulating in the shelter around 15,000 Cal BP, although human use of the shelter appears not to have begun until 500 or so years after this time. As the oldest date so far obtained for occupation in Wardaman Country, it is probably no coincidence that first occupation appears to coincide with a period of rapid climatic shift from cool/dry conditions to warm/wet conditions. This may have made the region vastly more inhabitable at this time than it had been previously.

Figure 5.25. Depth-age curve for M squares at Gordolya rockshelter.

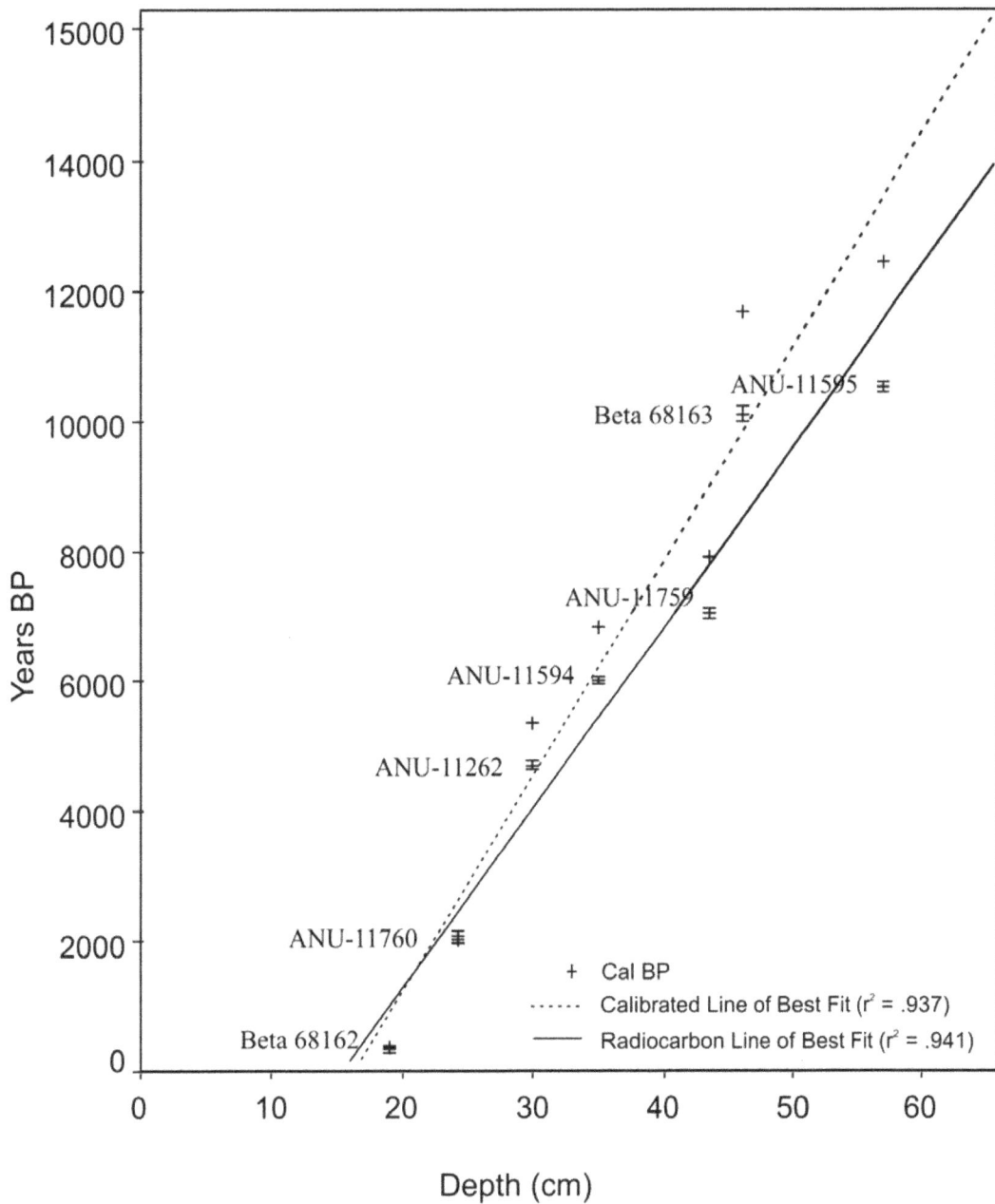

Cultural Materials

A range of cultural materials were found at Gordolya, including ochre, stone artefacts, European contact items and the largest bone assemblage yet recovered from the study region (Appendix E). While bone is abundant throughout the sequence with one clear peak in all squares (Spit 11 in M24, Spit 10 N25), other organic materials are less common and show complex patterns over the depth of the deposit.

Quantities of charcoal, for instance, vary for each square, with two peaks in M24 (Spit 5 and Spit 13), two peak in M25 (Spit 3 and Spit 6), one peak in N24 (Spit 10), and a gradual decline with depth in N25. Other organics (leaves, twigs, animal faeces, etc.) all peak within the top three spits, and greatly reduce in quantity below that depth. Ochre also has a complex distribution, with a single peak in M24 (Spit 2), two peaks in M25 (Spits 11 and 16), two peaks in N25 (Spits 1 and 17) and a single peak in N25 (Spit 2). The small quantities of ochre overall may have caused the noisiness in depositional frequencies. Stone artefacts show a single distinct peak in deposition in three squares (Spit 13 in M24, Spit 15 in M25, and Spit 15 in N25), but two peaks in Square N24 (Spit 14 and Spit 10).

Sample size is small, and fewer technological classes of stone artefacts are found at this site than the others, but a transition from earlier retouched flakes and cores to points, tulas and lancet flakes takes place in most squares, though with limited definition (Appendix E). Three raw materials are likely to be available close to the site: silcrete, hydrothermal chert and brown and grey quartzite of the nearby Antrim Plateau volcanics (Appendix E).

Conclusion

This chapter has presented information on the location, chronology and range of cultural materials found in the four excavated rockshelters. The rockshelters chosen for investigation all contain deposits spanning long periods and do not appear problematic in terms of the their age-depth relationships or the quantity of cultural materials recovered. This information provides the background context to the data that will be presented in the following two chapters. These chapters construct reduction sequences that help measure change and understand assemblage variation, and examine the changing systems of technological provisioning and land use that are expected to reflect changes in mobility, climate change, prey-structure and risk.

6. Reduction Sequences: Artefact Form and Manufacturing Technology in Wardaman Country

Understanding stone artefact manufacture and the effects of intensity of reduction on lithic implement form and other kinds of debris are crucial steps in understanding similarity, difference and change in Australian technological traditions. As explained in Chapter 1, such an understanding should also underwrite attempts to compare industries and to determine the ways in which people organised technologies to meet their various needs. This chapter constructs reduction sequence models for a range of common stone artefact forms found in Wardaman Country, including cores, flakes (including lancets), retouched flakes (scrapers), points, burins, tulas and burrens. I will begin by exploring the effects of reduction on core and flake form, and then documenting reduction continuums and blank selection for retouched implements.

Documenting Reduction Sequences: Core Reduction

It was argued in Chapter 3 that it is possible to model core reduction by exploring changes in geometry, force variables, morphology and various measures of the quantity of flake removals. As most platforms fail to produce flakes of consistent form beyond a certain point – often determined by the build up of step or hinge terminations, increases in platform angle and reductions in platform area – one measure of overall attempts to extract the maximum number of useable flakes from a core is the number of times it has been rotated to set up new platforms. This measure is employed here as a means of ranking core reduction so that the changes in core morphology, the frequency with which particular procedures are used, and the likelihood of insurmountable problems arising throughout the reduction process can be explored.

To track changes in core form and the use of different technological strategies over the sequence of core reduction, twelve variables are plotted against increasing number of core rotations in Figure 6.1. These changes are documented from a set of 200 chert and quartzite cores spanning all available periods of occupation. This diagram shows that many of the measured core characteristics show an increase over the sequence of reduction, while others decrease.

As might be expected, the number of scars found on cores increases with each rotation, as does the percentage of platforms that have more than one conchoidal scar, resulting from the use of a previous core face as the new platform (Figure 6.1a). The percentage of scars found on the core showing step and hinge terminations also increases as core rotation proceeds, as does the minimum external angle of the last platform used on cores. The use of overhang removal also increases steadily throughout the remainder of the reduction sequence. Overhang removal was presumably used to strengthen the platform to better receive the forceful blows required to remove flakes from small cores with increasingly high angled platform edges.

In contrast to these increasing trends, cortex diminishes rapidly in the early stages of reduction, indicating that more surface material was removed prior to the first rotation than at any stage subsequent to it (Figure 6.1b). This idea is supported by the rapid reduction in the weight of cores over the first few rotations. As the weight of cores reduces with more rotations, so does the size of the platform and the length of flake scars. As length reduces, so too does the elongation of flake scars. Finally, the used portion of the platform edge first increases and then decreases as the viable platform perimeter reduces. This is no doubt largely due to irregularities left on the core face and platform by previous rotations that constrict flaking to certain areas, but may also reflect decreasing control over force variables that allow successful flake detachments.

Figure 6.1. Changes in core morphology over the reduction sequence.

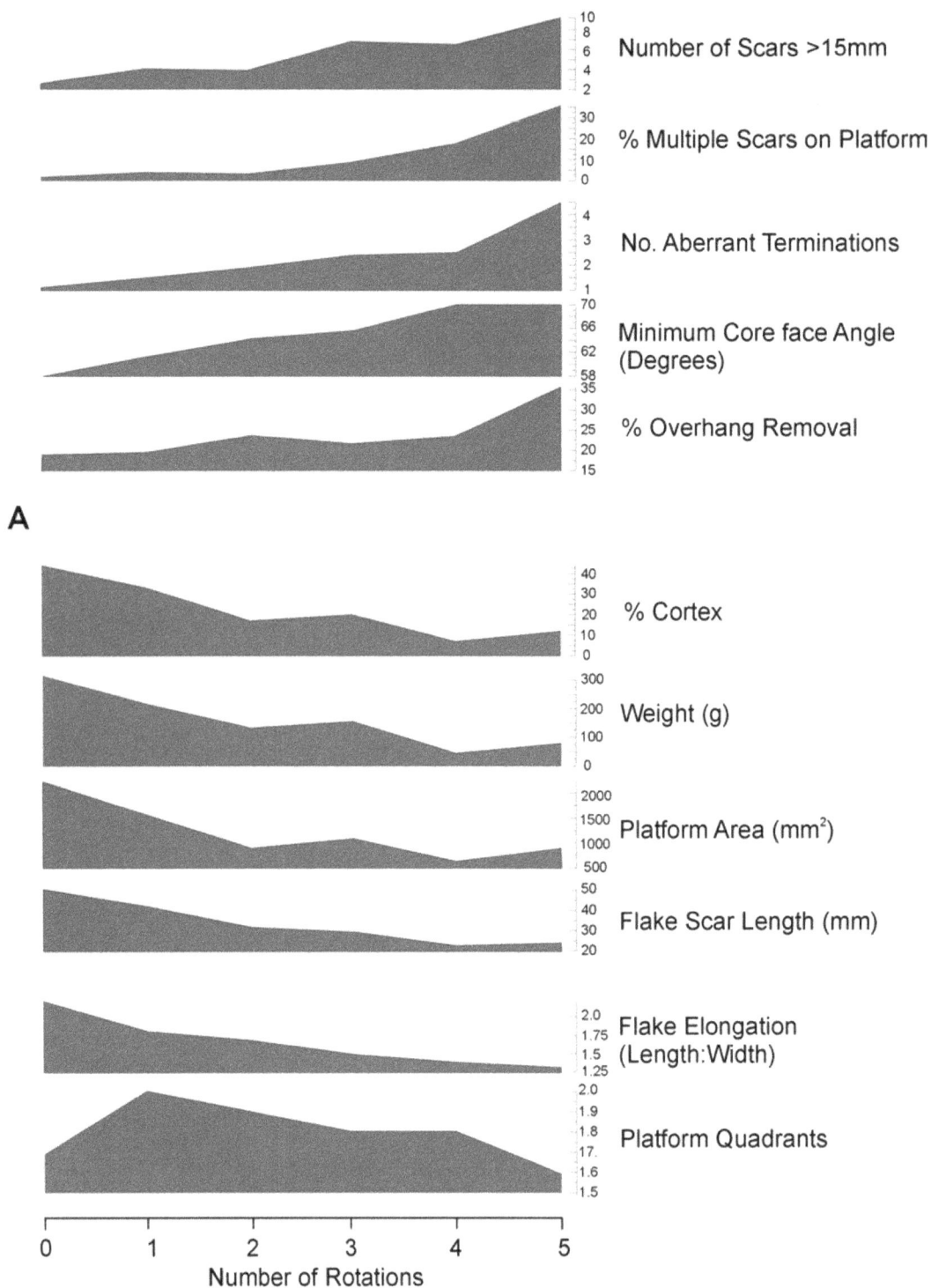

It is also possible to examine variation in each of these attributes as reduction proceeds. Tables 6.1 and 6.2 provide the means, standard deviations and coefficients of variation (CV) for nine of the metrical variables shown in Figure 6.1. CV is given as well as standard deviation as the size of the mean influences standard deviation, whereas CV removes any effect the mean has on the measure of variation. The CVs for most attributes are quite high (over 50%), but most show no directional changes in variation over the sequence of reduction. The exceptions are weight, which shows a marked increase in variation as rotation continues, and length and scar elongation which both show reductions in variation over the sequence. A suggested reason for increasing variation in weight is that most cores start large, but only some finish small, as cores can sometimes be rotated many times without reducing mass significantly. Another reason is that larger cores can be taken into later stages of reduction as their greater mass means inertia thresholds are reached later in the sequence than for smaller cores. Consequently, both large and small cores may reach late stages of reduction, creating more variation as the number of rotations increases. Reduced variation in flake elongation and length, on the other hand, probably reflects the reduced possibilities for producing long flakes later in the sequence as cores become shorter and squatter.

Table 6.1. Mean, standard deviation and coefficient of variation for four measures of core reduction, morphology and reduction technique over the sequence of core rotations.

Rotations	# Scars			% Cortex			Flake Elongation *			Flake Scar Length*		
	Mean	σ	c.v.	Mean	σ	c.v.	Mean	σ	c.v.	Mean	σ	c.v.
0	2.6	1.9	72.6	44	34.4	78.2	2.2	1.3	60.4	50.6	9.0	17.9
1	4.1	2.5	61.6	33	29.0	87.8	1.8	1.3	73.2	41.8	9.2	21.9
2	3.9	2.2	55.7	17	26.1	153.7	1.7	1.0	61.3	31.6	5.0	15.9
3	6.8	3.9	56.8	20	23.6	118.2	1.5	0.7	44.6	29.3	3.7	12.6
4	6.5	2.3	34.9	7	11.9	169.5	1.4	0.7	48.3	22.7	1.9	8.4
>/=5	9.2	6.5	71.1	12	11.2	93.5	1.3	0.8	59.5	24.0	4.1	17.2

* Average taken for the last four scars struck from cores.

Table 6.2. Mean, standard deviation and coefficient of variation for a further seven measures of core reduction, morphology and reduction technique over the sequence of core rotations.

Rotations	Weight (g)			Minimum Core Face Angle			% Overhang Removal	% Multiple Platform Scars	% Aberrant Terminations
	Mean	σ	c.v.	Mean	σ	c.v.	Mean	Mean	Mean
0	316	348.5	110.3	59	13.2	22.3	19.0	1.6	1.1
1	216	271.7	125.8	62	9.2	14.9	19.6	3.9	1.5
2	133	186.6	140.3	65	11.2	17.3	25.8	3.2	1.9
3	156	246.5	158.0	66	14.4	21.8	21.7	8.7	2.4
4	45	69.9	155.3	70	9.9	14.1	23.5	17.6	2.5
>/=5	80	123.2	153.9	70	7.8	11.1	35.7	35.7	4.5

Cores are more likely to become stabilised (i.e. unresponsive to freehand percussion) as reduction proceeds, and knappers faced with this situation might opt either to discard the core, or switch to the use of a strategy that can better overcome inertia thresholds, such as the use of bipolar technique. A small number of cores in the sample were further reduced using bipolar technique. That bipolar reduction formed the end point in the continuum of core reduction is demonstrated by Figure 6.2, which shows bipolar cores as the smallest and last in a continuum of core sizes.

Figure 6.2. Changes in core size associated with changes in reduction strategy.

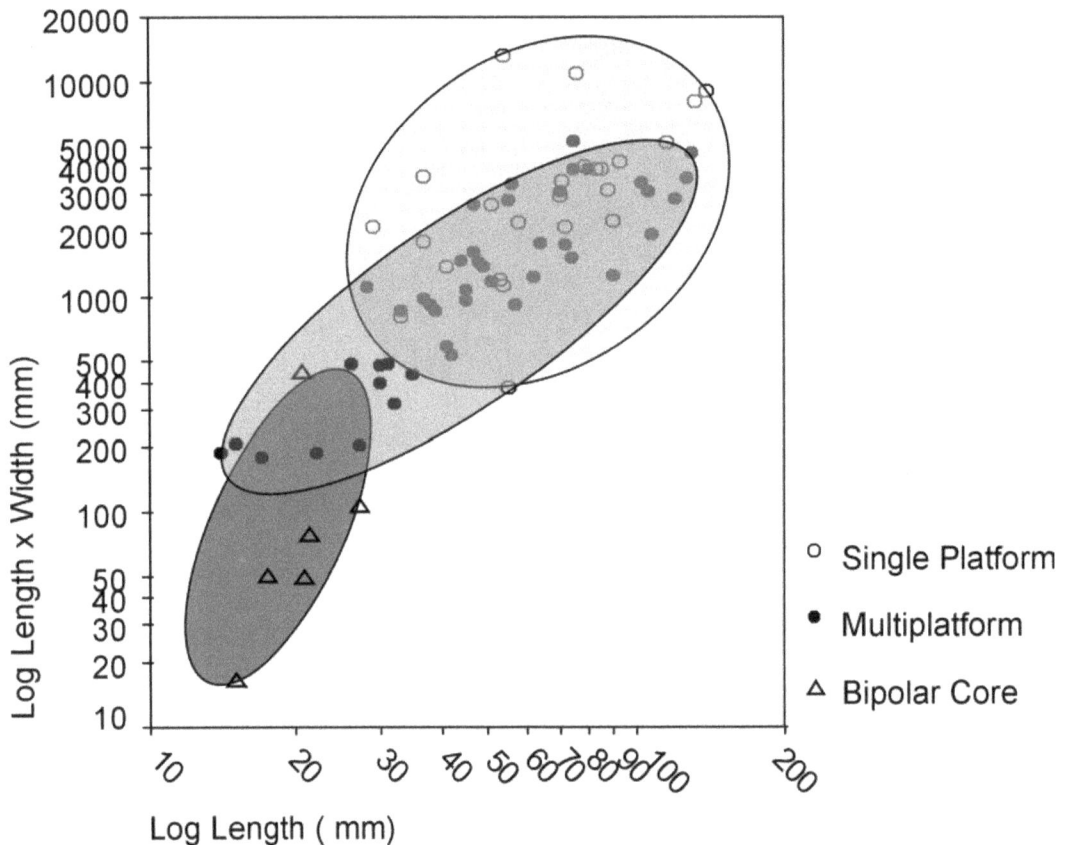

Changes in core morphology over the reduction sequence are illustrated as an event tree in Figure 6.3, which depicts a range of ways of flaking nodules that are commonly observed in sites in Wardaman Country. While archaeologists have sometimes used this type of chart to illustrate normative reduction sequences through which most forms are argued to pass, this chart ascribes frequencies to each stage in each sequence as determined from the assemblage itself (see also Bleed 1996). Reduction obviously begins with a single flake removed from a cortical platform. In the left-hand sequence (Sequence 1), new platforms are always created from the previous flaked surface via 90 degree core rotations. In the middle sequence (Sequence 2), new platforms are always created from cortical surfaces. In the right-hand sequence (Sequence 3), a single large scar is removed from each surface which then becomes the platform for the next removal. Also illustrated in Figure 6.3 are late stage rotated and bipolar cores, with and without cortex, which represent the very end stages of these sequences.

Figure 6.3. Event tree summarising the changes in core form that result from several modes of reduction, and their frequencies.

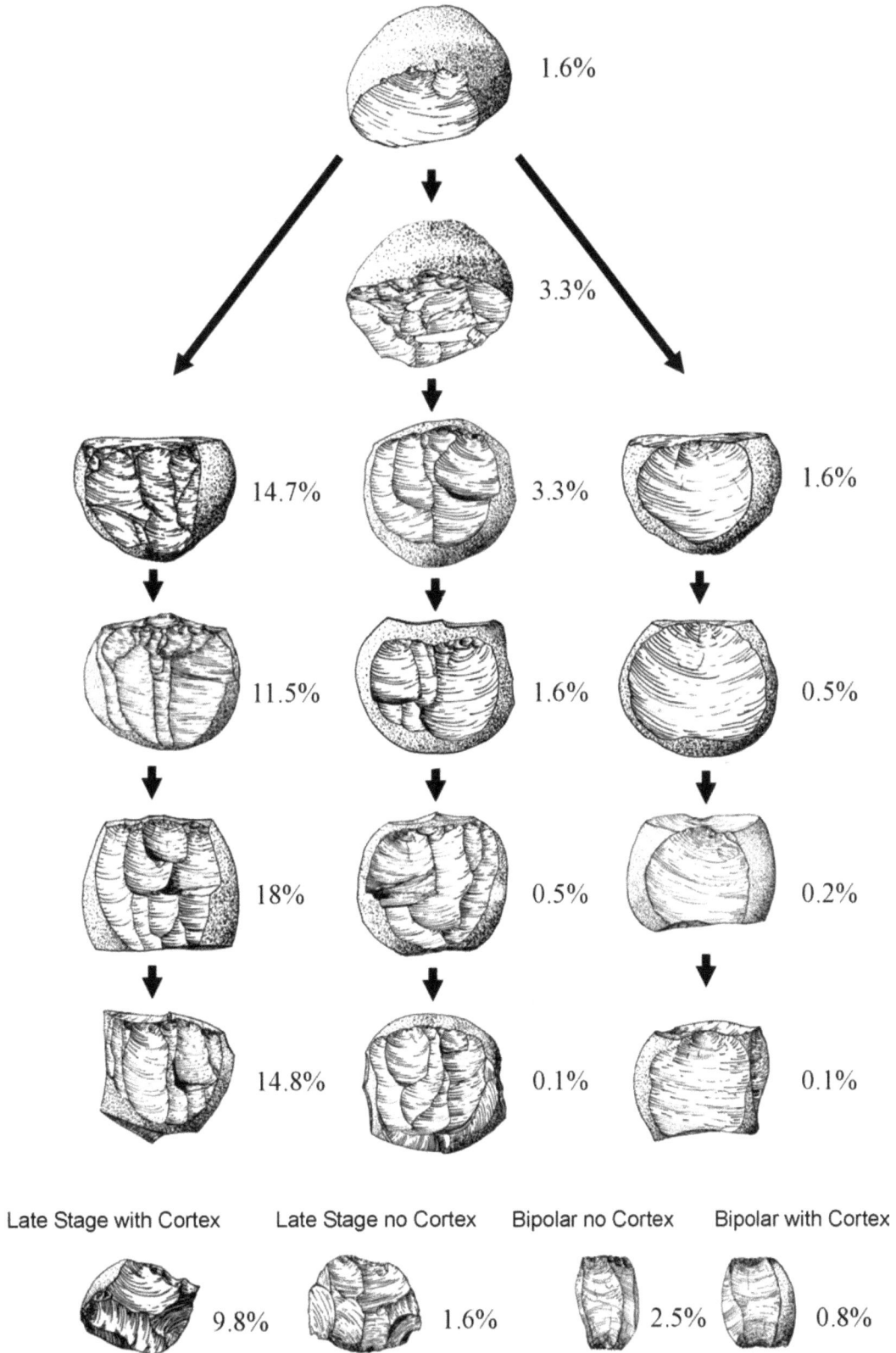

1.6%		
	3.3%	
14.7%	3.3%	1.6%
11.5%	1.6%	0.5%
18%	0.5%	0.2%
14.8%	0.1%	0.1%

Late Stage with Cortex	Late Stage no Cortex	Bipolar no Cortex	Bipolar with Cortex
9.8%	1.6%	2.5%	0.8%

From the percentage frequency figures provided in this diagram, it can be seen that Sequence 1 was most commonly practised in the study region, and that Sequence 2 was also a common alternative. Sequence 3 on the other hand was rarely practiced. Mapping reduction sequences in this way allows variation as well as the central tendency to be explored, and also demonstrates that core reduction was a highly variable process, with knappers responding to the results of each successful or unsuccessful blow in a flexible fashion, in which the options for rotation, discard or strategy switching (such as to bipolar reduction) were appraised at various points along the way (cf. Young and Bonnichsen 1984).

The preceding analysis suggests that the number of rotations found on cores is likely to be a useful and reliable measure of reduction intensity in most cases. Using the number of rotations to assign each core its likely stage in the reduction process will therefore allow the intensity of core reduction to be traced over time with implications for the range of issues relating to time-budgeting, risk, mobility, and land use discussed in later chapters.

Flake Reduction

Like core reduction, it is possible to order the stage in the reduction sequence at which individual flakes are produced. Separating flakes produced by retouch and those produced by core reduction is an important first step, however, because flakes produced via different reduction processes likely possess quite different characteristics (such as platform angles, size, platform and dorsal scar morphology, initiation type etc), such that analytical combination will result in a poor description of either population. Separating flakes on the basis of different reduction processes is also desirable if the information sought about each population differs, or if the focus of investigation is upon only one of these processes (i.e. core reduction vs. retouching). The rationale for separating flakes deriving from retouch from those struck from cores is to limit detailed flake analysis to the core-struck flakes only, and in so doing, drastically reduce the size of the assemblages analyzed while also focussing on potential 'blanks' for retouching and transport rather than the by-products of resharpening and implement manufacture. Of course, retouch flakes may also have been tools, but the decision is made here to overlook this possibility in order to make the analysis more manageable.

The systematic and quantitative approach to separating core and retouch struck flakes adopted here is an attempt to avoid subjective decisions about what constitutes a retouch flake. The literature abounds with attempts to recognize such flakes (e.g. billet flakes and bifacial thinning flakes), but a simpler approach is taken here.

When the length of the longest retouch flake scar on a sample of 334 retouched implements is measured, the maximum length of retouch scars is found to be 35 mm, while 99.8% of all maximum scar lengths are less than 21 mm in length. As a second independent test, the lengths of flakes found at quarries are plotted in Figure 6.4. The mean length of core-struck flakes on quarries is 66 ± 34 mm, while flakes less than 25 mm in length are very rare. Flake length is therefore taken as a simple and reasonably effective means of separating retouch from core struck flakes. Only complete flakes larger than 20mm are therefore included in the following analyses.

Flake Morphology and Reduction Intensity

Following the changes in core form depicted in Figure 6.1 and 6.3, flakes can be roughly ordered into reduction stages according to the nature of the platform surface, and changes in flake morphology examined as the reduction process progresses. The four platform types used to order flakes are cortical platforms, representing the first stages of core reduction, platforms formed from a single conchoidal flake scar, representing early to middle stages, platforms with multiple conchoidal scarring, representing late stages of freehand percussion, and crushed bipolar platforms, representing the last stage of the reduction continuum.

Figure 6.4. Histogram of the lengths of flakes found at quarries and inferred to be 'core-struck' flakes.

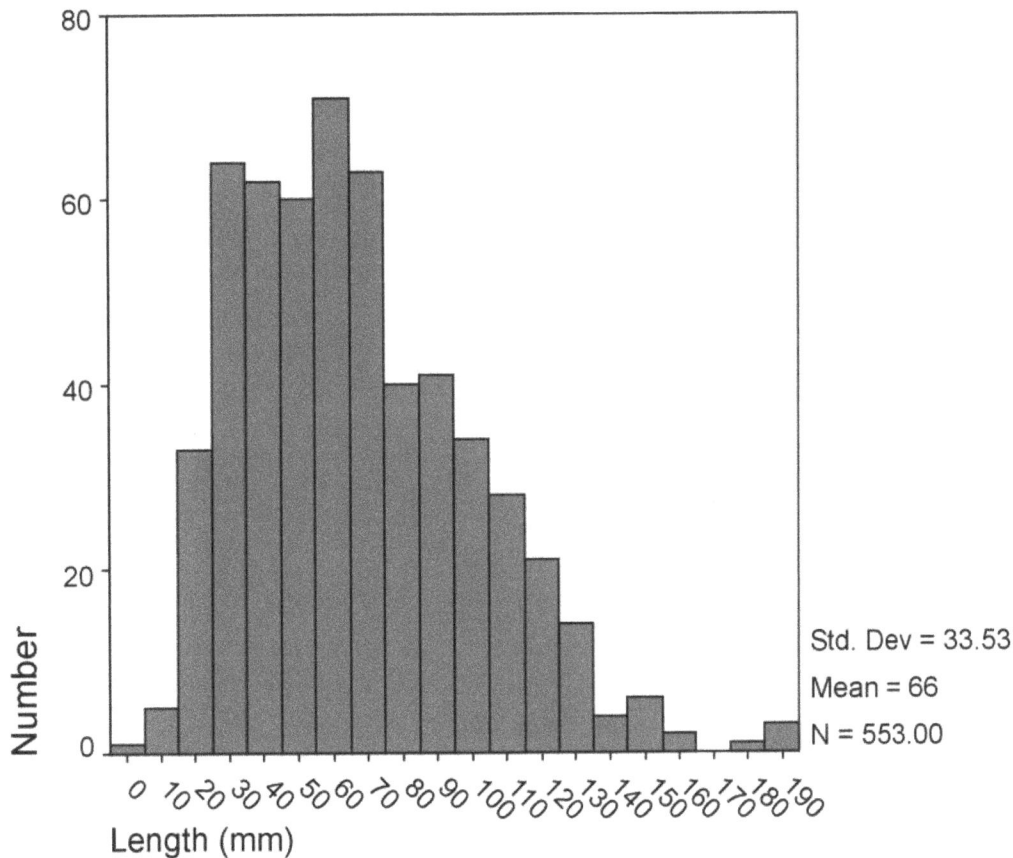

Figure 6.5 maps out the sorts of changes in flake characteristics that accompany each stage of reduction as inferred from platform surface type, including reductions in cortex, mean weight, and platform area that are consistent with the changes seen in core reduction above. Furthermore, there is evidence that knappers responded to changing force requirements by increasing the frequency of overhang removal as platform angle increased - a morphological change that is detected in core morphology as the number of rotations increases. Means and CVs are also provided in Table 6.3. No directional changes in variation are apparent from this data, and variation appears to peak in the middle-stages of reduction for most attributes. This suggests that the greatest range of flake shapes and sizes can be produced once effective platforms have been created, but before reduction proceeds too far and problems in core geometry and force input constrain the range of possible results. Interestingly, the greater number of flakes also belongs to the second and third stages when flake production was presumably under greatest control. Bipolar reduction, on the other hand, is extremely rare in Wardaman sites. No platform area is shown for bipolar flakes in Table 6.3 as bipolar reduction tends to entirely crush flake platforms.

Lancet and Leilira Flake Production

Lancets are long, elongate flakes with high length:thickness ratios, one or more dorsal ridges and parallel-sided or tapering margins, that are between 3 and 10 cm in length. We have seen from the previous analyses of core and flake reduction that elongate flakes tend to be produced early in the core reduction sequence, and hence knappers seeking these kinds of flakes would likely be most successful in the earlier stages of core reduction.

Indeed, analysis of the stages at which lancets are most commonly produced reveals a strong tendency toward early reduction stages, with most lancet flakes possessing either cortical or single conchoidal platforms, as shown in Figure 6.6. Cores found on quarries in association with lancet flakes also typically show large amounts of cortex and either cortical or single conchoidal platforms (Figure 6.7). Many cores used for lancet production found at quarries across Wardaman Country appear to have been discarded at this early stage, with a mean weight for discarded lancet cores of 623 ± 317 g, a mean length of 110 ± 23 mm and a mean thickness of 58 ± 36 mm. These dimensions place lancet cores very early in the reduction sequence if compared to Figure 6.2.

A limited number of successful conjoins from quarries also reveals a simple process used to set up platforms for lancet production on cores that lacked a suitable cortical platform. This typically involved the removal of a large flake from one end of an angular to sub-angular nodule, followed by removal of a large cortical flake along a natural ridge-line in the nodule, creating two arises on the core face. Subsequent blows remove elongate flakes from either side of this first scar. A number of lancet flakes are produced before step and hinge terminations accumulate on the core face. For two reconstructed cores used to produce lancets and shown in Figure 6.8, recurrent step and hinge terminations were encountered after removal 13 and 14, and the cores were later discarded as a result of changes in core geometry and increased force inputs arising from the instability created by these initial aberrantly terminated flake scars. Furthermore, more than 15% of refitted lancets in these conjoin sets had broken through end shock or cone splitting, and data taken from quarries reveals that up to 60% of lancets snapped transversely or longitudinally during manufacture in some locations.

Figure 6.5. Changes in flake morphology as reduction continues. Reduction stage is measured using four platform types: cortical, single conchoidal, multiple conchoidal and bipolar. Changes in morphology include: A: % dorsal cortex, B: mean weight, C: platform area, and D: frequency of overhang removal as platform angle increases.

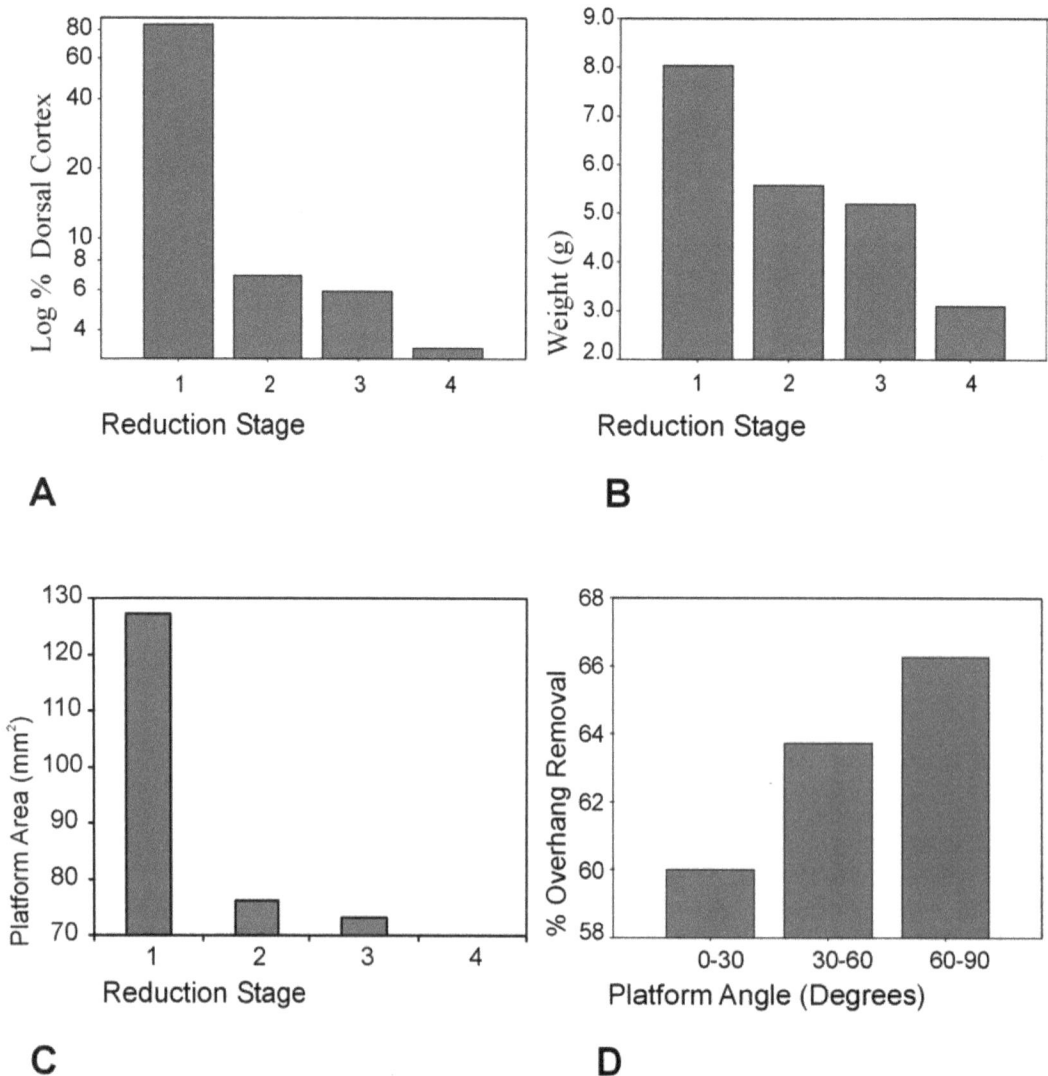

A

B

C

D

Table 6.3. Changes in flake morphology over the sequence of reduction, as inferred from platform surface type.

Platform Type	Number	Weight		Platform Angle		% Dorsal Cortex		Platform Area	
		Mean	c.v.	Mean	c.v.	Mean	c.v.	Mean	c.v.
Cortical	249	8.0	115.4	71.7	17.4	84.5	34.0	127.3	68.7
Single	1643	5.6	236.3	67.0	19.2	6.9	270.1	76.2	116.3
Multiple	371	5.2	121.9	67.6	20.1	5.9	298.1	73.2	109.8
Bipolar	5	3.1	89.4	--	--	3.3	173.2	0.0	0.0

Figure 6.6. A: lancet flake, and B: frequency of lancet flakes produced at each stage of reduction.

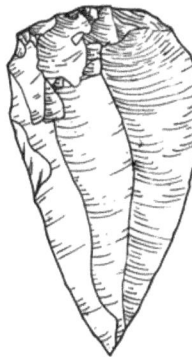

A

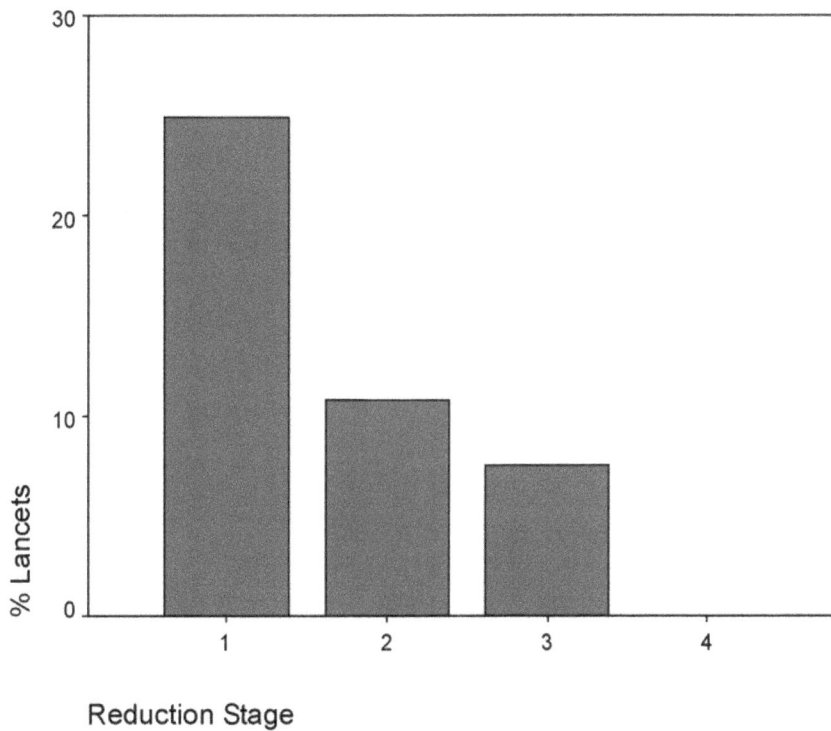

Reduction Stage

B

Figure 6.7. Cores found at quarries associated with lancet flakes. Note the large amounts of cortex on both cores, the cortical platform on one (A) and the single conchoidal scar on the platform of the other (B).

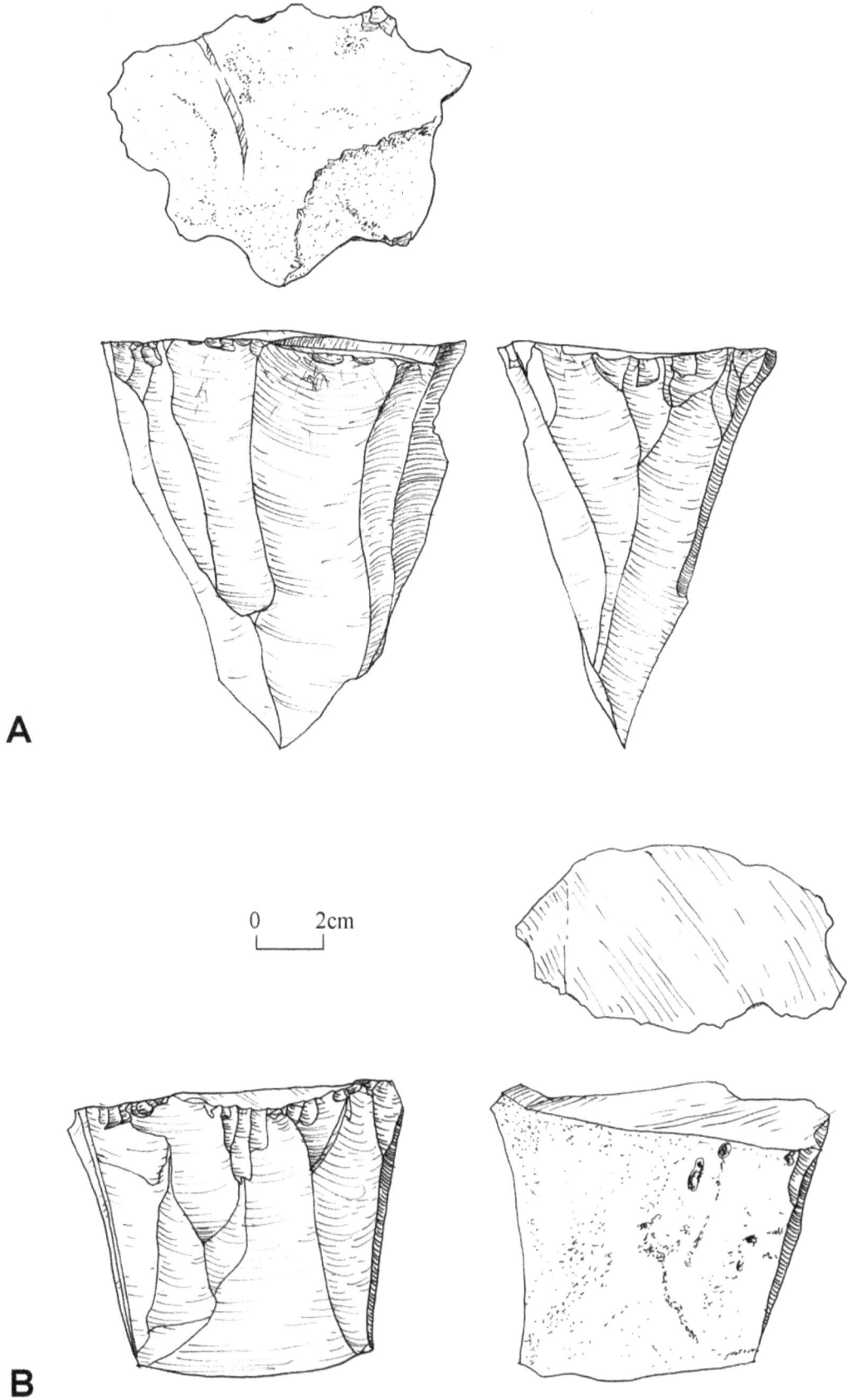

A

0   2cm

B

Figure 6.8. Conjoined quartzite cores and lancet flakes from A: a quarry near Wynbarr waterhole (Site 17), B and C: a quarry near Garnawala 2. Illustration C shows the actual conjoined core, while A and B show reconstructions of the original nodules and the series of flake removals taken as a slice through the centre of the platform.

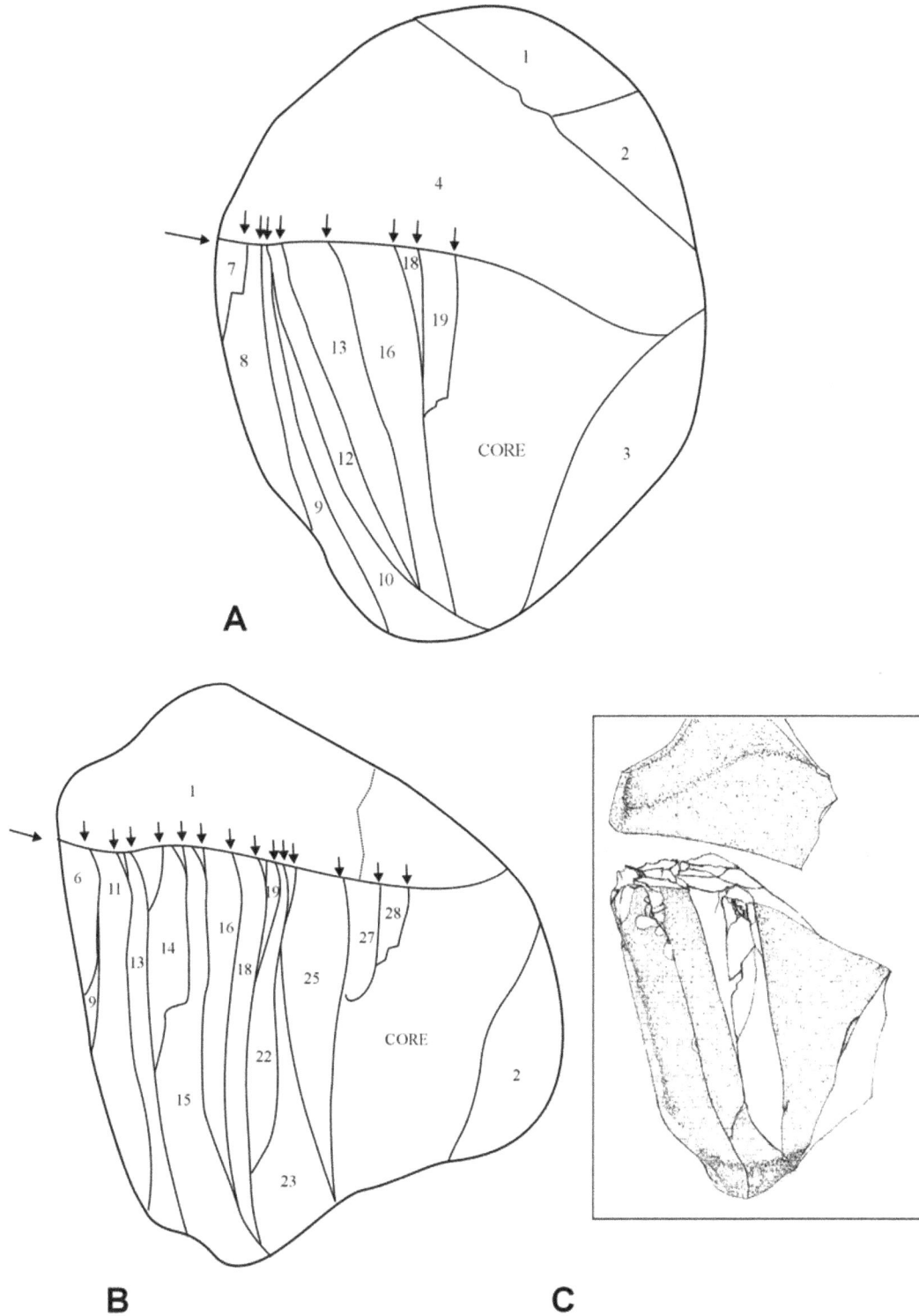

In summary, lancet production tends to be oriented toward early stages in the reduction process – essentially, single platform cores that have either been rotated once to create a large flat platform, or unrotated cores with cortical platforms. Most of these cores were discarded soon after lancet production began, relatively early in the reduction process and while much mass remained on cores. The large Leilira blades (defined here as lancets longer than 10 cm) found in Wardaman Country on the other hand, mostly appear to be the largest and typically earliest elongate flakes removed in the sequence. Leilira production therefore likely represents a more extreme version of lancet production in terms of being confined to even earlier stages of reduction and in making little use of the reduction potential of the core.

Retouched Flakes

One approach to exploring the continuums that underlie and connect various retouched implement forms is to develop sequence models that order individual artefacts according to the amount of retouch they have received. Most studies of reduction continuums for retouched implements have remained locked within normative typological schemes. This is best seen in the analyses of changing implement morphology that are undertaken through comparison of measures of central tendency between the type classes themselves (e.g. Dibble 1995), rather than using individual specimens removed from a typological framework.

While these type-based approaches nevertheless go some way toward demonstrating the changeability of implement forms, they are neither the most powerful nor useful means of depicting reduction continuums. This is because the type classes employed are not specifically designed to investigate reduction issues, and hence are unlikely to reveal sequential patterns to maximum effect. As Kuhn (1992) states, type classes are "created to describe formal variation as observed in the archaeological record, and not to measure the results of some specific prehistoric phenomenon or process. As such [they are] likely to embody the effects of *many* independent influences on artefact form".

An alternative approach to depicting reduction continuums in retouched flakes is adopted here which documents the series of changes to a number of important aspects of flake morphology as reduction intensity increases. This analysis is undertaken for scrapers (i.e. retouched flakes), points, tulas and burrens. This chapter therefore contributes to a small but growing body of studies that present sequence models for a variety of implement forms from different parts of the country (e.g. Clarkson 2002a, 2005; Clarkson and O'Connor 2005; Hiscock 1982b; Hiscock and Attenbrow 2003, 2005a, b; Lamb 2005, 2006).

Australian Approaches to Scraper Classification

Archaeologists have grappled with the interpretation and classification of scraper variability, or the 'amorphous' unifacially retouched flakes found in many assemblages, since archaeology began. This is best seen in Australia in the multitude of largely incompatible scraper typologies that found their most elaborate form in the period spanning the 1940s to 1970s (Clarke 2000). At this time scrapers were typically classified and named according to the location of retouch (e.g. side, end, side and end, double side and end etc), the nature of retouch (e.g. nosed, notched, denticulate), assumed function (e.g. knives, drills, piercers, adzes, choppers, planes, scrapers, spokeshaves), the curvature of the retouched portion (e.g. straight, round, convex, concave), overall shape and size (thumbnail, horsehoof, flat) and the steepness of the edge (e.g. low angled, steep edged) (Allen 1972; Bowler *et al.* 1970; Clegg 1977; Flood 1973, 1974; Jones 1971; Kenyon and Stirling 1900; McCarthy *et al.* 1946; Mitchell 1949; Mulvaney and Kamminga 1999; Sanders 1975; White 1969). Combinations of these attributes and names were also employed at various times, usually in unsystematic ways, and often ending in large and confusing taxonomies. Mirroring global trends, Australian archaeologists have tended to attribute the diversity of retouched forms to stylistic or ethnic variation (Bowdler 1981; McCarthy 1948, 1949, 1958; Mitchell 1949; Tindale 1957; White and O'Connell 1982); the functional efficiency of tool edges (usually tied to edge angle and edge shape) (Sanders 1975; White 1969), efficiency of raw material use

(Morwood and Hobbs 1995a:183), or design requirements related to hafting (Mulvaney and Joyce 1965).

The reduction sequence for north Australian scrapers is developed from observed variation in implement morphology, and by building on past observations of the interplay between various aspects of flake shape and fracture mechanics. This is achieved by observing changes in four aspects of flake morphology as retouch increases. These are edge angle, edge shape, retouch perimeter, and retouch termination type - the same four variables that are frequently used to classify scrapers into types (Clarkson 2005).

Measuring Scraper Reduction

As discussed in Chapter 3, reduction intensity is best measured on dorsally retouched flakes using Kuhn's (1990) Geometric Index of Reduction (GIUR). As the Wardaman scrapers are predominantly unifacial (82%), typically have at least one dorsal ridge (88%), and are rarely invasively retouched (mean Index of Invasiveness of 0.18), this index is highly suited to investigating scraper reduction in Wardaman Country.

The following tests employ a sample of 338 retouched flakes from the four rockshelter sites described in Chapter 5.

Edge Angle. A number of researchers (Dibble 1995; Hiscock 1982a; Morrow 1997; Wilmsen 1968) have drawn attention to the relationship that often exists between retouched edge angle and the amount of unifacial retouch a flake has received. In many cases, unifacial retouching reduces the width of a flake without reducing its thickness. This has the effect of moving the margins closer to the thickest (often central) section of the flake, causing an overall increase in the angle of the retouched edge.

To examine whether such a relationship holds for the sample of Wardaman scrapers, edge angle was recorded at the same three locations where retouch height and flake thickness were taken for measurement of Kuhn's GIUR. Figure 6.9a plots the mean edge angle and standard deviation of scrapers for six intervals along the GIUR, and indicates that mean edge angle increases appreciably over the reduction sequence, with all means showing an increase relative to the previous GIUR interval. The standard deviations, on the other hand, overlap to some degree, indicating that a single morphological continuum underlies these sequential changes.

Step Terminated Retouch. As the angle of the retouched edge increases with retouch, it is expected that step terminations should also accrue with increasing frequency as force requirements change, flake inertia thresholds are reached, and terminations become more difficult to control (Dibble and Pelcin 1995; Pelcin 1997c, 1998). To explore this relationship, the frequency of scrapers with pronounced stepped retouching is plotted at six intervals along the GIUR in Figure 6.9b. This graph reveals a gradual increase in the frequency with which areas of step terminated retouch build up on flake edges as reduction continues.

Percentage of Perimeter Retouched. The proportion of the retouched perimeter of an artefact might also be expected to increase if new and adjacent edges are used and resharpened as existing ones are exhausted. Figure 6.9c plots this relationship and reveals a strong trend toward the use of more of the perimeter as the GIUR increases. Standard deviations also reveal the existence of continuous variation that underlies and unites the observed changes in central tendency.

Edge Curvature. As retouched perimeter is observed to increase with retouch intensity, it might also be expected that the retouched edge should become more curved as more of the perimeter is worked. Edge curvature is here calculated by dividing the depth of retouch by its diameter as outlined in Chapter 3. Using this technique, concave edges give a negative result while convex edges yield a positive one. Figure 6.9d indicates that edges start out slightly concave but become highly convex as the percentage of the perimeter retouched increases, plotted at six intervals. Perimeter of retouch is used in place of the GIUR in this test as it reveals a stronger relationship, although both reduction measures return significant results (GIUR vs. Curvature, ANOVA, F = 18.8, df = 5, p = <.005; % Margin Retouched vs. Curvature, ANOVA, F = 164.1, df = 5, p = <.0005).

Figure 6.9. Graphs showing the mean and standard deviations for changes in various aspects of scraper morphology as reduction intensity increases, as measured using Kuhn's GIUR or % perimeter retouched. A: mean retouched edge angle, B: % step terminated retouch, C: % perimeter retouched, D: curvature of the retouched edge, and E: % with notches.

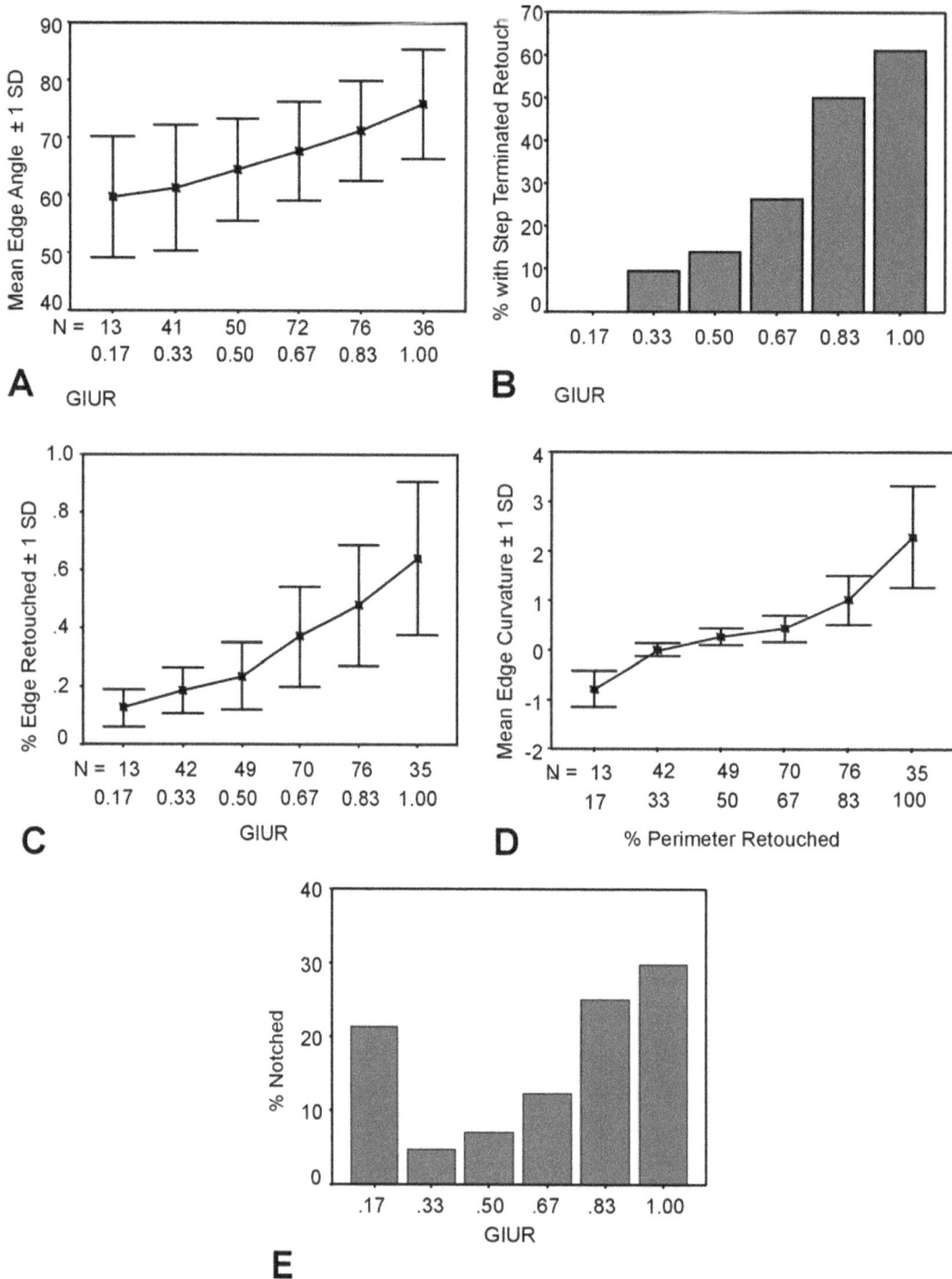

Notching. Notches, or deep retouched concavities on an otherwise straight or curved margin, are found on a small number of scrapers. In her study of the function of scrapers from Ingaladdi, Sanders (1975:44) noted that notches were most often represented by a single deep retouch flake scar, with a total absence of use-wear within these edge concavities, despite noting its occurrence along portions of the adjacent margins. In these cases it seems more likely that notches represent early stage retouching rather than a functionally specific feature.

White (1969:23) and Lenoir (1986) have both noted that heavily retouched and stepped edges can at times be rejuvenated by removing deep retouch flakes from the edge. If this is the case for the Wardaman scrapers, then the incidence of deep and adjacent concavities on the margins of flakes could represent an attempt to return a heavily stepped edge to good condition. It might also be expected that deep rejuvenating blows of this kind would have a significant subsidiary effect of reducing the average edge angle as well as the number of step terminations remaining on the margin.

Examining the incidence of notching throughout the sequence of reduction reveals that edge concavities are most common in the earliest and the latest stages of reduction (Figure 6.9e). The trend apparent in Figure 6.9e confirms the operation of two separate reduction processes that may both create concavities on scraper edges: single deep flake scars added to the edge at the outset of retouching, and deep rejuvenating blows delivered to remove stepped and exhausted sections of margins from more heavily reduced scrapers.

Retouch Location. Figure 6.10 plots the changing frequency and distribution of retouch found around the perimeter of flakes as the GIUR increases. For this analysis, flakes were divided into eight segments of equal length, with the central three segments divided into 'left' and 'right' cells. The intensity of shading represents the evenness with which retouch is distributed across each of the eight segments. The number in each cell indicates the frequency (expressed as a percentage of all retouched segments) with which that segment is retouched for that interval of the GIUR.

The results show a trend from an earlier uneven distribution of retouch that is centred on the distal end and left margin, to a later and more even distribution of retouch around the entire perimeter of the flake.

Figure 6.10. Graphic depiction of changes to the frequency and evenness with which retouch is distributed across eight segments as retouch increases.

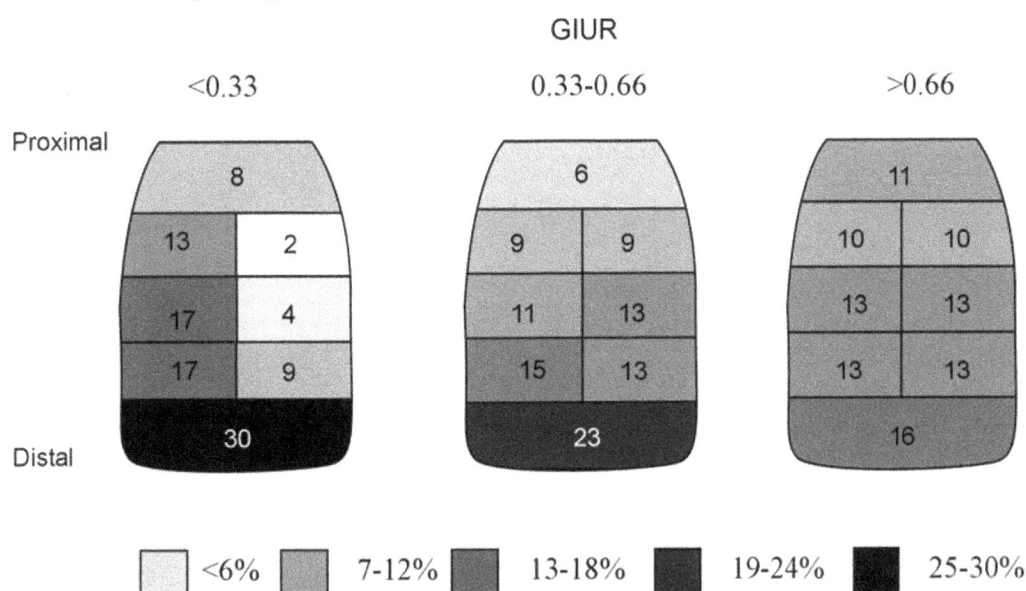

A Reduction Model for Scrapers

From the preceding tests it is clear that retouch intensity constitutes an important determinant of scraper morphology in the study region. To test the significance of the observed changes in implement morphology, *t*-tests were performed on adjacent GIUR categories for mean retouched edge angle, the percentage retouched perimeter and the index of edge curvature. The results are presented in Table 6.4 and indicate that almost all comparisons return significant results. The two comparisons that do not yield significant results are those between 0.17 and 0.33, and 0.33 and 0.5 on the GIUR for mean retouched edge angle. This result is quite understandable given that some flakes can be steep edged even before retouching begins, and these will overlap to some degree with flakes at later stages of reduction. This problem disappears, however, once flakes reach values of >0.5 on the GIUR, and all comparisons return significant results thereafter.

Table 6.4. *t*-test results for changes in measures of implement morphology for adjacent GIUR intervals.

GIUR Interval	t	F	p
Mean Retouched Edge Angle			
0.17 - 0.33	-0.504	0.194	0.551
0.33 – 0.50	-1.527	0.657	0.13
0.50 – 0.67	-2.022	0.036	0.045
0.67 – 0.83	-2.497	0.002	0.014
0.83 – 1.00	-2.588	0.022	0.011
% Perimeter Retouched			
0.17 - 0.33	-3.228	2.087	0.003
0.33 – 0.50	-2.425	3.477	0.018
0.50 – 0.67	-5.169	10.281	< .0005
0.67 – 0.83	-3.435	2.702	0.001
0.83 – 1.00	-3.487	3.967	0.001
Index of Edge Curvature			
0.17 - 0.33	-4.269	5.977	0.007
0.33 – 0.50	-2.249	0.111	0.027
0.50 – 0.67	-4.178	7.596	<0.0005
0.67 – 0.83	-3.404	16.529	0.001
0.83 – 1.00	-2.635	8.031	0.01

Figure 6.11. A reduction model for scrapers from Wardaman Country. A-C: increasing reduction.

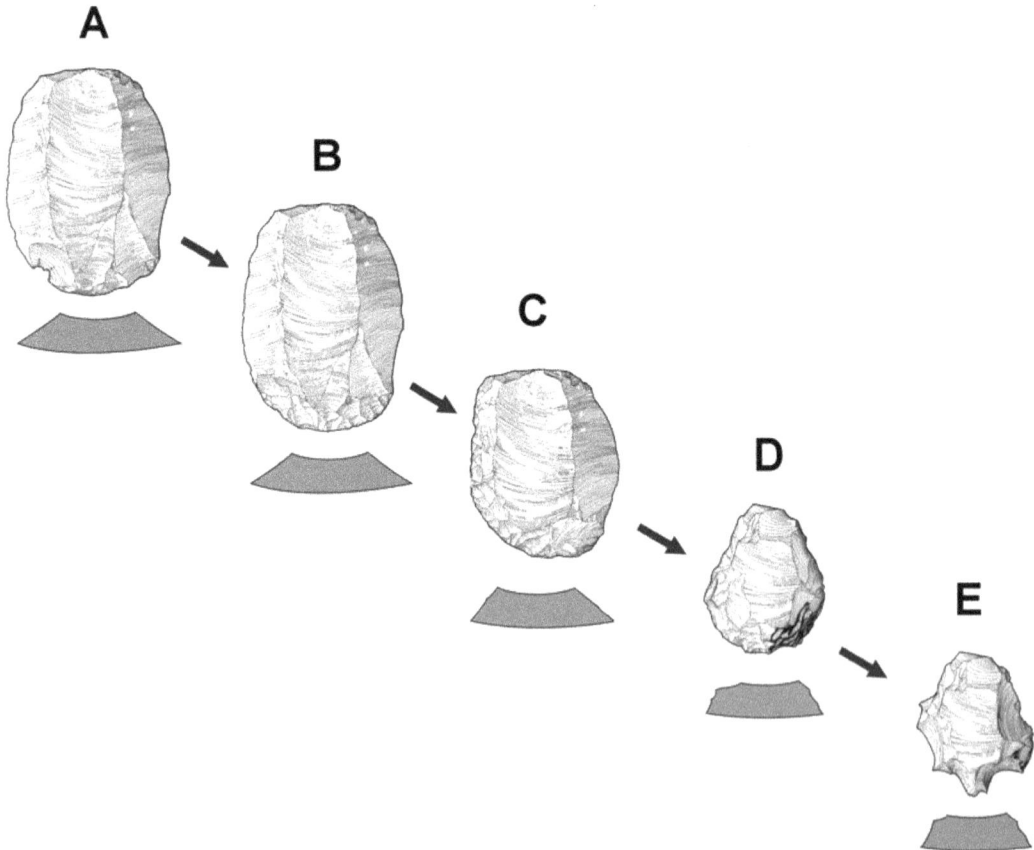

Chi-Square tests were also performed to measure the significance of changes in the frequency of step terminations, notches and the evenness of retouch distribution over the sequence of reduction. The results are shown in Table 6.5 and indicate that the changes over the reduction sequence are highly significant. A test of correlation between the GIUR and all measures of morphological change also returns Spearman's r and Kendell's tau results of 1, which are significant to the .01 level.

Thus, the morphological changes described above appear to take place in a consistent sequence that reflects the steady increase in reduction from relatively unworked through to relatively 'exhausted' forms. This sequence is illustrated in the reduction diagram shown in Figure 6.11, and depicts the changes to the extent, angle, shape, and location of retouch demonstrated to occur as reduction increases.

Table 6.5. Chi-Square statistics for percentages of step terminations and frequency of notching for each of the six intervals of the GIUR.

Variable	χ^2	df	p	Cramer's V	Sig.
% Step Terminated Retouch	55.8	5	<.0005	.419	<0.0005
% Artefacts with Notches	428.3	5	<.0005	.171	0.027
Distribution of Retouch	36.6	5	<.0005	.328	0.039

A typical sequence might therefore begin with the removal of a single deep flake scar on the left distal, or distal end of the flake, creating a small concavity or 'notch' (Figure 6.11A). This concavity is subsequently removed as retouch expands around more of the margin, creating a convex edge with a steeper edge angle (Figure 6.11B). By the time retouch spans around 50% of the perimeter, edge curvature and edge angle have both increased dramatically (Figure 6.11C). Towards the end of the sequence, retouch has increased to span the entire margin, has become very steep and exhibits areas of overlapping stepped scars in various places (Figure 6.11D). At this stage, edge rejuvenation may be attempted to remove accumulations of step terminations by delivering deep and forceful blows to the edge. This often creates a number of adjacent concavities that can give the implement a distinctive 'nosed' appearance (Figure 6.11E).

Blank Selection

It is often remarked in the Australian literature that scraper forms are highly variable in comparison to other retouched artefact forms, with little standardisation in the selection of flakes in terms of shape or size. Now that the reduction sequence for scrapers has been described in detail, it is possible to determine whether this is so for Wardaman scrapers, by examining the types of flakes commonly selected for this reduction process. This can be achieved by comparing the characteristics of scrapers that have received little overall modification, to the pool of complete unretouched flakes found in all four rockshelters in all time periods. Scrapers with little modification are here treated as those with a GIUR of less than or equal to 0.3. This cut off is implemented to ensure that flakes have begun the reduction process, and are not simply edge damaged flakes, yet are not so far advanced as to be significantly altered in size and shape by intensive retouching.

Figure 6.12 plots marginal angle against elongation (length/width) and cross-sectional shape (width/thickness) for complete unretouched flakes and lightly retouched scrapers. It is clear from this graph that flakes selected for retouch show a much reduced range to the total population of unretouched flakes, and that relatively thick, stout flakes were preferred over thin, elongate ones for scraper retouch. These flakes appear to derive predominantly from the second 'stage' of flake reduction, as 80% of lightly retouched scrapers have single conchoidal platforms.

Figure 6.12. Graphs showing the selection of a restricted range of flake shapes for scraper manufacture. A: marginal angle and elongation, and B: marginal angle and cross-section.

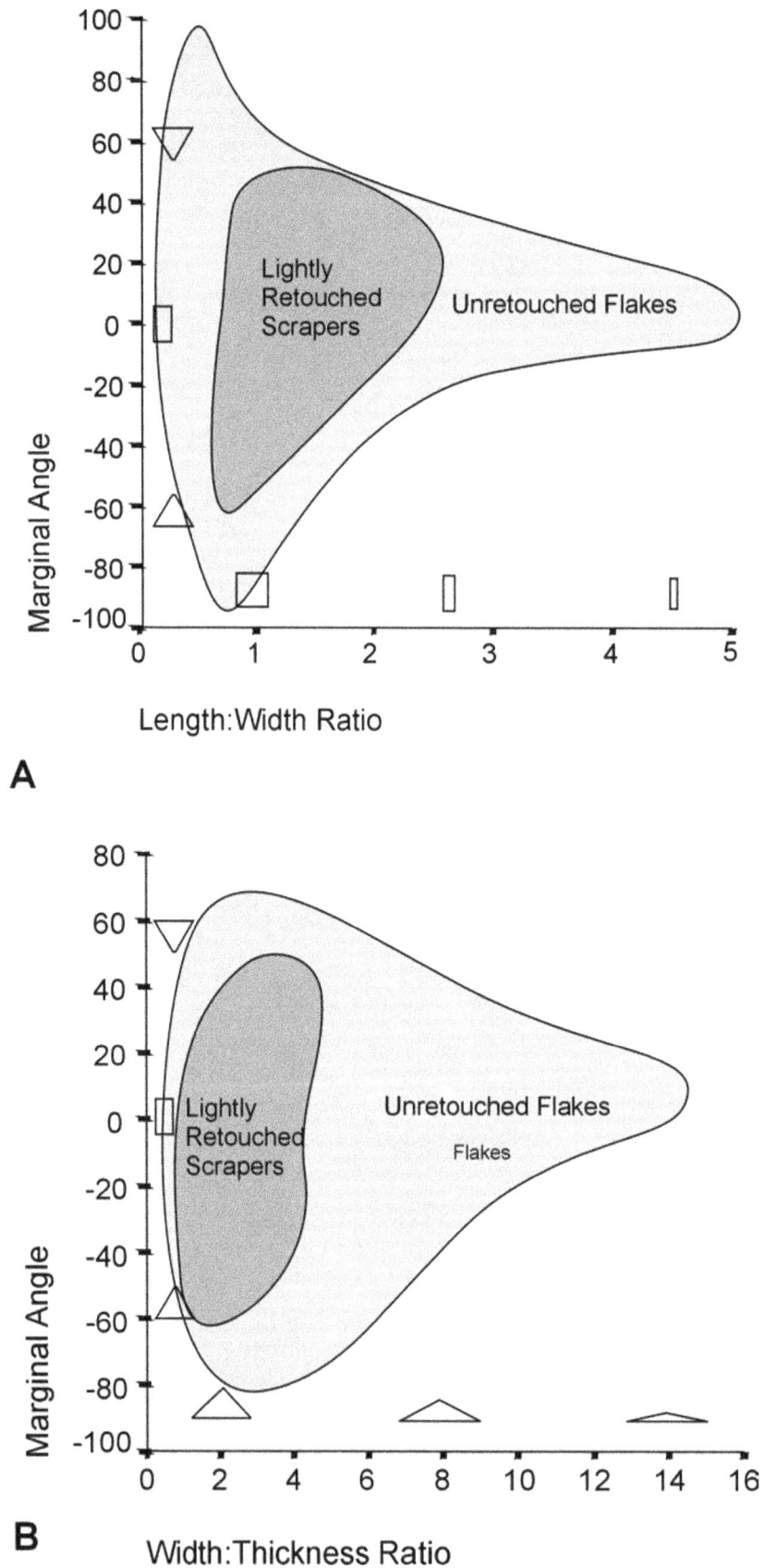

Variation in the size of scrapers over the reduction sequence also indicates that highly variable flakes were selected for retouching, with a mean weight of 21 ± 23 g and a coefficient of variation of 91%.

Discard Thresholds. Scrapers appear not to show any directional trend in weight loss over the sequence of reduction, with early stage scrapers (i.e. less than 0.3 GIUR) having a mean of 21 ± 18 g and late stage scrapers (i.e. GIUR of 1) a mean weight of 21 ± 26 g. This no doubt reflects the enormous variation in the size of flake blanks used. However, it also suggests that knappers were often unable to reduce scrapers down to very small sizes, probably due to the limiting variables identified above – that is, increasing edge angles and step terminations – both of which are likely to have resulted in terminating reduction prior to significant weight loss in most cases, despite the fact that most scrapers are heavily retouched (mode = 0.75).

Australian Approaches to Point Classification

Traditionally, two models of point production have proliferated in Australia, one that sees unifacial and bifacial points as unrelated and divergent forms, and another that views each type as having the potential to form stages in a continuum of reduction. Various tests and refutations of these models have been advanced over the years, although Hiscock (1994a) points out that it is the divergent model that has gained predominance in Australia. For example, differences in the types of raw material used in the manufacture of unifacial and bifacial points was cited by Schrire (1982) as evidence for divergence in point production in Arnhem Land, with unifacial points most commonly made from quartz and bifacial points from quartzite. Size differences were also advanced as evidence for the existence of a divergent model by Flood (1970) who argued that the smaller size of bifacial points at Yarrar shelter, southwest of Darwin, proved the existence of two separate types. Allen and Barton (n.d.) found the opposite pattern, with bifacial points from Ngarradj Warde Djobkeng in Kakadu tending to be larger than unifacial points, and likewise inferred from this that two discrete forms were represented. Flenniken and White (1985), on the other hand, argued on technological grounds founded in replicative experiments that true bifacial point reduction always commenced on the ventral face first, in order to move "the margins of the preform toward the middle of its mass so that flakes could be removed successfully from both faces" (Flenniken and White 1985:148). As unifacial points are typically reduced on the dorsal surface only, they reasoned that unifacial and bifacial points must be separate, as each entails a distinctive and mutually exclusive reduction sequence.

In a review of this literature, Hiscock (1994a) points to a number of flaws in the logic of arguments in favour of a divergence model. He also advances evidence from point assemblages from Kakadu and Lawn Hill in support of a sequence model. He points out that Schrire's case for a separation of point types on the basis of raw material useage is unconvincing as a number of studies have shown that both unifacial and bifacial points are made from a wide range of materials throughout Arnhem Land and Kakadu National Park (Allen and Barton n.d.; Brockwell 1989). The size differences noted by Flood also offer poor proof of the typological divergence model, and in fact, conform better to a reduction sequence model in which larger unifacial points are worked down to become smaller bifacial ones. At Ngarradj Warde Djobkeng, where unifacial points were on average smaller than bifacial points, Hiscock found the results not to be statistically significant.

Hiscock's own analysis focussed on the patterns of scar superimposition found on the ventral and dorsal surfaces of individual specimens at increasing distances to a stone source to determine the sequence of flake removals from each surface. The results showed that flaking began on the dorsal surface in the vast majority of cases for both unifacial and bifacial points, that points tended to decrease in size with distance from a stone source, and that bifacial forms became increasingly abundant in more distant assemblages. Hiscock interpreted this pattern to mean that unifacial points were often reworked into bifacial forms to extend their use-life as replacement stone became more difficult to obtain.

Roddam (1997) has also advanced evidence in support of a reduction continuum model using a sample of unifacial and bifacial points from sites across the Northern Territory. Roddam examined changes in the morphological characteristics of unifacial and bifacial points in relation to a number of indices of reduction, including size, frequency of invasive scar removals, and the frequency with which dominant dorsal surface scar patterns shifted from an alignment parallel to the percussion axis to one that was perpendicular to it, reflecting the gradual removal of older dorsal scars that were created prior to the removal of the blank from the core. Roddam found statistically significant correlations between changes in these aspects of point morphology, including a decrease in flake weight, length and thickness from unifaces to bifaces, an increase in the frequency of invasive retouch on bifaces (with forms intermediate between marginally retouched unifaces and invasively flaked bifaces), and a shift from scars that were predominantly aligned parallel (longitudinally) to the percussion axis on unifaces to those aligned predominantly perpendicular (laterally) to this axis on bifacial points. Roddam also found that bifacial points were more likely to exhibit modification of the proximal end (or butt) into a square or rounded shape, and that platforms were often entirely retouched on bifacial points but not unifacial points. Most importantly, Roddam observed that a large overlap existed between both unifacial and bifacial points for all the attributes tested, suggesting that the two forms are merely arbitrary subdivisions of an underlying reduction continuum.

A major limitation of all of these studies is the use of a bipartite system of division that allows only two artefact classes (unifacial and bifacial points) to be examined and compared. This drastically reduces the analytical power of arguments that seek to demonstrate continuous change. In the following analysis points are subdivided into six categories according to the amount of reduction they have received. This allows the reduction process, and the continuum that underlies morphological differences, to be teased out and depicted in greater detail.

In the following sections, the reduction sequence for points is explored for the study region using a number of tests. Kuhn's index is unsuited to the measurement of invasive bifacial retouch as typically found on northern Australian points as bifacial thinning changes the relationship between retouch height and flake thickness, so that the index need not increase as a factor of retouch intensity. The Index of Invasiveness (Clarkson 2002b) is therefore employed in its place. As described in Chapter 3, this index measures the extent and coverage of retouch scars across both faces of an artefact, and expresses this as a value between 0, indicating no retouch, and a value of 1, signaling that an artefact is completely invasively retouched on both surfaces. In the following sections, changes to the size and shape of points are plotted at six intervals on the Index of Invasiveness. Unifacial points can not of course increase beyond 0.5 (i.e. one surface completely retouched), whereas bifacial points may become bifacial early in the sequence and remain so until they reach a value of 1. The sample used in the following tests consists of 495 complete points of all lithologies and from the four Wardaman rockshelters.

Morphological Changes

Size. A number of researchers have used changes in the size of points either as evidence for or against a reduction sequence model. In the following test, artefact weight is plotted against the Index of Invasiveness for unifacial and bifacial points. Figure 6.13a plots the weight of points against the Index of Invasiveness. Figure 6.13b, on the other hand, plots the mean and standard deviations for the weight of points at six intervals along the Index of Invasiveness. Both figures indicate that points become progressively lighter as retouching continues, and that more variation exists in lightly reduced points than heavily reduced ones. Differences in weight over the sequence also prove significant (Table 6.5). Figure 6.13a also indicates that points may become bifacial very early in the reduction process, suggesting that an underlying continuum unites these two forms.

Figure 6.13. Changes in the morphology of points over the reduction sequence. A and B: changes in weight, and C: changes in the % of perimeter retouched.

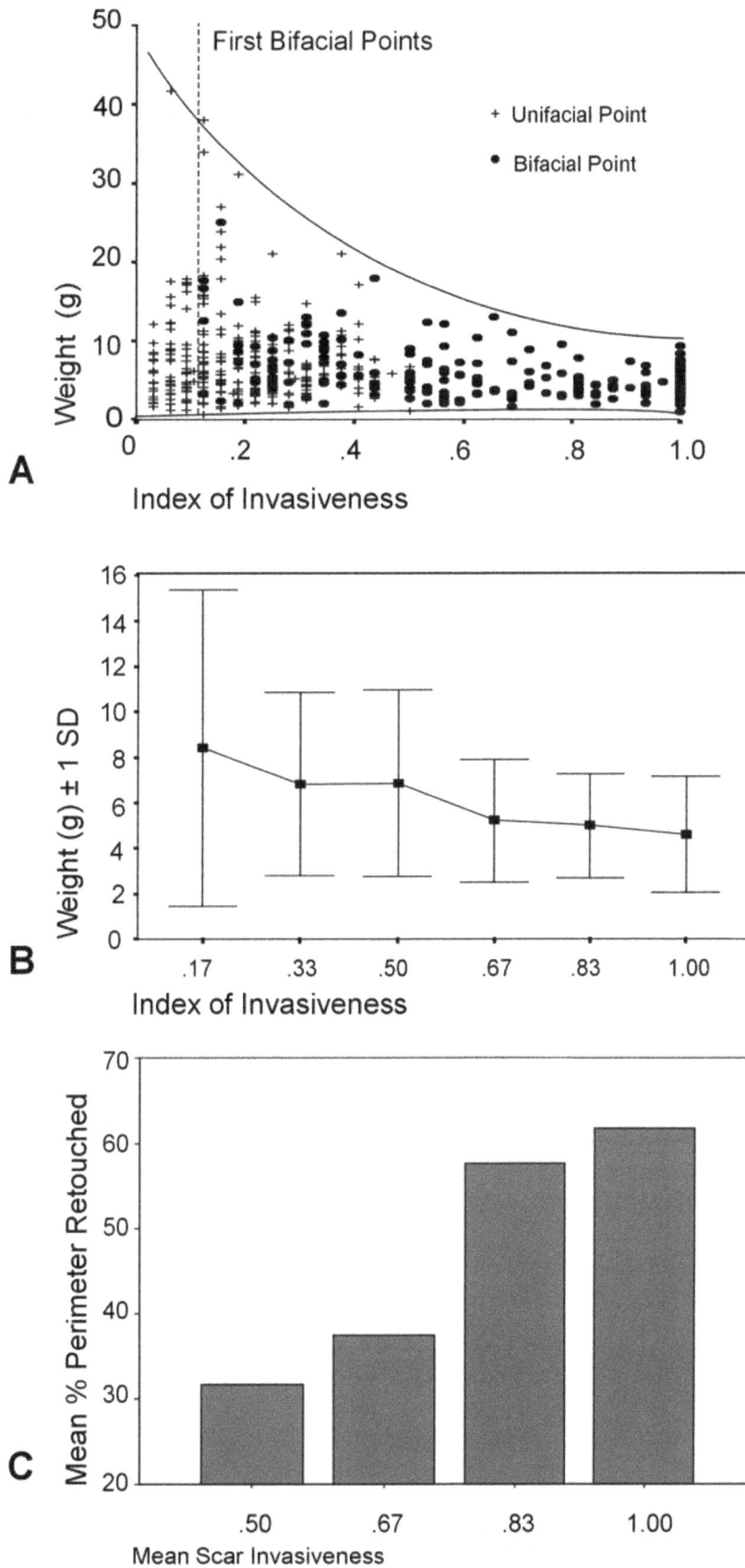

Percentage of Perimeter Retouched. In one sense the Index of Invasiveness already includes a measure of the perimeter of retouch, because the increasing number of segments required for the index to increase implies that retouch must be extending around more of the margin. To remove this effect, Figure 6.13c plots the changes in the percentage of the perimeter that has been retouched as the invasiveness of flake scars increases. Flake scar invasiveness calculates just the degree to which scars intrude onto the surface of an artefact by dividing the sum of all segment scores by the number of retouched segments rather than by all 16 segments. The graph shows a clear and steady increase in retouch perimeter as flake scar invasiveness increases. This relationship is also significant as shown in Table 6.6.

Table 6.6. ANOVA tests of significance for each of the attributes used to measure change in point morphology as reduction increases.

Attribute	df	F	p
Weight vs Index of Invasiveness	5	7.70	<0.0005
Width:Thickness vs Index of Invasiveness	5	17.35	<0.0005
Length:Thickness vs Index of Invasiveness	5	3.40	0.005
Base Curvature vs Index of Invasiveness	5	40.24	<0.0005
% Perimeter Retouched vs Scar Invasiveness	5	31.16	<0.0005

Cross-Sectional Shape. The cross-sectional shape of points has been observed to vary between different forms (Schrire 1982), principally with unifacial points tending to be thinner than bifacial points. The cross-sectional shape of points can be calculated by dividing width by thickness, for a lateral cross-section, and length by thickness for a longitudinal one. Figure 6.14a indicates that points begin as wide, thin flakes, but become narrower and thicker as reduction continues, taking on a lenticular cross-section in the later stages of bifacial reduction, before finally thinning again relative to width in the final stages. The capacity of invasive retouch to thin points is largely what allows edge angles to be maintained over the reduction sequence (with edge angles generally remaining in a narrow window of between 25 and 35 degrees). Length to thickness also reduces rapidly to begin with, but increases again in the final stages as thickness is further reduced through invasive flaking without further altering length (Figure 6.14b). ANOVA reveals both changes to be significant (Table 6.6).

Proximal Thinning and Butt Curvature. Another aspect of formal variation in points is whether the proximal end is trimmed (perhaps to better fit a haft), and the degree of curvature of the retouched base. Figure 6.15a and 6.15b indicates that the frequency with which points are thinned and shaped into a curved base at the proximal end increases significantly as retouching continues ($\chi^2 = 57.25$, df = 5, p = .005), and so too does the actual curvature of the base (Table 6.5). Lightly retouched points therefore tend to have straight and/or untrimmed butts.

Location and Distribution of Retouch. It is possible using patterns of scar location and superimposition to determine the general pattern of retouching on points, including the first surface to be retouched and the ordering of subsequent retouch on the dorsal and ventral surfaces. Shown in Figure 6.16a is a trend that confirms Hiscock's findings for points in Kakadu and Lawn Hill. Wardaman points begin in the majority of cases with retouch delivered to the dorsal face only. Then as reduction continues, the probability that retouch will be added to the ventral face increases, and this reaches its maximum likelihood by the time points have attained values of between 0.5 and 0.66 on the Index of Invasiveness.

Figure 6.14. Changes in point cross-section measured in two ways. A: lateral cross-section (width:thickness ratio), and B: longitudinal cross-section (length:thickness ratio).

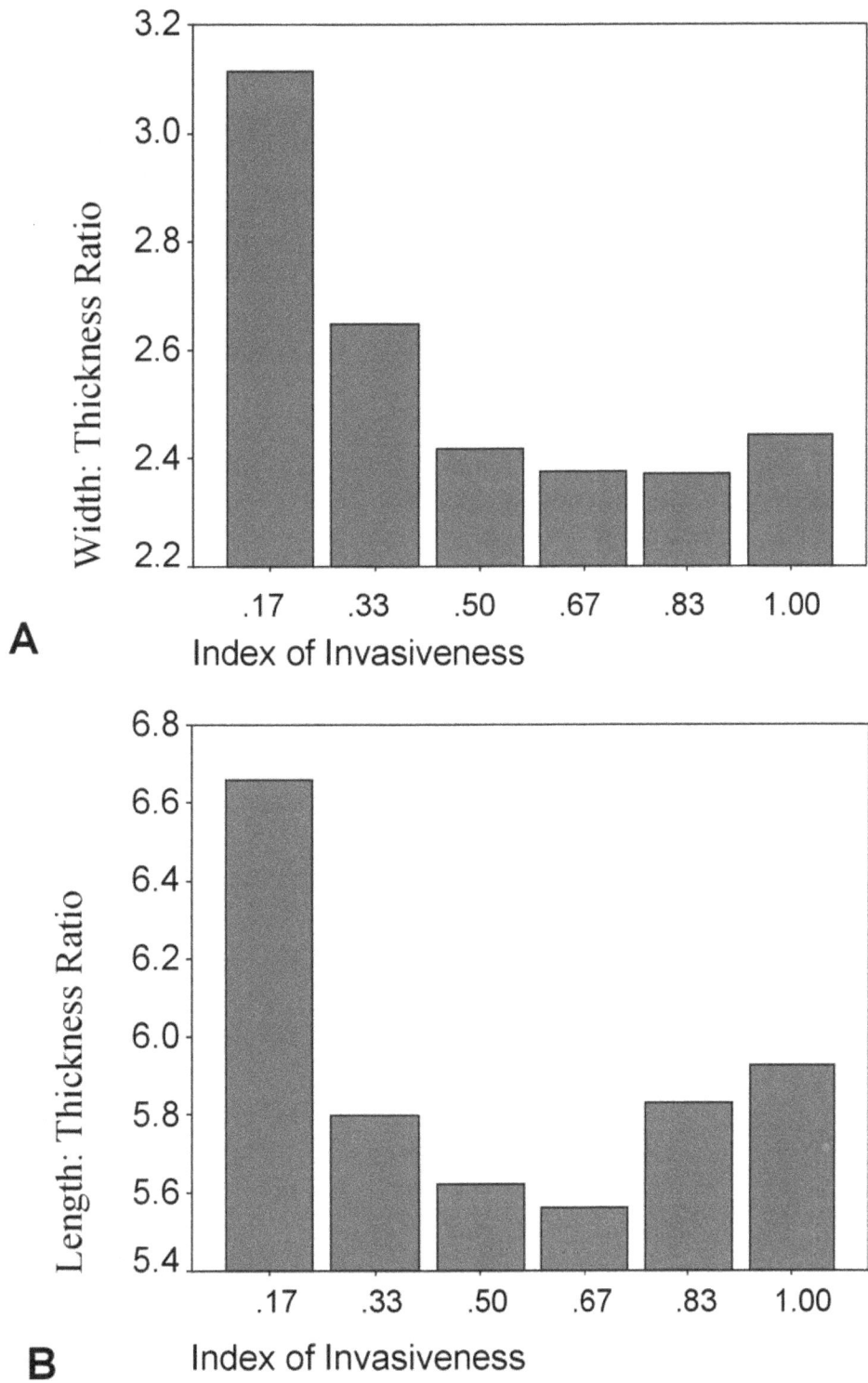

Figure 6.15. Changes in the proximal morphology of points. A: base curvature, and B: % proximal thinning.

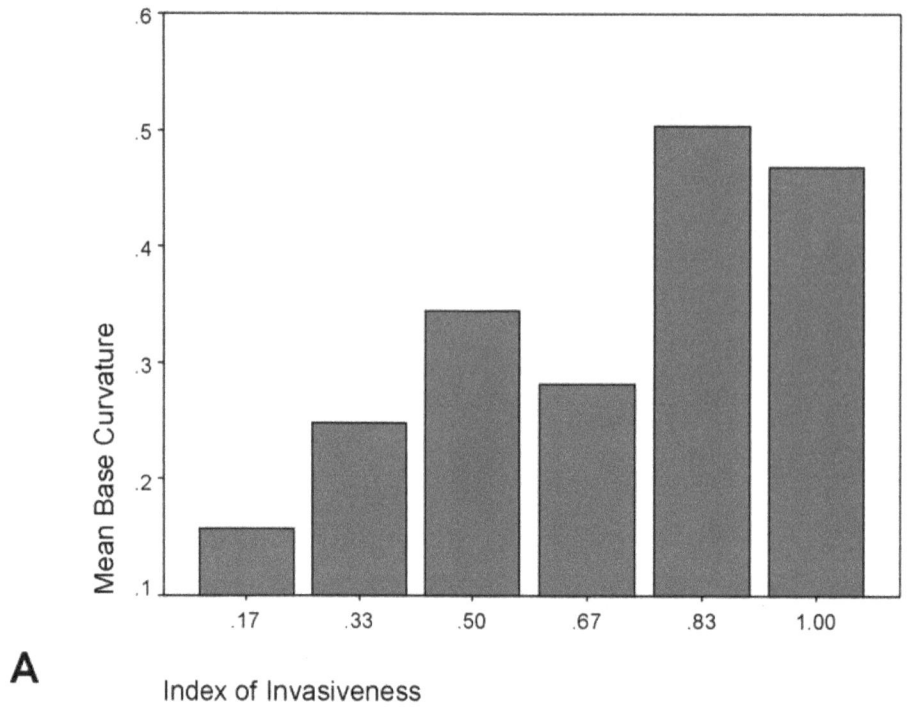

A

Index of Invasiveness

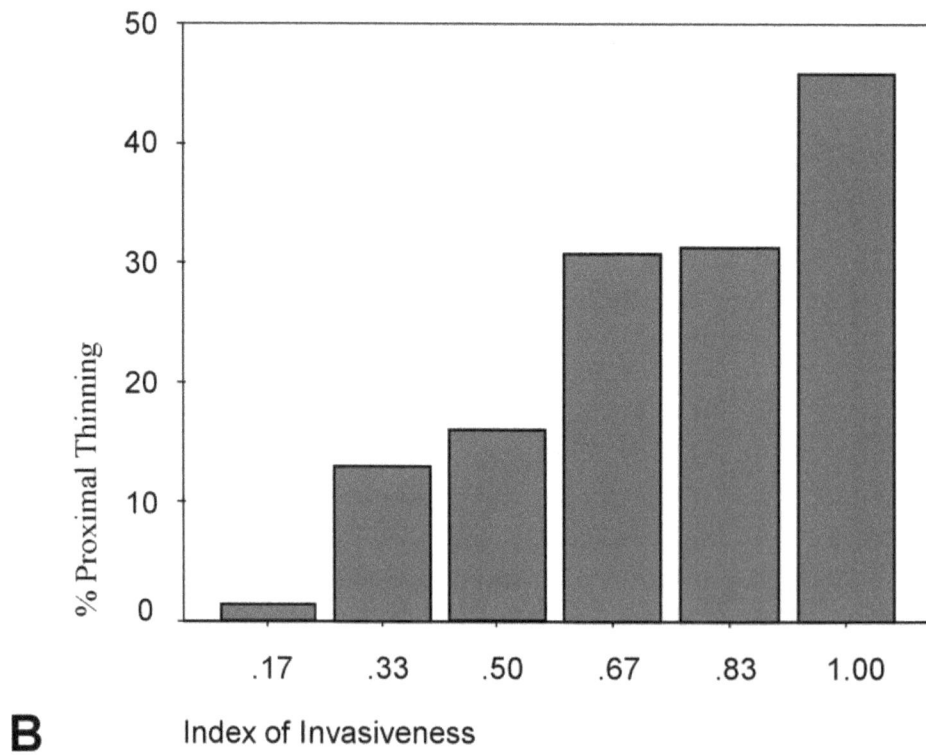

B

Index of Invasiveness

Figure 6.16. Changes to the location and ordering of retouch over the sequence of point reduction. A: order of retouch as determined from scar superimposition, and B: the evenness of retouch across 16 segments (changes in point shape and size are also represented).

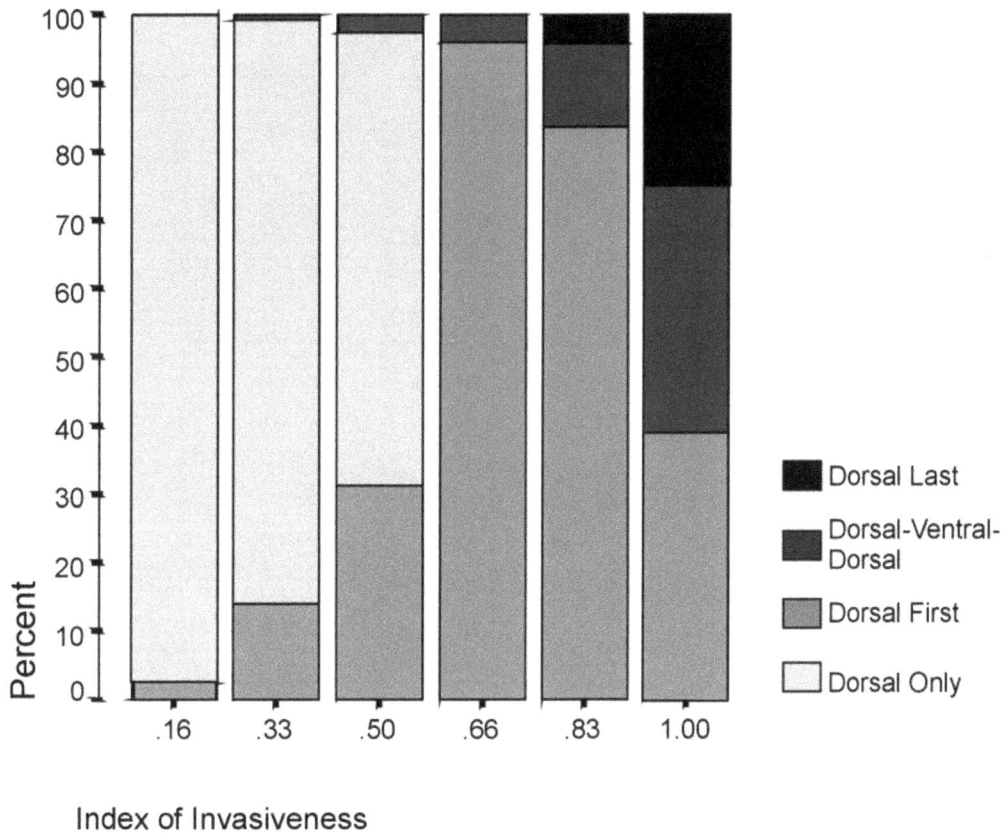

A

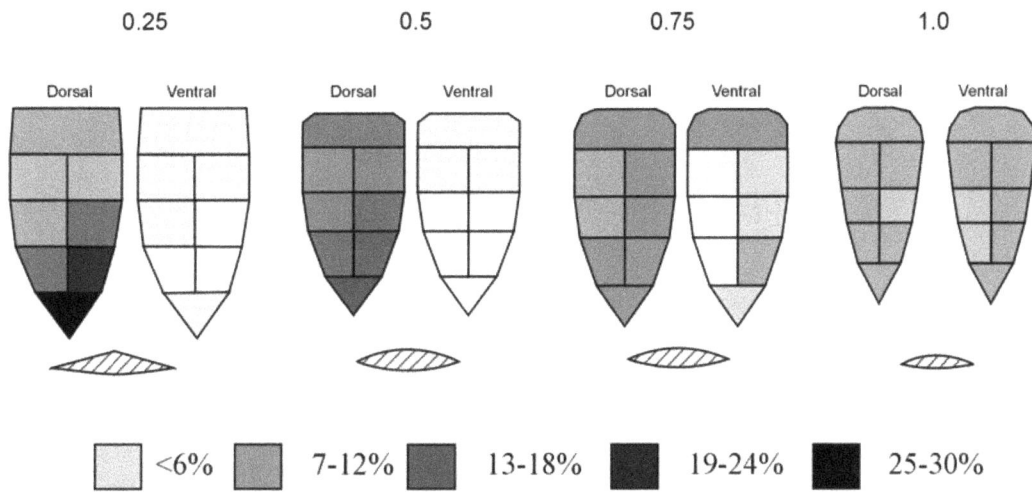

B

Figure 6.17. Variation in blank shape for points.

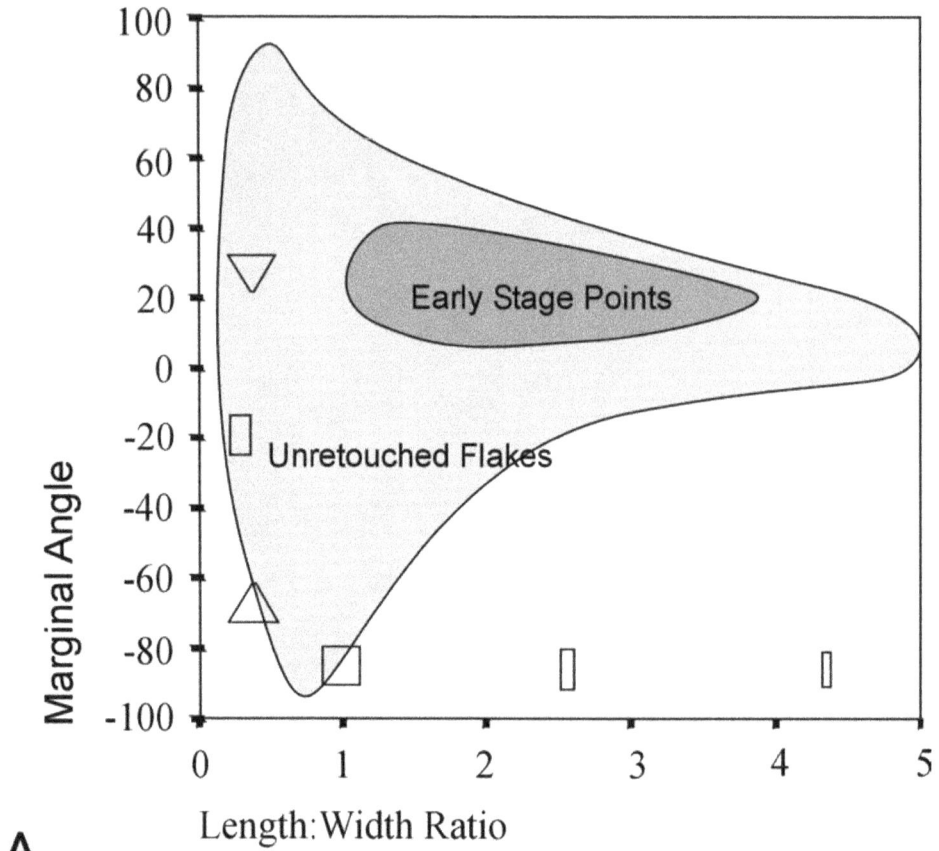

A

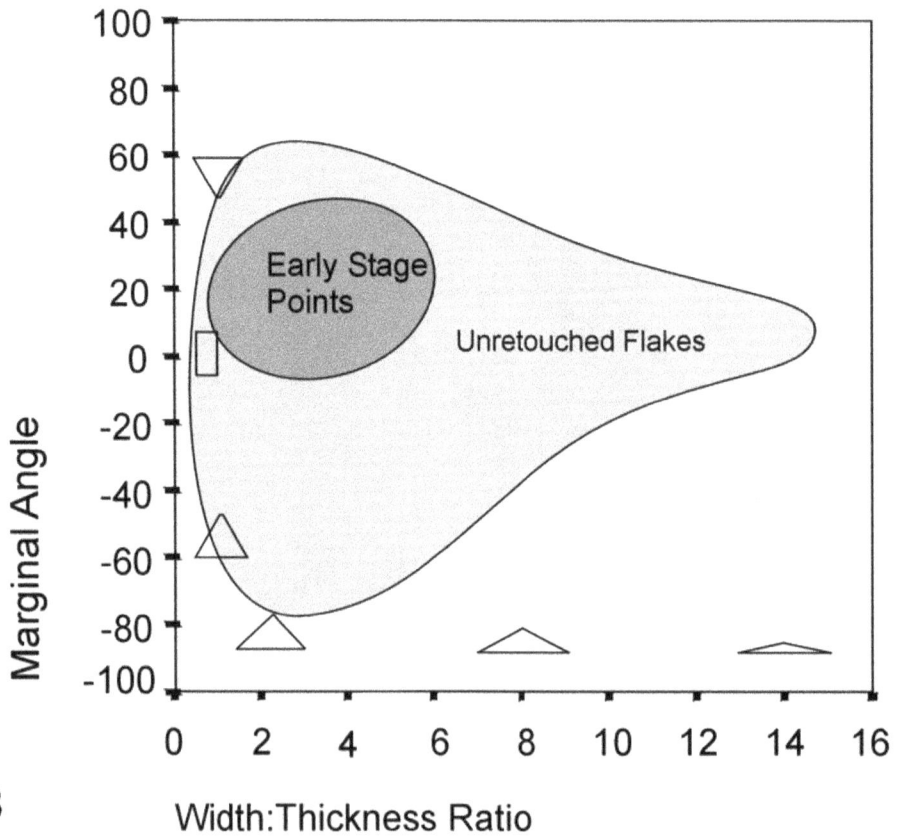

B

The second way of investigating changes in retouch location is to examine the evenness of retouch distribution across the 16 segments used to calculate the Index of Invasiveness. The results are shown in Figure 6.16b and show a progression from uneven retouch centred on the distal and right margin of the dorsal surface with a very low incidence of retouch on the ventral surface (mainly distal and proximal ends), steadily progressing to a very even distribution of retouch in all segments on both surfaces. Interestingly, the proximal end tends to receive more ventral retouch initially, a situation that probably reflects concern for the size and thickness of the proximal end for the purposes of hafting. Changes to the mean dimensions of points and the degree of curvature of the proximal end are also depicted in Figure 6.16b.

Blank Selection. It is possible to examine the types of flakes commonly selected for point manufacture by comparing the characteristics of lightly retouched points to the pool of complete unretouched flakes for which data exists. Points with little modification are defined as those with an Index of Invasiveness less than or equal to 0.3. This cut-off helps ensure that retouching has definitely begun but has not yet significantly altered flake form. The results are shown in Figure 6.17, and indicate that lightly retouched points represent a very narrow range of flake shapes. Examination of the attributes for this tight grouping of flakes reveals them to be predominantly lancet flakes. Lancets are elongate flakes, with low width:thickness and high length:thickness ratios and one or more arrises on the dorsal face – all of the attributes possessed by early stage points (Table 6.7).

Table 6.7. Mean attributes of lancets and lightly retouched points.

Type	Number	Length : Width Ratio		Length : Thickness Ratio		Width : Thickness Ratio		Marginal Angle		No Arises	
		Mean	C.V.	Mean	C.V.	Mean	C.V.	Mean	C.V.	Mean	C.V.
Lancet	173	2.50	23.9	7.80	32.9	3.18	27.7	22.34	21.6	1.30	83.0
Point	171	1.86	29.1	6.23	35.5	3.29	25.7	27.11	25.1	1.32	89.3

Examination of Table 6.6 reveals that all attributes except number of arrises have very low coefficients of variation, supporting the idea that points are made from a very select group of flakes best represented by lancets. However, Table 6.7 also reveals that elongation (length:width) and length:thickness ratios are lower for points than for lancets. This no doubt reflects the reduction in length that results from retouching the margins to form a strong point at the distal end. Alteration of the margins, even at this early stage of reduction means that platform attributes and weight are likely to be a better guide to similarities in the two populations than ventral measurements, as the platform is rarely altered at this early stage of reduction (see Figure 6.15b). Table 6.8 presents the results of *t*-tests on platform attributes between lancets and early stage points. None of the attributes compared show significant differences at the p = .05 level, and the two populations are therefore likely to be identical. It is therefore possible to conclude that points were manufactured from a narrow range of flake forms selected from a large overall pool of variation, and that selection was largely focused on the highly regular flake form represented by the lancet flake. As discussed above, lancets are best seen as flakes produced early in the process of core reduction when geometry and force variables were under the greatest control of the knapper.

Table 6.8. *t*-tests for differences in platform attributes between lancet flakes and lightly retouched points.

Attribute	t	df	p
Weight	-1.84	225.25	0.07
Proximal Width	-1.28	334.78	0.20
No. Arrises	0.15	322.18	0.88
Platform Width	-0.93	328.17	0.35
Platform Thickness	-1.81	177.55	0.07
Platform Angle	-1.38	305.92	0.17

The size of point blanks also seems to vary, but is much more standardized than for scrapers (mean = 6.3 ± 3.9), representing around 30% less variation in blank form than for scrapers.

Discard Thresholds. Not all points continue on into bifacial stages, and many very small, heavily worked unifacial points are found (down to 0.6 g). It also seems that only heavier (i.e. larger) points are taken into later stages of reduction, presumably because bigger artefacts possess greater reduction potential – and some support for this notion is found in Figure 6.13a, where the minimum weight of points at discard increases over the sequence of reduction from a minimum discard weight of around 0.6 g at an index of 0.1 to a minimum weight of 2.1 g at an index of 1.0. The success of invasive bifacial knapping in maximizing the reduction potential of artefacts is seen however in the mean loss of 60% of the original weight of points over the reduction sequence. This is therefore a vastly more successful approach to extending the reduction of flakes than is marginal, unifacial scraper reduction. Adding a bifacial stage to point reduction also leads to noticeable improvement in the degree to which points can be reduced. The mode weight of dorsal only unifacial points with an index of 0.5 is 5 g (equal to a 20% reduction of original mean weight), whereas the mode weight of fully invasive bifacial points is only 3 g. Adding this last stage in the reduction process therefore adds further maintenance and resharpening time amounting to the equivalent of an additional 32% of the original mean weight of points.

The Reduction Sequence Model for Points. It is now possible to summarise the reduction sequence for points found in Wardaman Country. This sequence is illustrated in Figure 6.18. Point blanks were selected from a highly standardised pool of lancet flakes, with high length:width, high length:thickness and high width:thickness ratios, all properties that were sought after for point manufacture (Figure 6.18a). Retouching of the point blank began on the distal and right margin of the dorsal surface of the lancet flake (Figure 6.18b). Some ventral retouch was added early in the sequence if points were destined for bifacial stages, whereas unifacial points continued to be retouched around the perimeter until the entire dorsal surface was entirely invasively flaked (Figure 6.18d). Generally, it seems that only larger points were selected for bifacial working, whereas smaller flakes were more likely to remain unifacial. Flakes entering truly bifacial stages still tended to be worked more heavily on the dorsal surface than the ventral, with ventral retouch mainly concentrated on shaping and/or thinning the proximal end (Figure 6.18c). Truly bifacial points began to take on quite thick cross-sections due to reductions in width and length (Figure 6.18e). Only late in the reduction sequence did bifacial points receive substantial thinning on both faces, with length:thickness ratios climbing again (Figure 6.18f). As the sequence continued, points were more likely to receive thinning and shaping of the proximal end, resulting in a bifacially trimmed base with a pronounced curve (Figure 6.18e and f).

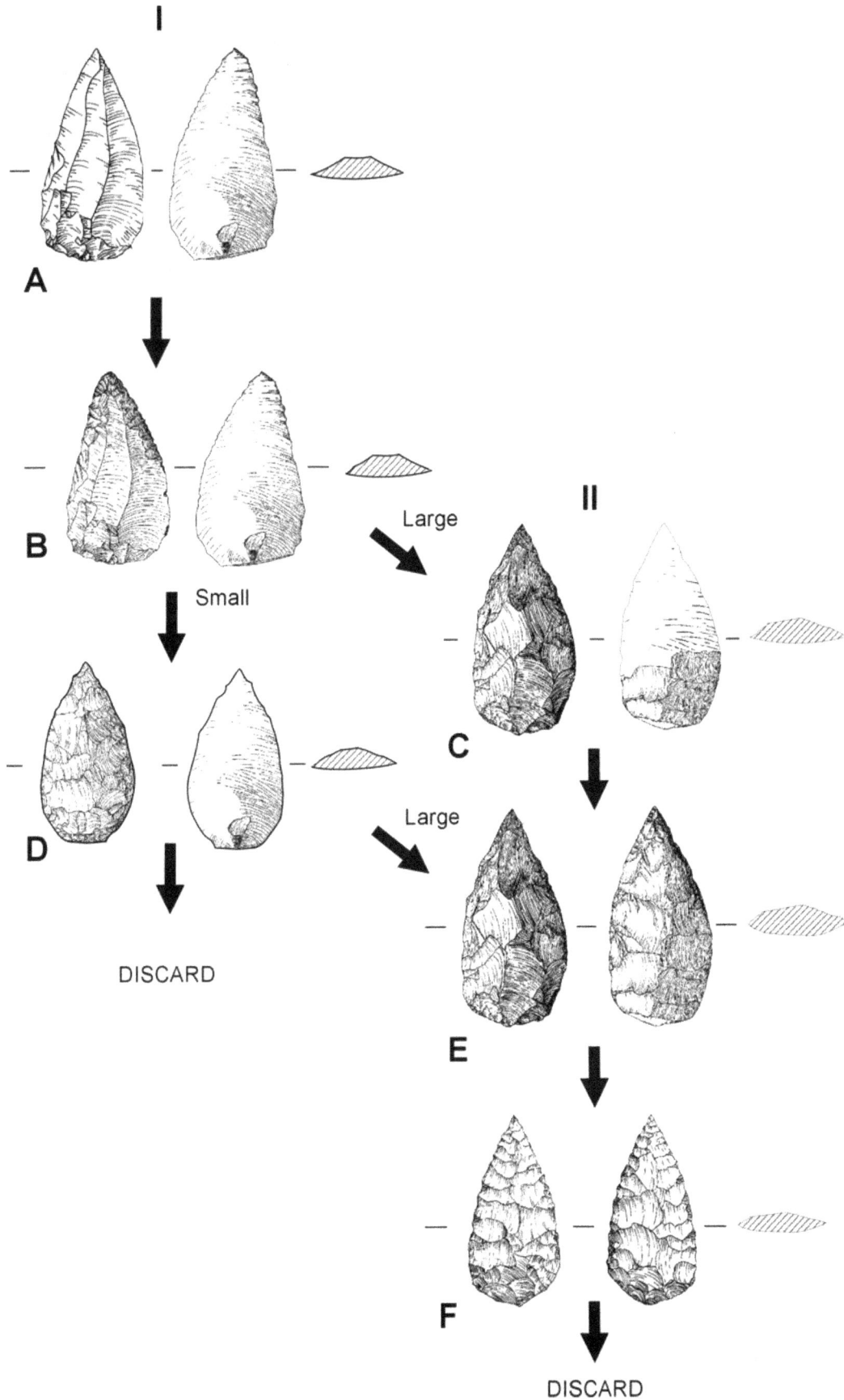

Figure 6.18. Reduction model for points, showing the flexibility in the system to either take points into a bifacial stage if large enough, or continue with unifacial reduction (generally if small).

This reduction model allows us to talk of a first and a second sequence. The first sequence is purely unifacial, while the second diverges at various points into sequence II bifacial point manufacture. No cases have yet been identified in Wardaman Country of the manufacture of bifacial points from blocks of stone rather than flakes (as seen for instance in the Camooweal district of north Queensland [Moore 2003]). There is some evidence for the existence of a potential third sequence involving alternative bifacial reduction from the very earliest stages, although this strategy is very rare (only 8.3% of early stage points, as opposed to 80% that show initial retouch on the dorsal only). Chapter 7 explores alterations in the frequency with which sequences I and II were used through time.

Non-Point Lancet and Leilira Reduction

While lancets appear to have commonly been used in point production, these regular flakes were often retouched into other forms as well. For instance, a large number of lancet and Leilira blades were retouched on the distal end to form a steep edge (Figure 6.19a). Some of these show signs of having snapped transversely prior to retouching the broken distal end. Leilira blades in particular also often possess steep, convex retouching along the lateral margins. Additionally, lancet flakes sometimes had their proximal ends smashed off using bipolar percussion directed onto opposed lateral margins. Cundy (1990) called the bipolar butts that are produced by this process 'bipolar cores', and while this is technically correct, it is likely that this common procedure was performed to thin the proximal end by removing the thick bulb of percussion, rather than to produce bipolar flakes *per se*.

Figure 6.19. Examples of non-point retouch on leiliras and lancets.

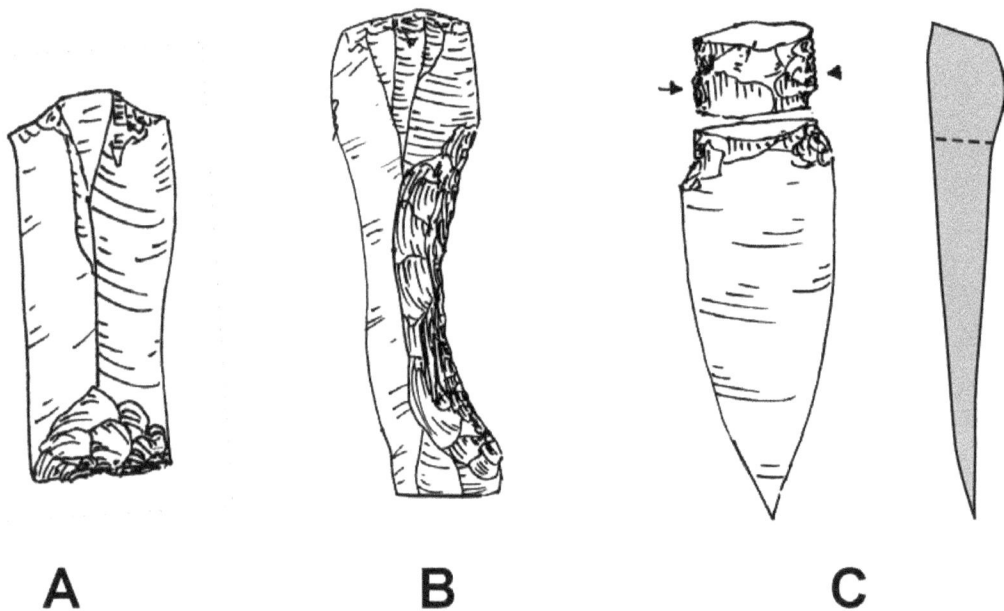

A   B   C

Burinate Reduction and Australian Classification

A distinctive characteristic of the Wardaman assemblages is the high prevalence of burinate retouch - or retouch that has removed one or more of the lateral margins of a flake by directing blows along the margins rather than away from them. Burins are known throughout much of Australia (Cundy 1977; Dortch 1977; Hiscock 1988, 1993a; McCarthy 1948; McCarthy 1964), but are generally poorly reported and their technological relationship to other classes of artefacts is not well understood (but see Hiscock [1993a] for a detailed reduction model for the Hunter Valley). The reduction process for burins is modelled here using a sample of 162 burins and spalls.

Blank Type Burinate retouch appears to have been delivered to a wide variety of flake forms, as shown in Figure 6.20a. Among these, flakes are most common, followed by unifacial points, then lancet flakes, then bifacial points, then scrapers and finally a single example of burinate retouch was found on a tula.

Figure 6.20. The nature of burinate reduction. A: frequency of burinate retouch on different artefact classes, B: frequency of different initiation surfaces, and C: the frequency of rotation.

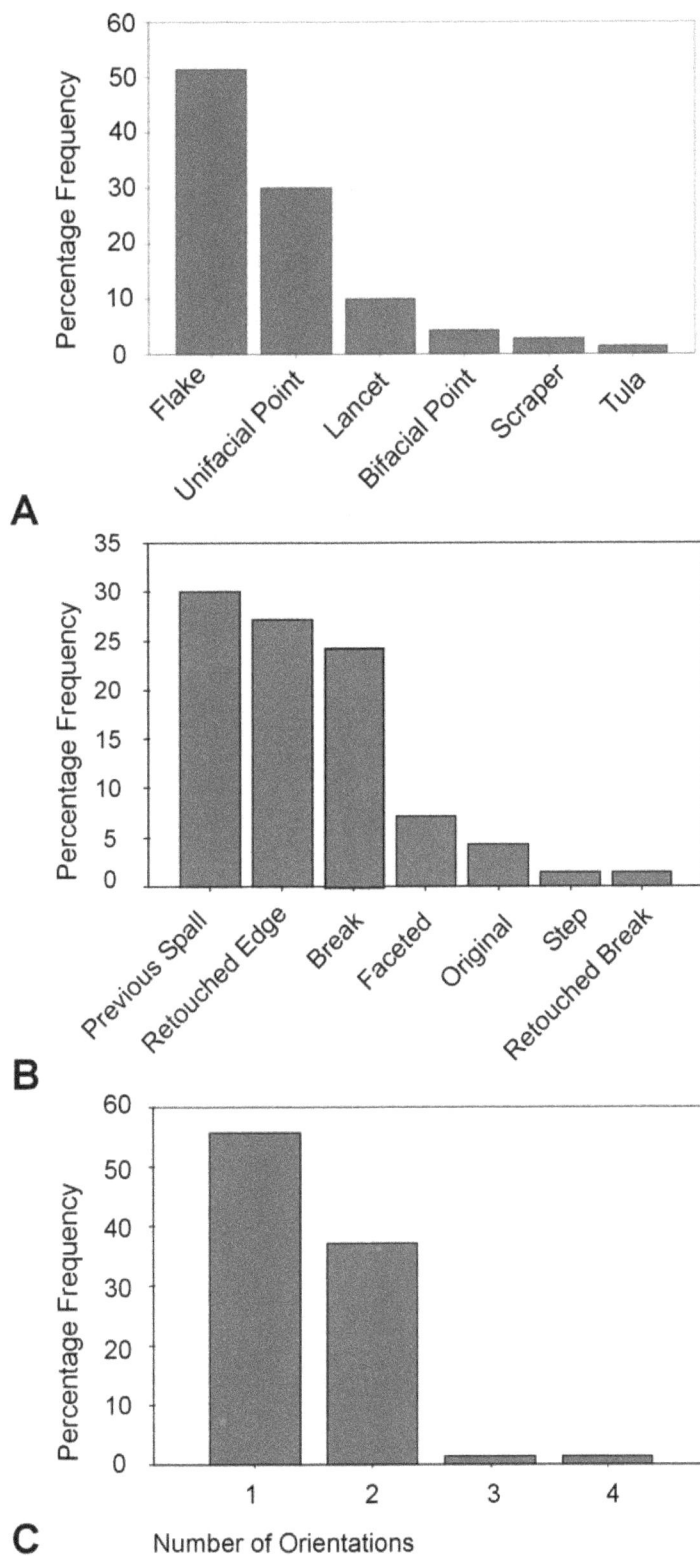

Burinate Initiation. An important step in understanding the nature of burinate reduction is to examine the point of initiation for burin spalls. The frequency with which spalls are initiated from different types of surfaces is shown in Figure 6.20b. Burin blows are most commonly initiated from the scars left by previous spalls with a different orientation (i.e. usually at less than 90 degrees to the second series). This means that spalls were often struck from burins in more than one direction, and that the scars left by the first series of detachments were often used as a platform for the next series. This use of previous burin spall scars to initiate reduction along a second margin often creates characteristic dihedral burins, particularly when both are initiated at the distal end (as is 75% of all burinate retouch). Despite the frequency of multiple burin platforms on flakes, single-platform spalling is most common in the sample of burins from rockshelters (Figure 6.20c).

The second most common initiation surface is retouched edges – essentially just sections of usually steep retouch close to the junction of two margins. A third common platform type for burinate retouch is a transverse break. Platforms are also often created by faceting a section of the end of one margin to form a flat surface suitable for use as a platform for striking blows along the adjacent margin. Original surfaces and step terminations are the next most common platform surfaces, while transverse breaks that have been retouched to provide a platform better suited to burination are the least common. Clearly, this set of platform surfaces suggests that burination was a common way of reusing flakes once they had broken, or of transforming plain and retouched edges for some specific purpose. This may have been to create a robust scraping implement, to make long thin spalls for a specific purpose, or simply to create fresh flakes with sharp edges when little other raw material was available.

Number of Spalls. Turning to the spalls themselves, Figure 6.21a indicates that the number of spalls struck from burins is strongly related to the number of initiation points (or orientations). As the number of spalls increases, the platform angle left after the last scar also gradually increases (Figure 6.21b), mirroring the changes in platform angle seen in core reduction described above. The frequency of step and hinge terminations also increases as the number of spalls increases ($\chi^2 = 4.18$, df = 1, p <.0005, V = 0.273), presumably as a result of increasing platform angle and excessive force requirements.

Spall Length. Burinate production tends to produce extremely elongate flakes (mean = 5.6, s.d. = 2.8, maximum = 16, N = 65) up to 50 mm long (mean = 26 mm, s.d. = 8), sometimes with a characteristic twist in the ventral face along the percussion axis. As burinate reduction continues, as measured by the number of spalls removed from burins, the length of burin spall scars decreases markedly as shown in Figure 6.22. ANOVA returns a significant result for changes in length as reduction continues (Table 6.9).

The Reduction Sequence for Burins. The analysis of the nature of burinate reduction as well as changes in the morphology of burins and the resulting spalls, allows a simple reduction model to be built for burins, as shown in Figure 6.23. Burin reduction appears to be principally focused on otherwise unretouched flakes, but unifacial points, lancets and other implement classes have all had burin spalls removed to varying degrees. The vast majority of spalls are oriented from the distal end, and initial spalls are struck either from retouched edges, breaks, plain or faceted margins. As the number of spalls struck from the burin increases, the chance of ending reduction from a specific platform also increases as platform angle and the frequency of step and hinge terminations increase. Knappers often responded by starting burinate flake production again on a new platform, most commonly the flat surfaces left by previous spall removals, sometimes creating classic dihedral burins on the distal margins of lancets (Figure 6.23a), points and other flakes. Rotation of flaking around the margin continued in some cases until up to 12 spalls have been removed from all four margins (Figure 6.23b).

Table 6.9. ANOVA tests for significant changes in burin morphology as reduction continues.

Attribute	df	F	p
No. Platforms vs No. Scars	3	34.03	<0.0005
Last Platform Angle vs No. Scars	3	4.55	0.06
Burin Length vs No. Scars	3	3.7	0.015

Figure 6.21. Changes in burin morphology as the number of platforms and scars increases. A: number of orientations, B: changes in mean platform angle, and C: changes in the frequency of step and hinge terminations.

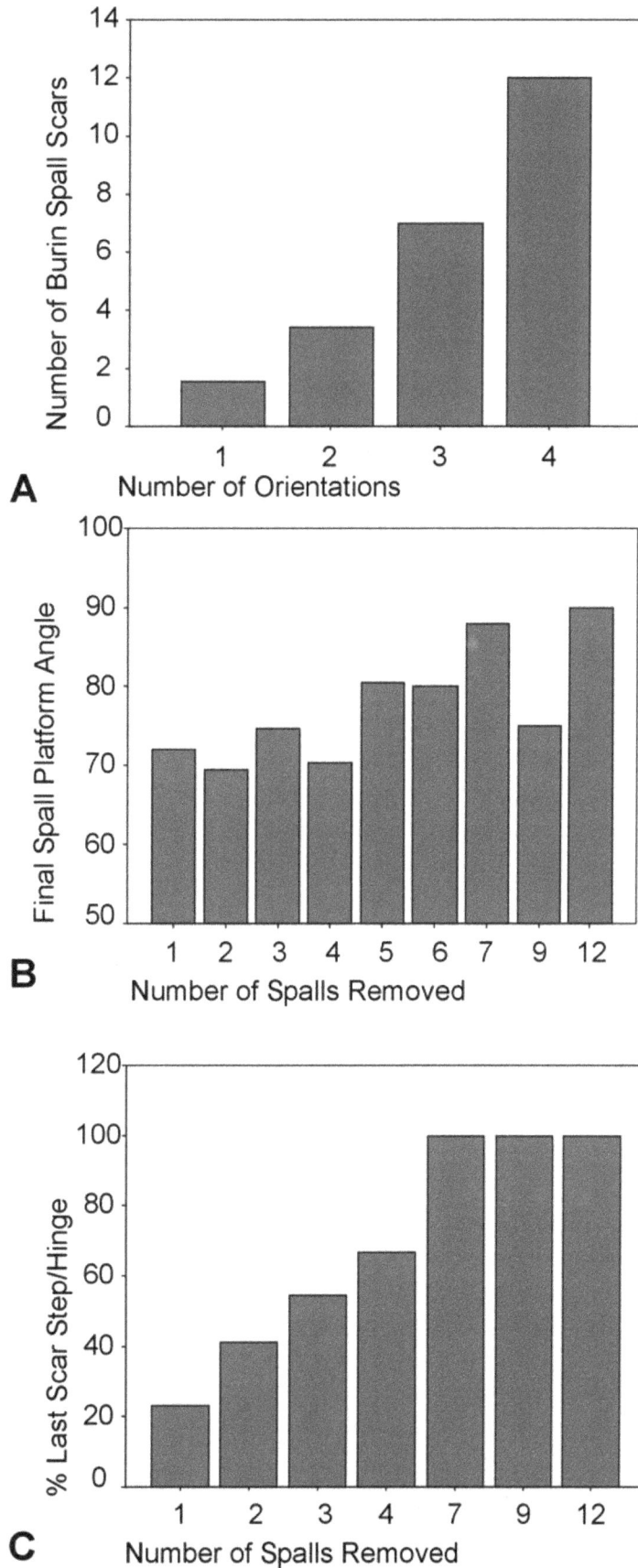

Figure 6.22. Changes to the length of burin scars as reduction continues.

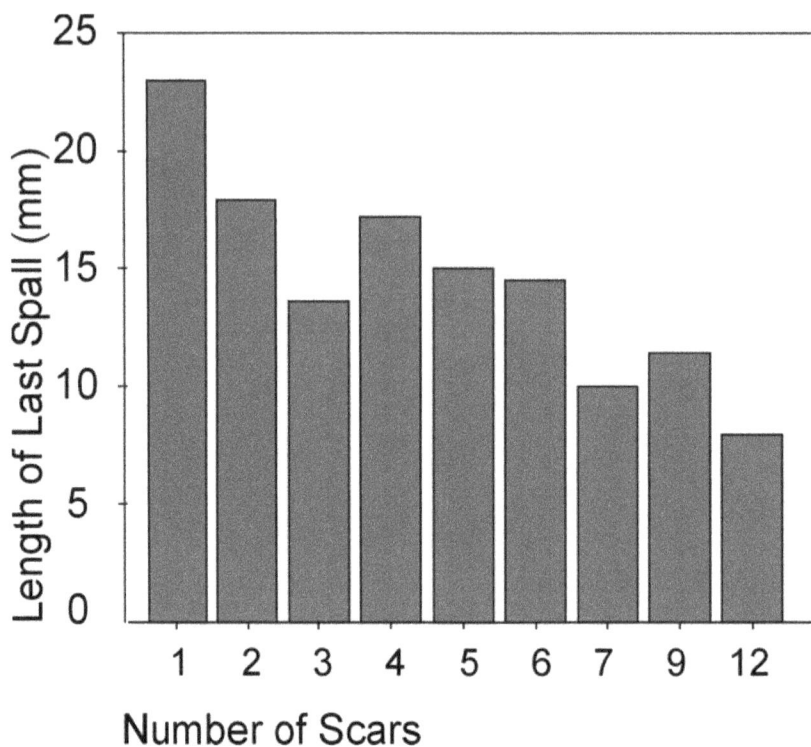

Tulas and Australian Classification Systems

Tulas are predominantly distally retouched flakes with a pronounced bulb of percussion where dorsal retouch has removed all excess ventral area, leaving only the bulb intact. Ethnographically they are known as specialized tools for adzing hard woods. Alongside points, tulas are perhaps the best recognized retouched implement form in Australia, and their reduction sequence has been well documented by early commentators such as Horne and Aiston (1924), and later by Cooper (1954), McCarthy *et al.* (1946), Tindale (1965) and Gould (1980), though not all Australian archaeologists have accurately identified these artefacts in archaeological contexts (see Hiscock and Veth 1991). Cooper (1954:92) summarized Horne and Aiston's earlier comments on the nature of tula reduction as follows: "Horne and Aiston (1924) remark that during the process of shaping a boomerang the native tradesman trims the Tula from time to time as its edge becomes blunted, by means of a hammerstone, until it is discarded and a fresh implement inserted in the gum. In consequence of continued use and the resultant symmetrical re-sharpening of the working edge to compensate for it, the Tula is gradually but evenly diminished in size and shape in the direction of its base... until it finally attains that state of diminution where it is no longer practical to embed it firmly in the gum or continue its employment economically."

Cooper's, and Horne and Aiston's, comments provide insight into some of the likely changes in morphology that should accompany continued reduction of tulas. They suggest that tulas are predominantly retouched in a succession of flake removals across the distal end, retaining the symmetry of the artefact, and ending when the flake is so shortened that it can no longer be reliably hafted. Hiscock and Veth's (1991) reanalysis of the tulas from Puntutjarpa found this progression in distal retouch to be readily identifiable on archaeological specimens, and were able to separate tulas and their heavily reduced slug forms from other retouched flakes on the basis of length:width ratios and the location of retouch. The sequence of changes to tula morphology is explored in this section using a number of measures of reduction, but primarily elongation (following Hiscock and Veth (1991)), for a sample of 66 tulas.

Size. If the reduction sequence outlined by Cooper and Hiscock and Veth holds for the Wardaman tulas, then changes in reduction intensity as measured by elongation should be accompanied by reductions in length, as length should show greater reductions than width. This turns out to be the case for the Wardaman tulas as shown in Figure 6.24a, with a significant decrease in the length of tulas occurring as elongation decreases (ANOVA, F = 23.3, df = 5, p <.0005).

Figure 6.23. A reduction model for burins. Two common sequences are illustrated. A: the sequence leading to dihedral burins, and B: a sequence of rotations leading to multiple orientations and the removal of substantial numbers of spalls.

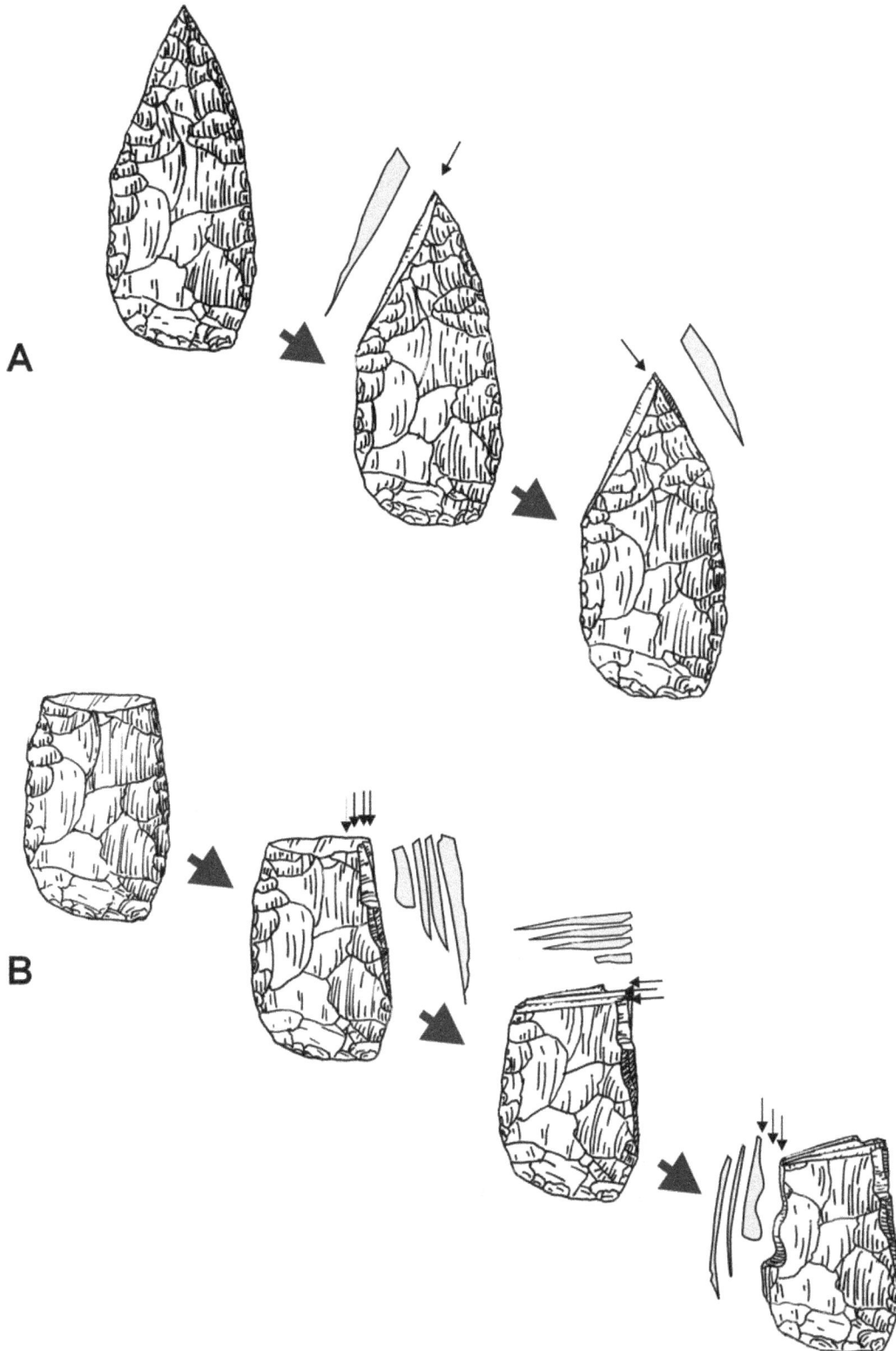

Figure 6.24. Changes in the morphology of tulas over the sequence of reduction. A: reduction in mean length, B: reductions in the % perimeter of retouch, and C: % platforms retouched.

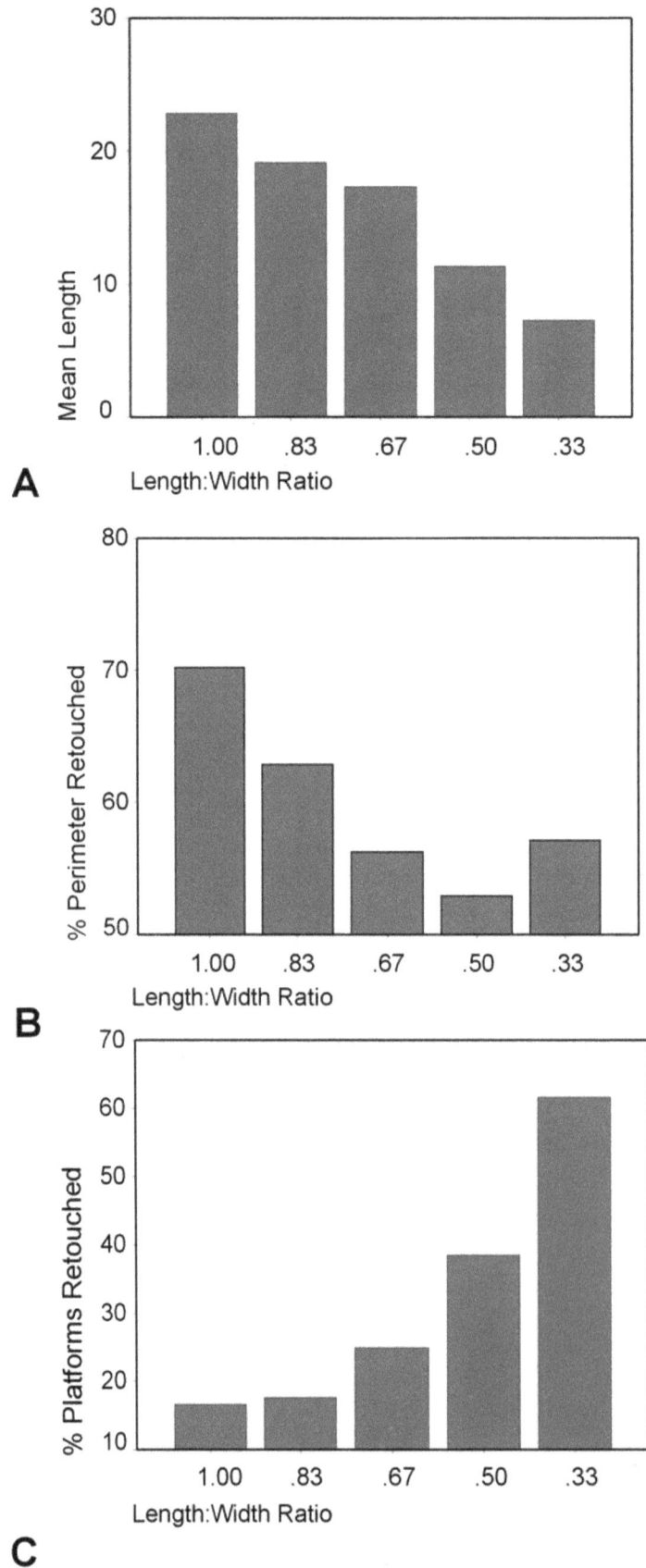

Percentage of Perimeter Retouched. According to ethnographic accounts of tula manufacture, an important first step is the removal of excess ventral area so that only the convex bulb of percussion is left intact. Tulas are then steadily dorsally trimmed from the distal end back toward the proximal end as use and resharpening continues. The result is a gradual loss of perimeter as reduction continues, but also a relative increase in the proportion of the unretouched edge as represented by the platform. This pattern should be represented by a decrease in the perimeter of retouch as reduction continues. This is exactly what is found for tulas, as shown in Figure 6.24b. However, in the final stage of reduction, perimeter of retouch increases again. This likely represents the reduction of the platform in the final stages of reduction. Turning the tula 180 degrees in the haft and retouching the old platform edge as the new working edge was observed ethnographically, and some tula slugs show signs of working on both proximal and distal ends. Figure 6.24c confirms that as tulas enter late stages of reduction, platforms are retouched with increasing frequency.

Edge Curvature. Cooper's description also suggests that sustained reduction of the distal end should result in decreases in the curvature of the edge. This is because the edge should be at its most curved once trimming of the bulbar area has finished, resulting in a wide arc of retouch around the bulb. As retouch continues, the edge straightens out and may finally become concave. This progression of changes in edge curvature is shown in Figure 6.25, and is measured using the same index as that used to describe scraper morphology. An ANOVA test also reveals the change to be significant (F = 4.39, p = .005).

Figure 6.25. Changes in edge curvature for tulas as reduction continues, measured using flake elongation (length:width ratio).

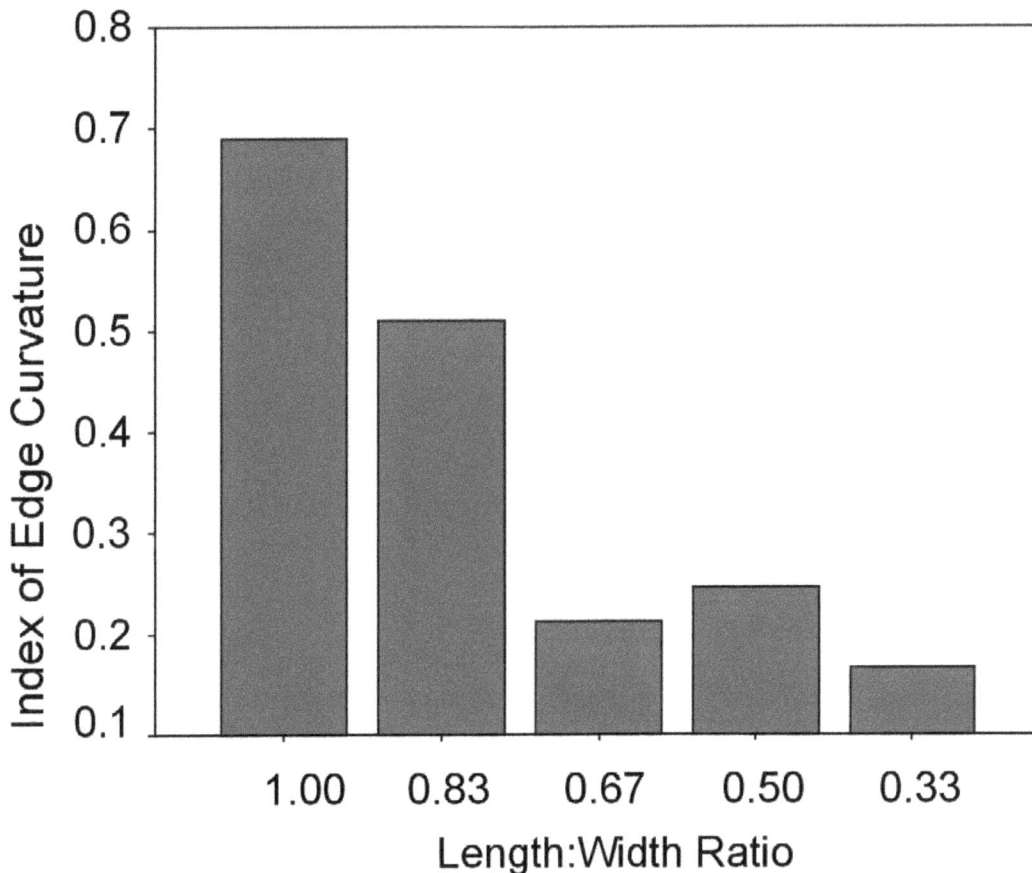

Blank Selection. Unfortunately there are next to no lightly retouched tulas in the sequence and so the dimensions of fully retouched tulas must be plotted instead, as shown in Figure 6.26. Perhaps not surprisingly given extensive reduction, tulas cluster together very tightly in terms of elongation, but vary extensively in cross-section and marginal angle.

Figure 6.26. Variation in tula shape in comparison with unretouched flakes.

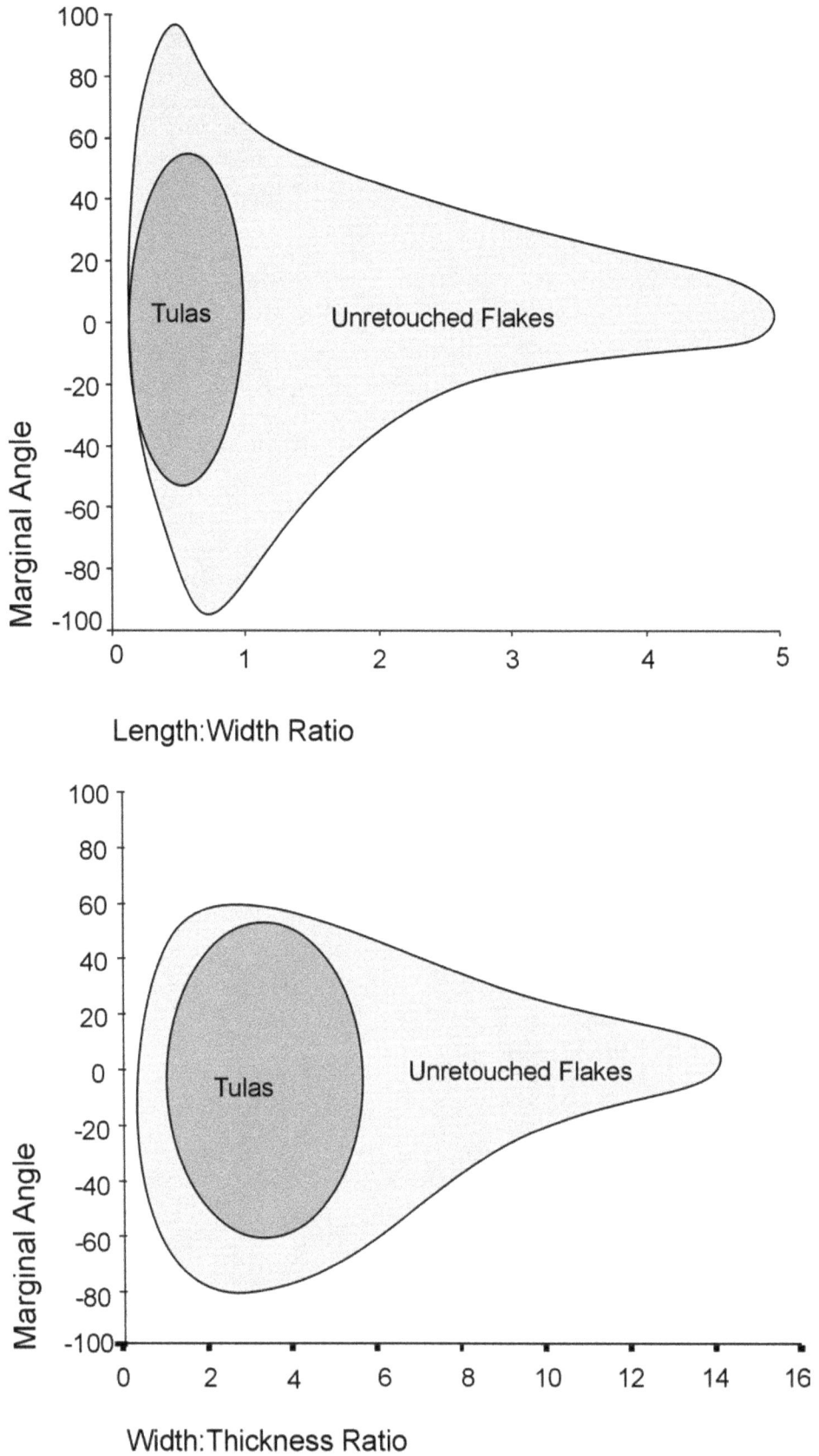

Length:Width Ratio

Width:Thickness Ratio

Discard Thresholds. Although no early stage tulas have been recovered at sites, mid-stage tulas weigh in at around 6 ± 4.2 g, and end up weighing around 3.8 ± 1.8 g. This represents nearly a 50% drop in weight just between middle and late stages, and suggests that tulas might be capable of sustaining use/maintenance adding up to around 80% of original weight lost. This is a very long use-life, especially for such a small artefact. The smallest 'slug' discarded weighed 1.5 g with an elongation of 0.2.

The Reduction Model for Tulas. The changes to size, shape and edge morphology documented here helps build a reduction sequence model for tulas like those for burins, points and scrapers above. Tulas begin as flakes with a pronounced bulb of percussion, and are first trimmed along the distal margin to leave only the bulb of percussion.

Figure 6.27. A reduction sequence for tulas. The A sequence represents continued reduction of the distal end. The B sequence results from turning the tula around and flaking the platform.

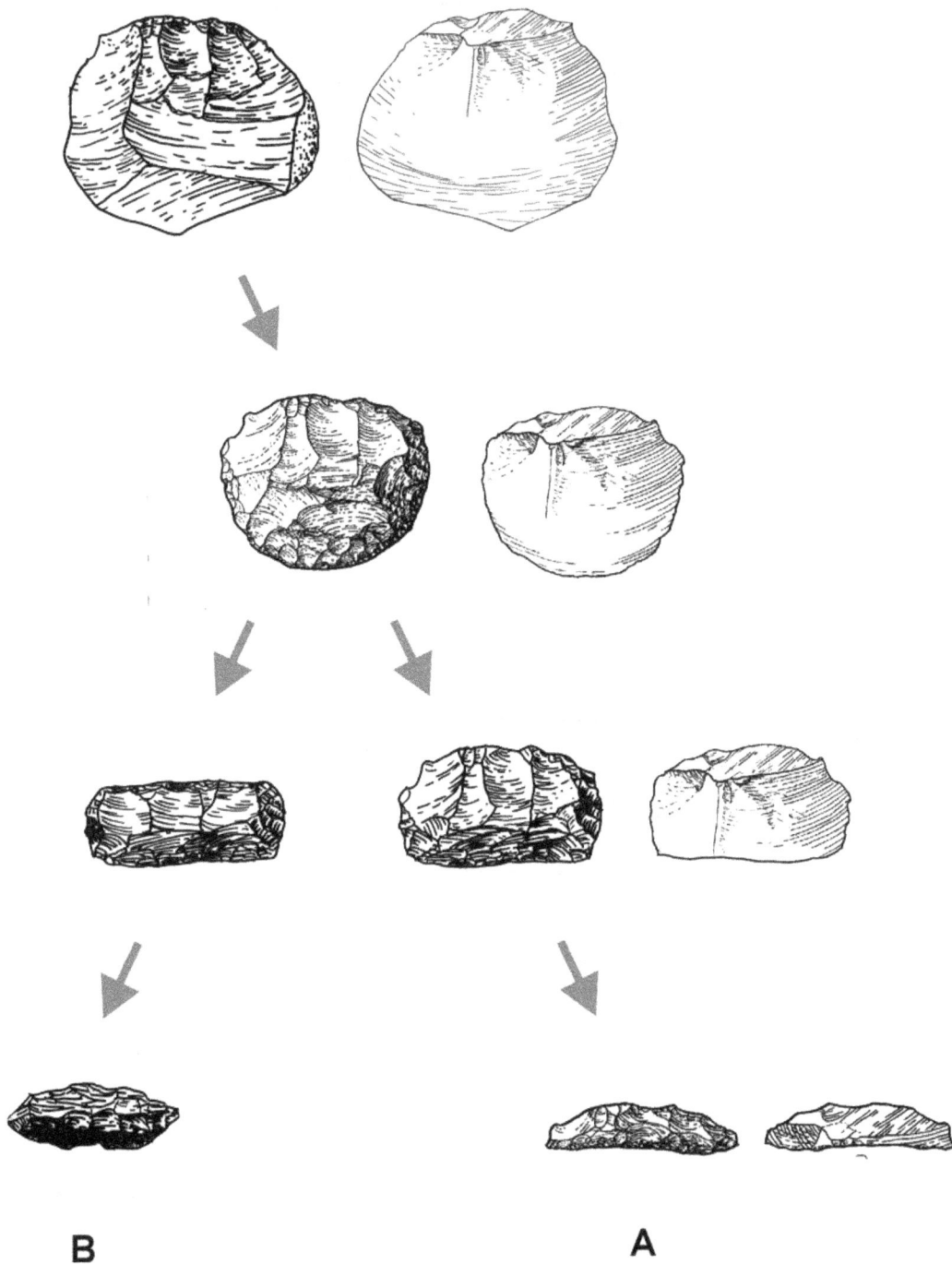

B   A

As retouch is added to tulas, length is reduced rather than width, the curvature of the distal margin straightens out and the unretouched platform represents an increasing proportion of the overall edge (Figure 6.27a). As tulas near the end of the sequence, they are sometimes flipped over and the platform is retouched to form a new edge, thereby maximizing the reduction potential of the implement (Figure 6.27b). This process takes place with increasing frequency as reduction continues. Finally, tulas are discarded once they have reached the point at which they can no longer be hafted. This usually takes place once tulas have been reduced to around 4 mm in length reaching a minimum weight of 1.2 g and an elongation of 0.2. Tulas have very much taken on their 'slug' form by this stage.

Burrens and Australian Classification

Burrens are essentially invasively retouched scrapers with retouch located on both lateral margins. Simultaneous reduction of both margins tends to result in an elongate slug-form. Burrens are perhaps the least well documented retouched artefact form discussed here, despite their frequent mention in the older Australian archaeological literature (Johnson 1979; Lampert 1971; McCarthy 1967; McCarthy *et al.* 1946). McCarthy argued that the burren was likely to be a functional equivalent of the tula, though with the haft set at 90 degrees to the lateral margins rather than parallel to it. Mulvaney (1969:82-83) also adopted the use of the term 'burren adze'. An adzing function for these implements seems unlikely, however, at least in the same manner as the tula, since most burrens lack the pronounced bulb of percussion that enables tulas to function as efficient adzing tools when encased in large amounts of resin. Others have tended to group burrens with other scrapers as a form of stylized scraper (Sanders 1975). While plausible, functional speculations of this kind are unhelpful in understanding the reduction process, and are not considered further here.

It is possible to test whether burrens stand out in any way from scrapers by examining their place within the continuum of retouch morphologies used for scrapers earlier in this chapter. This data is presented for 14 burrens and 341 scrapers in Figure 6.28. Burrens clearly sit neatly within the range for scrapers in terms of their edge curvature, perimeter of retouch, edge angle and invasiveness of retouch in relation to the GIUR. When the range of flake shapes associated with burrens and scrapers is examined, however, as in Figure 6.29, burrens do stand out as a sub-group of particularly parallel-sided implements with a narrow range of cross-sections in comparison to scrapers. The separation of burrens and scrapers is therefore likely to be an arbitrary one based on the straightness of the lateral margins, but no other aspect of formal variation. It therefore seems that burrens should not be considered a distinctive class in Wardaman Country, but rather one of a number of morphologies that could be teased out from the broader group of scrapers. In all other respects, burrens appear to fit neatly within the overall scraper reduction sequence.

Blank Selection and Flake Implement Standardisation

As the final piece of analysis for this chapter, the variation in shape for each group of retouched artefacts is overlayed in Figure 6.30. From these graphs, the degree of standardisation in implement form can be gauged. It is clear for instance that some forms are highly standardized, while others are extremely variable. Points and tulas, for instance, show highly restricted variation in shape, whereas scrapers and burins are highly variable. It can be inferred from these diagrams that much stronger selection criteria applied to the manufacture of points and tulas than to other classes (assuming that burrens are but an arbitrary sub-set of scrapers as argued above). This point will have significance in the discussion of temporal trends and provisioning discussed later.

Figure 6.28. Relationship between burrens and scrapers. A: % perimeter retouched, B: edge curvature (against perimeter of retouch), C: edge angle, and D: Index of Invasiveness.

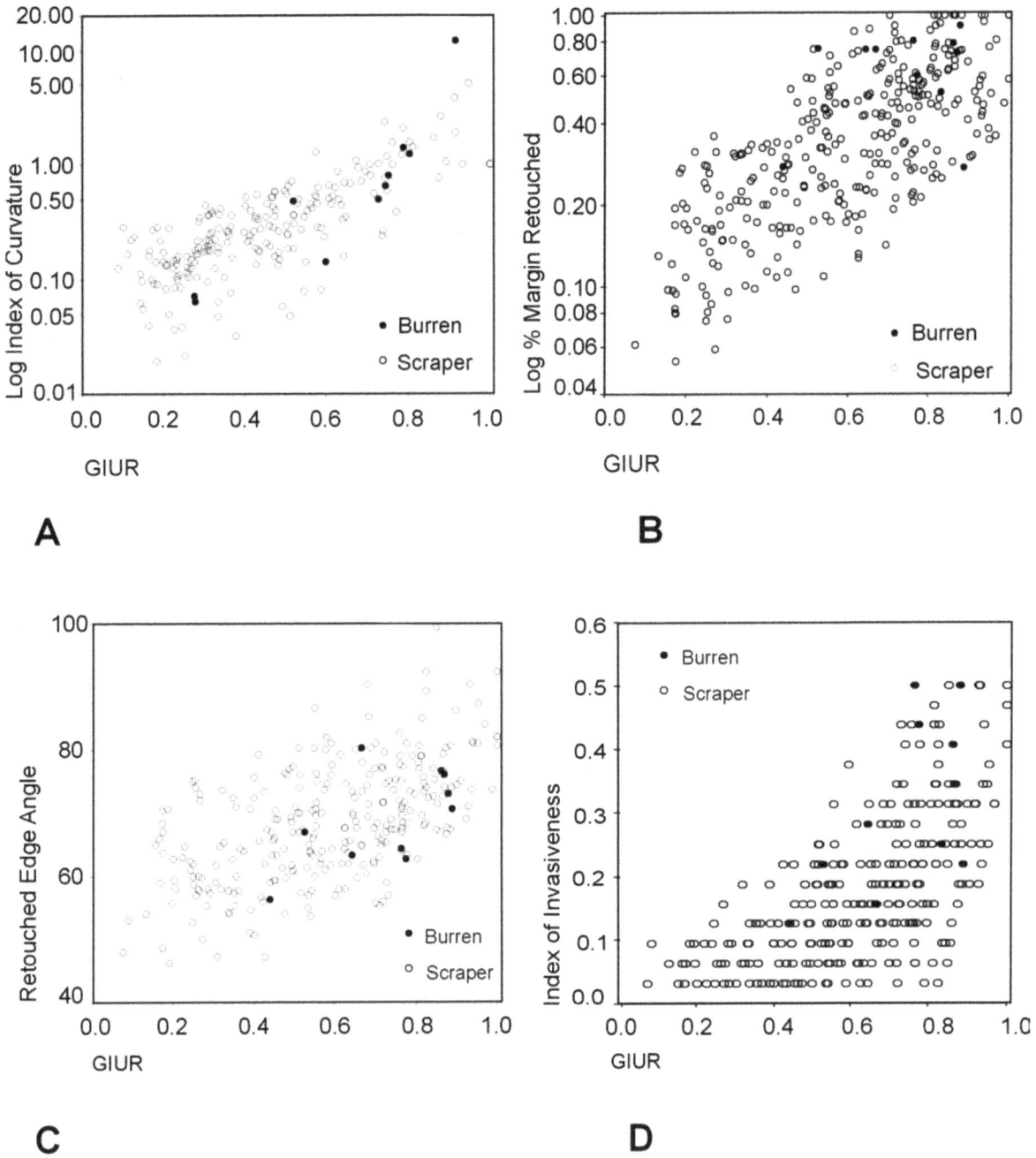

Figure 6.29. Variation in flake shape for burrens.

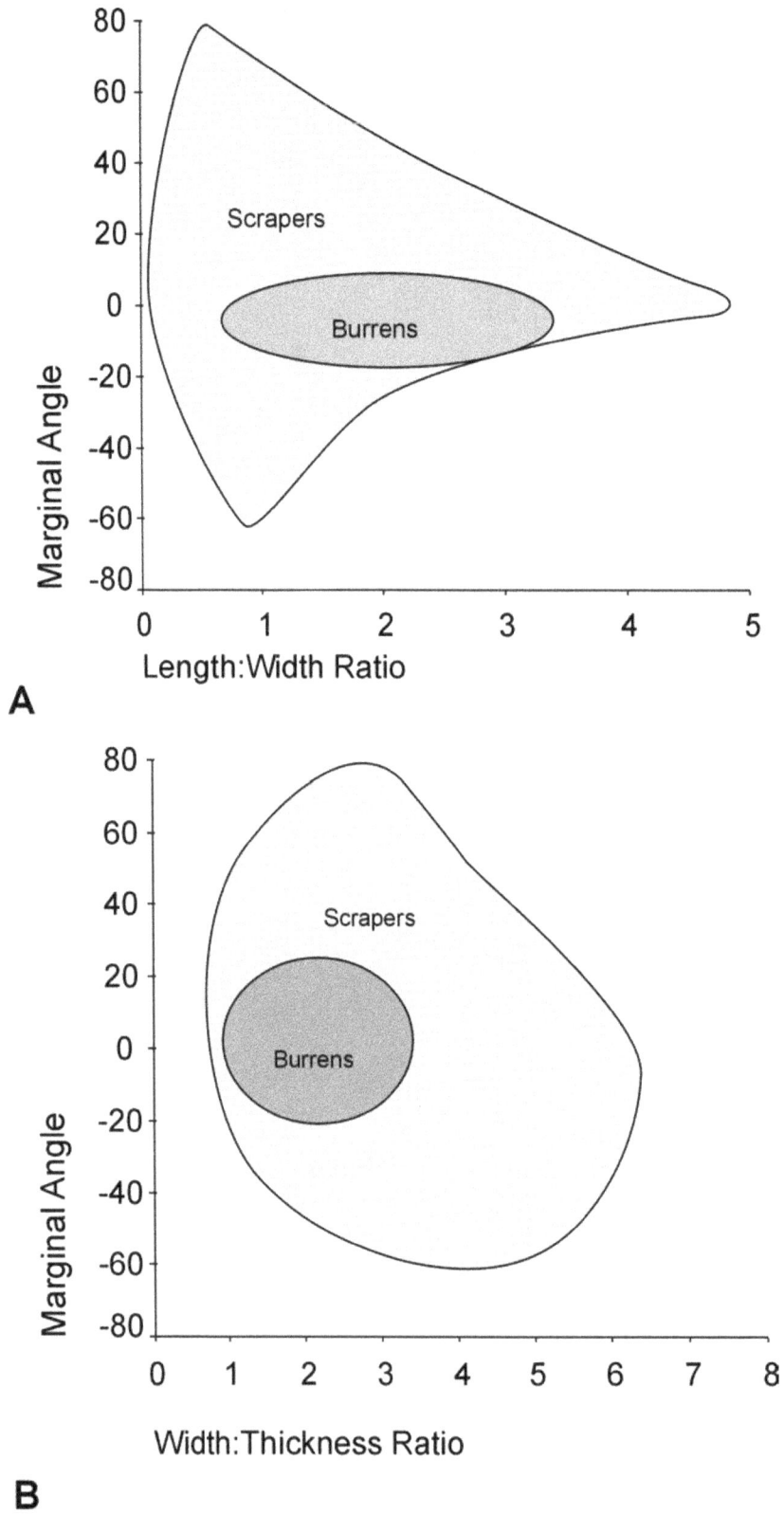

A

B

Figure 6.30. Overlay of the variation in retouched implement shapes by class. A: marginal angle plotted against elongation, and B: marginal angle plotted against longitudinal cross-section.

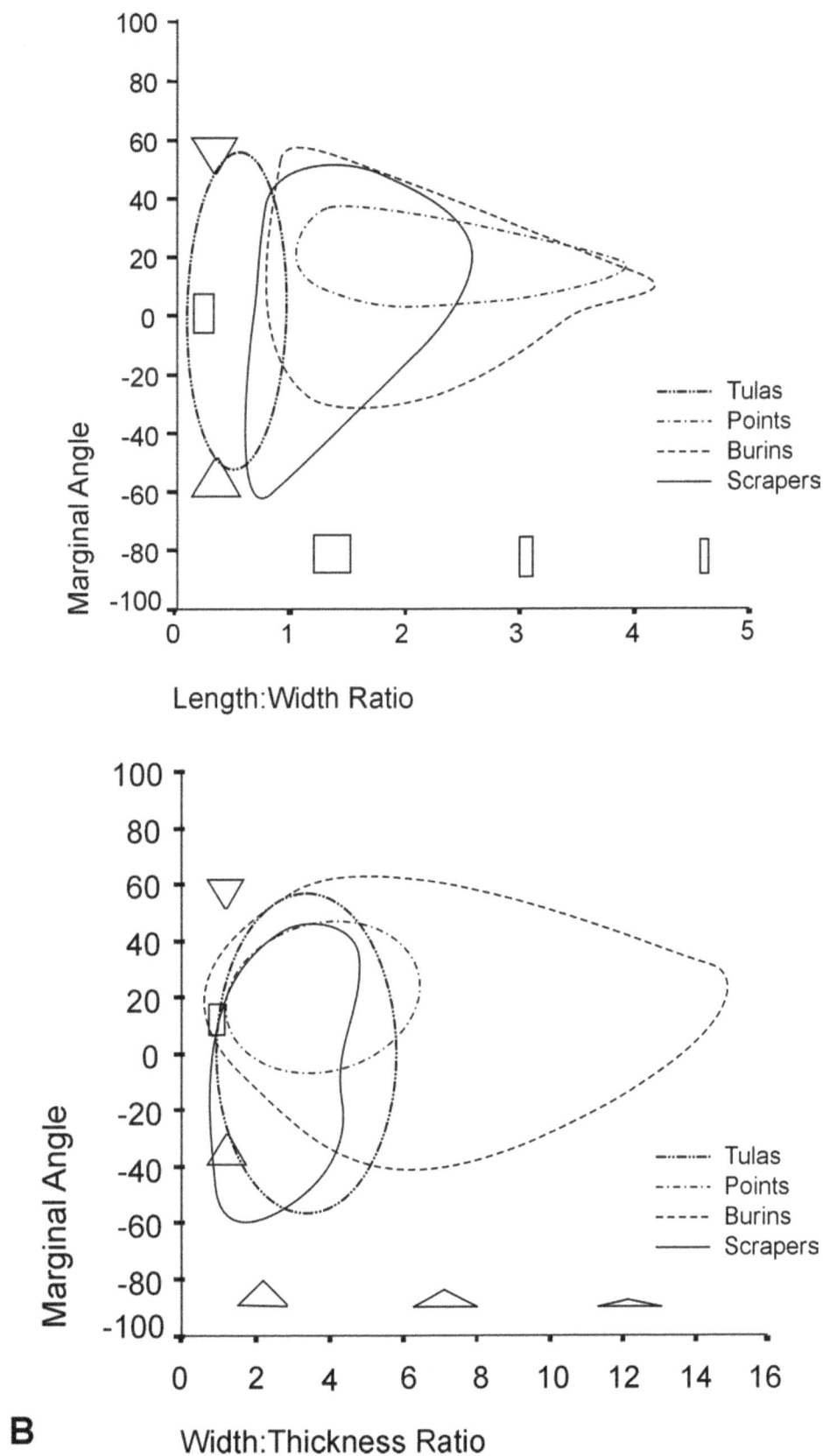

Reduction Sequences and Tool Design

Besides understanding the ways in which implements were manufactured and the reduction continuums that underlie variation in certain morphologies, reduction sequence models also allow us to speculate about the various advantages offered by certain tool designs in terms of standardisation, maintainability and reduction potential. It is clear from the descriptions of each mode of implement manufacture that certain trade-offs in design, investment and utility are at play. Firstly, implements such as lancet flakes are costly to produce in terms of the amount of core reduction potential foregone to make lancet flakes, which entails high breakage rates and early discard of the core. Because cores used to make lancets are often under-utilised in terms of their mass, they are also costly to transport since much unused weight must be transported along with the core to produce only a few unbroken lancets. These disadvantages are obviously traded against the highly standardized flakes that are produced through this manufacturing strategy.

Another set of trade-offs can be identified for scrapers. Scrapers are selected from a highly variable pool of blank sizes and shapes, and generally both begin large and end large (in terms of the reduction sequence). Furthermore, the exclusive use of unifacial reduction on irregular flake blanks means that there is great potential for the build up of step terminations and intractable edge angles to cause early termination of the reduction process in terms of the amount of weight left in the implement. Compared to points, which routinely result in the loss of more than 50% of original blank weight over the reduction sequence, scrapers are wasteful and unconducive to extended use-maintenance schedules. However, scrapers are obviously tools with minimum startup costs since little effort is expended in standardising blanks or shaping implements in particular ways, and it is therefore no surprise that scrapers are discarded early with regard to loss of original mass.

Points appear to represent the opposite extreme to scrapers. Points are regularly made from lancet flakes that are more difficult to produce, but provide the level of standardisation that might be required of a technology that was probably designed to perform in a relatively specialised role with high effectiveness (i.e. as projectile tips, although the possibilities do not end there). Maintainability is clearly also a focus of point design since invasive reduction of the sort employed in point reduction is capable of extending the use-life of the implement by a substantial degree, by maintaining platform angles and keeping step terminations to a minimum through opposed marginal thinning. The reduced variation in the size and shape of points that results from invasive flaking and the use of a standard blank form also likely enhanced the reliability of the technology by allowing modular replacement of the tip with another tip of similar size and shape, rather than make the entire tool again from scratch.

Tulas also appear to operate within a narrow morphological spectrum, but it is likely that most selection criteria were focused on the nature of the bulb of percussion. The tula shows the longest reduction sequence of any retouched implement documented here, with perhaps as much as 80% of original weight lost through maintenance and rejuvenation. The lengthy amount of time spent resharpening and resetting tulas into their hafting gum has been documented ethnographically (Gould 1980; Hayden 1979), and is consistent with the long reduction sequence documented for the Wardaman tulas.

Thus both tulas and points have remarkably long use-lives and appear to represent functionally effective tools designed for maximum performance in semi-specialised tasks (i.e. as spear points and hardwood working tools?). Their increased performance also likely comes at the expense of greater startup costs – making standardized blanks, constant resharpening, and the lengthy manufacture of hafting devices. Unfortunately, little is known about the methods of manufacture or selection of tula blanks, but the regularity of bulbar proportions and fine attention to bulbar trimming suggests there were initial start up costs to implementing this technology as well (not least of which is the manufacture of the haft). We should therefore expect both forms to have developed in response to strong pressures to increase the use-life and effectiveness of tools at the cost of greater manufacture and repair times, perhaps in response to increased mobility, risk and uncertainty. The issue of the origins, technological context and persistence of these implements will be dealt with in the next chapter.

Conclusion

Reduction sequences provide a means of tracking morphological transformation, and of reducing typological variability into a number of more meaningful units that are constructed via reference to the temporal process of reduction that unites various common forms. Knowledge of the number and nature of sequences allows us to identify the differential distribution of various stages of reduction, examine assemblage diversity in more meaningful terms than a simple tally of different forms, and to explore issues of reduction potential and provisioning through time. The reduction sequences constructed in this chapter therefore form the basis of the following analysis that examines temporal variation in stone artefact manufacture, transport and discard as a reflection of mobility, landuse and provisioning.

7. Change and Continuity in Stone Artefact Manufacture

Chronological changes in the organisation of technology in Wardaman Country can be seen from the sequence of stone artefacts deposited at the four rockshelter sites described previously. This chapter examines changes in technological design, organisation and provisioning in relation to changes in resource structuring, abundance and heightened climatic variability during the last 15,000 years that were discussed in Chapter 3. This is achieved by documenting fluctuating discard rates, changing reduction intensity, alterations to toolkit diversity and their relationship to resource stress, subsistence risk, changing levels of mobility and changes to technological provisioning. Changing patterns of stone artefact manufacture also form the basis for an examination of continuity in the social transmission of technological practices.

To examine such changes in lithic technology, we must begin by building a regional technological database that combines artefacts from units in all four rockshelter sites and assigns each unit an age in calibrated years BP, as determined through radiocarbon dating as well as cross-dating of major assemblage changes using the technique of interdigitation (Lyman *et al.* 1998). The purpose of this approach is to enlarge the sample size for periods of low stone artefact discard and to simplify the presentation and analysis of data. The following sections then examine changes in the rate of artefact discard over time. This is followed by analysis of the intensity of core and flake reduction, retouched implement reduction and changes in raw material procurement, transport and field processing. Having documented the changing nature of stone artefact manufacture in Wardaman Country, the next section turns to examining continuity in stone working traditions over time, and pays particular attention to evidence for possible breaks in transmission, or the appearance of new reduction sequences that could signal demographic changes or the emergence of new social networks. Finally, changes in technology are considered in terms of alterations to the design and organisation of technologies that help identify the nature and timing of changes in technological provisioning, mobility and risk over the last 15,000 years.

Building a Regional Technological Database

A regional database of stone artefacts tied to calibrated ages offers the potential to describe technological changes as a single set of results, making analysis and interpretation much simpler than if multiple sites and sequences are continually compared. This is achieved through use of a technique known as interdigitation, or the ordering of assemblages using both unit frequencies and superposed positions for each site (Lyman *et al.* 1998). For the Wardaman assemblages, cross-dating of spits and squares for each rockshelter was accomplished using the following temporal markers based on dating of distinctive peaks in various cultural materials and the ordering of these in each sequence:

1. The presence of glass flakes and beads was used to assign an age of less than 200 BP (i.e. European period) for spits near the surface of sites (here ascribed a notional age of 0 BP),
2. The first appearance of bifacial points in abundance in the region at c. 3,000 Cal BP, dated by four samples from three sites which overlap at two standard deviations (Nimji: ANU-57 2,890 ± 57, Garnawala 2: Beta 66434 2,920 ± 120, Garnawala 2: Wk-9252 2,751 ± 68, and Jagoliya: ANU 11364 2,780 ± 200).
3. Dates for two distinct peaks in artefact deposition. An upper post-bifacial point peak dated to c. 1,500 Cal BP at Garnawala 2 (Wk-9248 1640 ± 90), Jagoliya (ANU-11267 1,510 ± 90) and at Nimji (GX-03 1545 ± 75), and 7,294 Cal BP (ANU-11758 6255 ± 135) for a pre-bifacial point peak in stone artefact discard at Nimji. In cases where the exact location of the upper peak was indistinct (such as when two equivalent sized peaks occur close to each other with a small trough in between) a peak in unifacial point discard which is also dated to 1,500 BP was used to assign the date.

4. Maximum ages were set according to the maximum ages for sites as extrapolated from age-depth curves in Chapter 5. These are 15,000 BP for Gordolya, 6,500 BP for Jagoliya, 13,000 BP for Garnawala 2, and 10,000 BP for Nimji.

5. Calibrated radiocarbon dates. When available, radiocarbon dates were always used in place of estimated ages in determining the age of each spit.

The age of spits for which no temporal markers exist (i.e. those in between radiocarbon dates or cross-dated spits) was determined by averaging time over the number of intervening spits. This model is appropriate given the strong linear relationship between age and depth found at all sites. The results of interdigitation are shown in Figure 7.1 for Gordolya and Jagoliya and in Figure 7.2 for Garnawala 2 and Nimji. The calibrated ages assigned to each spit are shown in the right hand column for each square. This interdigitation is used to assign ages to every artefact in the database and provides the temporal framework for the following results.

Stone Artefact Discard Rates Through Time

A necessary starting point for much of the following analysis is documenting changes in stone artefact discard through time that may be informative about occupational intensities and fluctuations in resource abundance over time.

If hunter-gatherer foraging patterns and technologies responded to fluctuations in resource abundance and structuring in the ways they are posited to do in Chapter 2, then predictions can be made about the likely effects of climate change on foragers inhabiting this region over the last 15,000 years. It was predicted in Chapter 4, for instance, that the late Pleistocene/early Holocene should have been a period of high subsistence risk for hunter-gatherers newly occupying the region, as global climates were still in a state of major fluctuation with temperatures and rainfall undergoing substantial reversals. It was argued in Chapter 4 that such a situation would be unlikely to have favoured the establishment of large hunter-gatherer populations, and technologies might be expected to reflect low population numbers and high mobility as reflected in stone artefact discard rates, the nature of raw material transport and degree of reduction.

In contrast, the early to mid-Holocene climatic optimum, dated loosely to between 5 and 8,000 years BP, should have resulted in heightened resource abundance, greater stability in rainfall and temperature, and a more homogeneous distribution of resources than had existed for at least the last 20,000 years. An increase in environmental productivity of this kind should have provided an ideal situation for hunter-gatherers occupying the region, and one that might be expected to have resulted in larger populations living more sedentary lives with fewer constraints on subsistence and technology than in previous millennia.

At around 5,000 BP, climatic variability is believed to have increased dramatically, with much greater interannual variation in rainfall and a likely increased frequency of potentially catastrophic events such as cyclones, floods and prolonged droughts. These more severe perturbations are believed to be associated with an intensification of the El Niño/Southern Oscillation system, and would likely have resulted in resource depression (particularly in comparison to the former period), increased patchiness and reduced predictability that could have elicited a change in foraging behaviour as well as introducing significantly greater levels of subsistence risk for the inhabitants of the region. A reduction in population might well be expected as well as a technological response in terms of changes to toolkit design and the organisation of technology that might register as a significant overall change in technological provisioning in the region. Interannual variability in rainfall is believed to have reached its greatest severity in northern Australia between 3,500 and 2,000 BP.

At around 1,500 BP, interannual variability is thought to have ameliorated considerably and populations might again be expected to have increased and technologies to register a shift away from more pronounced forms of risk reduction and utility increase.

Figure 7.1. Method of interdigitation for each pit and each square for Gordolya and Jagoliya.

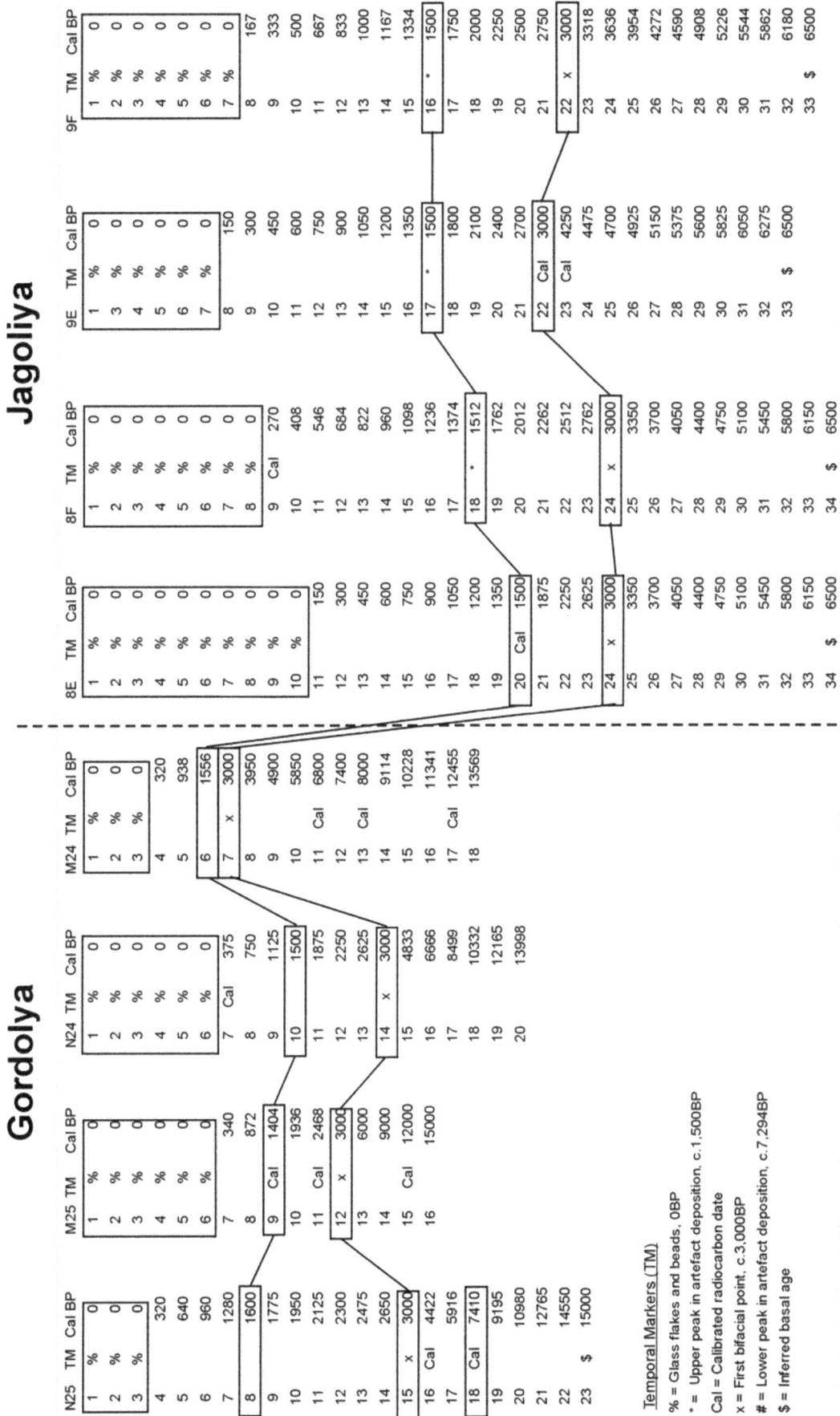

Temporal Markers (TM)

% = Glass flakes and beads, 0BP

* = Upper peak in artefact deposition, c.1,500BP

Cal = Calibrated radiocarbon date

x = First bifacial point, c.3,000BP

= Lower peak in artefact deposition, c.7,294BP

$ = Inferred basal age

Figure 7.2. Method of interdigitation for each spit and square for Nimji and Garnawala 2.

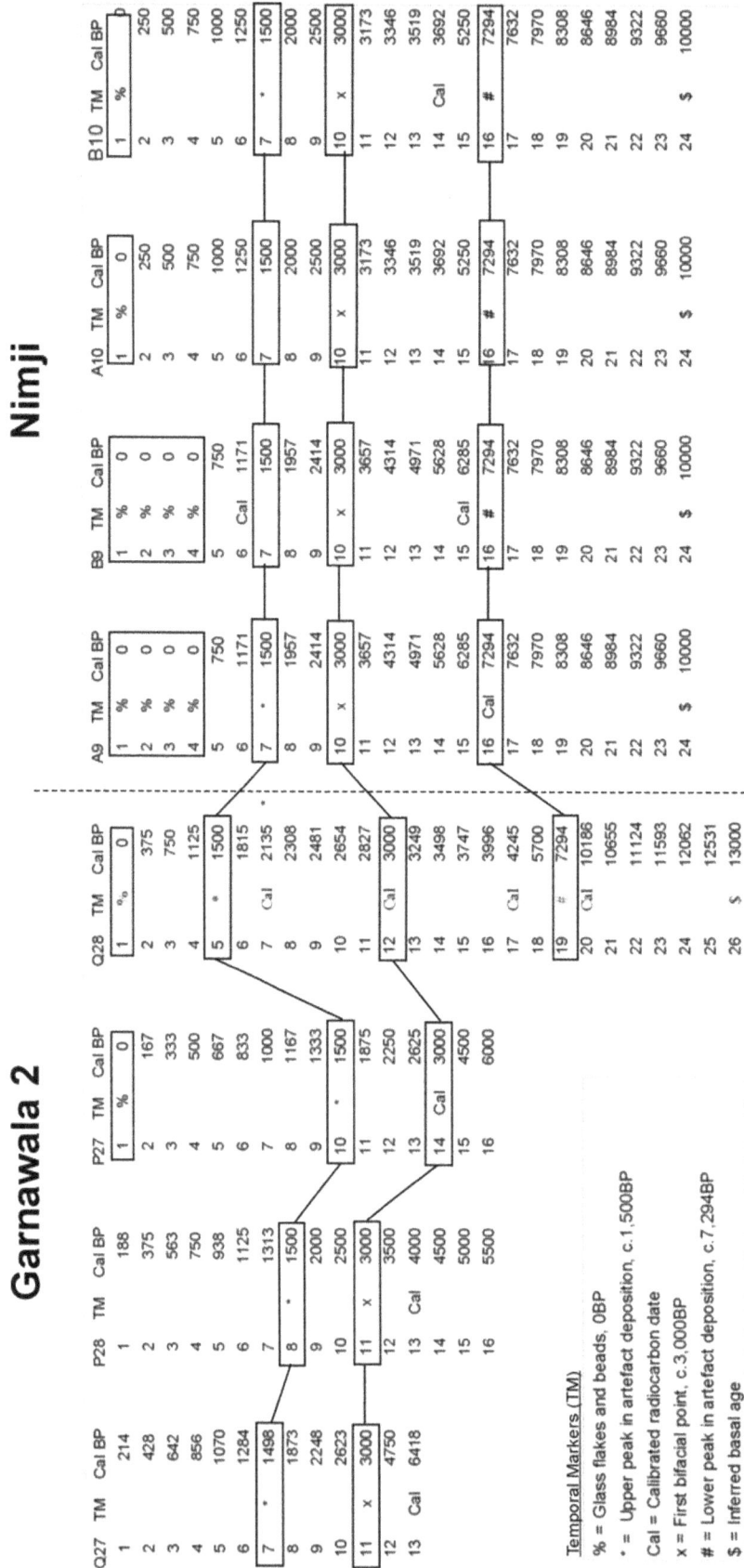

Figure 7.3. Changes in discard rates over the last 15,000 years. A: stone artefact numbers discarded per millennium for each site, and B: number of complete artefacts over 2cm in maximum dimension, bone weights (from Gordolya only), and charcoal and burnt earth weights overlayed over the average number of artefacts deposited over time for all sites.

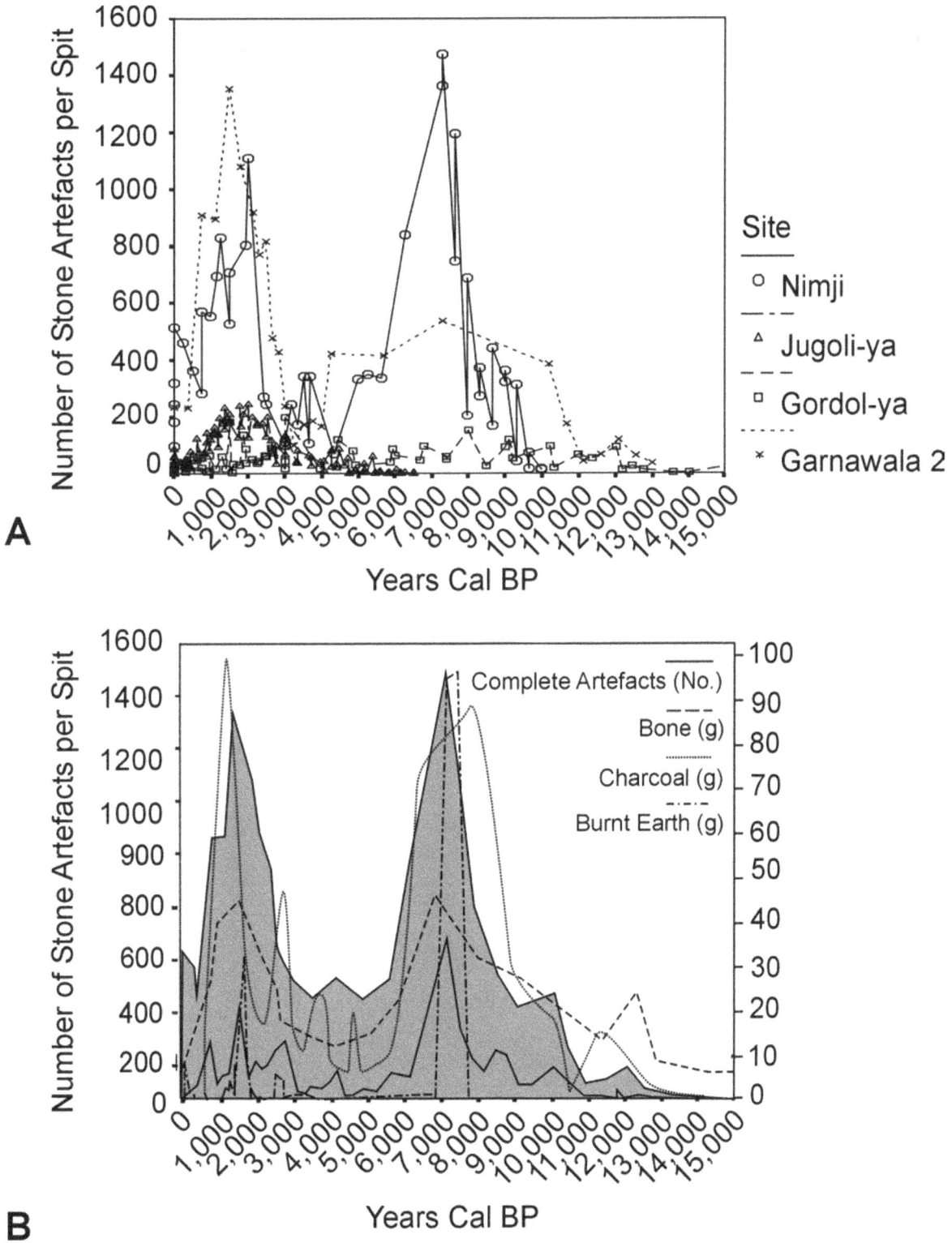

One way to explore whether these predictions are met for the study region is to examine discard rates to ascertain any possible changes in occupational intensity that might reflect changes in frequency of visitation, the size of visiting groups, length of stay or regional population size more generally. Figure 7.3a plots the changes in pooled stone artefact discard rate for all four rockshelters over the last ~15,000 years. Two distinct peaks in stone artefact discard are evident: one between 8,000 and 5,000 years ago, and the other centred on around 1,500 BP. Both peaks are in exact agreement with the predicted times at which populations might be expected to increase as foragers enjoyed favourable conditions. Between these two peaks is a pronounced trough in artefact discard, while artefact numbers gradually trail off over the several millennia preceding the mid-to early Holocene peak in artefact discard.

Raw stone artefact numbers may not always be a very accurate measure of occupational intensity, if for example taphonomic or technological factors have inflated artefact numbers in such a way that they no longer reflect numbers of people using the site. Plotting number of complete flakes over 2 cm length, however, makes little difference to the trend, as might be expected if fragmentation were a key factor contributing to assemblage size (Figure 7.3b).

Another possible measure of occupational intensity is the size of the faunal assemblage, which could loosely reflect the number of people consuming food in the shelter. Only one intact faunal assemblage has currently been obtained in Wardaman Country, and this is from Gordolya. The quantity of bone obtained from this site over time is overlayed on top of the graphs for total number of artefacts over time in Figure 7.3b. There is clearly a close relationship between the size of the faunal assemblage and the number of artefacts being deposited at sites over time. The weight of charcoal and burnt earth might also be expected to reflect occupational intensity if fires are routinely lit when people inhabit a shelter. The quantities of these materials also correspond closely to peaks in artefact deposition (Figure 7.3b). It therefore seems reasonable to assume that peaks in the discard of all of these cultural materials at 1,500 and at 7,000 BP represents an accurate picture of heightened intensity of occupation, and perhaps population size, in Wardaman country at certain times.

Changing Reduction Intensity

It was argued in Chapter 2 that intensity of reduction is likely to be a useful indicator of a number of technological strategies. One is the degree to which the use-life of artefacts is extended to recoup costs associated with more elaborate design and manufacture of implements, a second is the need to conserve and extend the life of implements when access to replacement raw material is difficult or uncertain, a third is to shape or transform implements for use in unanticipated tasks, and a fourth is to produce fresh flakes when other sources of raw material are scarce. Determining the intensity of reduction can therefore be a useful stepping stone in inferring changes in mobility, risk and technological investment.

Changing levels of core reduction can be measured by counting the number of rotations on cores. The proportions of flake platform types are also used as a measure of stages of flake production, and either the Index of Invasiveness or the GIUR is used to measure retouch. Figure 7.4 plots changes in the intensity of core, flake and retouched flake reduction, plotted against a background of total artefact discard over time. Mean retouch results are plotted for each flake for either the Index of Invasiveness or the GIUR depending on which index gave the greatest result for that specimen. Bipolar cores and flakes, representing the most heavily reduced forms, are found only in the last 4,000 years and before 7,000 BP, and are absent between 5 and 7,000 BP. The results indicate that levels of reduction are inversely related to the number of stone artefacts discarded until 3,000 BP, when reduction intensity remains high despite another peak in stone artefact discard at 1,500 BP. This suggests that climatic changes may have shaped hunter-gatherer responses in regular and predictable ways until the last 3,000 years, when changes in the nature of technology and provisioning appear to have taken place that meant levels of reduction remained high despite improved climatic conditions and a probable increase in population and/or site useage after this time.

Figure 7.4. Three measures of artefact reduction plotted against changes in artefact discard. A: numbers of core rotations, B: mean retouch intensity for either the GIUR or the Index of Invasiveness, and C: percentage of late stage flake platforms.

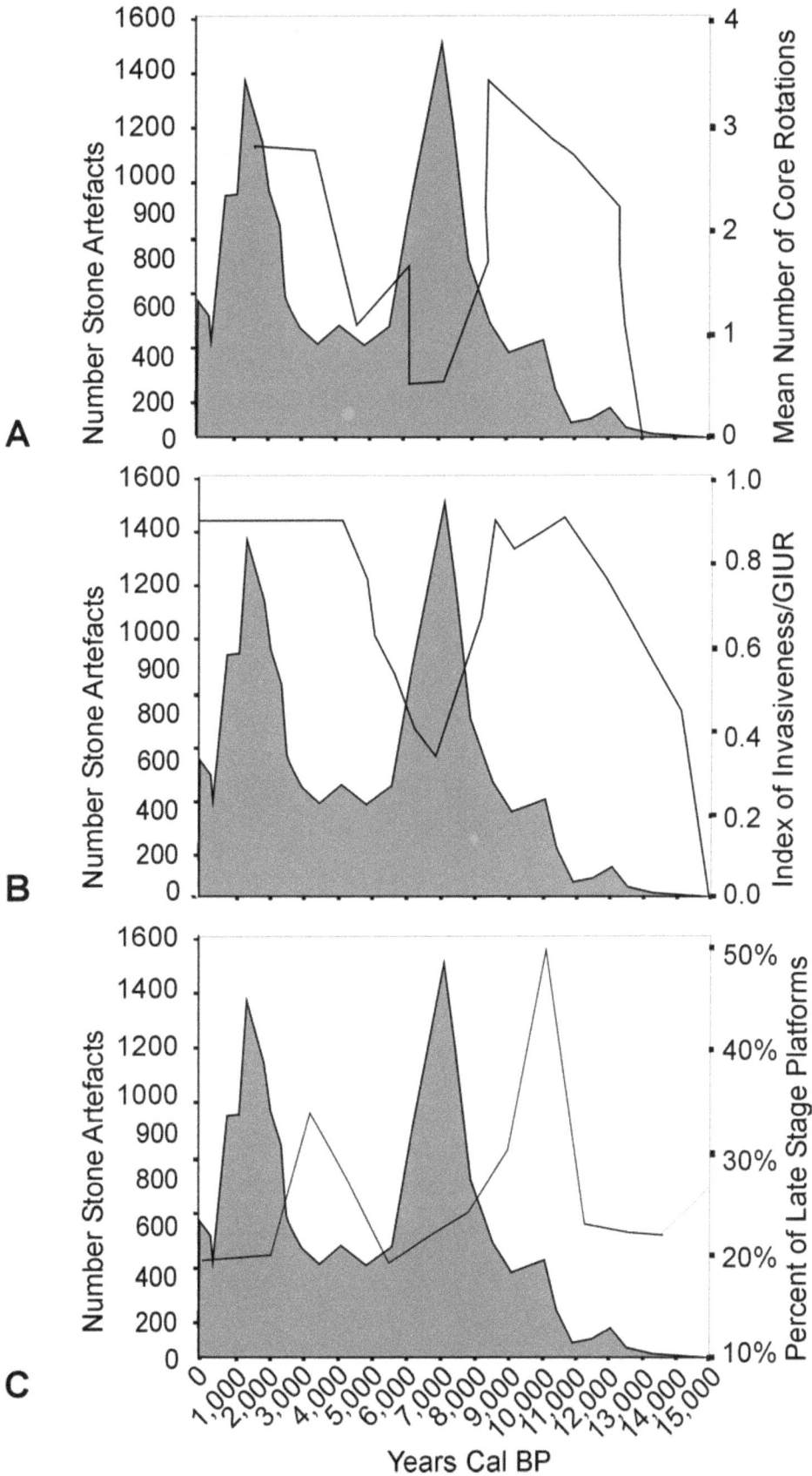

Core Reduction

The changes in reduction seen in Figure 7.4 are also reflected in the morphology of cores and flakes found in these sites. Changes in core morphology are plotted in Figure 7.5 for a sample of 56 cores. The overall sample of cores is too small to allow these changes to be plotted at millennial scales, and the data is therefore grouped into blocks of two thousand years. As only bipolar cores (which do not possess many of these attributes) and a single rotated core are found in the last 2,000 years, and no intact cores are found in sites before 12,000 BP, only the period 2,000-12,000 BP is plotted in Figures 7.4 and 7.5. The absence of cores before 12,000 BP is likely just an artefact of very small sample size.

Figure 7.5 indicates that as the mean number of core rotations increases, the weight, amount of cortex, and platform area all decrease, consistent with greater mass having been removed from the parent nodule. In contrast, the number of step and hinge terminations, platform quadrants, and platform angles all increase as the number of rotations increase.

Flake Reduction

Changes in flake characteristics over the sequence are shown in Figure 7.6 for a sample of 3,373 complete and unretouched flakes larger than 2cm in length. From this figure, it can be seen that the nature of flake production appears to change markedly in the last 4,000 years, with flakes becoming more pointed, longer relative to width and thickness, and lighter overall. Non-feather terminations also reduce in frequency, and platforms show more signs of preparation. As seen in Figure 7.4c, the majority of flakes also appear to derive from earlier stages of reduction in the last 3,000 years. Cores also become rare in the last 3,000 years (Table 7.1), suggesting that flakes produced during this time were not made on-site.

Table 7.1. Break down of core types found in each site per 1000 years.

Years Cal BP	Nimji Single Platform	Nimji Rotated Core	Nimji Bipolar Core	Garnawala 2 Single Platform	Garnawala 2 Rotated Core	Garnawala 2 Bipolar Core	Gordolya Bipolar	Total Single Platform	Total Rotated	Total Bipolar	Total
1,000					1			0	1	0	1
2,000						1		0	0	1	1
3,000		2						0	2	0	2
4,000		7			1		1	0	8	1	9
5,000								0	0	0	0
6,000		2		2	1			2	3	0	5
7,000		1						0	1	0	1
8,000	1	8	2					1	8	2	11
9,000	3	16						3	16	0	19
10,000	2	1			4			2	5	0	7
11,000				1				1	0	0	1
12,000								0	0	0	0
13,000								0	0	0	0
14,000								0	0	0	0
15,000								0	0	0	0
Total	6	37	2	3	7	1	1	9	44	4	57

Cores with many parallel flake scars and single or cortical platforms – in other words those identified in the previous chapter as the most likely source of lancet flakes – do not occur in the sample of cores found before 3,000 BP in rockshelters. They are however common at quarry sites, but these are likely to be younger than 3,000 BP (cf. Cundy 1990). The fact that lancet production was found to be somewhat 'wasteful' in the sense that these flakes are best produced early in the reduction sequence, have high failure rates, and cores are discarded when much of the original core mass still remains (yet also produce highly standardized flakes), might suggest high processing costs. This creates a situation where lancet production is likely to have taken place at quarries as a form of field processing, rather than transport cores to the central place for processing. The fact that lancet production appears almost never to have been undertaken away from quarries, and that many pre-processed lancet flakes of highly regular dimensions were selected for transport away from quarries suggests that mobility constraints were very high in the last 3,000 years. This point will be revisited later.

Figure 7.5. Changes in core morphology over time.

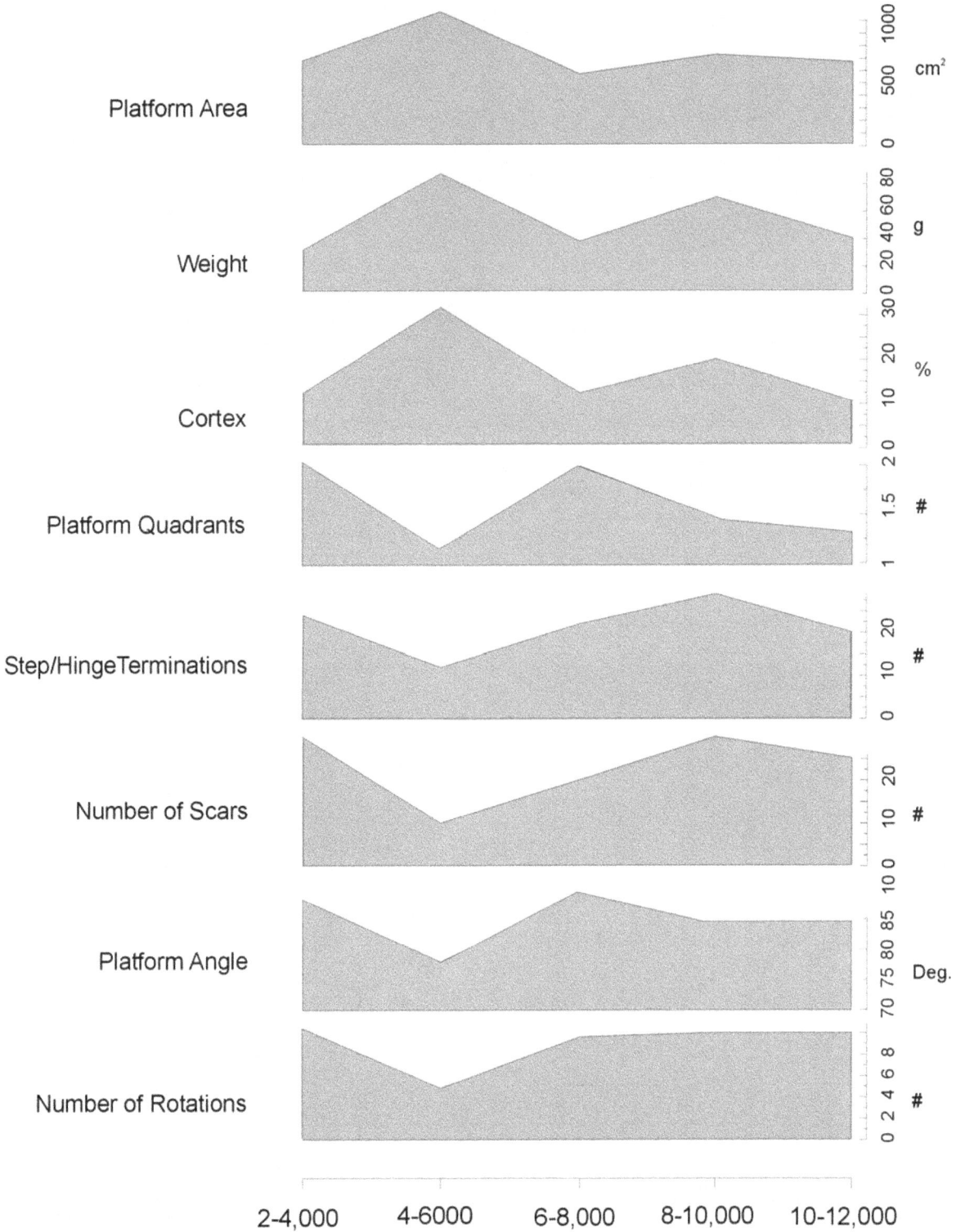

Figure 7.6. Changes in flake morphology over time.

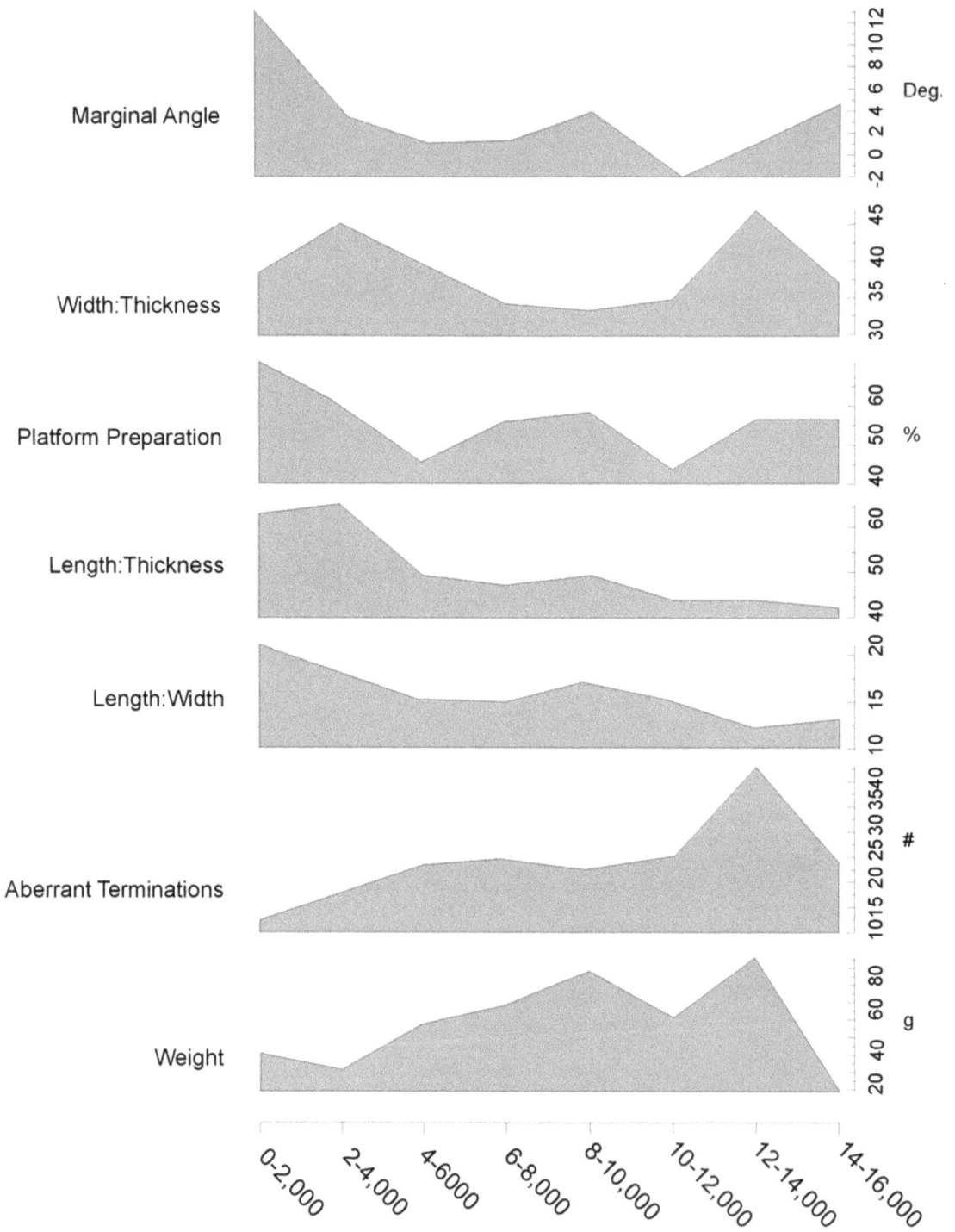

Retouched Flake Reduction

Changes in retouched flake reduction are also reflected in the frequency of implement types representative of different degrees of reduction. This can be seen in the last 3,000 years in changes in the frequency of various point forms shown in Figure 7.7. Bifacial points peak in frequency first at 2,000 BP, while unifacial points peak later at 1,500 BP. It is interesting to note that although lancets are commonly used as blanks for point manufacture, their peak comes later still. While this pattern of peak and decline may have many implications for functionality, style and transmission, it seems likely that it also represents a sliding up and down of the extendibility/reduction potential continuum through time, with an additional retouched face added to points early on that gives way gradually to the use of a single face, and then to little invasive retouch at all. As documented in Chapter 7, adding a second retouched face to points can add up to an additional 50% to reduction potential. Bifacial retouch also reaches its zenith by 2,000 BP, with bifacial points having a mean Index of Invasiveness of 0.8, which then drops back to 0.4 by 1,000 BP. Unifacial points also reach their highest mean Index of Invasiveness at 0.2 between 3,000 and 2,000 BP.

Figure 7.7. Temporal modes in the discard of various types of pointed flakes.

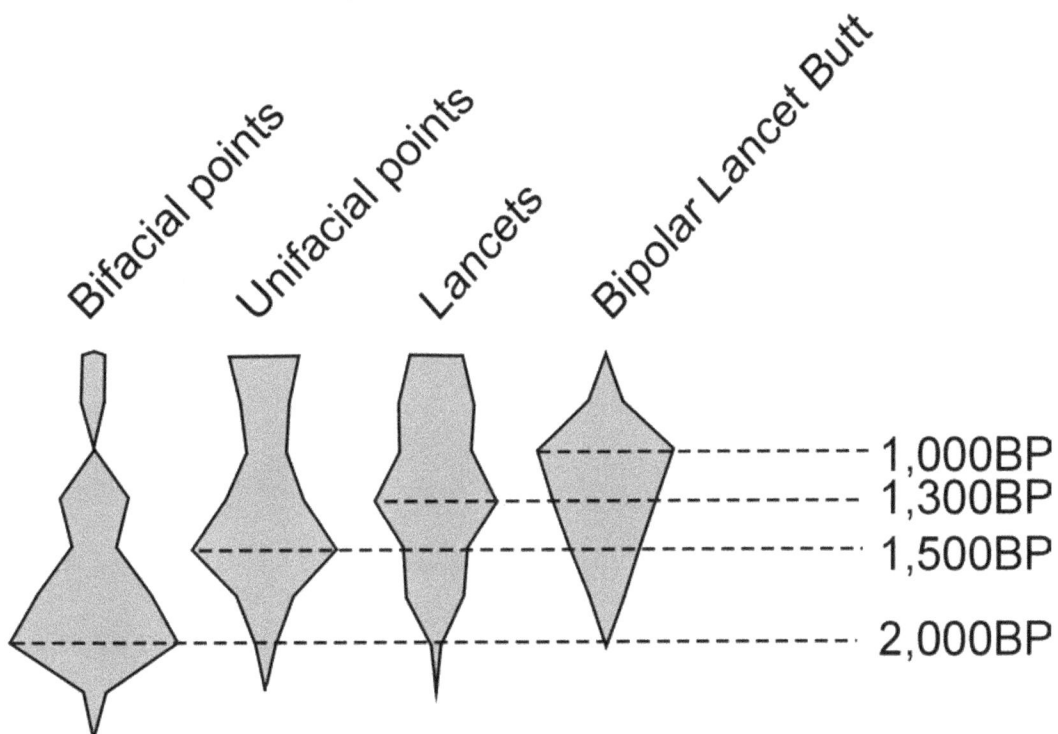

The review of theoretical models of tool design and technological investment presented in Chapter 2 identified higher levels of risk, greater focus on maintainability when access to replacement tools is limited, and the extension of use-life so as to recoup manufacture costs involved in producing more effective tools, as some of the likely reasons why shifts in reduction intensity like this might occur. The shift back from bifacial reduction toward less reduced (and reducible) forms is continued into later times, as unifacial points themselves wane and are replaced by a peak in unretouched lancet flake discard. As long, flat, pointed flakes, lancets are effective projectile points and require no additional retouch to serve in this role. Indeed, Davidson (1935) observed Wardaman people using unretouched lancets as spear points in the 1930s, and remarked that the use of bifacial points was unknown by this time and had clearly passed out of use since they were abundant in the eroding dripline and in lower levels of the rockshelters he visited and excavated.

Figure 7.8. Frequency of reduction sequences through time, as well as changing technological diversity for the region over time.

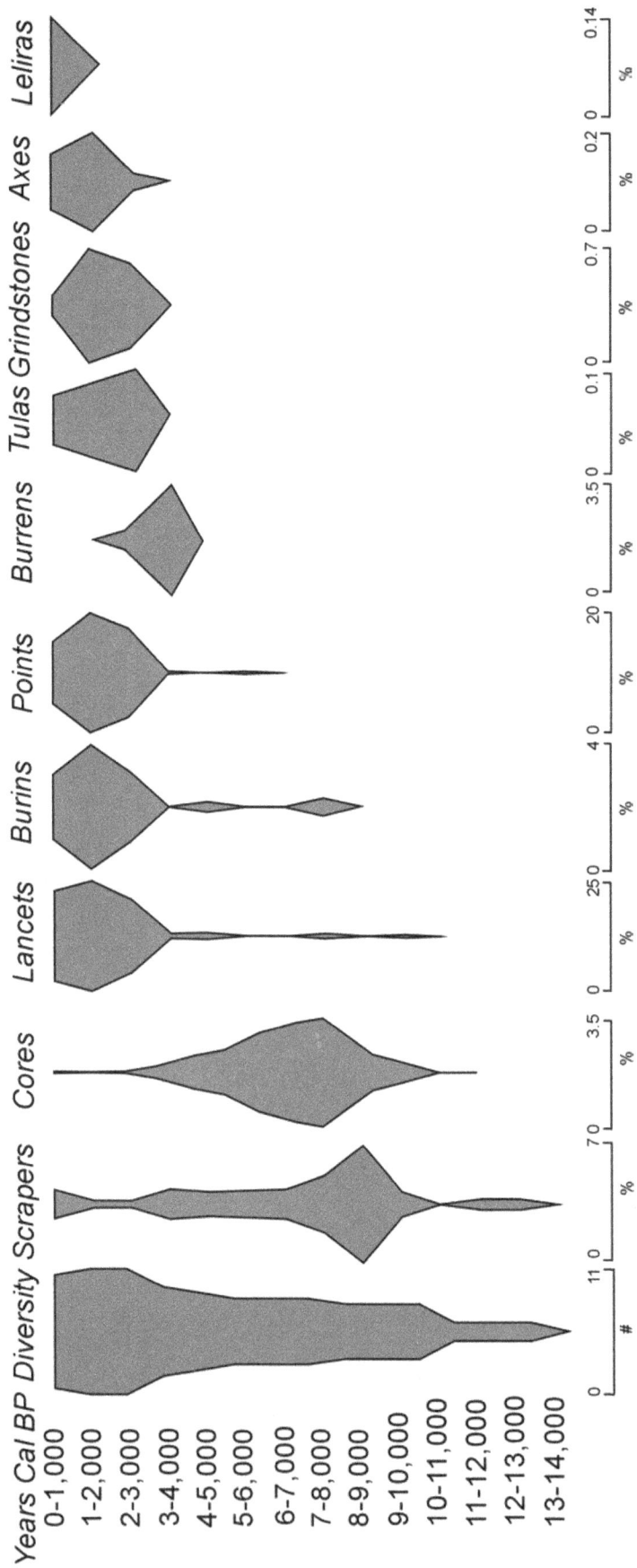

It therefore seems possible that the shift from predominantly bifacial to unifacial to unretouched points represents a move toward the use of a functionally equivalent form without the necessity for an extended use-life later in the sequence. The thinning of the proximal end of lancets using bipolar percussion in this late stage also suggests that this may have been an effective way of reducing basal thickness for hafting when extensive retouching of the margins and base was no longer practiced/required. In one sense then, there is good reason to believe that the progression of technologies seen in Figure 7.7 represents a series of functionally equivalent forms, where one of the design criteria – extendibility – gradually becomes obsolete over time. The significance of these changes for understanding land use and provisioning as well as for tracking heritable continuity is further discussed below.

Changes in the frequency of other heavily reduced types can also be seen, such as a peak in burrens - or heavily reduced scrapers - at around 3,657BP, just prior to the rise in frequency of points (Figure 7.8). This fits the pattern seen in reduction intensity for points, where extreme ends of the reduction spectrum peak and then slide quickly back toward less intensive reduction within 1,000 years or so of their greatest popularity. Tulas are also at their most reduced at around 3,000-2,500 BP with a mean elongation of 0.4. They then decrease in reduction intensity to a mean elongation of 0.6 by 1,500 BP. 'Slugs' too are most common between 2,500 and 2,000 BP. Burins also reach their most reduced stages after 3,000 BP. Most burins have between one and three spalls removed, but burins show a slightly greater number of spall removals between 2,000 and 3,000 BP, with cases of between 9 and 12 removals found at this time.

Also reflecting the decline in bifacial points after 2,000 years ago is the fact that 41% of spalls with old retouched margins on their dorsal ridges show unifacial invasive flaking only, whereas the 4% of spalls that preserve bifacially flaked edges are only found before 1,500 BP.

Changing Technological Diversity

Toolkit diversity was argued in Chapter 2 to provide a useful reflection of a number of features of past subsistence and technological systems. In particular, different levels of toolkit diversity were argued to be associated with limits on transportation and different kinds of mobility, and the level of task specificity and tool performance required of each technology.

Toolkit diversity cannot be measured directly, as it is impossible to differentiate 'tools' from 'non-tools' in archaeological assemblages without conducting use-wear and residue studies. However, it is possible to measure the level of diversity found in modes of implement production by counting the number of reduction sequences in existence in Wardaman Country at any one time (Table 7.2). Figure 7.8 maps the frequency of each of the major reduction sequences found in Wardaman Country over the last 15,000 years or so. The sequence of technologies is as follows. Unretouched and retouched flakes dominate assemblages when people first arrive in the region. Retouched flakes (scrapers) peak in frequency between 9,000 and 8,000 BP, and begin to decline in frequency as cores become a popular component in assemblages. Lancets and burinate retouch also appear in the early Holocene, though it is important to remember that a few lancets can be produced fortuitously from any core at early stages of reduction (e.g. Flenniken and White 1985), and their first appearance at this early time probably only reflects chance production. Burinate retouch on the other hand is a highly specific technique whose first appearance between 8,000 and 9,000 BP likely reflects a real technological change at this time.

Table 7.2. Numbers of artefacts over time grouped by reduction sequence and combined for all four rockshelters.

Years Cal BP	Technological Diversity	Total Number of Artefacts	Scrapers (including burrens)	Cores	Lancets	Burins	Points	Tulas	Grindstone Fragments	Axes and Axe Flakes	Leilira Blades
0-1,000	10	7604	122	3	318	28	294	3	2	13	17
1,000-2,000	11	12083	55	2	353	76	506	8	3	23	1
2,000-3,000	11	7223	29	4	218	45	312	16	4	4	
3,000-4,000	8	2249	40	9	3	1	2				
4,000-5,000	7	1451	20	15	2	4	1				
5,000-6,000	6	922	19	4	0	0					
6,000-7,000	6	1009	17	27	3	0					
7,000-8,000	6	6318	181	1	0	5					
8,000-9,000	5	977	65	33	0						
9,000-10,000	5	637	9	8	0						
10,000-11,000	5	768	0	5	1						
11,000-12,000	2	162	1								
12,000-13,000	2	169	1								
13,000-14,000	2	5									
14,000-15,000	1	45									

Points appear to have been manufactured in larger numbers in Wardaman Country after c. 3,000 BP, but make their first appearance in very low numbers at around 5,000 BP. Tulas, on the other hand, show a sudden introduction at c. 3,000 BP, but peak earlier than bifacial points at c.2,600 BP. They also decline in frequency soon after introduction, and are very rare within 1,500 years of their first appearance. Grindstones and edge ground axes both only appear in the last 3,000 years, and peak at 1,500 BP when discard rates are at their highest.

Although likely to be little more than an oversized, early-stage product of the lancet flake production system, 17 Leilira blades were found in the excavated deposits in levels inferred to be less than 1,000 years old, with only a single Leilira found before this time. This late date is in accordance with the usual occurrence of these large lancet flakes either on the surface or in the top few spits at most sites. Recent work at a rockshelter in close association with a massive quartzite quarry (Gindan) near Garnawala 2 has revealed that large numbers of Leilira blades were being produced at this quarry shortly after 330 BP (Clarkson 2001).

Shown at the left hand end of Figure 7.8 is a measure of changing technological diversity through time. Diversity can be seen to increase gradually between 14,000 and 4,000 years ago, increasing more dramatically after 3,000 BP, and then declining slightly in the last 1,000 years. This trend can probably be interpreted as a gradual shift from greater residential mobility (where few tools are employed) to logistical mobility through time (where many specialised tools are employed). This shift can probably be linked to increasing patchiness and a rise in mobile/clumped resources as rainfall became very variable between 3,500 and 2,000 years ago. Increasing the number of specialised tools in the toolkit would presumably have reduced time-stress and subsistence risk by increasing the chances of successful resource capture in more time-limited encounters with resources.

Rates of Implement Recycling

Another characteristic of retouched implements worth examining is the rate of implement transformation and recycling through time that might give an indication of changes in technological versatility and the use of situational gear. The importance of situational gear, particularly as a form of ensuring successful resource capture when replacement tools are unavailable, was outlined in Chapter 3, and a rise in frequency of use may point to an increase in time-limited foraging, and increased constraints on the transported supply. Figures 7.9a and b show the percentages of implement recycling found in sites through time, as indicated by the retouching of broken edges, and the scavenging of flakes, as indicated by retouch that is superimposed over older weathered surfaces. There is a clear increase in retouched implement scavenging at c. 4,000 BP and another before 8,000 BP (Figure 7.9b). No signs of the use of situational gear are found during the lower peak in artefact discard between 8,000 and 5,000 BP. This is consistent with the low intensity of flake, core and retouched flake reduction found in sites at this time, and suggests that situational gear only became important at times of greater subsistence stress associated with fluctuating climate and aridity, presumably as mobility, risk and time-limited foraging increased. The continued use of situational gear at around 1,500 BP suggests that although interannual variability may have lessened at this time, the subsistence system was still geared toward high mobility/high risk foraging.

Figure 7.9. Frequency of artefact reuse as a possible indicator of the use of situational gear. A: frequency of retouched broken edges, and B: reuse of flakes with old weathered surfaces.

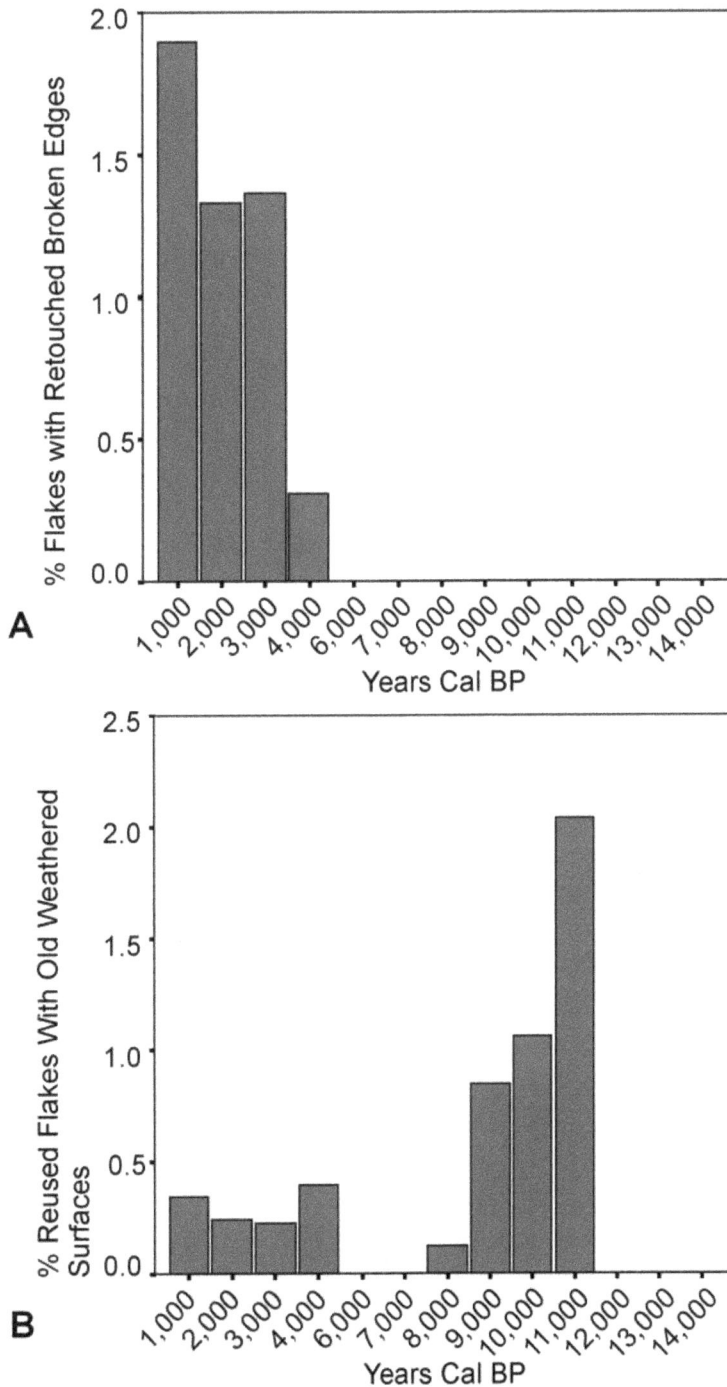

Changing Stone Procurement

Changes in the nature of stone procurement can be deduced from the types of raw materials used for stone artefact manufacture and the distances over which raw materials were transported.

Raw Material Richness and Patch Use

If raw material diversity reflects patch visitation, then changes in raw material richness (i.e. raw material diversity/sample size) should give an indication of the diversity of patches and stone sources visited, and hence of overall mobility and range of foraging. As seen in Figure 7.10, raw material richness is highest during periods of lower stone artefact discard, suggesting that mobility and patch visititation was also highest at this time. The same trend is noticeable at all three sites. The range of raw materials present therefore leads to speculation that people visited a greater range of patches while travelling to and from Nimji, Garnawala 2 and Gordolya during periods of low discard, indicating a higher level of either logistical or residential mobility at those times.

Raw Materials and Transport Distance

Changing procurement patterns can be explored by examining the changing proportions of local versus exotic stone over time. The data used for these tests is drawn from Nimji and Garnawala 2, rather than the entire combined sample of rockshelters, because the location of local raw materials is relatively well known for these two sites, but is less well known for Gordolya and Jagoliya. Stone types that cannot be reliably provenanced were excluded from this analysis, and these include most varieties of chert (but all non-hydrothermal chert has an origin at least 29 km away). The results are shown in Figure 7.11 for Nimji and Garnawala 2. Following initially high proportions of exotic stone, local stone dominates the assemblage from c. 9,000 BP until around 3,600 years ago, after which time there is a dramatic drop in frequency, and local stone is replaced by a huge increase in the importation of exotic stone. This suggests that people were travelling over much greater distances in the last 3,600 years.

Raw Material Quality

It is difficult to assess raw material quality, and no quantitative measures of fracture quality, toughness or brittleness have been obtained for the region's materials, but in terms of texture, homogeneity and outcrop size, the exotic raw materials brought to Nimji and Garnawala 2 tend to be the highest quality materials found in the region (apart from local Antrim Plateau Quartzite which is also of extremely high quality). This suggests that people may have preferentially selected high quality raw materials for transport while foraging in distant patches. This does not mean that raw materials do not reflect patch useage, only that patch use and toolkit diversity might be out of phase if poorer quality materials are cleared from the toolkit whenever higher quality ones are encountered. In a manner similar to prey choice models, foragers likely procure higher quality materials whenever they are encountered, and retain, conserve and transport these in prereference to lower quality ones. If raw material procurement was embedded, then foragers must have been more mobile to have encountered these distant, higher quality raw materials so often. If procurement was organised into specialised visits to quarries, the pattern likely indicates greater investment in long-distance journeys to procure higher quality materials.

Figure 7.10. Changes in raw material richness over time superimposed over changes in pooled artefact discard for all four sites. A: Nimji, B: Garnawala 2, and C: Gordolya.

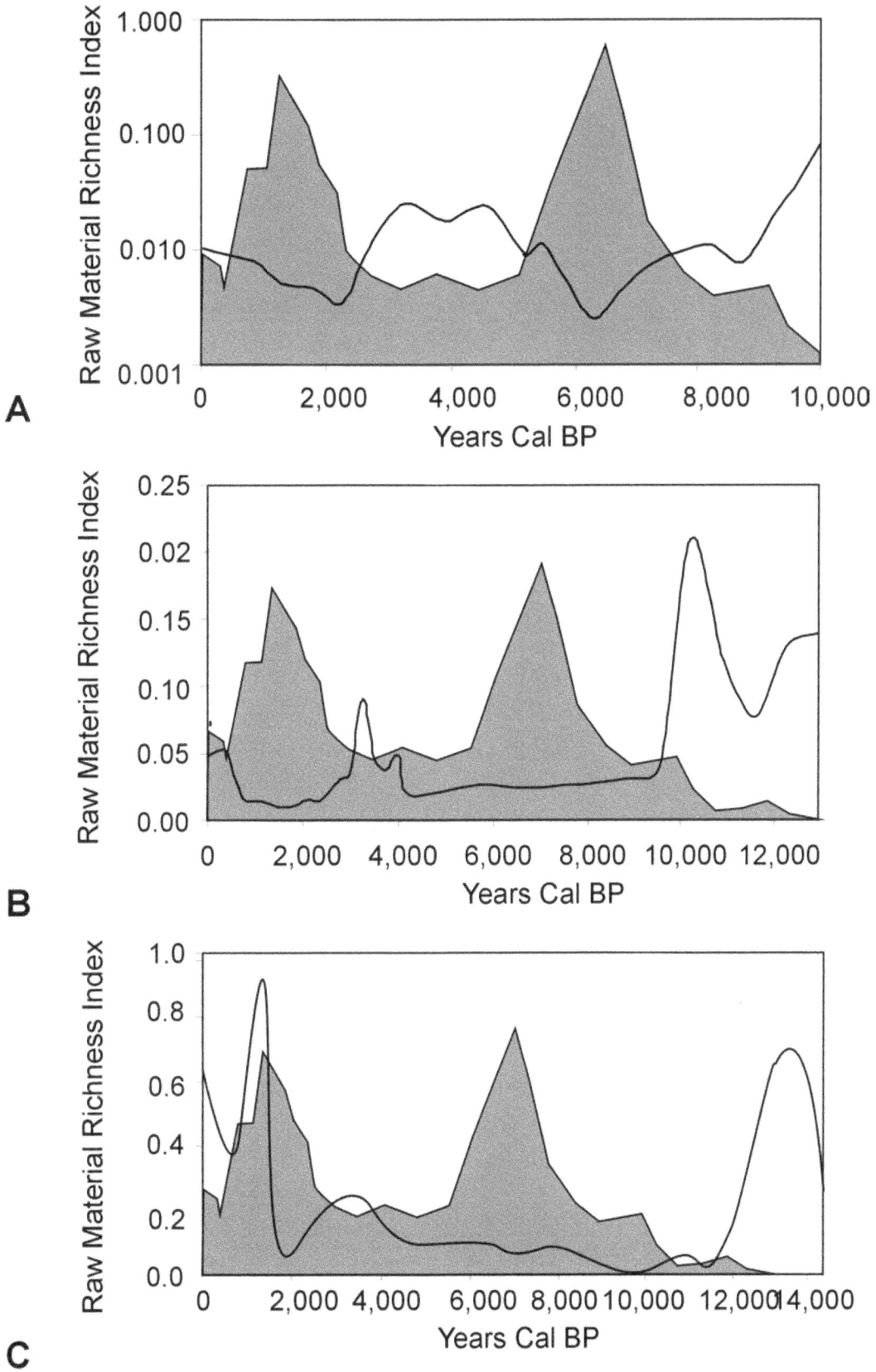

Figure 7.11. Changes in the proportions of local versus exotic raw materials. A: Nimji, and B: Garnawala 2

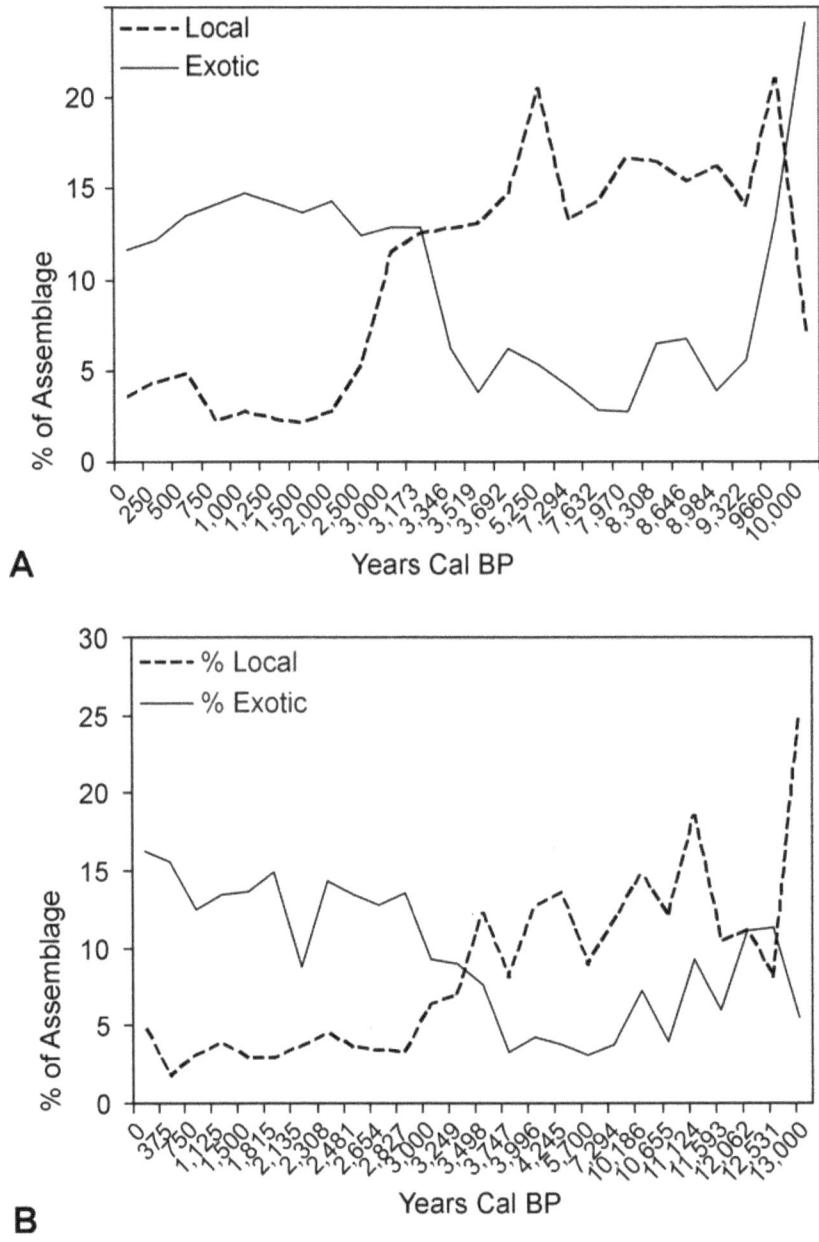

A

B

Figure 7.12. Changes in the size and abundance of cores transported over varying distances to Nimji. A: number of cores, and B: mean weight of cores.

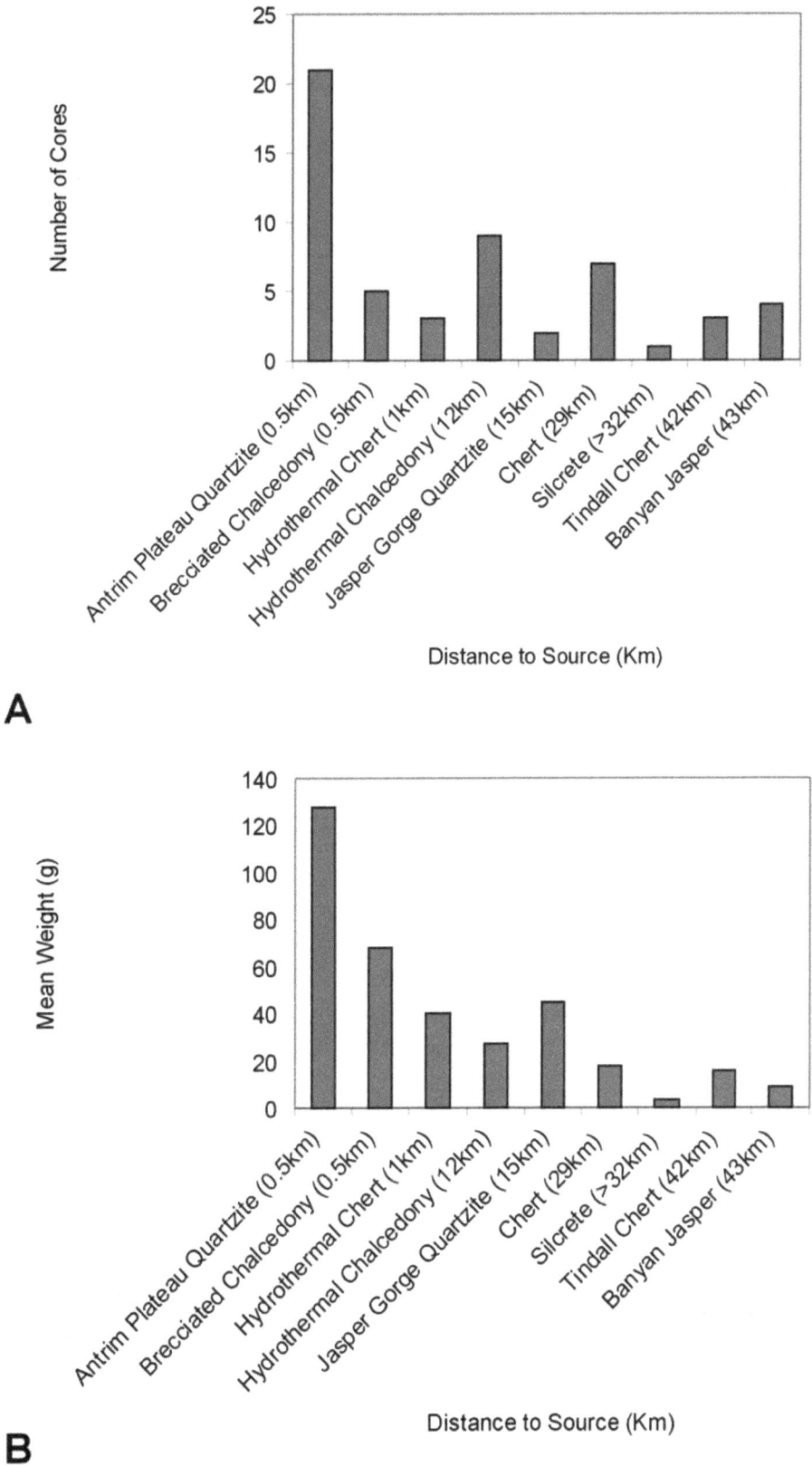

A

B

Figure 7.13. Evidence of continuity in stone artefact manufacturing technologies over the last 14,000 years.

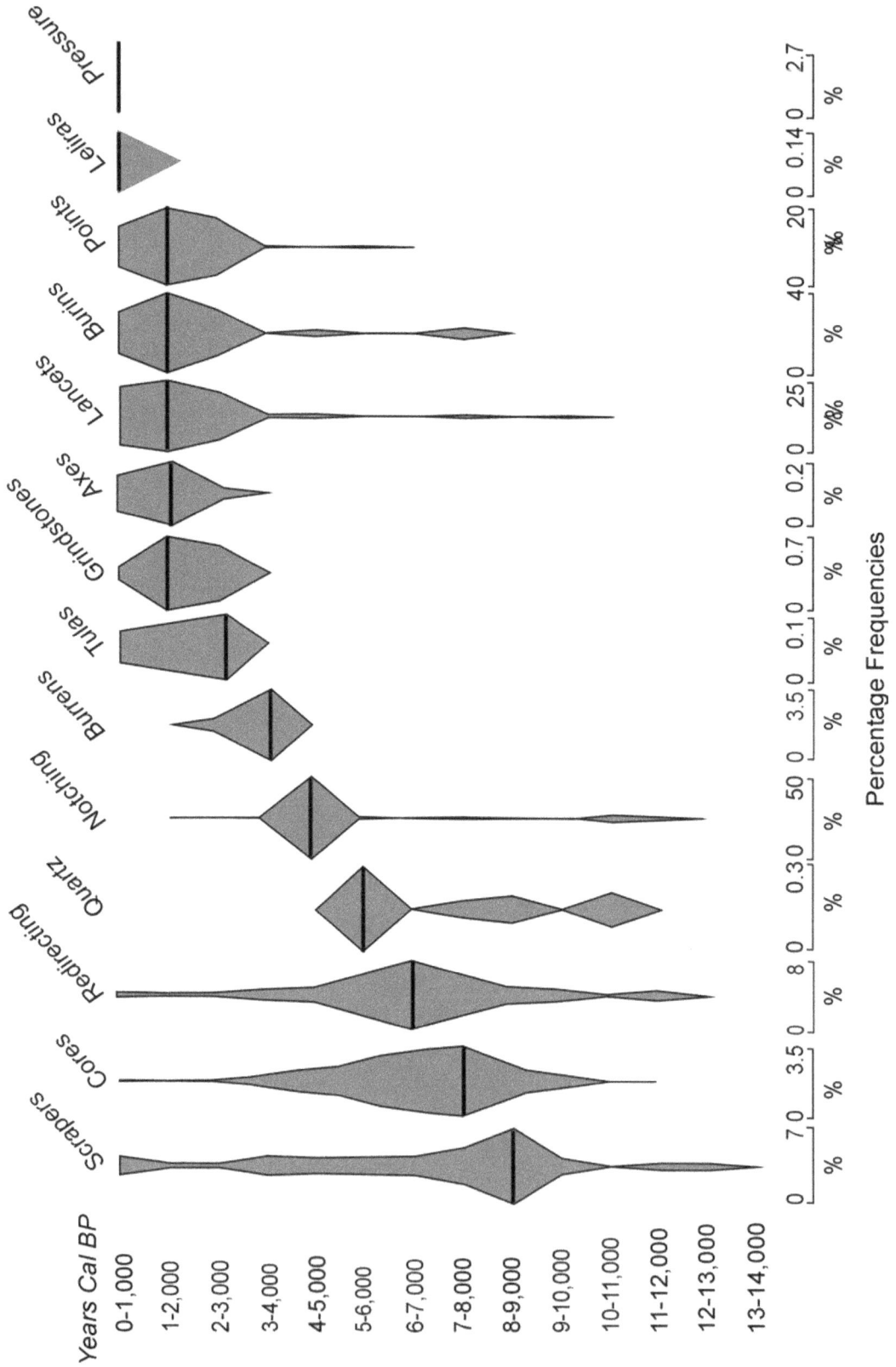

Field Processing and Distance Decay

It was argued in Chapter 2 that the transport of materials to a central place may be optimized through pre-processing of materials at the source to reduce transport costs, and that this might be detected archaeologically by certain distance-decay relationships in raw material size and weight. Essentially, the field processing model predicts that the further cores are to be transported to the place of reduction, the more superfluous mass should be removed from them before transport to increase utility:weight ratios. Figure 7.12 plots the mean weight and number of cores brought to Nimji from sources at differing distances to the shelter. Only data from Nimji is used here as Nimji has the largest sample of cores. The results show a strong distance decay relationship in the weight of transported cores (Figure 7.12b), but a weaker relationship for the number of transported cores (Figure 7.12a). The weaker relationship between distance and core numbers can be understood in relation to the argument made previously about preferential retention and transport of higher quality raw materials. Chalcedony, chert and jasper are all extremely high quality materials and cores made from these materials are proportionally more abundant than would be expected for a simple distance decay curve. The weight of cores transported, however, is strongly patterned by distance and hence likely reflects decisions about how much mass to remove from cores before tranport as well as how long they have been in the use/transport system.

Continuity in Stone Artefact Manufacture

So far this monograph has examined patterning in the manufacture, transport, and discard of stone as an indicator of the constraints and opportunities placed on foraging by local and long-term ecological variables. Another important issue centres on whether there is evidence for continuity in the transmission of cultural information over time, or in this case, in the ways of manufacturing stone artefacts to meet various needs. By examining the frequency distributions of major stone artefact manufacturing techniques and other more minor techniques (such as notching, serrated pressure retouch), as well as the use of distinctive raw materials over time, it is possible to determine whether overlap exists in manufacturing traditions that might point to continuous transmission of manufacturing practices over time. If overlap does not exist in the technological traditions found in the region, and major discontinuities in manufacturing traditions are evident, then there may be grounds on which to argue for breaks in transmission – perhaps as a result of demographic change (such as migration and population replacement), or overwhelming cultural replacement. It has been routine in archaeology since the 1930s to test for continuity in social transmission by searching for lenticular frequency distributions over time in cultural phenomena (i.e. battleship curves), and the theoretical basis for this approach has recently been reasserted by evolutionary archaeologists (Bentley and Shennan 2003; Neiman 1995 and many others)

Figure 7.13 displays the frequency of manufacturing techniques, sequences and distinctive raw materials found in the Wardaman sites over the last 14,000 years. There is clearly a great deal of overlap in the occurrence of these technological features through time, and all display unimodal, lenticular distributions. The apparent overlap in time between technologies suggests that there is no major break in cultural transmission in this region, despite waxing and waning in the frequency with which each component is represented through time. Of course, changes in the frequency of reduction sequences may track a combination of different traits (i.e. both functional and stylistic), and it is difficult to extend the same interpretive argument that might follow from seeing such a pattern in, say, decorative pottery motifs, to retouched implement forms. However, as the rise in frequency in many retouched implement forms at 3,000 BP takes place without a major break in the manner of retouched implement production (i.e. scraper reduction sequences after 3,000 BP appear to be identical to those before 3,000 BP), and since the changes in core and flake form and abundance can be seen as alterations to rates of core transport and reduction, technological changes appear to have taken place within a framework of continuous transmission and without any evidence of a dramatic break from what came before.

Standardization in Production Systems

To explore whether the observed changes in technology are also accompanied by changing levels of variation in the production process, changes in central tendency and variation are plotted for key indicators of retouched implement shape, size and retouch type over time in Figures 7.14 to 7.16. These traits are selected as they were hypothesized in Chapter 2 to be features that might be modified as elements of designs that seek to increase utility, and might therefore be expected to be heavily modified in certain contexts. Shape, for instance, was reasoned to strongly dictate the functional efficiency of a tool and its suitability for hafting, size to affect portability and hafting, and retouch type to effect extendibility and artefact use-life.

Shape. Figure 7.14 plots central tendency and variation for marginal angle, length:width, width:thickness and length:thickness. Only the last 10,000 years are plotted as sample size becomes too small before this time (n = 8). It is clear from these graphs that the distinctive upward trend in mean values in the last 3,000 years is accompanied by a marked decrease in variation, as indicated by the standard error of the mean. Furthermore, central tendency tends to move up and down in a pattern that is suggestive of stochastic variation prior to 3,000 BP, but holds a steadier trajectory after this time. These combined features of mode shift, variation reduction and random versus directional mode shift point to strong pressures to standardize aspects of lithic production and tool design.

Size. Variation and central tendency for the size of implements can also be examined by plotting the mean and standard error for a number of implement dimensions. Figure 7.15 plots changes in the mean and standard error for proximal width, thickness, distal width and weight. These graphs reveal an overall decline in both central tendency and variation over the sequence. Like those for shape, these graphs also show greater fluctuation in mean values prior to the last 3,000 years, with more steady and directional changes thereafter.

Retouch Type. Changes in central tendency and variation in retouch type can be assessed by use of the scar invasiveness index which examines the invasiveness of retouch scars when the effects of perimeter of retouch are removed from the equation. This index measures the tendency for retouch scars to run across the face of the artefacts toward the mid-line. Figure 7.16a plots mean and standard error for scar invasiveness over the occupational sequence. There is a marked trend toward increasing invasiveness through time, and a reduction in variation toward the end of the sequence. Another measure of change in retouch technology is the frequency of bifacial retouching. Bifacial retouching was argued in Chapter 2 to provide a solution to the problem of accruing step terminations on the margins of flakes that inhibit reduction and shorten the use-life of tools. Figure 7.16b plots the central tendency as well as standard error for the number of bifacially retouched segments found on retouched flakes out of a total of 16 possible segments. Not only does the mean number of bifacially retouched segments increase over time, but variation also reduces in the last 3,000 years. While these trends do of course reflect the manufacture of bifacial points in large numbers after 3,000 BP, many other retouched implements also possess bifacial retouch, and it is therefore not the case that points alone drive changes in retouch type. Indeed, bifacial flaking appears with increasing frequency from a very early date, and therefore is not only associated with points.

The results presented here suggest a trend toward reduced variation through time, which is what would be expected if the tendency were to standardize technologies and design features in periods of increased risk and resource depression. What does not appear to be in evidence, at least in terms of the attributes examined here, is an increase in variation immediately preceding the appearance of new implement types around 5,000 years ago of the kind Fitzhugh (2001) argues should occur as innovation increases in relation to heightened risk. This suggests either that periods of technological innovation were perhaps too rapid to be detectable in archaeological assemblages, or that that they did not take place in this case. Another possibility is that innovation is best represented by the sudden increase in implement diversity at 3,000 BP. These arguments are further discussed in the final chapter.

Figure 7.14. Changes in mean and standard error for four measures of retouched implement shape.

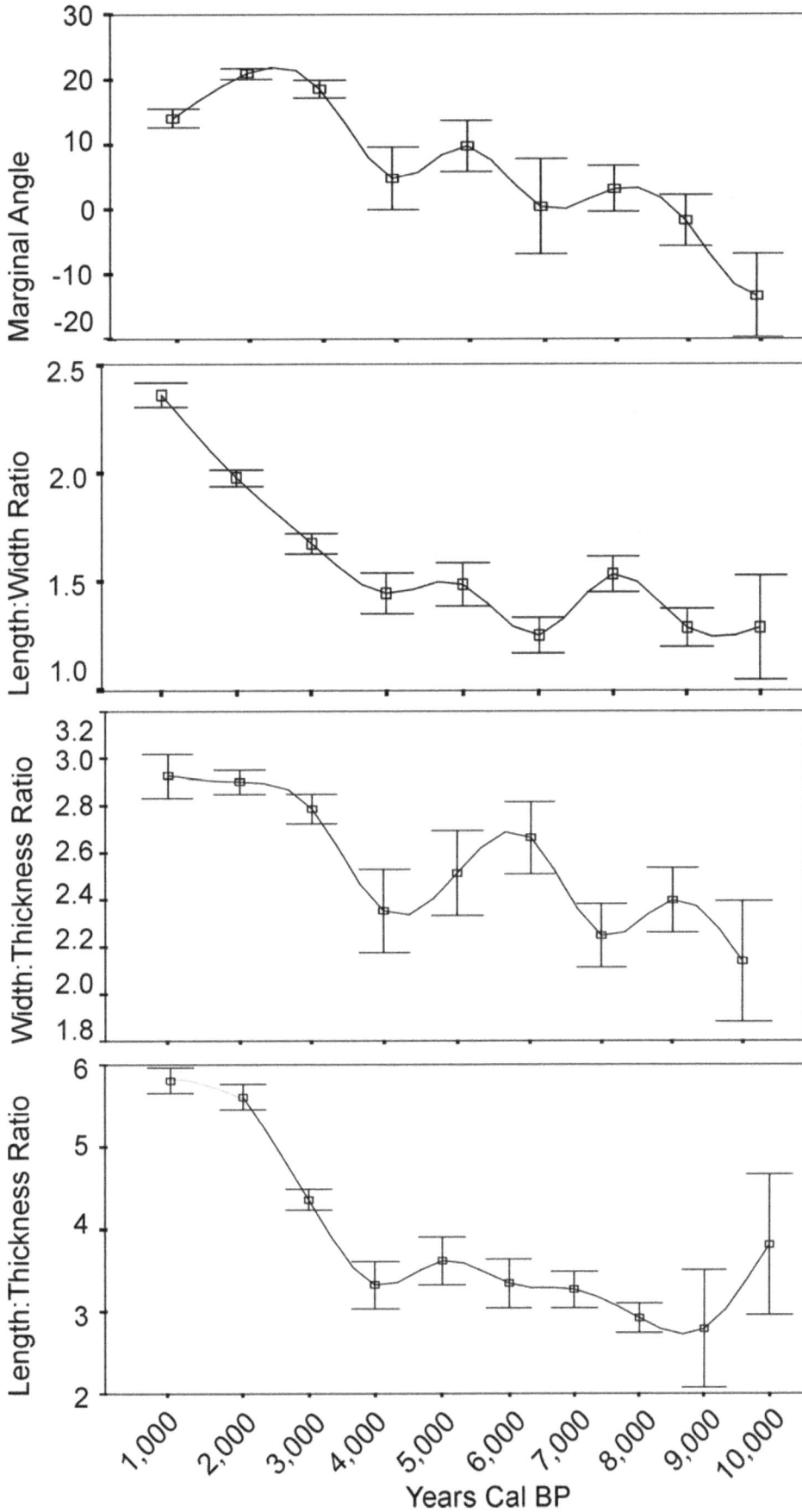

Figure 7.15. Changes in mean and standard error for several measures of retouched implement size.

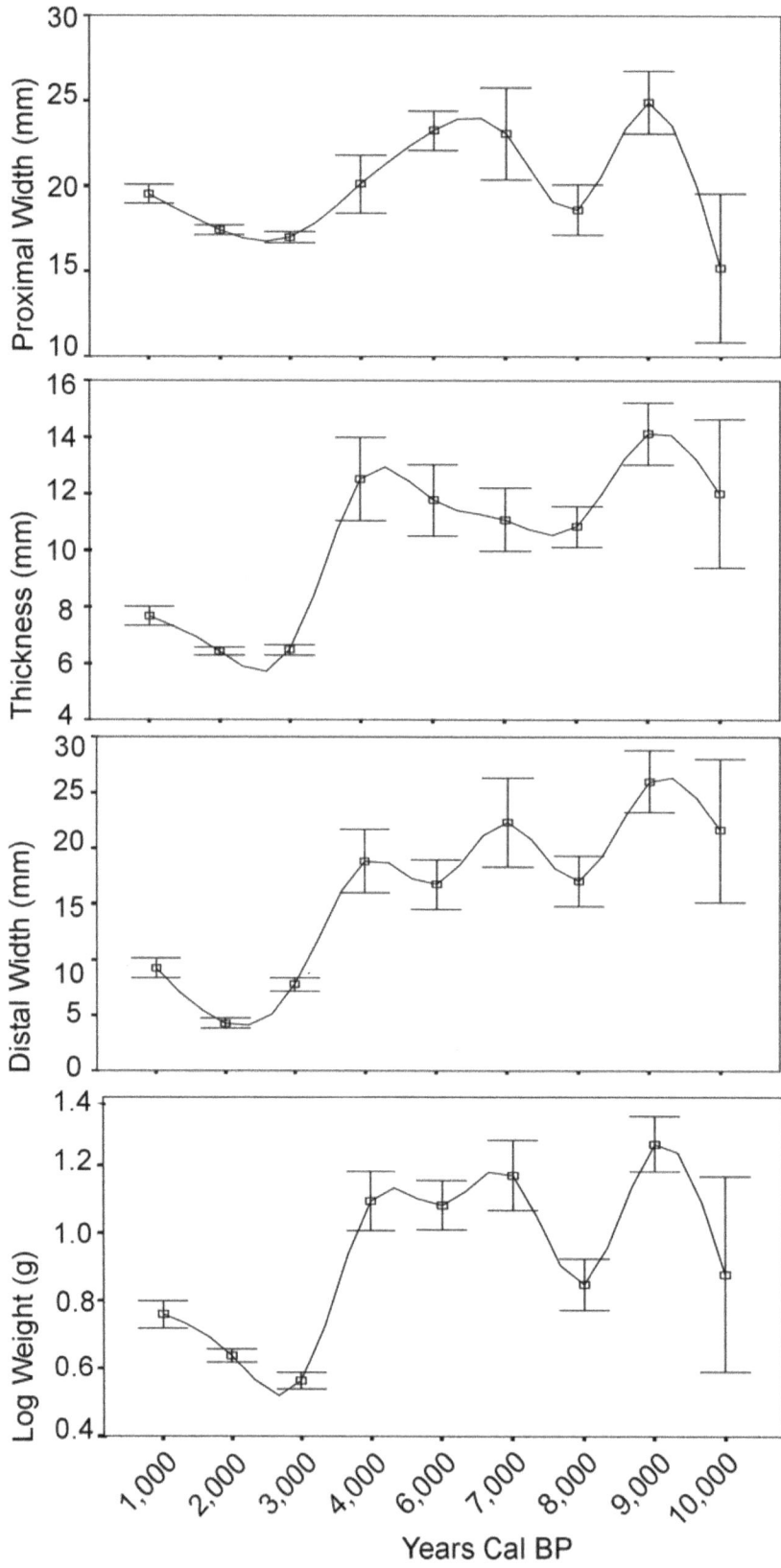

Figure 7.16. Changes in mean and standard error for two measures of flake retouching. A: the Index of Invasiveness, and B: the number of bifacially retouched segments.

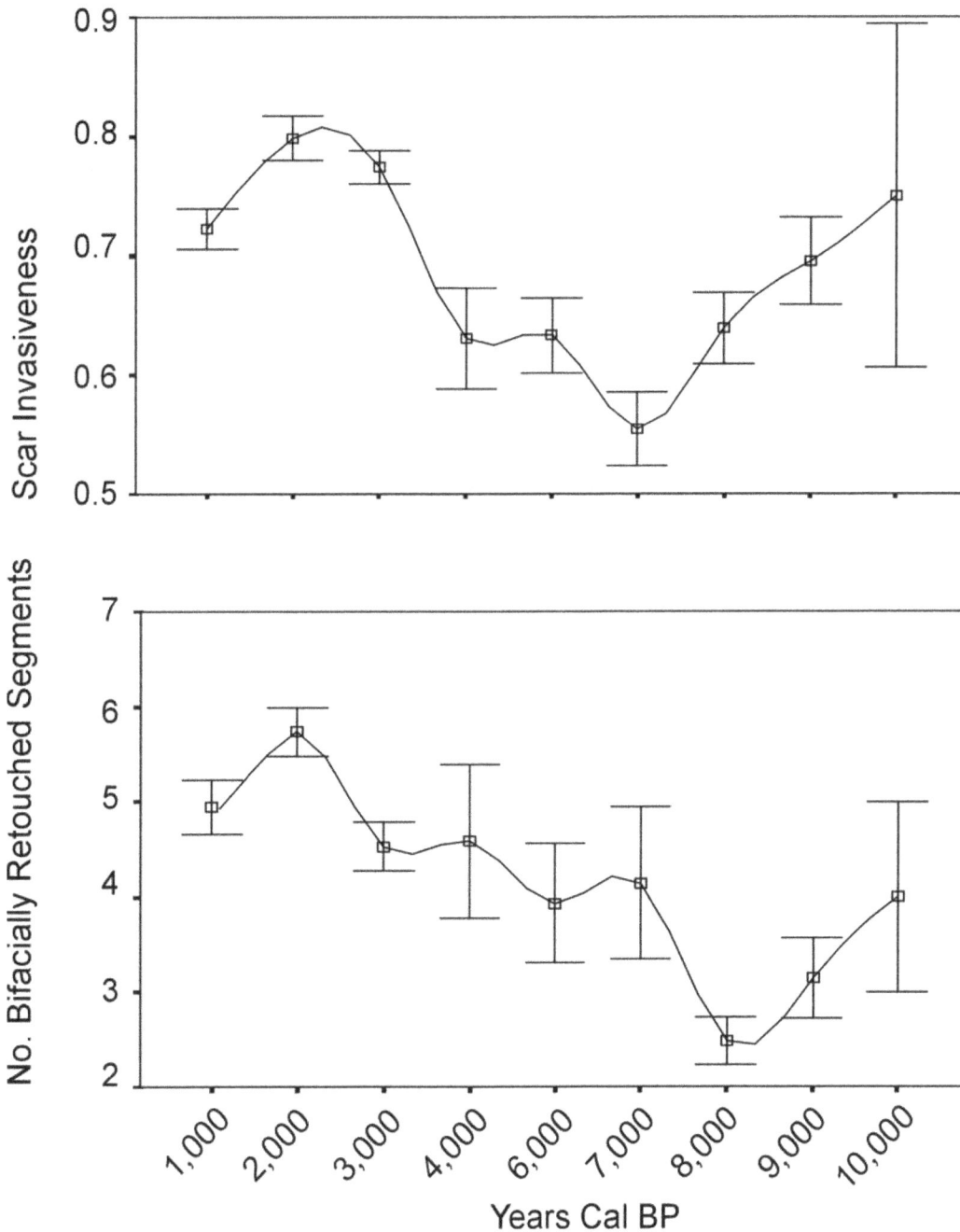

Technological Change, Toolkit Design and Provisioning

The analyses presented in this chapter have revealed major changes in technology that likely correspond to a complete shift in the way technologies were organised, toolkits were designed and raw materials were provisioned over the last 15,000 years. These changes will be interpreted in broader socio-economic terms in the next chapter, however, it is useful to conclude this analysis by briefly summarizing temporal changes into a coherent model of changing subsistence, mobility and land use and to review how closely the results match the predictions made in Chapter 3 about the effects of climate change on demography, subsistence and technology.

15,000 to 8,000 BP

The first signs of human occupation of the region appear at around 15,000 BP with very small numbers of stone artefacts and a wide range of raw materials. Flakes and retouched flakes are the only technological categories found at this time, but this is almost certainly a factor of low sample size. By 12,000 BP, numbers of stone artefacts had more than doubled, small heavily rotated cores were becoming a significant feature of assemblages, and reduction intensity was on the increase. By 10,000 years ago, stone artefact numbers were still increasing and reduction intensity had reached very high levels. Raw material richness remained high, and scavenged and recycled artefacts were in common use. By 8,000 years ago, retouched flakes (scrapers) have reached their peak, retouch intensity is very high, and new forms of artefact transformation appear with the first signs of burinate retouch at this time.

The progression of technological changes over this initial period of occupation from 15,000 to 8,000 BP seems to indicate increasing concern for the extension of artefact use-life, with cores, flakes and retouched implements all taken to later stages of reduction. Raw material richness, as a proxy measure of patch visitation, and the frequency of exotic raw materials, as a measure of foraging range, both indicate high mobility and long-range foraging over this period. Technological diversity, however, remains quite low at this time, suggesting that few if any specialised implements were being manufactured or transported. The signature for this early period therefore appears to be one of mostly individual provisioning, but with both small cores and retouched flakes forming a strong component of the transported toolkit. The transport of cores would have increased technological flexibility by allowing fresh flakes to be created from cores on demand. Transporting a supply of raw materials would also have lessened the need to extend the use-life of retouched implements beyond a certain point, and the exclusive use of relatively short use-life implements at this time (i.e. scrapers) is understandable as a low-investment/low-use-life strategy aimed at maximising toolkit flexibility at the expense of toolkit diversity and efficiency. This combination of design features as well as indications of high-frequency, relatively long-range mobility is what would be expected of a highly residentially mobile system of land use, where resources tend to be stable and evenly spaced rather than mobile and clumped.

8,000 to 5,000 BP

An apparent major reversal in trends takes place between 8,000 and 5,000 BP. This coincides with a major peak in stone artefact deposition which is argued to reflect an increase in occupational intensity. Reduction intensity decreases in cores, flakes and retouched flakes at this time, as does the proportion of exotic raw materials and raw material richness. The proportion of larger, more lightly reduced cores in the assemblage also increases, and the proportions of retouched flakes declines. The combination of factors points to reduced range and frequency of mobility, an increase in stockpiling of sites with raw materials from local sources as well as a reduced range of distant sources, and a discontinuation of artefact scavenging and recycling. The signature is clearly one of place provisioning – a strategy that is most suited to more regular movements within the landscape where the types and frequency of subsistence opportunities can be predicted. In the context of greater predictability of use and lower residential mobility, the peak in occupational intensity also suggests an increase in people visiting the shelters, more frequent visitation, longer visitations, or an overall increase in population density such that all forms of site use are intensified. Climatic data for this period indicate a time of increased rainfall and reduced interannual variability. Phytolith analyses undertaken using sediments from these sites also point to a wet phase at this time (Clarkson and Bowdery 2005; Clarkson and Wallis 2003). These are exactly the sorts of conditions under which we should expect population growth to take place and technological strategies to emerge that take advantage of higher resource abundance and more predictable availability of food and raw materials.

5,000 to 1,500 BP

After 5,000 BP there is a change in technology back toward the higher levels of reduction that existed in the initial period of occupation. However, the nature of technological strategies employed after

5,000 BP appears to differ from those employed earlier on. Standardised retouched implements begin to make their appearance from 5,000 BP, including unifacial points and late reduction stage scrapers (identified as burrens), and raw material richness and the proportion of high quality exotic stone increases once again. Cores too begin to drop out of the record and the size of artefacts begins to decrease markedly.

The rate of change intensified at 3,000 BP, including a marked increase in technological diversity, with up to five new reduction sequences appearing in the region, and a rapid increase in the recycling of artefacts. Reduction intensity and the extension of reduction potential also peaks between 2,000 and 3,000 BP, with the most reduced stages of many retouched implement forms (i.e. bifacial points, tulas and burins) and the end points in core reduction (i.e. bipolar cores) peaking at this time, and then declining soon after. Edge ground axes, arguably the most extendable and most costly implements to produce, also make their first appearance at this time. The rise in diversity represents a far greater investment in technology in terms of time and labour that can only have been recouped through the extension of artefact use-lives. The greater attention to design and standardisation of form at this time was no doubt targeted at increasing the efficiency of tools in performing particular tasks and may also have aided in reducing the risk of subsistence failure by increasing capture rates for mobile prey (as in the case of points), reducing handling times (as in grindstones and tulas), while also building in an element of flexibility through the transformation and recycling of tool-bits to guard against potential technological shortfall (in the case of burination and the reworking of broken artefacts).

Hafting was almost certainly a key element in technological change after 5,000 BP, as seen in the diminution of implement forms, and an increased concern for standardising the proximal dimensions of flakes. Standardisation and the use of invasive retouching and bifacial reduction over this period also likely improved the maintainability of tools, by allowing the use of interchangeable forms within costly, pre-designed hafts, and by ensuring that problems in implement geometry (such as steep edge angles and the accumulation of step and hinge terminations) could be overcome through careful invasive flaking across the surfaces of implements.

The nature of technological change over the period from 5,000 to 1,500 BP can be characterised as a shift from place provisioning toward an extreme form of individual provisioning, where very little besides small, standardised, and highly retouched implements were transported. Rates of diverse patch visitation were high, as was the long distance import of raw materials, implying mobility had greatly increased over this period. The increase in toolkit diversity, on the other hand, points to higher logistical rather than the earlier residential mobility. This implies that resources may have become more mobile/clumped after 5,000 BP, and that longer, dedicated foraging trips under increased time-limited circumstances were required after this time. The rise in risk reduction strategies after 5,000 BP, such as increased maintainability of toolkits, use of higher quality raw materials and increased diversity and increased effectiveness of tools points to a period of increased subsistence risk at this time. Climatic data indicate that interannual variability peaked between 3,500 to 2,000 BP. The change in technology toward pronounced individual provisioning points to the use of mechanisms that evolved to cope with decreased certainty over access to resources like food, water and stone, and increased logistical mobility to reconcile the differences between the location of people and fluctuating resources. Interestingly, Fitzhugh (2001) predicts that foragers facing less than minimum subsistence returns are more likely to focus efforts on improving technologies that enhance capture rate of larger, high-ranked prey, but as these are driven to decline, the focus should shift to hardier, and more reproductively stable r-selected species. The appearance of points after 5,000 BP, and around the time of intensified climatic variation, may represent an instance in which foragers attempted first to improve success rates in hunting larger, higher ranked game such as macropods, but were also led to improve handling times for more reliable, lower ranking resources like seeds (as represented by a later rise in the frequency of grindstones) once high ranked game became depleted.

Other forms of risk reduction are also hinted at. The origins of the new standardised retouched implement forms that appear around 5,000 years ago and which appear widely distributed across large parts of northern and central Australia has always been a source of speculation about inter-regional contacts. Since it is unlikely that these technologies were independently invented many times in various regions of northern Australia, it seems highly likely that the appearance of these new forms in Wardaman Country is a measure of social transmission between this and neighbouring regions that already possessed these technologies, such as Arnhem Land to the northeast where points appear to have been in use since before 6,000 years ago[1] (Hiscock 1993b; Jones and Johnson 1985; Kamminga and Allen 1973), and central Australia to the south where tulas seem to have their origins around 5,000 BP (Gould 1967; Law 2005). It is intriguing to consider why these new technologies might have begun appearing in Wardaman Country after this time, and why they did not appear in abundance until 2,000 to 3,000 years later. One possibility is that people inhabiting this region began to experience greater subsistence risk after 5,000 BP with the onset of ENSO-driven variability, and began to establish forms of social storage through risk reduction reciprocity with neighbouring groups. Such social networks brought the inhabitants of Wardaman Country into contact with new technologies that were successful in reducing risk. Their gradual appearance in Wardaman Country after 5,000 BP might therefore represent a gradual trickle of information across kinship and linguistic boundaries after this time. The fact that much of the rock art of Wardaman Country also bears close ties to the rock art of more northern regions (Attenbrow *et al.* 1995; Clarkson and David 1995; David *et al.* 1990; David *et al.* 1994) suggests that social ties to neighbouring regions, possibly begun as early as 5,000 BP, resulted in the transmission of a great deal of cultural information between regions over long periods.

Figure 7.17. Examples of pressure flaked points from Nimji dating to the last 1,000 years.

1,500 to 0 BP

The final phase of technological change takes place after 1,500 BP at which point a second peak in stone artefact discard occurred. This last period also witnessed a decline in reduction intensity as seen in the frequencies of highly reduced implement forms. Raw material richness and the proportion of exotic materials decreased, and therefore so presumably did the level of logistical mobility. The fact that most technologies persisted throughout this last period, however, suggests that changes back toward a system of lower mobility and increased abundance and predictability of resource availability after this time were likely to be minor in comparison with the complete system change that took place between 5 and 8,000 BP. This is understandable given that interannual variation in rainfall continued to the present day, and that despite a reduction in overall amplitude, oscillations are still capable of producing regular floods and droughts. Subsistence risk therefore likely remained high right up until

[1] Hiscock (1994b, 1996, 1999) argues that points arose earlier in Arnhem Land than in other regions because the sub-coastal plain was undergoing extremely rapid changes in salinity, hydrology and vegetation that were related to sea level rise. He argues that these changes created increased subsistence risks for hunter-gatherers occupying this region. These changes likely pre-date the onset of ENSO and may have given rise to an earlier emergence of new technologies there than in nearby regions.

the arrival of Europeans, and many of the technological and social strategies set in place after 5,000 BP for coping with risk, unpredictable resource abundance and increased mobility appear to have continued to some degree until historical times.

New technologies and implement forms, such as large Leilira blades and serrated pressure retouching, also appear in the last 1,000 years (Figure 7.17). Leilira blades are ethnographically known to have been traded over large areas (Allen 1997) and are dated in Wardaman Country to the last 330 years. The appearance of serrated pressure retouch in the last 1,000 years may also indicate inter-regional contacts with the Kimberley region at this time, as this technique is common (although in undated contexts) in that region but appears always to have been rare in Wardaman Country. Kimberley points are also a well-documented exchange item, traded over many hundreds of kilometres in the recent past. The emergence of both of these new systems of manufacture and exchange may signify ongoing, albeit altered, social networks for the purpose of (among other things) social storage and ensuring access to resources in bad times.

Conclusion

It is clear that major changes in stone artefact production and design took place over the last 15,000 years in Wardaman Country. The results point to major alterations in provisioning and land use that are probably closely tied to changing resource abundance, stability and structure over time. In the final chapter these observations will be drawn together to offer new insights into Wardaman Prehistory and socio-demographic changes in northern Australia more generally.

8. Wardaman Country in Broader Context: A New Look at North Australian Prehistory

Based on the preceding observations of changing lithic technology, land use and provisioning we can begin to formulate a new and perhaps more dynamic interpretation of cultural change in Wardaman County than those presented before. There may also be potential to discover similar trends in other sites across the 'Top End'. Following David's (2002) recent work on pre-understanding and ontology, it is probably appropriate to suggest that major changes in subsistence and ecology were accompanied by significant alterations to the way people conceived of places, themselves and others in the landscape. The final chapter of this monograph deals with all of these issues, and places the sequence of cultural changes in Wardaman Country into a broader north Australian context.

The Nature of Technological Change in Wardaman Country

An accurate description of technological change is essential to understanding the nature of cultural changes in Wardaman Country since stone artefacts form the bulk of the archaeological record and reflect important aspects of the daily life of past occupants. Much of this monograph has been dedicated to building an accurate picture of the nature of technological change in this region. Through detailed analyses of rockshelter assemblages I have revealed a huge number of technological changes in Wardaman Country, including changes to the number of reduction sequences present through time, changes to the nature of stone procurement from the use of predominantly local to predominantly exotic stone, fluctuations in reduction intensity which have in turn affected the typological composition of assemblages, and many changes in the design and organisation of the transported component of toolkits. These changes have never been adequately documented before in northern Australia, and hence our understanding of technological change has been seriously compromised by poor information about the nature of assemblage variability itself. The now vastly improved picture of technological change in Wardaman Country allows a completely new depiction of changing mobility and landuse in northern Australia over time, as summarised in following sections.

Another goal of this research has been to better understand the nature of the transition between earlier and later industries which were previously thought to be discrete periods lacking technological innovation and displaying few signs of continuity across the mid-Holocene industrial transition. Instead, a set of gradual and continuous technological changes has been identified, beginning with the first detectable sings of human habitation and continuing right up until the last stone artefacts were deposited in the early contact period. Although the pace of technological change undoubtedly accelerates between 5,000 and 3,000 years ago, continuous change is nevertheless apparent over the entire period of occupation. Continuous and overlapping changes in many aspects of the production system also appear to indicate unbroken cultural transmission (i.e continuous inter-generational ancestor-descendent relations) over the last 15,000 years, which underlie the significant changes taking place in the design and organisation of technology over this period. Such a signature, coupled with the complex regional distributional pattern of implement production systems in Australia, leaves no doubt in my mind as to the indigenous development of Australian Holocene technologies, as well as the high level of ingenuity and creativity which formed the basis for solutions to the increasing problems of interannual variability and aridity during the mid to late Holocene.

Models of technological change in Australia must therefore look to internal factors as a source of explanation rather than diffusion as migration of new technologies into Australia from elsewhere. Recent work on the genetics of Aboriginal Australians in relation to global populations supports the view of long-term isolation of Australia from the rest of the world, including Papua New Guinea, and reinforces the point that technologieal innovation in Australia is of indigenous origin (Hudjashor *et al*. 2007; Huoponen *et al*. 2001; Rayser *et al*. 2001).

Many of the technological changes documented in this monograph also appear consistent with the emergence of strategies that could be argued to have facilitated the capture and extraction of resources through better design and organisation of technology. In so doing, there are grounds to argue that technological changes were geared to the optimization of settlement and subsistence practices by pursuing the dual goals of utility increase and risk reduction. Evidence for such practices includes:

- use of a greater range of technologies geared to specific tasks during periods of heightened economic risk
- increased portability of toolkits during periods of high mobility magnitude
- greater field processing of stone during periods of high mobility magnitude
- greater standardisation of implement forms and increased reliability and efficiency during periods of economic risk
- the emergence of new ways of introducing flexibility into standardised tools as uncertainty over opportunities to reprovision with new tools increased
- lengthening artefact use-lives to recover the costs of greater technological investment during periods of high economic risk
- lengthening artefact use-lives to better ensure tool functionality in time-limited foraging during periods of greater uncertainty in resource availability
- increased use of high quality exotic stone to improve tool performance and reliability during periods of greater demands on tool performance

The sequence of technological changes documented in sites over the last 15,000 years therefore appears to indicate a gradual rise in the degree of investment in subsistence related technologies that increased utility (i.e. returns on energy expended) and reduced risk, with a big increase in technological investment and rates of technological change taking place between 5,000 and 3,000 years ago. That the optimality models used in this monograph appear to explain even some behaviour attests to their utility in anthropology and their ongoing importance in helping explain cultural change and assemblage variability in hunter-gatherer societies.

Kinds or Continuums?

North Australian prehistory is largely built on stone typologies, yet the relationships between various implement forms has remained poorly understood, as has the sequence of manufacture involved in their production and the changes in morphology they undergo throughout their use-lives. To help redress this situation, a number of reduction sequence models were constructed that demonstrated the connections between apparently distinctive implement forms, as well as various offshoots and points of convergence. Four distinctive reduction sequences were documented for retouched flakes which have effectively united tens of typological classes within a series of connected sequences. While this approach might seem to have unnecessarily reduced typological diversity, the goal was to arrive at an accurate description of changing technological diversity over time that is highly resistant to the effects of greater or lesser classificatory sub-division. By ranking individual specimens according to their place in a reduction sequence, it has become possible to explore changing intensity of reduction over time using continuous rather than categorical measurement systems.

It seems that much of the diversity in northern Australian assemblages can be explained by changes in reduction intensity. Implement diversity is highest in Wardaman assemblages between 4,000 and 2,000 years ago (Figure 7.8), reflecting the occurrence of late reduction stage classes such as bifacial points, bipolar cores, reversed and plain platformed tula slugs, burrens and dihedral burins, effectively doubling the range of implement types in common circulation before or after this period, but with no change in the number of reduction sequences in existence (i.e. changes in the diversity of reduction sequences largely took place prior to 4,000 BP). Nevertheless, there is undoubtedly an increase in technological diversity in this region through time, as well as real changes in manufacturing traditions and the organisation of technology, and not all changes in assemblage composition can be explained by mere fluctuations in reduction intensity.

The importance of an improved understanding of implement manufacture and reduction sequences therefore lies not in challenging existing typologies or reducing the number of types recognised in an assemblage, but in determining real rather than apparent changes in technological diversity over time, the place of each type in a continuum such that reduction intensity can be measured over space and time, and the overall length of reduction sequences such that extendibility and use-life can be quantified for each individual production strategy.

Documenting reduction sequences is a relatively new field of enquiry in Australian lithic studies, but it is possible to imagine many future applications for this type of analysis. These might include examining the growth of regional differences in production systems across space and time (e.g. scraper reduction that produces predominantly convex forms vs those that produce predominantly concave forms), comparing the effects of raw materials on reduction potential, examining changes in modes of use over the life of an artefact as its morphology changes, or even devising classifications with wide-ranging utility that are closely tied to the reduction process, rather than continuing to use dimensions of artefact variability that obscure those processes. These avenues of research are only just beginning to be explored, and future studies should be able to make broad-based comparisons of the cost-benefit trade-offs and similarities and differences in knapping technologies as these sequences become better understood for a number of regions.

Changing Land Use and Mobility

A major aim of this study was to identify patterned behaviour in the way sites are provisioned across the landscape, and how changes in resource structuring and abundance influenced technology as a reflection of changing land use over time.

Long-term changes in technology do indeed seem to reflect major alterations in mobility, forward planning and technological investment. These in turn appear to be closely tied to significant climatic changes, and by inference, changes in the abundance and structuring of resources over time. The regional sequence essentially appears to be one of reversals between periods of individual provisioning and place provisioning, but with a major shift in the degree of logistical mobility and subsistence risk over time.

The first inhabitants of the region appear to have begun moving into the area in low numbers after about 15,000 BP, at a time when major reversals between tropical and glacial conditions were taking place at millennial scales. These first occupants left few traces of their presence besides flakes and an occasional retouched implement. By the time a considerable signature of occupation had accumulated at around 12,000 BP, people seem to have adopted a highly mobile pattern of residential movement through the landscape. Subsistence risk appears either to have been fairly low – perhaps implying that interannual variation was quite low despite massive longer-term fluctuations in temperature and rainfall - or it was adequately kept in check by the nature of the settlement and subsistence system without need for major investment in technology. The technological strategy in place at this time appears to reflect low-investment in manufacture, with implements typically displaying short use-lives as new flakes could be easily obtained from the transported supply of small cores. This technological signature and low toolkit diversity points to resources having been fairly evenly distributed and stable over time, with high residential mobility the most effective form of land use.

Occupational intensity appears to have steadily increased with time, either as conditions improved toward the early to mid-Holocene optimum, or because people developed strategies to better exploit local resources during this period. In any case, there is a pronounced peak in occupational intensity between 8,000 and 5,000 years ago that likely reflects increased population size. At this time there is a marked reversal in technological trajectories, with a shift to the provisioning of places with large, lightly reduced cores, less reduction and recycling of artefacts, a decline in raw material diversity and less use of high quality, exotic raw materials. Improved rainfall and low interannual variability likely increased the abundance of resources and populations appear to have increased and adopted fairly sedentary lifestyles centred on the exploitation of more locally available resources.

After 5,000 BP, mobility appears to have increased again, and the technological system changed once more. This time a suite of new technologies made their appearance between 5,000 and 3,000 BP, often in low numbers to begin with, but vastly increasing in frequency after 3,000 BP. This change is argued to mark the onset of ENSO-driven interannual variability in rainfall, with reduced effective precipitation overall and the emergence of a regime of severe drought and flood that was revisited in quasi-cyclical fashion at frequent intervals. Resource abundance may have dropped at this time, but would certainly have fluctuated more severely than previously, and resources may also have become patchier as populations of plants and animals retreated to refuges or others were driven to local extinction. These conditions reached their greatest severity from 3,500 to 2,000 years ago. The technological response was a massive increase in investment in tool design, with increased technological diversity, standardisation, quality of materials and use-life. Retouched implements also became more portable and were likely hafted to increase effectiveness, perform certain functions and prevent loss. This new toolkit is indicative of an extreme form of individual provisioning, where toolkits are made to last and continue to perform for an unknown duration, with the potential for maintainability, rejuvenation and recycling if and when circumstances dictate. Such an extreme provisioning strategy, high toolkit diversity and frequent importation of exotic stone was likely associated with high logistical mobility, which is most effective for dealing with time-limited, mobile and/or clumped resources.

The last 1,500 years saw another peak in occupational intensity which appears to be correlated with a marked reduction in interannual rainfall variability. The provisioning system appears to have remained much the same, however, although maximising implement use-life appears not have been so important after this time. This suggests that resource access became somewhat more predictable and technological investment had also reduced, such that tools needn't function for quite so long.

Overall, the sequence of technological changes appears to be closely tied to climate change and resource abundance, but the nature of technological response was different in each period. This implies an historical component to technological change, in which the particular technologies that arose were at least partly dependent on what came before, as well as a functional component, whereby new technologies arose to meet particular needs, and their overall forms were constrained by subsistence requirements.

Thus climate, resource structure and subsistence strategy could have played a very strong role in shaping technologies in Wardaman Country over the past 15,000 years. The exact nature of those changes, however, is complex and historically contingent rather than simple and deterministic. A number of the particular technologies that rose to prominence in the last 3,000 years, for instance, are those that had already existed in the system for some time, but at low frequency. Later changes in technology seem to be an example of solving current problems using existing ways of doing things.

The resulting picture is one of constant and dynamic change, with populations, mobility, and degrees of future planning against anticipated risks all fluctuating significantly over the last 15,000 years. This stands in stark contrast to the picture painted in Chapter 1 of northern Australian technologies as composed of two clearly divided periods of typological stasis – one diverse and the other depauperate. There is probably much potential to identify such dynamic changes in other northern Australian sites, though insight will be limited so long as our evidence is constrained by currently published data. Future studies would do well to draw on older, well-dated sites to explore whether technological changes take place at these sites that may be indicative of alterations to provisioning, mobility, and resource structuring. Searching for evidence for continuities in manufacturing strategies that point to changes from within the pool of technological variants as well as transmission between regions will also be an important step in determining the origins and broader significance of technological change.

Wardaman Country in Regional Context

The ultimate value of regional studies of technology lies in their contribution to answering the 'big questions' in Australian archaeology. The final objective is therefore to consider how changes in one small region may reflect and inform on socio-demographic changes in Aboriginal society over a much larger area. This last question involves consideration of multiple lines of evidence, including archaeological, linguistic, skeletal, genetic and environmental data to build an interpretive model of Holocene changes in Aboriginal society. In this role, the study of stone artefact assemblages has the potential to contribute a vital and unique perspective on the past because they provide a tangible record of human behaviour intimately linked to the means by which people extracted a living from their environment. To address this question, four issues of significance for Australian prehistory are considered:

1. the degree to which the timing of first occupation of Wardaman Country fits with evidence for the re-occupation of large areas of Northern Australia after a prolonged hiatus spanning the Last Glacial Maximum,

2. the significance of demonstrated continuity and regionalisation of retouched implement distributions for models of linguistic diffusion and migration in Australia,

3. evidence for similar changes in technology and occupational intensity that may point to a broadly similar pattern of changes in Aboriginal society and environment over the last 15,000 years, and

4. the implications of changes in land use and technology for changes in Wardaman ontology and regional social relations.

Occupational Intensity and Re-Colonisation Around the LGM

The extrapolated dates for initial occupation of Wardaman Country fit reasonably well with other evidence for colonisation/reoccupation after the LGM of large areas of northern Australia at around 10,000 to 15,000 years ago. In Arnhem Land for instance, most sites located in large outliers on the flood plains have extrapolated basal ages of between 9,000 and 15,000 BP (e.g. Jimeri I, Ngarradj Warde Djobkeng, Jimeri II, Burial Cave, Angbangbang 1, Leichardt Site). The four exceptions to this trend are Malakananja II, Nauwalabila I, Nawamoyn and Malanagangerr which appear to have occupation spanning the LGM back to a maximum (OSL dated) age of around 50,000 to 60,000 BP (Jones and Johnson 1985; Morwood and Hobbs 1995b; but see O'Connell and Allen 2004). These last four sites are all situated in well-watered gorges where permanent water was probably available throughout the LGM. The west Kimberley sites (e.g. Mandu Mandu, Widgingarri Shelter 2, Koolan Shelter 2), on the other hand, predominantly show a long occupational hiatus spanning the LGM, with first signs of re-occupation at around 10,000 BP (Morwood and Hobbs 1995b; O'Connor et al. 1993). The exception in this region is Carpenter's Gap 1, where occupation appears to span the LGM despite a truncation of sediments in the late Pleistocene (O'Connor 1995). This site is located in the well-watered limestone of the King Leopold Ranges. Sites in Cape-York also show either occupational hiatuses over the LGM until around 15,000 BP or later (e.g. Sandy Creek 2, Magnificent Gallery, Mushroom Rock, and Early Man, Ngarrabulgan Cave), or else much reduced occupational intensities (e.g. Yam Camp and Sandy Creek 1) (David 2002; Morwood and Hobbs 1995b). Some sites located in sandstone gorges and limestone outcrops close to permanent water in this region show an increase in occupational intensity over this period, such as at Fern Cave (Lamb 1996). The same is true at Lawn Hill close to the Gulf of Carpentaria where occupation of caves in well-watered limestone gorges intensified over the LGM (Hiscock 1988).

Overall, hiatuses and changes in occupational intensity over the LGM indicate that large areas of northern Australia were either abandoned or left unoccupied until climatic amelioration and the onset of very tropical conditions at around 15,000 BP, while occupation tended to intensify over the LGM in well-watered gorges, karst limestone and uplands. Following initial post-LGM occupation, most sites appear to show continuous occupation throughout the Holocene, though fluctuations in occupational intensity are common. These results suggest that people were repopulating large tracts of land either from more habitable, now drowned, land on the Arafura shelf, or from refuges in the few places were reliable water sources existed throughout the LGM. Interestingly, no demographic expansion is registered in the genetics of Aboriginal Australians at any time except following initial occupation, and here it seems likely that recolonisation of landscapes after the LGM more likely involved population reconfigurations and gradual population growth than a large and sudden demographic expansion (Clarkson and Ricaut 2006). If ever there was a time to identify the movement of populations across large areas of northern Australia, however, then around 15,000 BP is it. Yet this is not the time at which retouched implements like points, burins, burrens and tulas make their first appearance in sites, and hence arguments for these implements accompanying a migration of people at around 5,000 BP seems unlikely, at least for this part of Australia. This leads to the second issue discussed here – heritable continuity and language spread.

Re-Occupation, Continuous Transmission and Linguistic Origins

Strong evidence for continuous transmission of stone artefact manufacturing traditions spanning the last 15,000 years was presented for Wardaman Country in Chapter 7. These results make the sudden appearance of new retouched technologies between 5,000 and 3,000 BP as a signal for the incursion of new populations or language speakers into the region at this time highly unlikely, especially in the light of the recent genetic evidence for long-term population isolation. Furthermore, it seems likely that some of the new retouched implements found in Wardaman Country in large numbers after 3,000 BP are indigenous to the region (such as lancets and burins), while some likely have a northern origin (i.e. points), and others a southern one (i.e. tulas). This situation points more toward medium to long-term social contacts between regions resulting in gradual diffusion of new technologies across large areas, than it does to regional populations being overrun by new arrivals or the spread of technological ideas and/or new languages out of a single homeland and in a single direction.

McConvell's (1990, 1996) and Evans and Jones's (Evans and Jones 1997) ideas of linguistic spread did not take account of the problem of widespread northern bifacial point technologies, except to make the link with northern non-Pama-Nyungan (NPN) languages that are supposedly older, *in situ* developments. Yet the appearance of bifacial points across a region of vast linguistic diversity and therefore supposed great antiquity in its current spatial configuration also requires explanation – particularly since this study offers some evidence of heritable continuity in one region over this period.

Unifacial points, found in both northern and southern Australia, are usually lumped together with the hypothesized outward spread of Pama-Nyungen (PN) languages with other new implement types (such as tulas and backed artefacts) at around 5,000 BP from a supposed homeland in the Gulf of Carpentaria and into most parts of southern Australia. The unity of this southern spread is supposedly confirmed by the homogeneity and ancestral connections between languages spoken across the southern two thirds of Australia. Yet this argument for southern homogeneity may not be entirely correct. The people of large areas of southeastern Australia were almost entirely decimated by disease before much linguistic information could be recorded for these areas (Butlin 1983). Little linguistic material exists for the Murray River corridor, for instance, a region containing the greatest diversity in skeletal populations known in Australia (Pardoe 1984, 1993), and hence it is surely difficult to appraise how diverse the languages of southern Australia were before contact. New linguistic evidence suggests that the southeast may in fact have been an area of very high linguistic diversity (Clendon 2006). The differences between northern and southern language groups is still not well understood, and there are at least some linguists who would argue that differences do not exist on a large enough scale to advocate migration and language replacement (e.g. Dixon 1997).

The real problem with current models of linguistic spread from a technological point of view, however, is that much of the variation in the spatial distribution of distinctive regional technologies is ignored, as pointed out in Chapter 1 and illustrated in Figure 1.3. For such a complex distribution to have emerged means either that the spread of individual stone implement manufacturing traditions is not coincident with the spread of languages in the mid-Holocene, and/or that a single spread did not take place. The technological evidence seems in favour of both of these explanations. The regionalized nature of technologies suggests that the advent of new standardized implement forms may represent a series of localized solutions to the problem of increased risk and climatic variability from the mid-Holocene on, with the later spread of these technologies perhaps resulting from transmission and information exchange between neighbouring groups. Social networks that facilitate the transfer of information, goods and genes have probably always existed to some degree between hunter-gatherer populations in Australia (Edwards and O'Connell 1995), but these may have strengthened and become more wide-reaching over the last 5,000 years. Increased unpredictability in resource abundance would have created a need for social storage as a form of risk reduction, creating alliances based on reciprocal access to resources in the territories of other groups during bad times.

Clendon (2006) makes the argument that a northern and southern language division may have existed since the separation of northern and southern populations by the broad expanse of an emptied central Australian arid zone during the LGM. The linguistic picture might therefore represent two *sprachbünde* of great antiquity rather than the results of phylogenetic spreading from proto-language ancestors. The linguistic division seen today might therefore represent the meeting of northern and southern populations repopulating the interior once climate ameliorated in the last 15,000 years (with some areas of central Australia probably not colonized until the mid-to-late Holocene – thereby accounting for pockets of extreme linguistic homogeneity) (Veth 1989).

The isolation of northern and southern populations in fact finds some support in non-linguistic evidence as well. Genetic studies of Australian mt-DNA suggests some deep divisions could exist within the Australian Aboriginal population (Huoponen *et al.* 2001; Ingman and Gyllensten 2003; van Holst Pellekaan *et al.* 1998), possibly running along north-south lines. Our own reanalyis of the mt-DNA data, however, points to more complex patterns of interaction and isolation (Clarkson and Ricault 2006). Pardoe's (1984, 1990) study of non-metric cranial traits also found a major division between northern and southern populations. Claims for a northern rock art province have also been mirrored in claims for a pervasive southern Panaramitee style. Layton (1997:384) proposed a similar model to Clendon's to explain such geographic divisions: "the simplest model might conceive of two refuge areas during the last Glacial, the southeast (home of geometric art) and the north coast (home of large silhouettes)."

Dixon (1997) has argued that such periods of punctuated language division as might result from separation of a northern and southern population over the LGM can be later smoothed over by long-periods of equilibrium, as might have occurred after recolonisation of previously abandoned areas and the continuous occupation of both north and south Australia since the terminal Pleistocene. Clendon sees widespread sharing of linguistic features since reoccupation as a likely explanation for widespread phonological and grammatical similarities in Australia, and also for a fuzzy band of overlap in linguistic features between northern NPN (or what he calls *Arafuran Languages*), and southern PN languages. The pattern of distribution seen in retouched technologies could therefore represent localised adaptations to changing environmental conditions overlayed over a linguistic divide of much greater antiquity (i.e. since before the LGM). The spread of technologies across much smaller areas likely indicates nothing more than the continued regional interaction and transmission that characterizes all human groups in all times and places (Edwards and O'Connell 1995), resulting in the spread of new and regionally specific approaches to dealing with increased stochastic variation in resource abundance after 5,000 BP. In many cases, these technologies likely had their origins as variants that had already been in existence for some time in some regions, and burgeoned and spread only once local conditions brought them to prominence in some areas and favoured their adoption as 'optimal solutions' in others. Hiscock (2002) has recently made essentially the same argument in relation to the advent and spread of backed artefacts out of a southeastern Australian homeland, though new Pleistocene dates for backed artefacts from North Queensland suggest some revision of Hiscock's model is necessary (Slack *et al.* 2004).

ENSO and Regional Technological Change

If my model of fluctuations in mobility, risk and provisioning in Wardaman Country can be linked to changes in the predictability and quantity of rainfall over time, then we should expect similar changes to take place over wide areas of northern Australia. Unfortunately, comparable technological studies are non-existent for the Top End of Australia. There are, however, glimpses in the published literature which suggest that broadly similar changes, both in terms of their gradual nature and directionality, were taking place in other parts of northern Australia throughout the Holocene. A classic case is to be found in the rockshelter sequences from the gorges and flood plains of Arnhem Land. These sites display a series of gradual changes in stone artefact production systems and raw material selection that are closely timed with major environmental changes in flood plain evolution and increased climatic variability in that region over the Holocene (Allen and Barton n.d.; Hiscock 1994b; Jones and Johnson 1985; Kamminga and Allen 1973; Schrire 1982; White 1971). These include a shift from core and scraper manufacture early on, to a later use of points and bipolar cores after 6,000 BP. In the case of Nauwalabila, the changes in raw materials and flake size are gradual, with peaks in one raw material gradually giving way to peaks in another, as the average size of artefacts also decreased (Jones and Johnson 1985). Several of Schrire's (1982) plain (Malangangerr, Nawamoyn) and plateau sites (Jimeri II) as well as Jones and Johnson's (1985) excavations at Nauwalabila, indicate two distinct peaks in charcoal and artefact deposition, with the lower peak situated between 6,000 and 8,000 BP, and an upper peak somewhere between 1,000 and 3000 BP, similar to Wardaman Country. These sites also show signs of the gradual adoption of bifacial flaking techniques leading up to the first appearance of points. It is difficult to assess changes in reduction intensity in this region over time as numbers of unifacial and bifacial points have not been published for any of the main sites, and nor have core types such as single platform, multiplatform or bipolar, that might allow broad changes in reduction intensity to be identified. These patterns are nevertheless suggestive that significant, and possibly broadly similar patterns of technological change in parity with those taking place in Wardaman Country may have occurred in this neighbouring region.

Other faint traces of similar patterning come from Cape York Peninsula in Queensland, the Port Keats region of the Joseph Bonaparte Gulf in the Northern Territory and the western Kimberley of Western Australia. Mackay (2005), for instance, has documented increasing mobility from 5,000 until 1,000 BP as indicated by changing technology at three rockshelters on Ngarrabulgan Mountain in southeast Cape York Peninsula. Mackay was able to demonstrate a move away from place provisioning toward greater reliance on individual provisioning, particularly between 3,000 and 2,000 BP, despite an absence of formal types in these assemblages. This shift in provisioning and increased mobility was followed by apparent total abandonment of the mountain and surrounds at 900 BP.

At Yarrar rockshelter, in the Port Keats region south of the Daly River, Gregory (1998) has documented a peak in intensity of occupation at c. 1,500 BP. However, Gregory also argues that mobility was very high over the 3,000 to 5,000 years of occupation contained within the shelter. Flood (1970) also found in her analysis of point manufacture at Yarrar that flake blanks and bifacial blanks were transported to the site from quarries at medium distances to the shelter, suggestive of the transport of only those implements with high utility to weight ratios. Most significantly, Flood found that bifacial points were more abundant in the lower than the upper levels, where unifacial points dominated the assemblage. This change in proportions proved significant as indicated by a chi square test.

At Widgingarri 2, there is a peak in artefact discard at c .7,000 BP and another one around 1,000 years ago (O'Connor 1999). Cores and scrapers also gradually decrease in number as points increase, with the first points dated to around 4,970 ± 60 BP (Wk 1398). It is difficult to tell whether bifacial points occur earlier in the sequence, but it may be significant that many of the bifacial points occur in the bottom spits at both Widgingarri 1 and 2.

In summary, there are tantalising indications that broad patterns in occupational intensity, changing extent of reduction and provisioning are mirrored in other sites in the region during the Holocene. Furthermore, there is clearly evidence of gradual changes and *in situ* developments in technologies that are more suggestive of continuous cultural transmission than of a sudden break in technologies accompanying the first appearance of points and other heavily retouched forms. This suggests that regional transmission through social networks that were perhaps geared toward social storage could provide a plausible model of the spread of new technological ideas in the last 5,000 years. Unfortunately, the data is too coarse-grained to get much of an idea of the subtle and gradual changes in technology taking place in regions neighbouring Wardaman Country. There is therefore a great deal of research that still needs to be conducted to place the trends in mobility, provisioning and land use documented in Wardaman Country into a regional context. It is clear, however, that potential exists to build an exciting and dynamic picture of long-term cultural change from stone artefact assemblages, and to understand the nature of the feedback relationship between ecological and social processes and pressures that have shaped northern Australian prehistory since humans first entered this continent more than 45,000 years ago.

Land Use, Sociality and Ontology

The results of detailed technological investigations need not end at discussion of economic and environmental changes, but may also shed light on shifting world views and relationships between people and landscape over time. David (2002) sees ontology - or the system of meaning with which people interpret the world and their own place in it - as fundamentally shaped by our experience of the landscape, material objects and other people, such that a change in any one of these variables will likely also result in a change in belief systems. This idea has important implications for the way we should view the sorts of changes in technology, subsistence and land use argued to have taken place over many thousands of years in Wardaman Country. Although change is continuous over this period, increases in the rate of change have also been identified that points to major and rapid readjustments to the way people related to the landscape over time, albeit within the context of broad cultural continuities. If David is correct in this view, then we should expect such periods of major economic and technological restructuring to be accompanied by alterations in systems of signification and world view, as well as perhaps a reconfiguration of the ways in which people related to each other.

For example, a relatively sedentary group spending large amounts of time in each other's company and tethered to only a few resource patches, a few large waterholes, and a number of familiar rockshelters, and possessing clearly demarcated boundaries with frequently encountered neighbours, may relate quite differently to each other, and to the landscape around them, than to those living in, say, dispersed groups, moving constantly over large areas with which they are less familiar, and potentially travelling long distances to make contact with neighbouring groups whom they encounter more rarely. David argues on this basis that major discontinuities in the archaeological record should also signify rapid changes in world view, because the material world is meaningful, and any change in the patterning of material phenomena will likely also indicate a change in the meanings ascribed to them.

Following this argument, we might expect the changes in subsistence, technology and land use documented in Wardaman Country to be accompanied by major changes in social relationships, rock art styles and signification and even the mythological basis of the Dreaming itself. David et al. (1994) found two peaks in ochre deposition in excavations beneath large painted panels in Wardaman Country dating to 1,500 BP and 380 BP. At Menngen-ya where occupation is dated to greater than $2,109 \pm 60$ (NZA 1624) radiocarbon years, the younger peak in ochre is thought to relate to the painting of two large striped anthropomorphic figures that dominate the panel, while the older peak probably dates faded paintings that are of a different style and which underlie the striped anthropomorphs. If this is correct, and changes in rock art styles indicate changes in ontology, then the timing of changes in art styles and world view are neatly coincident with two important technological changes in Wardaman Country – the peak in occupational intensity at 1,500 BP and the first appearance of Leilira blades in large numbers at 330 BP. In the latter case, these blades are known to have been traded over very large areas, and point to the emergence, or more likely a change in nature and orientation, of regional networks of social interaction at this time. Technology and social changes therefore seem closely tied to one another as David predicts they should be.

Technology can therefore indirectly inform us about many of the larger issues in northern Australian prehistory that have proved more difficult to access through conventional archaeological techniques of excavation and cataloguing. As yet, the data and interpretation offered can only take us so far, because so few detailed regional studies of technology have been undertaken in Australia. Perhaps our most pressing need in northern Australian archaeology then is a wide-ranging program of interconnected regional studies that will help us to comment on the specific nature of technological, economic and social change in this region for the tremendous span of human occupation of the country.

Conclusion

Writing prehistory is a difficult business no matter what the theoretical stance or the type of data chosen to base it on. It is arguably at its most difficult, however, when trying to extract an understanding of the past lives of complex cultural beings from variation in chipped pieces of stone.

This research has been successful in so far as it has documented major changes in the system of stone artefact procurement, manufacture, transport and discard through time, and has identified general ecological processes as important factors shaping assemblage variability in this region. Seemingly, increased inter-annual variability in rainfall after 5,000 BP is a major factor that has noticeably transformed Aboriginal technologies and modes of land use across northern Australia, with likely consequences for the way people related to each other, assimilated each other's ideas and maybe even used each other's resources. Such major alterations to the social and physical environment must also have had ramifications for the ontologies of people and the way they graphically depicted their world.

The apparent success of this research both confirms the importance of ecological modelling as a useful tool in exploring the forces that partly shaped past human behaviour, and the value of stone artefact assemblages as an important interpretive window on the past. It is a great pity that so few detailed analyses of this kind have appeared in Australia, for much of their impact is lost without companion studies in nearby regions with which to compare results. The need for regional studies that connect broad geographic areas and provide the necessary comparative data for expansive treatments of socio-demographic change has perhaps never been more urgent than at present, since theoretical modelling of Aboriginal cultural changes appears to be outstripping the rate at which the necessary data required to test these models is gathered.

This monograph has proposed a very specific model of technological, economic and social change that has many testable components within and outside of Wardaman Country and involving many independent lines of enquiry. Changes in mobility range, mobility frequency and mobility type could be easily explored using faunal data from sites in nearby areas with well-preserved faunal assemblages. The Kintore Caves site excavated by Mulvaney and Golson in 1963 and located near Katherine, for instance, has a very large and intact faunal assemblage, that could be used to explore these questions on a different class of material with a different set of methods. Evidence of intensified inter-regional exchange and social storage, on the other hand, could be addressed by gradually building a database of geochemical fingerprints for stone sources, such that exotic materials (especially for trade items such as Leilira blades) may be traced to particular distant quarries. The use of changing artefact discard numbers at sites to represent fluctuations in occupational intensity could be further tested by examining changes in site formation, the taphonomy of artefacts and the changing nature of prey selection, faunal reduction and exploitation. The notion that technological changes across the Top End represent continuous transmission through time rather than significant breaks could also be further explored by examining evidence for fine-grained, continuous and overlapping technological change in other rockshelters with large and well-stratified assemblages in nearby regions. Such studies are relatively straightforward and yet they are rare despite the massive amount of information they can provide about the prehistory of northern Australia.

In conclusion, an approach that unites processual and behavioural archaeologies with evolutionary ecology and design theory offers us clear direction as to how we should structure our observations of the record, construct temporal and spatial frames of reference, and begin interpreting our data with relevant models in mind. The ultimate measure of success in attempting to understand the past will likely rest on our ability to develop explanations of social and economic processes that take us from subsistence into the more complex domain of social structure and ontology.

References

Adams, J., Malsin, M. and Thomas, E. 1999 Sudden climate transitions during the Quaternary. *Progress in Physical Geography* 23:1-36.

Abbott, M.B., Leonard, R.D. and Jones, G.T. 1996 Explaining the change from biface to flake technology. In Maschner, H.D.G. (ed.) *Darwinian Archaeologies*, pp.33-42. New York: Plenum.

Adams, J., Malsin, M. and Thomas, E. 1999 Sudden climate transitions during the Quaternary. *Progress in Physical Geography* 23:1-36.

Ahler, S.A. 1989 Mass analysis of flaking debris: studying the forest rather than the trees. In Henry, D.O. and Odell, G.H. (eds) *Alternative Approaches to Lithic Analysis*, pp.85-118. Archaeological Papers of the American Anthropological Association 1.

Ahler, S.A. and Geib, P.R. 2000 Why flute? Folsom point design and adaptation. *Journal of Archaeological Science* 27:799-820.

Akerman, K. 1981 Notes on the Kimberley stone-tipped spear focussing on the point hafting mechanism. *Mankind* 11:486-489.

Akerman, K. and Bindon, P. 1995 Dentate and related stone biface points from northern Australia. *The Beagle* 12:89-99.

Allan, R., Lindesay, J. and Parker, D. 1996 *El Niño, Southern Oscillation and Climatic Variability*. Collingwood: CSIRO Australia.

Allen, H. 1972 Where the Crow Flies Backwards: Man and land in the Darling Basin. Ph.D. Thesis: The Australian National University.

Allen, H. 1997 The distribution of large blades (leilira): evidence of recent changes in Aboriginal ceremonial exchange networks. In McConvell, P. and Evans, N. (eds) *Archaeology and Linguistics: Aboriginal Australia in Global Perspective*. Oxford: Oxford University Press.

Allen, H. and Barton, G. n.d. Ngarradj Warde Djobkeng. *Oceania Monograph 37*.

Anderson, A., Gagan, M. and Schulmeister, J. 2006 Mid-Holocene cultural dynamics and climatic change in the western Pacific. In Sandweiss, D.H. and Maasch, K.A. (eds) *Climate Change and Cultural Dynamics: A Global Perspective on Holocene Transitions*. San Diego: Academic Press.

Anderson, R.Y. 1992 Long-term changes in the frequency of occurrence of El Niño events. In Diaz, H.F. and Markgraf, V. (eds) *El Niño: Historical and Paleoclimatic Aspects of the Southern Oscillation*, pp.193-200. Cambridge: Cambridge University Press.

Andrefsky, W. 1998 *Lithics - Macroscopic Approaches to Analysis*. Cambridge: Cambridge University Press.

Andrus, C.F.T., Crowe, D.E., Sandweiss, D.H., Reitz, E.J. and Romanek, C.S. 2002 Otolith d18O record of mid-Holocene sea surface temperature in Peru. *Science* 295:1508-1512.

Attenbrow, V., David, B. and Flood, J. 1995 Mennge-ya and the origins of points: new insights into the appearance of points in the semi-arid zone of the Northern Territory. *Archaeology in Oceania* 30:105-119.

Austin, R.J. 1997 Technological characterization of lithic waste-flake assemblages: multivariate analysis of experimental and archaeological data. *Lithic Technology* 24:53-68.

Bamforth, D.B. 1986 Technological efficiency and tool curation. *American Antiquity* 51:38-50.

Bamforth, D.B. and Bleed, P. 1997 Technology, flaked stone technology, and risk. In Barton, C.M. and Clark, G.A. (eds) *Rediscovering Darwin: Evolutionary Theory in Archaeology*. Archaeological Papers of the American Anthropological Association, No.7, pp.109-140. Washington: American Anthropological Association.

Baulmer, M.F. and Downum, C.E. 1989 Between micro and macro: a study in the interpretation of small-sized lithic debitage. In Amick, D.S. and Mauldin, R.P. (eds) *Experiments in Lithic Technology*, pp.110-116. Oxford: British Archaeological Reports.

Beck, C. 1995 Functional attributes and the differential persistence of Great Basin dart forms. *Journal of California and Great Basin Anthropology* 17:222-243.

Beck, C. 1998 Projectile point types as valid chronological units. In Ramenofsky, A.F. and Stefen, A. (eds) *Unit Issues in Archaeology: Measuring Time, Space, and Material*, pp.21-40. Salt lake City: University of Utah Press.

Beck, C., Taylor, A.K., Jones, G.T., Fadem, C.M., Cook, C.R. and Millward, S.A. 2002 Rocks are heavy: transport costs and Paleoarchaic quarry behaviour in the Great Basin. *Journal of Anthropological Archaeology* 21:481-507.

Bender, B. 1981 Gatherer-hunter intensification. In Sheridan, A. and Bailey, G. (eds) *Economic Archaeology*, pp.149-157. Oxford: British Archaeological Reports, International Series, 96.

Bentley, R.A. and Shennan, S.J. 2003 Cultural transmission and stochastic network growth. *American Antiquity* 68:459-485.

Bettinger, R.L., Mahli, R. and McCarthy, H. 1997 Central place models of acorn and mussel processing. *Journal of Archaeological Science* 24:887-899.

Binford, L.R. 1977 Forty seven trips. A case study in the character of archaeological formation processes. In Wright, R.V.S. (ed.) *Stone Tools as Cultural Markers*, pp.24-36. Canberra: Australian Institute of Aboriginal Studies.

Binford, L.R. 1979 Organizational and formation processes: looking at curated technologies. *Journal of Anthropological Research* 35:255-273.

Binford, L.R. 1980 Willow smoke and dog's tails: Hunter-gatherer settlement systems and archaeological site formation. *American Antiquity* 45:4-20.

Binford, L.R. and Binford, S.R. 1966 A preliminary analysis of functional variability in the Mousterian of Levallois facies. *American Anthropologist* 68:238-295.

Bird, D., Bliege Bird, R. and Parker, C. 2005 Aboriginal burning regimes and hunting strategies in Australia's Western Desert. *Human Ecology* 33.

Bleed, P. 1986 The optimal design of hunting weapons: maintainability or reliability. *American Antiquity* 51:737-747.

Bleed, P. 1991 Operations research and archaeology. *American Antiquity* 56:19-35.

Bleed, P. 1996 Risk and cost in Japanese microcore technology. *Lithic Technology* 21:95-107.

Bleed, P. 2001 Trees or chains, links or branches: conceptual alternatives for consideration of stone tool production and other sequential activities. *Journal of Archaeological Method and Theory* 8:101-127.

Bleed, P. 2002 Obviously sequential, but continuous or staged? Refits and cognition in three late paleolithic assemblages from Japan. *Journal of Anthropological Archaeology* 21:329-343.

Bourke, R.M. 1998 Impact of the 1997 drought and frosts in Papua New Guinea. Unpublished manuscript held on file, Department of Human Geography, Research School of Pacific and Asian Studies, The Australian National University, Canberra.

Bowdler, S. 1981 Stone tools, style and function: evidence from the Stockyard Site, Hunter Island. *Archaeology in Oceania*:64-69.

Bowdler, S. and O'Conner, S. 1991 The dating of the Australian Small Tool Tradition, with new evidence from the Kimberley, WA. *Australian Aboriginal Studies* 1991/1:53-62.

Bowler, J.M. 1983 32+/-5ka Northern Australia: Hydrological Evidence. In J., C. and Grindrod, A. (eds) *CLIMANZ 1*, pp.4-6. Canberra: The Australian National University.

Bowler, J.M., Jones, R., Allen, H. and Thorne, A. 1970 Pleistocene Human remains from Australia: a living site and human cremation from Lake Mungo, western New South Wales. *World Archaeology* 2:39-60.

Bradbury, A.P. 1998 The examination of lithic artefacts from an Early Archaic assemblage: strengthening inferences through multiple lines of evidence. *Midcontinental Journal of Archaeology* 23:263-288.

Bradbury, A.P. and Carr, P.J. 1999 Examining stage and continuum models of flake debris analysis: an experimental approach. *Journal of Archaeological Science* 26:105-116.

Bradley, B.A. 1975 Lithic reduction sequences: a glossary and discussion. In Swanson, E.H. (ed.) *Lithic Technology: Making and Using Stone Tools*, pp.5-14. The Hague: Mouton Publishers.

Brantingham, P.J. 2003 A neutral model of stone raw material procurement. *American Antiquity* 68:487-509.

Bright, J., Ugan, A. and Hunskar, L. 2002 The effect of handling time on subsistence technology. *World Archaeology* 34:164-181.

Brockwell, C.J. 1989 Archaeological Investigations of the Kakadu Wetlands, Northern Australia. MA Thesis: The Australian National University.

Brookfield, H. and Allan, B. 1989 High-altitude occupation and environment. *Mountain Research and Development* 9:201-9.

Broughton, J.M. 2003 Prey spatial structure and behaviour affect archaeological tests of optimal foraging models: examples from the Emeryville Shellmound vertebrate fauna. *World Archaeology* 34:60-83.

Broughton, J.M. and O'Connell, J.F. 1999 Evolutionary ecology, selectionist archaeology, and Behavioural Archaeology. *American Antiquity* 64:153-165.

Butlin, N. 1983 *Our Original Agression*. Sydney: Allan and Unwin.

Cane, S. 1984 Desert camps: a case study of stone artefacts and Aboriginal behaviour in the Western Desert. Ph.D. Thesis: The Australian National University.

Caraco, T. 1979a Time budgeting and group size: A test of theory. *Ecology* 60:618-627.

Caraco, T. 1979b Time budgeting and group size: A theory. *Ecology* 60:617-617.

Caraco, T., Martindale, S. and Whittam, T.S. 1980 An empirical demonstration of risk-sensitive foraging preferences. *Animal Behaviour* 28:820-830.

Cashdan, E. 1985 Coping with risk reciprocity among the Basara of northern Botswana. *Man* 20:454-474.

Cashdan, E. 1992 Spatial organization and habitat use. In Smith, E.A. and Winterhalder, B. (eds) *Evolutionary Ecology and Human Behaviour*, pp.237-266. New York: Aldine de Gruyter.

Chappell, J. 2001 Climate before agriculture. In Anderson, A., Lilley, I. and O'Connor, S. (eds) *Histories of Old Ages: Essays in Honour of Rhys Jones*, pp.171-183. Canberra: Pandanus Books, Research School of Pacific and Asian Studies, The Australian National University.

Charnov, E.L. 1976 Optimal foraging: the marginal value theorem. *Theoretical Population Biology* 9:129-136.

Charnov, E.L., Orians, G.H. and Hyatt, K. 1976 Ecological implications of resource depression. *American Naturalist* 110:247-259.

Chippindale, C. and Taçon, P.S.C. 2000 The many ways of dating Arnhem land rock art, north Australia. In Chippindale, C. and Taçon, P.S.C. (eds) *The Archaeology of Rock-Art*, pp.90-111. Cambridge: Cambridge University Press.

Christenson, A.L. 1982 Maximizing clarity in economic terminology. *American Antiquity* 47:419-426.

Clarke, J.E. 2000 Hunting the Classifier: Ambiguity in Stone Artefact Classification - An Australian Perspective. B.A.Hons Thesis: The Australian National University.

Clarkson, C. 2001 Technological Change in Wardaman Country: Report on the 1999 Season. *Australian Aboriginal Studies* 2001:63-68.

Clarkson, C. 2002a Holocene scraper reduction, technological organization and landuse at Ingaladdi Rockshelter, Northern Australia. *Archaeology in Oceania* 37:79-86.

Clarkson, C. 2002b An Index of Invasiveness for the measurement of unifacial and bifacial retouch: a theoretical, experimental and archaeological verification. *Journal of Archaeological Science* 1:65-75.

Clarkson, C. 2005 Tenuous Types: 'Scraper' reduction continuums in Wardaman Country, Northern Australia. In Clarkson, C. and Lamb, L. (eds) *Lithics 'Down Under': Australian Perspectives on Stone Artefact Reduction, Use and Classification*. BAR International Series S1408, pp.21-34. Oxford: Archaeopress.

Clarkson, C. J. 2006 Interpreting surface assemblage variation in the eastern Victoria River region. In Lilley, I. and S. Ulm (eds) *An Archaeological Life: Essays in Honour of Jay Hall* pp. 177-190. Aboriginal and Torres Strait Islander Studies Unit. Brisbane: The University of Queensland.

Clarkson, C. J. 2006 Explaining point variability in the eastern Victoria River region, Northern Territory. *Archaeology in Oceania* 41: 97-106.

Clarkson, C. and Bowdery, D. 2005 *Report to the Centre for Archaeological Research on the result of phytolith analyses undertaken for Nimji and Gordol-ya rockshelters, as part of the 2002 New Initiatives Scheme*. The Australian National University.

Clarkson, C. and David, B. 1995 The antiquity of blades and points revisited: investigating the emergence of systematic blade production south-west of Arnhem Land, northern Australia. *The Artefact* 18:22-44.

Clarkson, C. and O'Connor, S. 2005 An introduction to stone artefact analysis. In Balme, J. and Patterson, A. (eds) *Archaeology in Practice: A Student Guide to Archaeological Analyses*. New York: Blackwell.

Clarkson, C. and F. X. Ricault 2006 Interaction and isolation: mt-DNA evidence for regional gene flow, demography and isolation in Australia. Paper presented at the 2006 meetings of the Australian Archaeological Association, Beechworth, Australia.

Clarkson, C. and Wallis, L.A. 2003 The search for El Nino/Southern Oscillation in archaeological sites: Recent phytolith analysis at Jugali-ya rockshelter, Wardaman Country, Australia. In Hart, D.M. and Wallis, L.A. (eds) *Phytolith and Starch Research in the Australian-Pacific-Asian Regions: The State of the Art*. Terra Australis 19, pp.137-152. Canberra: Pandanus Books.

Clegg, J.K. 1977 The four Dimensions of Artificial Variation. In Wright, R.V.S. (ed.) *Stone Tools as Cultural Markers: Change, Evolution and Complexity*, pp.60-66. New Jersey: Humanities Press.

Clendon, M. 2006. Reassessing Australia's Linguistic Prehistory. *Current Anthropology* 47:39-62.

Colson, E. 1979 In good years and in bad: Food strategies of self-reliant societies. *Journal of Anthropological Research* 35:18-29.

Cooper, H.M. 1954 Material culture of Australian Aborigines Part 1. Progressive modification of a stone artefact. *Records of the South Australian Museum* 11:91-7.

Cotterell, B. and Kamminga, J. 1987 The formation of flakes. *American Antiquity* 52:675-708.

Crabtree, D.E. 1968 Mesoamerican polyhedral cores and prismatic blades. *American Antiquity* 33.

Crabtree, D.E. 1972a The cone fracture principle and the manufacture of lithic materials. *Tebiwa* 15:29-42.

Cundy, B.J. 1977 An analysis of burins from New England and Capertee. Unpublished B.A. (Hons) Thesis: The Australian National University.

Cundy, B.J. 1990 An Analysis of the Ingaladdi Assemblage: critique of the understanding of lithic technology. Ph.D. Thesis: The Australian National University.

David, B. 1991 Archaeological excavations at Yiwarlarlay 1: Site Report. *Memoirs of the Queensland Museum* 30:373-380.

David, B. 2002 *Landscapes, Rock-art and the Dreaming: An Archaeology of Preunderstanding*. London: Leicester University Press.

David, B., Chant, D. and Flood, J. 1992 Jalijbang 2 and the distribution of pecked faces in Australia. *Memoirs of the Queensland Museum* 32:61-77.

David, B., David, M., Flood, J. and Frost, R. 1990 Rock Paintings of the Yingalarri region: preliminary results and implications for an archaeology of inter-regional relations in Northern Australia. *Memoirs of the Queensland Museum* 28:443-462.

David, B. and Lourandos, H. 1998 Rock art and socio-demography in northeastern Australian prehistory. *World Archaeology* 30:193-219.

David, B., McNiven, I., Attenbrow, V. and Flood, J. 1994 Of Lightning Brothers and White Cockatoos: dating the antiquity of signifying systems in the Northern Territory, Australia. *Antiquity* 68:241-251.

Davidson, D.S. 1935 Archaeological Problems of Northern Australia. *Journal of the Royal Australian Institute* 65:145-182.

Dawkins, R. 1982 *The Extended Phenotype: The Long Reach of the Gene*. Oxford: Oxford University Press.

De Deckker, P. 2001 Late Quaternary cylcic aridity in tropical Australia. *Paleogeography, Paleoclimatology, Paleoecology* 170:1-9.

Devitt, G. 1988 Contemporary Aboriginal Women And Subsistence In Remote, Arid Australia. Ph.D. Thesis: The University of Queensland.

Dewar, R. 2003 Rainfall variability and subsistence systems in Southeast Asia and the Western Pacific. *Current Anthropology* 44:369-388.

Diaz, H.F. and Markgraf, V. 1992 Introduction. In Diaz, H.F. and Markgraf, V. (eds) *El Niño: Historical and Paleoclimatic Aspects of the Southern Oscillation*, pp.1-16. Cambridge: Cambridge University Press.

Dibble, H. 1995 Middle Paleolithic scraper reduction: background, clarification, and review of evidence to date. *Journal of Archaeological Method and Theory* 2:299-368.

Dibble, H. and Pelcin, A. 1995 The effect of hammer mass and velocity on flake mass. *Journal of Archaeological Science* 22:429-439.

Dibble, H. and Whittaker, J. 1981 New experimental evidence on the relation between percussion flaking and flake variation. *Journal of Archaeological Science* 8:283-296.

Dixon, R.M.W. 1997 *The Rise and Fall of Languages*. Cambridge: Cambridge University Press.

Dortch, C.E. 1977 Early and late industrial phases in Western Australia. In Wright, R.V.S. (ed.) *Stone Tools as Cultural Markers*, pp.104-132. Canberra: Australian Institute of Aboriginal Studies.

Ebert, J.I. 1979 An ethnoarchaeological approach to reassessing the meaning of variability in stone tool assemblages. In Kramer, C. (ed.) *Ethnoarchaeology: Implications of Ethnography for Archaeology*, pp.59-74. New York: Columbia University Press.

Edwards, D. and O'Connell, J.F. 1995 Broad spectrum diets in arid Australia. *Antiquity* 69:769-783.

Elkin, A.P. 1948 Pressure flaking in the northern Kimberley, Australia. *Man* 48:110-113.

Ely, L.L., Enzel, Y., Baker, V.R. and Cayan, D.R. 1993 A 5000-year record of extreme floods and climate change in the southwestern United States. *Science* 262:410-2.

Enfield, D.B. 1989 El Niño, past and present. *Review of Geophysics* 27:159-87.

Enfield, D.B. 1992 Historical and prehistorical overview of El Niño/Southern Oscillation. In Diaz, H.F. and Markgraf, V. (eds) *El Niño: Historical and Paleoclimatic Aspects of the Southern Oscillation*, pp.96-118. Cambridge: Cambridge University Press.

Evans, N. and Jones, R. 1997 The cradle of the Pama-Nyungans:archaeological and linguistic speculations. In McConvell, P. and Evans, N. (eds) *Archaeology and Linguistics: Aboriginal Australia in Global Perspective*, pp.385-418. Melbourne: Oxford University Press.

Faulkner, A. 1972 Mechanical Principles of Flint Working. PhD Thesis: Washington State University, University Microfilms, Ann Arbor.

Fitzhugh, B. 2001 Risk and invention in human technological evolution. *Journal of Anthropological Archaeology* 20:125-167.

Flenniken, J.J. 1981 *Replicative Systems Analysis: A Model Applied to the Vein Quartz Artefacts from the Hoko River Site*. Reports of Investigations, Np.59. Pullman: Washington State University Laboratory of Anthropology.

Flenniken, J.J. and White, J.P. 1985 Australian flaked stone tools: a technological perspective. *Records of the Australian Museum* 36:131-151.

Flood, J. 1970 A point assemblage from the Northern Territory. *Archaeology and Physical Anthropology in Oceania* 5:27-52.

Flood, J. 1995 *Archaeology of the Dreamtime: The Story of Prehistoric Australia and its People*. Sydney: Angus & Robertson Publication.

Flood, J.M. 1973 The Moth-Hunters. Ph.D. Thesis: The Australian National University.

Flood, J.M. 1974 Pleistocene man at Clogg's Cave: his tool kit and environment. *Mankind* 9:175-178.

Frakes, L.A., McGowran, B. and Bowler, J.M. 1987 Evolution of Australian environments. In Dyne, G.R. and Walton, D.W. (eds) *Fauna of Australia*, pp.1-16. Canberra: Australian Government Publishing Service.

Friis-Hansen, J. 1990 Mesolithic cutting arrows: functional analysis of arrows used in hunting of large game. *Antiquity* 64:494-504.

Frison, G.C. 1989 Experimental use of Clovis weaponry and tools on African elephants. *American Antiquity* 54.

Gagan, M.K., Chivas, A.R. and Isdale, P.J. 1994 High-resolution isotopic records of the mid-Holocene tropical Western Pacific. *Earth and Planetary Sciences* 121:549-558.

Gagan, M.K., E.J. Hendy, S.G. Haberle, W.S. Hantaro 2004 Post-glacial evolution of the Indo-Pacific Warm Pool and El Niño-Southern oscillation. *Quarternary International* 118-119: 127-143.

Gillieson, D., Smith, D.I., Greenaway, M. and Ellaway, M. 1991 Flood history of the limestone ranges in the Kimberley region, Western Australia. *Applied Geography* 11:105-23.

Glantz, M.H. 1991 Introduction. In Glantz, M.H., Katz, R.W. and Nicholls, N. (eds) *Teleconnections Linking World-Wide Climate Anomalies. Scientific Basis and Societal Impact*, pp.1-11. Cambridge: Cambridge University Press.

Glantz, M.H. 1996 *Currents of Change: El Niño's Impact on Climate and Society*. Cambridge: Cambridge University Press.

Glantz, M.H., Katz, R.W. and Nicholls, N. 1991 *Teleconnections Linking World-Wide Climate Anomalies. Scientific Basis and Societal Impact*. Cambridge: Cambridge University Press.

Glover, I. 1973 Island southeast Asia and the settlement of Australia. In Strong, D.E. (ed.) *Archaeology Theory and Practice*. London.

Goodyear, A.C. 1989 A hypothesis for the use of crypto-crystalline raw materials among Paleoindian groups of North America. In Ellis, C.G. and Lothrop, J.C. (eds) *Eastern Paleoindian Lithic Resource Use*, pp.1-9. Boulder (Co): Westview Press.

Gorecki, P., O'Connor, S., Grant, M. and Veth, P. 1997 The morphology, function and antiquity of Australian grinding implements. *Archaeology in Oceania* 32:141-150.

Gould, R.A. 1967 Notes on hunting, butchering, and sharing of game among the Ngatatjara and their neighbours in the west Australian desert. *Kroeber Anthropological Society Papers* 36:41-66.

Gould, R.A. 1980 *Living Archaeology*. New Studies in Archaeology. Cambridge: Cambridge University Press.

Gould, R.A. and Saggers, S. 1985 Lithic procurement in Central Australia: a closer look at Binford's idea of embeddedness in archaeology. *American Antiquity* 50.117-136.

Graumlich, L.J. 1993 A 1000-year record of temperature and precipitation in the Sierra Nevada. *Quaternary Research* 39:248-55.

Green, R.F. 1980 Bayesian birds: a simple of Oaten's stochastic model of optimal foraging. *Theoretical Population Biology*:244-256.

Gregory, R.L. 1998 Aboriginal Settlement Patterns in the Ord-Victoria River Region. PhD Thesis: Northern Territory University.

Gremillion, K.J. 2002 Foraging theory and hypothesis testing in archaeology:" An exploration of methodological problems and solutions. *Journal of Anthropological Archaeology* 21:142-164.

Guthrie, R.D. 1983 Osseous projectile points: biological considerations affecting raw material selection and design among Paleolithic and Paleoindian peoples. In Clutton-Brock, J. and Grigson, C. (eds) *Animals and Archaeology: 1. Hunters and Their Prey*. BAR International Series 163, pp.273-294. Oxford: Oxbow.

Halstead, P. and O'Shea, J. 1989 Introduction. In Halstead, P. and O'Shea, J. (eds) *Bad Year Economics*, pp.1-8. Cambridge: Cambridge University Press.

Hames, R. 1980 Game depletion and hunting zone rotation among the Ye'kwana and Tanomamo of Amazonas, Venezuela. In R. Hames (ed.), *Working Papers on South American Indians*, pp.24-62. Bennington, VT: Bennington College.

Harpending, H.C. and Davis, H. 1977 Some implications for hunter-gatherer ecology derived from the spatial structure of resources. *World Archaeology* 8:275-286.

Hawkes, K. 1990 Why do men hunt? Benefits for risky choices. In Cahsdan, E. (ed.) *Risk and Uncertainty*, pp.145-166. Boulder: Westview Press.

Hawkes, K. 1991 Showing off: Tests of an explanatory hypothesis about men's foraging goals. *Ethology and Sociobiology* 12:29-54.

Hawkes, K. and Bliege Bird, R. 2002 Showing off, handicap signalling, and the evolution of men's work. *Evolutionary Anthropology* 11:58-67.

Hawkes, K. and O'Connell, J.F. 1992 On optimal foraging models and subsistence transitions. *Current Anthropology* 33:63-66.

Hayden, B. 1979 *Paleolithic Reflections: Lithic Technology and Ethnographic Excavations among Australian Aborigines*. Canberra: Australian Institute of Aboriginal Studies.

Hayden, B. 1981 Subsistence and ecological adaptations of modern hunter-gatherers. In Teleki, R. (ed.) *Omnivorous Primates: Hunting and Gathering in Human Evolution*, pp.344-422. New York: Columbia University Press.

Hayden, B., Franco, N. and Spafford, J. 1996 Evaluating lithic strategies and design criteria. In Odell, G.H. (ed.) *Stone Tools: Theoretical Insights into Human Prehistory*, pp.9-50. New York: Plenum Press.

Hiscock, P. 1982a The meaning of edge angles. *Australian Archaeology*.

Hiscock, P. 1982b A technological analysis of quartz assemblages from the south coast. In Bowdler, S. (ed.) *Coastal Archaeology in Eastern Australia*, pp.32-45. Canberra: Department of Prehistory, Research School of Pacific and Asian Studies, The Australian National University.

Hiscock, P. 1988 Prehistoric Settlement Patterns and Artefact Manufacture at Lawn Hill, Northwest Queensland.: University of Queensland.

Hiscock, P. 1993a Bondaian technology in the Hunter Valley, New South Wales. *Archaeology in Oceania* 28:64-75.

Hiscock, P. 1993b Interpreting the vertical distribution of stone points within Nauwalabila 1, Arnhem Land. *The Beagle* 10:173-178.

Hiscock, P. 1994a The end of points. In Sullivan, M., Brockwell, S. and Webb, A. (eds) *Archaeology in the North*, pp.72-83. Darwin: The Australian National University (NARU).

Hiscock, P. 1994b Technological responses to risk in Holocene Australia. *Journal of World Prehistory* 8:267-292.

Hiscock, P. 1996 Mobility and technology in the Kakadu coastal wetlands. *Bulletin of the Indo-Pacific Prehistory Association* 15:151-157.

Hiscock, P. 1999 Holocene coastal occupation of Western Arnhem Land. In Hall, J. and McNiven, I. (eds) *Australian Coastal Archaeology*, pp.91-103. Canberra: ANH Publications, Department of Archaeology and Natural History, The Australian National University.

Hiscock, P. 2001a Looking the other way: a materialist/technological approach to classifying tools and implements, cores and retouched flakes, with examples from Australia. In McPherron, S. and Lindley, J. (eds) *Tools or Cores? The Identification and Study of Alternative Core Technology in Lithic Assemblages*. Pennsylvania: University of Pennsylvania Museum.

Hiscock, P. 2001b Sizing up prehistory: sample size and the composition of Australian artefact assemblages. *Australian Aboriginal Studies* 2000.

Hiscock, P. 2002 Pattern and context in the Holocene proliferation of backed artefacts in Australia. In Elston, R.G. and Kuhn, S.L. (eds) *Thinking Small: Global Perspectives on Microlithization*. Archaeological Papers of the American Anthropological Association (AP3A) No. 12, pp.163-177.

Hiscock, P. 2005 Blunt and to the point: changing technological strategies in Holocene Australia. In Lilley, I. (ed.) *Archaeology in Oceania: Australia and the Pacific Islands*. Blackwell.

Hiscock, P. and Attenbrow, V. 2002 Early Australian implement variation: a reduction model. *Journal of Archaeological Science* 30:239-249.

Hiscock, P. and Attenbrow, V. 2003 Morphological and reduction continuums in eastern Australia: measurement and implications at Capertee 3. *Tempus* 7:167-174.

Hiscock, P. and Attenbrow, V. 2005a *Australia's Eastern Regional Sequence Revisited: Technology and Change at Capertee 3*. BAR S1397. Oxford: Archaeopress.

Hiscock, P. and Attenbrow, V. 2005b Reduction continuums and tool use. In Clarkson, C. and Lamb, L. (eds) *Lithics 'Down Under': Australian Perspectives on Stone Artefact Reduction, Use and Classification*. BAR International Series S1408, pp.43-56. Oxford: Archaeopress.

Hiscock, P. and Clarkson, C. 2000 Analysing Australian stone artefacts: an agenda for the Twenty First Century. *Australian Archaeology* 50:98-108.

Hiscock, P. and Clarkson, C. 2005a Experimental evaluation of Kuhn's Geometric Index of Reduction and the flat-flake problem. *Journal of Archaeological Science* 32:1015-1022.

Hiscock, P. and Clarkson, C. 2005b Measuring Artefact Reduction - An Examination of Kuhn's Geometric Index of Reduction. In Clarkson, C. and Lamb, L. (eds) *Lithics 'Down Under': Australian Perspectives on Stone Artefact Reduction, Use and Classification.* BAR International Series S1408, pp.7-20. Oxford: Archaeopress.

Hiscock, P. and Hughes, P.J. 1980 Backed blades in Northern Australia: evidence from Northwest Queensland. *Australian Archaeology* 10:86-95.

Hiscock, P. and Veth, P. 1991 Change in the Australian Desert Culture: a reanalysis of tulas from Puntutjarpa. *World Archaeology* 22:332-345.

Holdaway, S. 1995 Stone artefacts and the transition. *Antiquity* 69:784-97.

Hope, G. and Golson, J. 1995 Late Quaternary change in the mountains of New Guinea. *Antiquity* 69:818-30.

Horn, H.S. 1968 The adaptive significance of colonial nesting in the Brewer's Blackbird (*Euphagus cyanocephalus*). *Ecology* 49:682-694.

Horne, G. and Aiston, G. 1924 *Savage Life in Central Australia.* London: Macmillan.

Horton, D.R. 1993 Here be dragons: A view of Australian archaeology. In Smith, M.A., Spriggs, M. and Fankhauser, B. (eds) *Sahul in Review: Pleistocene Archaeology in Australia, New Guinea and Island Melanesia*, pp.11-16. Canberra: Department of Prehistory, Research School of Pacific Studies, The Australian National University.

Hughes, M.K. and Brown, P.A. 1992 Drought frequency in central California since 101 B.C. recorded in giant sequoia tree rings. *Climate Dynamics* 6:161-7.

Hudjashov, G., Kivisild, T., Underhill, P.A., Endicott, P., Sanchez, J.L., Alice, A.L., Shen, P., Oefuer, P., Renfrew, C., Villems, R., and P. Forster 2007. Revealing the prehistoric settlement of Australia by Y chromosome and mt-DNA analysis. *Proceedings of the National Academy of Sciences* 104(21): 8726-8730.

Huoponen, K., Schurr, T.G., Yu-Sheng, C., and D.C. Wallace 2001 Mitochondrial DNA variation in an Aboriginal Australian population: evidence for genetic isolation and regional differentiation. *Human Immunology* 62:954-969.

Ingman, M. and U. Gyllensten 2003 Mitochondrial genome variation and evolutionary history of Australian and New Guinean Aborigines. *Genome Research* 13:1600-1606.

Jeske, R.J. 1992 Energetic efficiency and lithic technology: A Mississipean example. *American Antiquity* 57:467-481.

Johnson, I. 1979 The Getting of Data. Unpublished PhD Thesis: The Australian National University.

Jones, K.T. and Madsen, D.B. 1989 Calculating the cost of resource transportation: A great basin example. *Current Anthropology* 30:529-534.

Jones, R. 1969 Firestick farming. *Australian Natural History* 16:224-228.

Jones, R. 1971 Rocky Cape and the problem of the Tasmanians. Ph.D. Thesis: University of Sydney.

Jones, R. and Johnson, I. 1985 Deaf Adder Gorge: Lindner Site, Nauwalabila 1. In Jones, R. (ed.) *Archaeological Research in Kakadu National Park*, pp.165-228. Canberra: Australian National Parks and Wildlife Service.

Jones, T.L., Brown, G.M., Raab, L.M., McVicker, J.L., Spaulding, W.G., Kennet, D.J., Tyork, A. and Walker, D.L. 1999 Environmental imperatives reconsidered. Demographic crises in western North America during the Medieval Climatic anomaly. *Current Anthropology* 40:137-70.

Kamminga, J. and Allen, H. 1973 *Report of the archaeological survey. Alligator Rivers Environmental Fact-Finding Study.*

Kaplan, H. and Hill, K. 1992 The evolutionary ecology of food acquisition. In B. Winterhalder (ed.), *Evolutionary Ecology and Human Behaviour*, pp.167-202. New York: Aldine De Gruyter.

Kayser, M., Brauer, S., Weiss, G., Schiefenhövel, W., Underhill, P., and M. Stoneking 2001 Independent histories of human Y chromosomes from Melanesia and Australia. *The American Journal of Human Genetics* 68(2001): 173-190.

Keeley, L.H. 1982 Hafting and retooling: Effects on the archaeological record. *American Antiquity* 47:798-809.

Kelly, R.L. 1988 The three sides of a biface. *American Antiquity* 53:717-734.

Kelly, R.L. 1992 Mobility/sedentism: concepts, archaeological measures and effects. *Annual Review of Anthropology* 21:43-66.

Kelly, R.L. and Todd, L.C. 1988 Coming into the country: early paleoindian hunting and mobility. *American Antiquity* 53:231-244.

Kenyon, A.S. and Stirling, D.L. 1900 Australian Aboriginal stone implements, a suggested classification. *Proceedings of the Royal Society of Victoria* 13:191-197.

Kerr, R.A. 1998 Warming's unpleasant surprise: shivering in the greenhouse? *Science* 281:156-8.

Kerr, R.A. 1999 Big El Niños ride on the back of slower climate change. *Science* 283:1108-9.

Kershaw, A.P. 1983 The vegetation record from northeastern Australia 7±2ka. In Chappell, J. and Grindrod, A. (eds) *CLIMANZ 1*, pp.100-1. Canberra: The Australian National University.

Kershaw, A.P. 1995 Environmental change in Greater Australia. *Antiquity* 69:656-76.

Kershaw, A.P. and Nix, H.A. 1989 The use of bioclimatic envelopes for estimation of quantitative paleoclimatic values. In Donnelly, T.H. and Wasson, R.J. (eds) *CLIMANZ 3 Proceedings of the Symposium*, pp.78-85. Canberra: Division of Water Resources, CSIRO.

Knox, J.C. 1993 Large increases in flood magnitude in response to modest changes in climate. *Nature* 361:430-2.

Kooyman, B.P. 2000 *Understanding Stone Tools and Archaeological Sites*. Calgary: University of Calgary Press and University of New Mexico Press.

Koutavas, A., Lynch-Steiglitz, J., Marchitto, T.M.j. and Sachs, J.P. 2002 El Niño-like pattern in Ice Age tropical Pacific sea surface temperature. *Science* 297:226-231.

Kuhn, S. 1990 A geometric index of reduction for unifacial stone tools. *Journal of Archaeological Science* 17:585-593.

Kuhn, S.L. 1992 On planning and curated technologies in the Middle Paleolithic. *Journal of Anthropological Research* 48:185-207.

Kuhn, S.L. 1995 *Mousterian Lithic Technology*. Princeton: Princeton University Press.

Lamb, L. 1996 Investigating changing stone technologies, site use and occupational intensities at Fern Cave, north Queensland. *Australian Archaeology* 42:1-6.

Lamb, L. 2005 Backed and forth: an assessment of typological categories and technological continuums. In Clarkson, C. and Lamb, L. (eds) *Lithics 'Down Under': Australian Perspectives on Lithic Reduction, Use and Classification*. BAR International Series S1408, pp.35-42. Oxford: Archaeopress.

Lambeck, K. and Chappell, J. 2001 Sea level change through the last glacial cycle. *Science* 292:679-86.

Lampert, R.J. 1971 *Burrill Lake and Currarong*. Canberra: Department of Prehistory, The Australian National University.

Larson, D.O., Neff, H., Graybill, D.A., Michaelsen, J. and Ambos, E. 1996 Risk, climatic variability, and the study of Southwestern prehistory: an evolutionary perspective. *American Antiquity* 61:217-241.

Law, B. 2005 Stone artefact reduction, mobility and arid zone settlement models: A case study from Puritjarra Rockshelter, Central Australia. In Clarkson, C. and Lamb, L. (eds) *Lithics 'Down Under': Australian Perspectives on Lithic Reduction, Use and Classification*. BAR International Series S1408, pp.81-94. Oxford: Archaeopress.

Layton, R. 1997 Small tools and social change. In McConvell, P. and Evans, N. (eds) *Archaeology and Linguistics*, pp.377-384. Oxford: Oxford University Press.

Lees, B. 1992a The development of chenier sequence on the Victoria delta, Joseph Bonaparte Gulf, northern Australia. *Marine Geology* 103:214-24.

Lees, B. 1992b Geomorphological evidence for late Holocene climate change in northern Australia. *Australian Geographer* 23:1-10.

Lees, B., Lu, Y. and Head, J. 1990 Reconnaissance thermoluminescence dating of northern Australian coastal dune systems. *Quaternary Research* 34:169-185.

Lees, B., Lu, Y. and Price, D.M. 1992 Thermoluminescence dating of dunes at Cape Lampert, east Kimberleys, northwestern Australia. *Marine Geology* 106:131-9.

Lenoir, M. 1986 Un mode d'obtention de la retouche "Quina" dans la Moustérian de Combe Grenal (Domme, Dordogne). *Bulletin de la Société Anthropologique de la Sud Ouest* 21:153-160.

Leonard, R.D. 1989 Resource specialization, population growth, and agricultural production in the American southwest. *American Antiquity* 54:491-503.

Lourandos, H. 1985 Intensification and Australian prehistory. In Price, T.D. and Brown, J.A. (eds) *Prehistoric Hunter-Gatherers: The Emergecne of Cultural Complexity*, pp.385-423. Orlando, Florida: Academic Press.

Lyman, R.L., Wolverton, S. and O'Brien, M.J. 1998 Seriation, superposition, and interdigitation: a history of Americanist graphic depictions of culture change. *American Antiquity* 63:239-261.

MacArthur, R.H. and Pianka, E.R. 1966 On optimal use of a patchy environment. *American Naturalist* 100:603-609.

MacDonald, D.H. 1998 Subsistence, sex and cultural transmission in Folsom culture. *Journal of Anthropological Archaeology* 17:217-239.

Macgregor, O. 2001 Controlled experimental research into the mechanics of flaked stone artefact production. Unpublished BA (Hons) Thesis: The Australian National University.

Macgregor, O. 2005 Abrupt terminations and stone artefact reduction potential. In Clarkson, C. and Lamb, L. (eds) *Lithics 'Down Under': Australian Perspectives on Stone Artefact Reduction, Use and Classification*. BAR International Series S1408, pp.57-66. Oxford: Archaeopress.

Mackay, A. 2005 Informal movements: changing mobility patterns at Ngarrabullgan, Cape York Australia. In Clarkson, C. and Lamb, L. (eds) *Lithics 'Down Under': Australian Perspectives on Stone Artefact Reduction, Use and Classification*. BAR International Series S1408, pp.95-108. Oxford: Archaeopress.

McCarthy, F. 1948 The Lapstone Creek Excavation: two culture periods revealed in eastern New South Wales. *Records of the Australian Museum* 22:1-34.

McCarthy, F. and McArthur, M. 1960 The food quest and the time factor. In Mountford, C.P. (ed.) *Records of the American-Australian Scientific Expedition to Arnhem Land*, pp.145-194. Melbourne: Melbourne University Press.

McCarthy, F.D. 1949 The prehistoric cultures of Australia. *Oceania* 19:305-19.

McCarthy, F.D. 1958 Culture succession in south eastern Australia. *Mankind* 5:177-190.

McCarthy, F.D. 1964 The archaeology of the Capertee Valley, N.S.W. *Records of the Australian Museum* 26:197-246.

McCarthy, F.D. 1967 *Australian Aboriginal Stone Implements*. Sydney: Australian Museum.

McCarthy, F.D., Brammell, E. and Noone, H.V.V. 1946 The Stone Implements of Australia. *Memoirs of the Australian Museum* 9:1-94.

McCarthy, L. and Head, L. 2001 Holocene variability in semi-arid vegetation: new evidence from *Leporillus* middens from the Flinders Ranges, South Australia. *The Holocene* 11:681-689.

McConvell, P. 1990 The linguistic prehistory of Australia: Opportunities for dialogue with archaeology. *Australian Archaeology* 31:3-27.

McConvell, P. 1996 Backtracking to Babel: the chronology of Pama-Nyungan expansion in Australia. *Archaeology in Oceania* 31:125-44.

McGlone, M.S., Kershaw, A.P. and Markgraf, V. 1992 El Niño/Southern Oscillation climatic variability in Australasian and South American paleoenvironmental records. In Diaz, H.F. and Markgraf, V. (eds) *El Niño: Historical and Paleclimatic Aspects of the Southern Oscillation*, pp.435-462. Cambridge: Cambridge University Press.

McNamara, J.N. 1982 Optimal patch use in a stochastic environement. *Theoretical Population Biology* 21:269-288.

McNiven, I. 1992 Delamere 3: Further excavations at Yiwarlarlay (Lightning Brothers Site), Northern Territory. *Australian Aboriginal Studies* 1992:67-73.

McPhail, M.K. and Hope, G.S. 1985 Late Holocene mire development in montane southeastern Australia: a sensitive climatic indicator. *Search* 15:344-9.

Merlan, F. 1989 *Report to Australian Heritage Commission Survey of Aboriginal Sites in the Northwest of the Northern Territory*. Canberra: Australian Heritage Commission.

Metcalfe, D. and Barlow, K.R. 1992 A model for exploring the optimal trade-off between field processing and transport. *American Anthropologist* 94:340-356.

Minc, L. and Smith, K. 1989 The spirit of survival: Cultural responses to resource variability in north Alaska. In Halstead, P. and O'Shea, J. (eds) *Bad Year Economics*, pp.8-39. Cambridge: Cambridge University Press.

Mitchell, S.R. 1949 *Stone-Age Craftsmen. Stone Tools and Camping Places of Australian Aborigines*. Melbourne: Tait Book Company.

Mithen, S.J. 1990 *Thoughtful Foragers: A Study of Prehistoric Decision Making*. Cambridge: Cambridge University Press.

Moore, M.W. 2003 Flexibility of stone tool manufacturing methods on the Georgina River, Camooweal, Queensland. *Archaeology in Oceania* 38:23-37.

Morrow, T.A. 1997 End scraper morphology and use-life: an approach for studying paleoindian lithic technology and mobility. *Lithic Technology* 22:51-69.

Morwood, M. 2002 *Visions from the Past: The archaeology of Australian Aboriginal Art*. Crows Nest: Allen and Unwin.

Morwood, M. and Hobbs, D.R. 1995a Quinkan Prehistory: The archaeology of Aboriginal art in S.E. Cape York Peninsula, Australia. *Tempus* 3.

Morwood, M. and Hobbs, D.R. 1995b Themes in tropical prehistory. *Antiquity* 265:747-768.

Mulvaney, D.J. 1969 *The Prehistory of Australia*. London: Thames and Hudson.

Mulvaney, D.J. and Joyce, E.B. 1965 Archaeological and Geomorphological Investigations on Mt. Moffatt Station, Queensland, Australia. *Proceedings of the Prehistoric Society* 31:147-212.

Mulvaney, D.J. and Kamminga, J. 1999 *Prehistory of Australia*. Allen and Unwin.

Myers, A. 1989 Reliable and maintainable technological strategies in the Mesolithic of mainland Britain. In Torrence, R. (ed.) *Time, Energy and Stone Tools*, pp.78-91. Cambridge: Cambridge University Press.

Nagooka, L. 2002 The effects of resource depression on foraging efficiency, diet breadth and patch use in southern New Zealand. *Journal of Anthropological Archaeology* 21:419-442.

Neeley, M.P. and Barton, C.M. 1994 A new approach to interpreting late Pleistocene microlith industries in southwest Asia. *Antiquity* 68:275-288.

Neiman, F.D. 1995 Stylistic variation in evolutionary perspective: implications for decorative diversity and inter-assemblage distance in Illinois Woodland ceramic assemblages. *American Antiquity* 60:7-36.

Nelson, M.C. 1991 The study of technological organization. *Archaeological Method and Theory* 3:57-100.

Newcomer, M.H. 1971 Some quantitative experiments in handaxe manufacture. *World Archaeology* 3:85-92.

Newcomer, M.H. 1975 "Punch technique" and Upper Paleolithic blades. In Swanson, E.H. (ed.) *Lithic Technology: Making and Using Stone Tools*, pp.97-102. The Hague: Mouton Publishers.

Nix, H.A. and Kalma, J.D. 1972 Climate as a dominant control in the bio-geography of northern Australia and New Guinea. In Walker, D.L. (ed.) *Bridge and Barrier: the Natural and Cultural History of Torres Strait*, pp.61-92. Canberra: The Australian National University Press.

Nott, J. and Price, D. 1999 Waterfalls, floods and climate change: evidence from tropical Australia. *Earth and Planetary Science Letters* 171:267-276.

O'Connell, J.F. and Allen, J. 2004 Dating the colonization of Sahul (Pleistocene Australia–New Guinea): a review of recent research. *Journal of Archaeological Science* 32:1-19.

O'Connell, J.F. and Hawkes, K. 1984 Food choice and foraging sites among the Alyawara. *Journal of Anthropological Research* 40:504-535.

O'Connor, S. 1995 Carpenter's Gap rockshelter 1: 40,000 years of occupation in the Napier Ranges, Kimberley, W.A. *Australian Archaeology* 40:48-9.

O'Connor, S. 1999 *30,000 Years of Aboriginal Occupation*. Terra Australis. 14. Canberra: Department of Archaeology and Natural History and Centre for Archaeological Research.

O'Connor, S., Veth, P. and Hubbard, N. 1993 Changing interpretations of postglacial human subsistence and demography in Sahul. In Smith, M., Spriggs, M. and Fankhauser, B. (eds) *Sahul in Review: Pleistocene Archaeology in Australia, New Guinea and Island Melanesia*, pp.95-108. Canberra: Department of Prehistory, Research School of Pacific Studies, The Australian National University.

Odell, G.H. 1989 Experiments in lithic reduction. In Amick, D.S. and Mauldin, R.P. (eds) *Experiments in Lithic Technology*, pp.163-198. Oxford: British Archaeological Reports.

Odell, G.H. 1994 Prehistoric hafting and mobility in the North American Midcontinent: Examples from Illinois. *Journal of Anthropological Archaeology* 13:51-73.

Orians, G.H. and Pearson, N.E. 1979 On the theory of central place foraging. In Horn, D.J., Mitchell, R.D. and Stairs, G.R. (eds) *Analysis of Ecological Systems*, pp.154-177. Columbus: Ohia State University.

Pardoe, C. 1984 Prehistoric human morphological variation in Australia. PhD Thesis: The Australian National University.

Pardoe, C. 1990 The demographic basis of human evolution in southeastern Australia. In Meehan, B. and White, N. (eds) *Hunter-Gatherer Demography: Past and Present*, pp.59-70. Sydney: University of Sydney Press.

Pardoe, C. 1993 The Pleistocene is still with us: Analytical constraints and possibilities for the study of ancient human remains in archaeology. In Smith, M., Spriggs, M. and Fankhauser, B. (eds)

Sahul in Review: Pleistocene Archaeology in Australia, New Guinea and Island Melanesia, pp.81-94. Canberra: Department of Prehistory, Research School of Pacific Studies.

Parry, W.J. and Kelly, R.L. 1987 Expedient core technology and sedentism. In Johnson, J.K. and Morrow, C.A. (eds) *The Organization of Core Technology*, pp.285-304. Boulder: Westview Press.

Patterson, L.W. 1982 Replication and classification of large sized lithic debitage. *Lithic Technology* 11:50-8.

Patterson, L.W. 1990 Characteristics of bifacial-reduction flake-size distribution. *American Antiquity* 55:550-8.

Patterson, L.W. and Sollberger, J.B. 1978 Replication and classification of small size lithic debitage. *Plains Anthropologist* 23:103-112.

Pelcin, A. 1997a The effect of core surface morphology on flake attributes: evidence from a controlled experiment. *Journal of Archaeological Science* 24:749-756.

Pelcin, A. 1997b The effect of indentor type on flake attributes: evidence from a controlled experiment. *Journal of Archaeological Science* 24:1107-1113.

Pelcin, A. 1997c The formation of flakes: the role of platform thickness and exterior platform angle in the production of flake initiations and terminations. *Journal of Archaeological Science* 24:1107-1113.

Pelcin, A. 1998 The threshold effect of platform width: a reply to Davis and Shea. *Journal of Archaeological Science* 25:615-620.

Phagan, C.J. 1985 Lithic technology: flake analysis. In MacNeish, R., Nelken-Terner, A., Phagan, C.J. and Vierra, R. (eds) *Prehistory of the Ayacucho Basin, Peru*, pp.233-281. Michigan: The University of Michigan Press.

Pontifex, I.R. and Mendum, J.R. 1972 *Fergusson River, Northern Territory*. 1:25,000 Geological Series - Explanatory Notes. Sheet SD/52-12. Department of National Development. Bureau of Mineral Resources, Geology and Geophysics.

Prentiss, W.C. 1998 The reliability and validity of a lithic debitage typology: implications for archaeological intepretation. *American Antiquity* 63:635-650.

Prentiss, W.C. and Romanski, E.J. 1989 Experimental evaluation of Sullivan and Rosen's debitage typology. In Amick, D.S. and Mauldin, R.P. (eds) *Experiments in Lithic Technology*, pp.89-99. Oxford: British Archaeological Reports.

Ramp, D. and Coulson, G. 2002 Density dependence in foraging habitat preference of eastern grey kangaroos. *OIKOS* 98:393-402.

Rhode, D. 1990 On transportation costs of Great Basin resources: an assessment of the Jones-Madsen model. *Current Anthropology* 31:413-419.

Richerson, P.J., Boyd, R. and Bettinger, R.L. 2001 Was agriculture impossible during the Pleistocene but mandatory during the Holocene? A climate change hypothesis. *American Antiquity* 66:387-411.

Rodbell, D.T., Seltzer, G.O., Anderson, D.M., Abbott, M.B., Enfield, D.B. and Newman, J.H. 1999 A ~15,000-year record of El Niño-driven alluviation in southwestern Ecuador. *Science* 283:516-21.

Roddam, W. 1997 Like, --But Oh How Different: stone point variability in the Top End, N.T.: Northern Territory University.

Root, M.J. 1997 Production for exchange at the Knife River flint quarries, North Dakota. *Lithic Technology* 22:33-50.

Roth, W.E. 1904 *Domestic Implements, arts and manufactures*. North Queensland Ethnography, Bulletin No.7.

Rowland, M.J. 1999a Holocene environmental variability: have its impacts been underestimated in Australian pre-History? *The Artefact* 22:11-48.

Rowland, M.J. 1999b The Keppel Islands - a '3000 year' event revisited. In Hall, J. and McNiven, I. (eds) *Australian Coastal Archaeology*. Research Papers in Archaeology and Natural History, No.31, pp.141-156. Canberra: The Australian National University.

Sahlins, M.D. 1972 *Stone Age Economics*. Chicago: Aldine.

Sanders, B. 1975 Scrapers from Ingaladdi. MA Thesis: The Australian National University.

Schiffer, M.B. and Skibo, J.M. 1987 Theory and experiment in the study of technological change. *Current Anthropology* 28:595-622.

Schiffer, M.B. and Skibo, J.M. 1997 The explanation of artefact variability. *American Antiquity* 62:27-50.

Schindler, D.L., Hatch, J.W., Hay, C.A. and Bradt, R.C. 1984 Thermal alteration of Bald Eagle Jasper. *American Antiquity* 49:173-177.

Schrire, C. 1982 *The Alligator Rivers: Prehistory and Ecology in Western Arnhem Land*. Terra Australis. 7. Canberra: Department of Prehistory, Research School of Pacific Studies, The Australian National University.

Schulmeister, J. and Lees, B. 1992 Morphology and chronostratigraphy of a coastal dunefield; Groote Eylandt, northern Australia. *Geomorphology* 5.

Schulmeister, J. and Lees, B. 1995 Pollen evidence from tropical Australia for the onset of ENSO-dominated climate at c.4000 BP. *The Holocene* 5:10-18.

Sellet, F. 1993 Chaîne opératoire; the concept and its applications. *Lithic Technology* 18:106-112.

Shennan, S. 2003 Learning. In Hart, J.P. and Terrell, J.E. (eds) *Darwin and Archaeology: A Handbook of Key Concepts*, pp.201-224. Westport, Connecticut: Bergin & Garvey.

Shott, M. J.1986 Technological organization and settlement mobility: An ethnographic examination. *Journal of Anthropological Research* 42:15-51.

Shott, M.J. 1989 On tool-class use lives and the formation of archaeological assemblages. *American Antiquity* 54:9-30.

Shott, M.J. 1994 Size and form in the analysis of flake debris: review of recent approaches. *Journal of Archaeological Method and Theory* 1.

Shott, M.J. 1996 Stage versus continuum models in the debris assemblage from production of a fluted biface. *Lithic Technology* 21:6-22.

Shott, M.J. 2003 Chaine operatoire and reduction sequence. *Lithic Technology* 28:95-105.

Singh, G. and Luly, J. 1991 Changes in vegetation and seasonal climate since the last full glacial at Lake Frome, South Australia. *Paleogeography, Paleoclimatology, Paleoecology* 84:75-86.

Slack, M.J., Fullagar, R.L.K., Field, J.H., and Border, A. 2004 New Pleistocene ages for backed artefact technology in Australia. *Archaeology in Oceania* 39: 131-138.

Slayter, R.O. 1970 Climate of the Ord-Victoria area. In Stewart, G.A. (ed.) *Lands of the Ord-Victoria Area, W.A. and N.T.* Land Research Series. Commonwealth Scientific and Industrial Research Organization, Australia.

Smith, E.A. 1983 Anthropological applications of optimal foraging theory: a critical review. *Current Anthropology* 24:625-651.

Smith, M. 1985 A morphological comparison of Central Australian seedgrinding implements and Pleistocene-age grindstones. *The Beagle* 2:23-38.

Smith, M. and Cundy, B.J. 1985 Distribution maps for backed blades and flaked stone points in the Northern Territory. *Australian Aboriginal Studies* 1985:32-37.

Sobel, E. and Bettles, G. 2000 Winter hunger, winter myths: subsistence risk and mythology among the Klamath and Modoc. *Journal of Anthropological Archaeology* 19:276-316.

Speth, J.D. 1974 Experimental investigations of hard-hammer percussion flaking. *Tebiwa* 17:7-36.

Speth, J.D. 1975 Miscellaneous studies in hard-hammer percussion flaking. *American Antiquity* 40.

Speth, J.D. 1981 The role of platform angle and core size in hard-hammer percussion flaking. *Lithic Technology* 10:16-21.

Stahle, D.W. and Dunn, J.E. 1984 An analysis and application of the size distribution of waste flakes from the manufacture of bifacial stone tools. *World Archaeology* 14:84-97.

Steffen, A., Skinner, E.J. and Ainsworth, P.W. 1998 A view to the core: technological units and debitage analysis. In Ramenofsky, A. and Steffen, A. (eds) *Unit Issues in Archaeology*, pp.131-146. Salt Lake City: University of Utah Press.

Stephens, D.W. and Charnov, E.L. 1982 The logic of risk-sensitive foraging. *Animal Behaviour* 29:628-629.

Stockton, E.D. 1973 Shaw's Creek Shelter: Human displacement of artefacts and its significance. *Mankind* 9:112-117.

Sullivan, A.P. and Rozen, K.C. 1985 Debitage analysis and archaeological interpretation. *American Antiquity* 50:755-779.

Sweet, I.P. 1972 *Delamere, Northern Territory*. 1:250 000 Geological Series. Canberra: Australian Government Publishing.

Thompson, W.A., Vertinsky, I. and Krebs, J.R. 1974 The survival value of flocking in birds: A simulation model. *Journal of Animal Ecology* 43:785-820.

Tindale, N.B. 1957 Cultural succession in South-Eastern Australia from Late Pleistocene to the Present. *Records of the South Australian Museum* 13.

Tindale, N.B. 1965 Stone implement making among the Nakako Ngadadjara, and Pitjantjara of the Great Western Desert. *Records of the South Australian Museum* 15:131-164.

Tindale, N.B. 1985 Australian Aboriginal techniques of pressure-flaking stone implements. In Plew, M.G., Woods, J.C. and Pavesic, M.G. (eds) *Stone Tool Analysis: Essays in Honour of Don E. Crabtree*, pp.1-33. University of New Mexico Press.

Torrence, R. 1983 Time budgeting and hunter-gatherer technology. In Bailey, G. (ed.) *Hunter-Gatherer Economy in Prehistory*, pp.11-22. Cambridge: Cambridge University Press.

Torrence, R. 1989 Re-tooling: towards a behavioral theory of stone tools. In Torrence, R. (ed.) *Time, Energy and Stone Tools*, pp.57-66. Cambridge: University of Cambridge.

Trenberth, K.E. and Hoar, T.J. 1996 The 1990-1995 El Niño-Southern Oscillation event: longest on record. *Geophysical Research Letters* 23:57-60.

Tudhope, A.W., Chilcott, C.P., McCulloch, M.T., Cook, E.R., Chappell, J., Ellam, R.M., Lea, W.L., Lough, J.M. and Shimmield, G.B. 2001 Variability in the El Niño-Southern Oscillation through a glacial-interglacial cycle. *Science* 291:1511-1517.

Ugan, A., Bright, J. and Rogers, A. 2003 When is technology worth the trouble? *Journal of Archaeological Science* 30:1315-1329.

van Holst Pellekaan, S. M., M. Frommer, J. A. Sved, and B. Boettcher. 1998. Mitochondrial control-region sequence variation in Aboriginal Australians. *American Journal of Human Genetics* 62:435-449.

Veth, P. 1989 Origins of the Western Desert Language: convergence in linguistic and archaeological space and time models. *Archaeology in Oceania* 24:81-92.

Veth, P. 1993a Islands in the Interior: A Model for the Colonisation of Australia's Arid Zone. *Archaeology in Oceania* 24:81-92.

Veth, P.M. 1993b *Islands in the Interior: The Dynamics of Prehistoric Adaptations Within the Arid Zone of Australia*. International Monographs in Prehistory, Archaeological Series 3. Michigan: Ann Arbor.

Webster, P.J. and Palmer, T.N. 1997 The past and the future of El Niño. *Nature* 390:562-4.

Webster, P.J. and Streten, N.A. 1978 Late Quaternary ice age climates of tropical Australasia: interpretations and reconstructions. *Quaternary Research* 10:279-309.

Weissner, P. 1982 Risk, reciprocity and social influence on!Kung economics. In Leacock, E. and Lee, R. (eds) *Politics and History in Band Societies*, pp.61-84. Cambridge: University of Cambridge Press.

White, C. 1971 Man and Environment in Northwest Arnhem Land. In Mulvaney, D.J. and Golson, J. (eds) *Aboriginal Man and Environment in Australia*, pp.141-157. Canberra: ANU Press.

White, J.P. 1969 Typologies for some prehistoric flaked stone artefacts of the Australian New Guinea Highlands. *Archaeology and Physical Anthropology in Oceania* 4:18-46.

White, J.P. and O'Connell, J.F. 1982 *A Prehistory of Australia, New Guinea and Sahul*. Sydney: Academic Press.

Whittaker, J. 1994 *Flintknapping: Making and Understanding Stone Tools*. Austin: University of Texas Press.

Wilmsen, E.N. 1968 Functional analysis of flaked stone artefacts. *American Antiquity* 33:156-161.

Winterhalder, B. 1986 Diet choice, risk and food sharing in a stochastic environment. *Journal of Anthropological Archaeology* 5:369-392.

Winterhalder, B. 2002 Models. In Hart, D.M. and Terrell, J.E. (eds) *Darwin and Archaeology: A Handbook of Key Concepts*, pp.201-224. Westport, Conneticut: Bergin and Garvey.

Winterhalder, B., Lu, F. and Tucker, B. 1999 Risk-sensitive adaptive tactics: Models and evidence from subsistence studies in biology and anthropology. *Journal of Anthropological Research* 7:301-348.

Wylie, A. 1989 Archaeological cables and tacking: the implications of practice for Bernstein's 'Options beyond objectivism and relativism'. *Philosophy of the Social Sciences* 19:1-18.

Young, D.E. and Bonnichsen, R. 1984 *Understanding Stone Tools: A Cognitive Approach*. Peopling of the Americas Process Series Volume 1. Orono: Centre for the Study of Early Man, University of Maine.

Appendix A. Attributes recorded on stone artefacts

Attributes recorded on broken artefacts or artefacts smaller than 2cm in maximum dimension.

Information – All Artefacts

*   Site
*   Record Number
*   Heat Affected?

Technological Type – All Artefacts

*   Core
*   Flake
*   Retouched Flake
*   Flaked Piece

Raw Material Type – All Artefacts

*   Chert (Unprovenanced, Tindall, Banyan)
*   Quartzite (Jasper gorge, Antrim Plateau)
*   Silcrete
*   Basalt
*   Chalcedony
*   Quartz
*   Glass
*   Other

Dimensions – All Artefacts

*   Weight
*   Percussion Length
*   Proximal Width
*   Width
*   Distal Width
*   Thickness

Dorsal Scar Characteristics of Flakes

*   No Arrises
*   Old Platform Angle

Flake Platform Characteristics

*   Platform Width
*   Platform Thickness
*   Platform Angle
*   Platform Preparation

Flake Platform Type

*   Focalised
*   Multiple Conchoidal
*   Single Conchoidal
*   Crushed
*   Cortical
*   Combination of Above

Flake Termination Type

*   Feather
*   Hinge
*   Step
*   Outrépassé
*   Crushed

Flake Cortex

*   % Cortex
*   Cortex Location (Platform, Dorsal, Both)
*   Cortex Type (Rounded, Irregular, Angular)

Typology – All Artefacts

*   Unifacial Pont
*   Bifacial Point
*   Burin
*   Burren
*   Spall
*   Tula
*   Tula Slug
*   Lancet
*   Leilira
*   Kimberley Point
*   Grindstone
*   Grindstone Flake
*   Ground Edge Axe
*   Ground Edge Axe Flake
*   Redirecting Flake
*   Combination of the Above
*   Single Platform Core
*   Multiplatform Core
*   Bipolar Core

Retouch Characteristics – Retouched Flakes

*   Retouched Break?
*   Marginal (For Each Segment)
*   Invasive (For Each Segment)

Retouched Platform – Retouched Flakes

*   Base Shape
*   Base Height
*   Base Width

Marginal Attrition – All Artefacts

*   Edge Damage?

Recycling – Retouched Flakes

- Retouched Break?

Burinate Retouch – Retouched Flakes (Burins)

- Number of Burin Spalls

Location of Retouch – Retouched Flakes

- Dorsal Proximal End
- Dorsal Left Proximal
- Dorsal Right Proximal
- Dorsal Left Medial
- Dorsal Right Medial
- Dorsal Left Distal
- Dorsal Right Distal
- Dorsal Distal End
- Ventral Proximal End
- Ventral Left Proximal
- Ventral Right Proximal
- Ventral Left Medial
- Ventral Right Medial
- Ventral Left Distal
- Ventral Right Distal
- Ventral Distal End
- Number of retouched Segments

Retouch Order – Retouched Flakes

- Dorsal Only
- Ventral Only
- Dorsal First
- Ventral First
- Alternating
- DVD
- VDV

Core Scar Characteristics

- Number of Scars >15mm
- Number of Rotations
- Bipolar?
- Longest Face
- No of Aberrant Terminations
- No of Parallel Arrises

Core Dimensions

- Length
- Width
- Thickness
- Base Thickness

Core Platform Characteristics

- Platform Preparation
- No Platform Quadrants
- Last Platform Angle

Core Cortex

- Cortex Location (Platform, Face, Distal, All)

Core Scar Dimensions

- Length1
- Face Length1
- Width1
- Termination 1
- Length2
- Face Length2
- Width2
- Termination 2
- Length3
- Face Length3
- Width3
- Termination 3
- Length4
- Face Length4
- Width4
- Termination 4

Attributes recorded on complete artefacts greater than 2cm in maximum dimension.

Information – All Artefacts

- Site
- Square
- Spit
- Record Number
- Heat Affected?
- Resin?
- Resin Location

Technological Type – All Artefacts

- Core
- Flake
- Retouched Flake
- Flaked Piece

Raw Material Type

- Chert (Unprovenanced, Tindall, Banyan, Black, Oolitic, Montejinni, Hydrothermal Red)
- Quartzite (Jasper gorge, Antrim Plateau)
- Silcrete
- Basalt
- Chalcedony (Hydrothermal, Montejinni)
- Soft Grey Volcanic/Metamorphic
- Quartz
- Glass
- Other

Dimensions – All Artefacts

- Weight
- Percussion Length
- Proximal Width
- Width
- Distal Width
- Thickness
- Perimeter of Margins

Dorsal Scar Characteristics of Flakes

- No Arrises
- Old Platform Angle

Flake Platform Characteristics

- Platform Width
- Platform Thickness
- Platform Angle
- Platform Preparation

Flake Platform Type

- Focalised
- Multiple Conchoidal
- Single Conchoidal
- Crushed
- Cortical
- Combination of Above

Flake Termination Type

- Feather
- Hinge
- Step
- Outrépassé
- Crushed

Flake Cortex

- % Cortex
- Cortex Location (Platform, Dorsal, Both)
- Cortex Type (Rounded, Irregular, Angular)

Typology – All Artefacts

- Unifacial Pont
- Bifacial Point
- Burin
- Burren
- Spall
- Tula
- Tula Slug
- Lancet
- Leilira
- Kimberley Point
- Grindstone
- Grindstone Flake
- Ground Edge Axe
- Ground Edge Axe Flake
- Redirecting Flake
- Combination of the Above
- Single Platform Core
- Multiplatform Core
- Bipolar Core

Retouch Characteristics – Retouched Flakes

- Retouch Length
- Base Shape (if retouched)
- Retouched Break?
- Serrated Pressure?
- Stepped?
- t/T1
- t/T2
- t/T3
- Retouch Edge Angle 1
- Retouch Edge Angle 2
- Retouch Edge Angle 3

- Retouch Depth
- Number of Notches
- Notch Type
- Notch Location
- Notch Width
- Notch Depth
- Bipolar Butt Removal?
- Marginal (For Each Segment)
- Invasive (For Each Segment)

Retouched Platform – Retouched Flakes

- Base Shape
- Base Height
- Base Width

Marginal Attrition – All Artefacts

- Edge Damage?
- Edge Rounding?

Recycling – Retouched Flakes

- Old Weathered Surface?
- Retouched Break?

Burinate Retouch – Retouched Flakes (Burins)

- Number of Burin Spalls
- Orientation of Burin Blow
- Number of Steps
- Number of Platforms
- Platform Type (Flaked, Plain, Break)
- Last Platform Angle
- Platform Width
- Platform Thickness
- Spall Length1
- Spall Length 2
- Spall Length 3
- Spall Length 4
- Deepest Step Length
- Deepest Step Depth
- Opposed Platforms?

Burinate Retouch – Burin Spalls

- No Previous Spalls
- Nature of Previous Margin (Unifacial Retouch, Bifacial Retouch, Plain, Edge Damage, Edge Rounding)

Location of Retouch – Retouched Flakes

- Dorsal Proximal End
- Dorsal Left Proximal
- Dorsal Right Proximal
- Dorsal Left Medial
- Dorsal Right Medial

- Dorsal Left Distal
- Dorsal Right Distal
- Dorsal Distal End
- Ventral Proximal End
- Ventral Left Proximal
- Ventral Right Proximal
- Ventral Left Medial
- Ventral Right Medial
- Ventral Left Distal
- Ventral Right Distal
- Ventral Distal End
- Number of retouched Segments

Retouch Order – Retouched Flakes

- Dorsal Only
- Ventral Only
- Dorsal First
- Ventral First
- Alternating
- DVD
- VDV

Core Scar Characteristics

- Number of Scars >15mm
- Number of Rotations
- Bipolar?
- Longest Face
- No of Aberrant Terminations
- No of Parallel Arrises

Core Dimensions

- Length
- Width
- Thickness
- Base Thickness

Core Platform Characteristics

- Platform Thickness
- Platform Width
- Platform Preparation
- No Platform Quadrants
- Last Platform Angle

Core Cortex

- Cortex Location (Platform, Face, Distal, All)

Core Scar Dimensions

- Length1
- Face Length1
- Width1
- Termination 1
- Length2

- Face Length2
- Width2
- Termination 2
- Length3
- Face Length3
- Width3
- Termination 3
- Length4
- Face Length4
- Width4
- Termination 4

Appendix B. Descriptions of excavated materials from Nimji

Table B.1. Stratigraphic descriptions for Squares AB 8-10 from the 1966 excavation at Nimji (Ingaladdi) (after Cundy 1990).

Layer	Cumulative Depth (cm)	Spits	Description	Munsell
I	0-70	1-10	Finely sorted yellow/red sand containing a high charcoal fraction, contributing to its dark grey colour. The sand is generally free of roof fall. This layer grades into Unit II.	5YR 2.75/1
II	70-100	11-13	Unit II is transitional between Unit I and III and is not as well defined. It is composed of yellow/red sand and contains a small number of medium sized rocks (10-20cm diameter).	5YR 3/2
III	100-170	14-21	Unit III matrix is a mixture of orange sand and sub-rounded sandstone rubble (3-10cm diameter).	5YR 3/4
IV	170-190	22-25	Unit IV is comprised of bright orange sand gravel mix (gravel size range is 2-6mm diameter). The units depth varies from 10-20cm depending on the density of the underlying bedrock from which it appears to be derived.	5YR 4-5/6

Table B.2. Non-Stone cultural materials from Squares AB9, Nimji.

Spit	Cumulative Depth (cm)	Exfoliation (g)	Large Quartz Crystals (#)	Calcite Crystals (#)	Teeth and Jaws (g)	Bone (g)	Mussel Shell (g)	Burnt Earth (g)	Ochre (g)
1	6.4				0.3	0.4	4.9		
2	14.0		1	1					0.1
3	21.6		1						
4	29.2								
5	36.8								0.4
6	44.5								2.6
7	52.1								0.3
8	59.7								4.8
9	62.2					0.1	0.1		0.5
10	74.9								1.6
11	82.6								
12	90.2								
13	97.8	186.0							61.8
14	105.4								62.4
15	113.0								135.7
16	120.7		2	2				1.0	20.7
17	128.3							0.8	3.3
18	135.9			1				85.2	1.8
19	143.5							86.5	31.0
20	151.1								
21	158.8	2.0							
22	166.4								
23	174.0								
24	181.6								

Table B.3. Non-stone cultural materials from Squares AB10, Nimji.

Spit	Cumulative Depth (cm)	Ochered Exfoliation	Exfoliation	Large Quartz Crystals (#)	Calcite Crystals (#)	Teeth & Jaws (g)	Bone (g)	Mussel Shell (g)	Burnt Earth (g)	Ochre (g)
1	11.4			1.0		0.4	1.7	4.7		2.5
2	19.1									
3	26.7								0.5	
4	34.3				2.0	0.2				16.2
5	41.9	2	1		1.0					10.0
6	49.5									1.0
7	57.2									1.5
8	64.8								0.4	1.1
9	67.3									
10	80.0									
11	87.6									13.8
12	95.3									
13	102.9						0.5			13.4
14	110.5									
15	118.1									
16	125.7			2.0						0.1
17	133.4			2.0					0.4	1.0
18	141.0									
19	148.6									
20	156.2								28.0	
21	163.8									
22	171.5									
23	179.1									
24	186.7									

Table B.4. Stone artefact counts from Squares AB9, Nimji.

Spit	Cumulative Depth (cm)	Hammerstone Fragments	Cores	Core Fragments	Glass Kimberley Fragments	Bifacial points	Unifacial Points	Lancets	Leiliras	Tulas	Retouched Flakes	Bipolar Lancet Butts	Bipolar Lancet Distal	Bipolar Distal Unifacial Points	Burrens	Burins	Redirecting Flakes	Spalls	Axe Flakes	Grindstone Fragments	Bipolar Flakes	Bipolar Cores
1	11.4				1	8	18	13	11		13					2	1	2	2			
2	19.1						12	8	1		8						2					
3	26.7					1	7	6	1		4						1	3				
4	34.3					2	18	14			8	1	2	1	1		1		1	2		
5	41.9						24	31	1	2	3	6					1	6	4			
6	49.5					11	60	66		2	10				1			3	1			
7	57.2					12	38	33		1	8					1		1				
8	64.8					26	38	28		2	8						1					
9	67.3					2	36	11			6							1		1		
10	80.0		1			1	4	6			3											
11	87.6	1	1								5											
12	95.3						2	1			2						3					
13	102.9	1	2	4							7						3					
14	110.5	1		1							3						2					
15	118.1										15						8					
16	125.7		1	2							33					1	10	1			1	1
17	133.4		1	1							26						8				2	
18	141.0		2	6							27					2	12				2	
19	148.6		1	1							6						2					
20	156.2		5	2							11						6					
21	163.8		5	2							10						7					
22	171.5		2	7							5						3					
23	179.1		2	5							3						4					
24	186.7																2					

Table B.5. Stone artefact counts from Squares AB10, Nimji.

Spit	Cumulative Depth (cm)	Hammerstones	Hammerstone Fragments	Cores	Core Fragments	Pressure Retouch	Bifacial Points	Unifacial Points	Recycled Unifacial Points	Lancets	Leilliras	Tulas	Retouched Flakes	Bipolar Lancet Butts	Bipolar Distal Unifacial Points	Burins	Redirecting Flakes	Spalls	Axe Flakes	Bipolar Cores	Heat Affected	Chert Manuports	Quartzite Manuports
1	11.4						4	40		31	2	2	21	2		1		1	2		9		
2	19.1							19		23			13				1	1			5		
3	26.7			1			7	15		17	1	1	8	2	1	1		2	1		17		
4	34.3					1	6	20		29	1		22	2		1	1	3	1		10		
5	41.9					2	3	45	2	72		2	13	9		1		4			12		
6	49.5						11	56		69			14	6		2	2	14	2		28		
7	57.2				1		29	79		25		4	11	1				5			14		
8	64.8						50	71		49		3	13	1			1	2			14		
9	72.3				1		3	12		15			8	1			1						
10	80.0			1			1	3		1			3				2	1			7		
11	87.6			5	3								9				1	1			14		
12	95.3									1			3				2				4		
13	102.9	2			2					1			2				5				17		
14	110.5												8				6				9		
15	118.1												9				3						
16	125.7	2	1	4	5								40				16	1		1	30		
17	133.4												14				4				22		
18	141.0	2	4	2	1								4				1				10		
19	148.6	2	1	3	1								9				4				26	1	2
20	156.2	1		10	1								21				7	1			37		
21	163.8			1	1								8				2				12		
22	171.5			1									1				1				3		
23	179.1																1						
24	186.7																						

Table B.6. Raw material counts from Squares AB9, Nimji.

Split	Cumulative Depth (cm)	Glass	Unprovenanced Chert	Yellow Tindall Chert	Local Hydrothermal Chert	Local Brecciated Chalcedony	Hydrothermal Chalcedony	Red Banyan Chert	Antrim Plateau Quartzite	White Jasper Gorge Quartzite	Basalt	Silcrete	Other Volcanic	Oolitic Chert	Sandstone	Black Chert	Quartz	Soft Grey Volcanic / Metamorphic	Stone Artefacts (g)	Total No.
1	11.4	4	43	7	9	10	9	4	200	18	13	2						1	892	320
2	19.1		25	1	4	14	13	5	169	8	1							5	377	245
3	26.7		11	1	10	1	9	4	50	5		2						1	150	94
4	34.3	2	12	3	6	3	19	5	111	16	2							2	387	181
5	41.9		39	12	4	10	11	15	174	13		4			2	2		3	721	283
6	49.5		96	18	6	22	26	23	455	34		3						8	931	694
7	57.2		50	3	8	11	18	13	398	21		10				2		2	634	527
8	64.8		48	14	17	15	8	17	646	26		4				1		1	837	804
9	67.3		34	3		20	1	8	395	3					1				534	269
10	80.0		14	2	5	7	6	1	59	3								2	283	98
11	87.6		19	3	3	16	4	3	51	3		1			2	2		1	460	106
12	95.3		8	1		7	3	1	50	1						2		4	214	70
13	102.9		57	6	7	24	17	7	224						1			3	721	333
14	110.5		68	10	7	29	62	6	182	5		1			5			4	499	335
15	118.1		150	25	57	104	55	12	413	7	2	2		2				3	1605	841
16	125.7		194	8	66	100	50	14	1009	22			3	1			1	1	2962	1474
17	133.4		123	5	41	118	33	11	830	9	1	1	2	1		2	2	1	3108	1196
18	141.0		97		28	56	4	4	455	8			1		1	1			2110	688
19	148.6		37	2	7	29	9	9	178	4			3			1			904	272
20	156.2		26	3	5	10	14	6	100	5									1851	168
21	163.8		68	4	13	30	12	2	226	5		1				1			1865	362
22	171.5		49	3	13	19	7	7	202	5									1466	312
23	179.1		9		3	9		2	42	1									877	73
24	186.7		3					2	5	4									56	14

Table B.7. Raw material counts from Squares AB10, Nimji.

Spit	Cumulative Depth (cm)	Glass	Other	Unprovenanced Chert	Montejinni Chalcedony	Yellow Tindall Chert	Local Hydrothermal Chert	Local Brecciated Chalcedony	Hydrothermal Chalcedony	Red Banyan Chert	Antrim Plateau Quartzite	White Jasper Gorge Quartzite	Basalt	Silcrete	Other Volcanic	Oolitic Chert	Sandstone	Black Chert	Quartz	Crystal Quartz	Volcanic / Metamorphic	Stone Artefacts (g)	Total Number
1	11.4	2		10	8	4	11		65	24	334	30	10	8	6		1					1375	513
2	19.1			9	27	4	4	1	74	33	269	25		10	4		1					625	461
3	26.7			12	6	6	11		53	20	224	21	6	3	1							464	363
4	34.3			10	22	5	6	2	88	27	351	35	2	15	6							696	570
5	41.9			11	15	7	8	1	77	37	351	24		15	5						1	568	552
6	49.5		1	13	34	5	5	1	138	51	492	57	1	25	1			2			4	1028	830
7	57.2			13	11	7	5	2	73	28	473	34		60							1	881	707
8	64.8			19	14	16	15	5	77	35	764	73	1	83				4			4	1358	1110
9	67.3			4	12		5	1	33	23	141	14		9			1					359	243
10	80.0			11	0	1	2	10	14	8	53	7		5								378	111
11	87.6			16	38	1	12	11	26	22	103	11		2							2	558	244
12	95.3			11	10		7	17	5	5	109	4		2							2	394	172
13	102.9			22	26	3	31	24	29	7	196	2		1		1					1	1006	342
14	110.5			19	33	1	21	29	30	13	187	5	1	2							3	893	344
15	118.1			1	82		25	22	22	17	179	2										711	349
16	125.7			54	77	3	60	114	55	50	921	11		9			1	1	1		8	5231	1364
17	133.4			21	48	5	38	52	38	14	508	9		3			1		3		4	2152	746
18	141.0			11	9		12	24	18	6	118	6						1			1	1249	205
19	148.6			22	20	6	30	37	23	7	205	14						2			6	2163	371
20	156.2			38	22	4	36	36	26	9	251	10		4							3	4553	441
21	163.8			14	22		15	42	27	9	186	7				1					1	1435	323
22	171.5			1	3	1	3	6	2	1	22	3									2	196	44
23	179.1							3		1	5	7										241	17
24	186.7						1	1			11	1						1				126	15

Appendix C. Descriptions of excavated materials from Garnawala 2

Table C.1. Description of stratigraphic layers from the 1990 and 1991 excavations at Garnawala 2.

Layer	Cumulative Depth (cm)	Colour	Texture	pH	Description
Ia	0-2	2.5YR 4/3 Reddish-brown	Loamy sand	6.5	Loose surface sediments containing organic macro-remains (e.g.macropod and cattle faeces, leaves, twigs). Stone artefacts and contact items are also present. Sediments are very loose and disturbed.
Ib	2-16	2.5YR 4/3 Reddish-brown	Loamy sand	6.5	Sediments are similar to those of SU1a in their cultural and non-cultural contents. The only difference between Layer Ia and Layer Ib is that the latter is more compact than the former. In most squares the changeover from Layer Ia and Layer Ib is marked.
II	16-24	2.5YR 3/1 Dark reddish-grey	Clayey sand	5.5	A well defined layer of white and grey ash. It is relatively loose but appears to be undisturbed. This layer consists almost entirely of ash and charcoal with many *in situ* materials observed during the excavation (including contact items). The boundary between Layer IIb and overlying Layer Ib and Layer IIa is well defined. The boundary with underlying Layer III is well defined.
III	24-35.7	2.5YR 4/2 Weak red	Loamy sand	5.5	Layer III is a well defined layer containing cultural materials. It is more compact and immediately overlies the bedrock. In some parts of the excavated area the upper surface of the bedrock itself broke-up as small flat plates of sandstone which were excavated as part of Layer III. In one part of the excavated area a currently active termite nest appeared at the base of Layer III. This termite nest was isolated from Layer III during excavation, and was left *in situ* (i.e. termite contamination was clearly demarcated stratigraphically and isolated from the *in situ* deposits).
IV	35.7-120.7	2.5YR 4/3 Reddish-brown	Loamy sand	5.5	Uniform sediments. Loose, decomposed sandstone fragments are abundant. This layer is very rocky, in the sense that sandstone pieces are common, including large pieces.
V	120.7				This is the sandstone bedrock, the upper surface of which is fragmenting in flat plates in parts of the excavation.

Table C.2. Size and stratigraphic association of excavation units from Square Q28, Garnawala 2.

Spit	Stratigraphic Unit	Mean Spit Thickness (cm)	Cumulative Depth (cm)	Area Excavated (m²)	Sediments Excavated (kg)
1	Ia	1.2	1.2	0.25	3.5
2	III	2.1	3.3	0.25	4.0
3	III	3.5	6.8	0.25	11.5
4	III	1.7	8.5	0.25	12.5
5	III	4.3	12.8	0.25	13.0
6	III	3.2	16.0	0.25	11.0
7	III	1.8	17.8	0.25	11.0
8	III	2.6	20.4	0.25	11.0
9	III	3.2	23.6	0.25	11.0
10	III	3.8	27.4	0.21	11.0
11	III	4.3	31.7	0.17	10.0
12	III	4.0	35.7	0.15	10.0
13	III/IV interface	4.6	40.3	0.12	12.0
14	IV	3.5	43.8	0.18	26.5
15	IV	4.2	48.0	0.16	10.0
16	IV	4.2	52.2	0.16	12.0
17	IV	3.0	55.2	0.20	12.0
18	IV	5.0	60.2	0.22	11.0
19	IV	3.3	63.5	0.22	11.0
20	IV	5.0	68.5	0.15	12.0
21	IV	7.0	75.5	0.14	10.5
22	IV	7.2	82.7	0.14	9.0
23	IV	6.9	89.6	0.19	12.0
24	IV	6.7	96.3	0.14	14.5
25	IV	10.3	106.6	0.14	13.0
26	IV	14.1	120.7	0.17	6.5

Table C.3. Non-stone cultural materials from Square Q28, Garnawala 2.

Spit	Cumulative Depth (cm)	Charcoal (g)	Animal Faeces (g)	Organics (g)	Bone (g)	Ochre (g)
1	1.2	5.5		18	2	3
2	3.3	4.1		4	1	6
3	6.8	9.4		4	0	11
4	8.5	12.7		1	1	14
5	12.8	20.3		2	<0.1	2
6	16	21.3		2		9
7	17.8	14.1		1	0	1
8	20.4	13.2	14	2	0	
9	23.6	18.4		2	<0.1	2
10	27.4	15.0	1	2		
11	31.7	2.9		3		5
12	35.7	5.1		1		9
13	40.3	0.6		0		0
14	43.8	0.8		2		0
15	48	0.5		0		1
16	52.2	0.3		0		1
17	55.2	1.6		1		10
18	60.2	0.4		0		1
19	63.5	0.4		1		3
20	68.5	0.7		1		1
21	75.5	0.1		1		1
22	82.7			0		
23	89.6			2		
24	96.3	<0.1		0		0
25	106.6	0.1		0		
26	120.7	0.3		1		

Table C.4. Stone artefact counts from Square Q28, Garnawala 2.

Spit	Cumulative Depth	Cores	Core Fragments	Serrated Pressure Retouch	Bifacial Points	Unifacial Points	Transformed Unifacial Points	Lancets	Leiliras	Tulas	Retouched Flakes	Bipolar Lancet Butts	Burins	Burrens	Redirecting Flakes	Spalls	Ground Edge Axes	Axe Flakes	Grindstone Fragment	Bipolar Core	Heat Affected
1	1.2	1		3		12	1	21							1	1		1			13
2	3.3					5		5			1		1			1		2			8
3	6.8	1				10		29	1				1		4	1		2			26
4	8.5	1		2	2	6		19			1	1	2		2	2					16
5	12.8					14		42				4	2		5	8	1	1	1		27
6	16					11	2	25			1			1		5		3			13
7	17.8				1	17	1	26				4	1			3					23
8	20.4				4	16	1	23				3	1		1	6					15
9	23.6				1	24		28					2		1	9					10
10	27.4				1	23	1	38		1		1	2		2	5		1			15
11	31.7				6	27	1	28		2			1			2					15
12	35.7				12	8		5							1						8
13	40.3				2																6
14	43.8	1						1							1						6
15	48																				3
16	52.2							2							2						3
17	55.2														1						6
18	60.2	1						1			1				4						9
19	63.5														4					2	27
20	68.5	4													1						27
21	75.5	1	1																		11
22	82.7																				1
23	89.6		1												1						5
24	96.3																				6
25	106.6																				2
26	120.7																				

Table C.5. Raw material counts from Square Q28, Garnawala 2.

Spit	Cumulative Depth	Glass	Chert	Montejinni Chalcedony	Tindall Yellow Chert	Local Hydrothermal chert	Nimji Brecciated Chalcedony	Local White Chert	Local Hydrothermal Chalcedony	Red Banyan Chert	Antrim Plateau Quartzite	Jasper Gorge Quartzite	Basalt	Silcrete	Other Volcanic	Oolitic chert	Sandstone	Black Chert	Quartz	Calcite Crystal	Crystal Quartz	Soft Grey Metamorphic / Volcanic	Total No.
1	1.2		13		2	11		8	40	6	114	27		3			9					1	234
2	3.3	3	7		1	4		9	17	8	152	24	2	3								1	231
3	6.8		67		2	28		23	179	20	487	83	5	7	1	1	4	1				2	910
4	8.5		55		2	35		16	223	28	439	81	1	6			1	3				4	894
5	12.8		76		2	39		56	359	41	627	132	1	6				3		1		9	1352
6	16		67		4	31		29	238	30	549	105		22			1					4	1080
7	17.8		41		6	34		30	262	24	471	41		9		1		1	3			1	920
8	20.4		29			34		37	140	28	415	67		9		1		5				1	769
9	23.6		51		2	29		42	221	37	361	62		6				2				1	815
10	27.4		23		1	16		24	148	23	206	33		2				2					478
11	31.7		32		4	14		19	63	21	239	15		15		1		2				1	427
12	35.7		21			15	1	19	32	8	127	10		4									236
13	40.3		14	1		7		7	14	2	48	4		3									100
14	43.8		24			21		6	2	5	105	5		3									171
15	48		32			15		7	27	4	98	2											185
16	52.2		21			21		3	30	6	81	1											166
17	55.2		91			57	2	19	31	10	208	4				2							422
18	60.2		56		1	37	7	6	36	6	262	5				1	3	1	3				415
19	63.5		44	1	1	63	3	11	38	12	351	5		1				1	1				536
20	68.5		43			57		23	16	12	212	12		2		1			2				384
21	75.5		27			21		11	21	3	88	4											175
22	82.7		3		1	8	2	1	3	1	24	0		2									43
23	89.6		9		1	7	1	2	2	1	43	2											67
24	96.3		10			13		10	6	7	63	3						3					117
25	106.6		9			5.0		2	7	3	31	4											62
26	120.7		4			9			4	2	17												36

Appendix D. Descriptions of excavated materials from Jagoliya

Table D.1. Stratigraphic description for the 1998 excavation at Jagoliya.

Layer	Depth (cm)	Munsell	Colour	pH	Texture	Description	9E Spits	9F Spits	8E Spits	8F Spits
I	0-4.2	5YR 5/3	Dark reddish grey	6	Loamy Sand	Loose ashy sand with abundant charcoal and organic matter. Kangaroo/feral pig wallows have disturbed the surface in places.	1	1	1	1
II	4.2-5	5YR 5/2	Reddish grey	6.5	Clayey Sand	More compact ashy sand. Undulating surface due to wallows. Organic matter reduced significantly.	1	2	2-4	2-3
III	5-9.4	10YR 4/2	Dark grayish brown	6.5	Loamy Sand	Compact ashy sand. Roots mark the interface with Layer IV.	2	3-5	5-8	6-8
IVa	10-12.9	5YR 5/2	Reddish grey	5.5-6	Clayey Sand	A thin lens of charcoal and burnt earth.	4 & 5	7	11	10-11
IVb	19-29	10YR 4/2	Dark greyish brown	6	Clayey Sand	A thick lens of burnt earth.	7	12-13	14	16-17
IV	12.9-32.2	5YR 4/2	Dark reddish grey	6	Clayey Sand	A uniform, compact ashy sand. Roots are particularly common.	3, 6 & 8-10	6, 8-11, 14	9-10, 13, 15-17	9, 12-15, 18
V	32.2-48.5	5YR 4/2	Dark reddish grey	5	Clayey Sand	A dark coloured sand with abundant stone artefacts. This layer is clearly visible as a much darker band in all sections.	11-15	15-20	18-19	19-22
VI	48.5-57.2	5YR 6/3	Light reddish brown	6.5	Loamy Sand	A lighter coloured loose layer directly overlying rubble layer. Rubble content is increasing.	16-17	21-24	20-24	23-25
VII	57.2-125	5YR 6/3	Light reddish brown	6.5	Loamy Sand	Extremely rubbly layer with loose sand in between large pieces of sandstone and unsorted gravel of all sizes. This layer becomes more compact with depth.	18-29	25-37	25-34	26-34

Table D.2. Spit depths by square for Jagoliya.

Spit	8E Mean Depth (cm)	8E Cumulative Depth (cm)	8F Mean Depth (cm)	8F Cumulative Depth (cm)	9E Mean Depth (cm)	9E Cumulative Depth (cm)	9F Mean Depth (cm)	9F Cumulative Depth (cm)
1	4.2	4.2	1.0	1.0	7.5	7.5	3.8	3.8
2	0.8	5.0	1.5	2.5	1.0	8.5	0.7	4.5
3	1.2	6.3	1.5	4.0	1.0	9.5	0.5	4.9
4	--	--	2.1	6.1	3.2	12.7	1.7	6.6
4b	3.2	9.4	--	--	--	--	--	--
5	2.2	11.6	1.5	7.6	3.2	15.9	3.1	9.7
6	0.6	11.6	2.9	11.2	1.0	15.9	0.4	10.1
6b	1.3	12.9	--	--	2.4	18.4	--	--
7	3.9	16.8	2.7	13.9	2.1	20.5	3.0	13.1
8	1.3	18.2	1.9	15.8	2.2	22.7	2.3	15.5
9	2.8	21.0	1.9	17.7	3.5	26.2	2.2	17.6
10	2.7	23.7	3.0	20.7	5.4	31.6	2.4	20.0
11	3.0	26.7	3.0	23.7	1.7	33.4	3.1	23.1
12	2.4	29.0	1.7	25.5	1.7	35.1	2.2	25.2
13	3.1	32.2	2.8	28.3	2.8	37.9	0.8	26.1
14	2.9	35.1	3.6	31.8	2.8	40.8	1.8	27.9
15	3.0	38.0	3.2	35.0	2.0	42.8	2.1	30.0
16	3.3	41.4	3.2	38.1	2.4	45.2	3.4	33.4
17	2.0	43.3	2.2	40.4	2.9	48.1	3.4	36.8
18	2.8	46.1	3.1	43.5	2.2	50.3	2.0	38.8
19	2.4	48.5	1.5	44.9	3.5	53.8	2.0	40.8
20	2.4	51.0	2.2	47.2	1.1	54.9	3.1	43.9
21	1.7	52.7	2.7	49.8	2.8	57.7	3.2	47.1
22	3.1	55.7	3.4	53.2	2.6	60.3	0.7	47.9
23	1.5	57.2	1.8	55.0	1.8	62.1	2.8	50.7
24	2.2	59.4	2.5	57.5	2.9	65.1	2.3	53.0
25	1.9	61.3	1.2	58.7	2.3	67.4	2.4	55.4
26	5.2	66.5	1.5	60.1	2.8	70.1	2.5	57.9
27	2.0	68.5	3.8	64.0	5.4	75.5	1.9	59.8
28	2.0	70.4	3.3	67.3	3.1	78.7	4.9	64.7
29	2.4	72.8	3.7	70.9	4.7	83.4	3.6	68.3
30	3.9	76.7	7.8	78.7	16.4	99.8	3.7	72.1
31	6.6	83.3	6.0	84.7	6.2	106.0	4.8	76.9
32	13.7	97.0	10.0	94.7	24.7	130.7	4.9	81.8
33	9.2	106.2	4.9	99.6			5.1	86.9
34	10.5	116.7					9.9	96.8
35	6.6	123.3					5.8	102.6
36	1.5	124.8						

Table D.3. Non-stone cultural materials for Square 8E, Jagoliya.

Spit	Depth (cm)	Charcoal (g)	Matrix (g)	Faecal Pellets (g)	Seeds (g)	Organics (g)	Teeth (g)	Bone (g)	Mussel Shell (g)	Land Snail (g)	Resin (g)	Beads	Burnt Earth (g)	Ochre (g)	Insect (g)	Termite Nest (g)
1	3.8	42.4	352.8	2.3	2.3	66.4		1.4	2.8			1	2.3	4.4	2	8.1
2	4.5	7.3	93.7	0.8	0.8	4.8	1	0.2	0.8		1.5		0.2	0.6	<0.1	1.7
3	4.9	4.6	51.1		0.6	5.8		0.1					0.1	0.2	0.2	1.8
4	6.6	12.4	124.7		1.3	5.6		0.1					0.5	<0.1	0.4	2.1
5	7.0	7.3	114.5		<0.1	8.4		0.3	<0.1	<0.1			0.1	0.2	0.2	3.6
6	8.4	14.2	126.1		0.3	11						1	1.1	1.1	1.3	1.7
7	11.4	34.4	203		0.1	9.8		0.2	<0.1				0.9	0.2	0.5	5.3
8	13.7	17.4	118.2		<0.1	8.4		0.1					0.3	0.6	0.7	11.2
9	15.8	12.7	170.2		<0.1	7.3		0.8					0.2	<0.1	4.2	
10	18.2	15	139.8	<0.1		82.5		<0.1					0.3	0.5	0.1	2.4
11	21.3	11.1	115.8		<0.1	14.4							1.7	1.4	0.2	153
12	23.5	11.2	151.4			15.4							0.7			323
13	24.3	6	50.9			32.6							0.2	<0.1	<0.1	2.1
14	26.1	3.8	85.4			48.9								0.7		46.2
15	28.2	12.1	122.1			50.4							2	0.3		21.8
16	31.6	13.5	247.7		<0.1	8.6							3.7	1.5	<0.1	12.1
17	35.0	10.6	454.4			23.5							6.1		0.1	
18	37.0	4	279.9			16		<0.1					1.1	1		
19	39.0	3.7	277.3			2							1.7	2.5	<0.1	
20	42.2	2.7	340.3			1.3		<0.1					1.1	<0.1	<0.1	
21	45.3	1.8	426.4			1.6							9.4			
22	46.1	0.9	260.8			1.7							0.2	<0.1	<0.1	
23	48.9	0.5	334.3			4.1								11		
24	51.2	0.9	616.4			1.4								1.9		
25	53.6	0.3	774.5			1.3							1	0.2		
26	56.1	0.2	655.2			1.3										
27	58.0	<0.1	1126.4			0.2							0.1			
28	62.9	0.1	1482.8			0.6										
29	66.6	0	2858			0.5										
30	70.3	<0.1	3879.7			1.8										
31	75.1	0	3108			1										
32	80.0	<0.1	2086.1			0.2										
33	85.1	<0.1	4970.6			2.2										
34	95.0		1528.6			0.4										
35	100.8		3610.4			0.9										

Table D.4. Non-stone cultural materials for Square 8F, Jagoliya.

Spit	Depth (cm)	Charcoal (g)	Matrix (g)	Faecal Pellets (g)	Seeds (g)	Organics (g)	Bone (g)	Mussel Shell (g)	Beads	Burnt Earth (g)	Ochre (g)	Resin (g)	Insect (g)	Termite Nest (g)
1	1	17.1	146	2.4	1.8	23.4	0.2	0.3		0.6	0.8		0.4	1.5
2	2.49	20	145.5	0.3	0.9	12.2	0.3	4.6	1	1	0.8	0.2	0.5	0.6
3	3.98	12.4	99.6	2.2	0.4	7.2	2.2	0.2		0.4	1		0.4	0.9
4	6.12	30.1	193.5	1.7	1.6	8.5	1.1	1.7		0.4	1.5		0.7	7.2
4b		1.8	7.5			0.7								0.1
5	7.6	8.7	58.8			3.6	0.3	0.3		0.5			1.2	2.3
6	8.3	19.4	115.6	0.2	0.1	6.5	0.2	<0.1		0.2	0.3		0.6	3.2
7	11.2	20.8	98.6	0.2	<0.1	4.6	0.2			0.4	0.2		0.7	1.6
8	13.9	25.8	166.4			10.1		<0.1		0.9			<0.1	62.1
9	15.8	8.8	129.4			20.8				1			0.3	13.9
10	17.7	12.9	94.4			11.8	<0.1			3	0.8		0.5	9.3
11	20.7	22.1	136.8		<0.1	21.5				<0.1	0.5		<0.1	0.2
12	23.7	10.3	130.3			6.4				1			0.1	61.9
13	25.5	17.3	165			8.5				0.1				11.3
14	28.3	10	151.4		<0.1	30				0.1	1.1		<0.1	0.4
15	31.8	16.4	211.2			16	<0.1			2.2	1.6			
16	35	11	297.5			2.9	<0.1			3.6	0.2			
17	38.1	5	13.3							2.3	1.5			
18	40.4	3.8	297.7			45.3	<0.1							
19	43.5	1.6	698.5			19.8				2.4	6.2			
20	44.9	0.7	375.1			2.3				0.4				
21	47.2	1.2	350.5			1.51								
22	49.8	1.7	952			1.6				5	0.3			
23	53.2	0.3	1245.7			1.5				3.8				
24	55	0.5	1084.6			2.1								
25	57.5	0.2	795.8			0.4				0.7				
26	58.7	0.2	454.4			0.6								
27	60.1	<0.1	749.4			0.4								
28	64	0.1	1241.2			1.2								
29	67.3	<0.1	3012.8			0.4								
30	70.9	0	4360.8			2.5								
31	78.7	<0.1	5565.3			2.7								
32	84.7	0	3151.3			2.5								
33	94.7	0	1883.5			0.6								
34	99.6	0	3344.4			0.6								

Table D.5. Non-stone cultural materials for Square 9E, Jagoliya.

Spit	Depth (cm)	Charcoal (g)	Ochre Stained Rock	Matrix (g)	Faecal (g)	Seeds Pellets (g)	Organics (g)	Bone (g)	Mussel Shell (g)	Fish Bone (g)	Land Snail (g)	Beads	Burnt Earth (g)	Ochre (g)	Resin (g)	Insect (g)	Termite Nest (g)
1	7.5	107		918	2.2	20	70.3	3.8	13	<0.1	<0.1		7.6	6.1	6.5	6.1	22.6
3	8.5	0		0			0										
4	9.5	0.1		2.5			0.1							<0.1		<0.1	
5	12.7	0.7		7.4			2.2	0.2	<0.1							<0.1	0.3
6a	12.7	0.5		3.6			0.2										
6b	12.7	14.6		98.6	0.1	0.8	6.8	0.2	<0.1					0.3		0.1	7
7	12.7	34.5		231		0.4	7.7	1.3				1	1.3	0.6		1.8	26.1
8	14.8	21.4		136.7			4.3	0.1					0.3	0.1		1.5	16
9	17.0	18.8		136.5			5.1	<0.1	<0.1				1.6	0.9		0.3	11.4
10	20.5	35.7		282.1			26.1	0.2					1.2			0.2	24.8
11	25.9	28.1		321.9			9.5						0.5	0.9		0.6	86.8
12	27.7	12.6		104.5			10.9						1.2	3.8		0.1	1.6
13	29.4	15.8		177.1			8.9						1.4	0.4			0.6
14	32.2	13.1		261.3			9						1.5	15			6.7
15	35.1	4.5		212.8			3.6						2	4.1		<0.1	
16	37.1	4		342.6			2.6						7	0.8			
17	39.5	2.4		685.5			2.1						29	0.1		<0.1	
18	42.4	1.3		372.7			1.1						0.9	1.5		<0.1	
19	44.6	1.4		529.5			0.7	0.1					0.1	1.3		<0.1	
20	48.1	1.8		522			1.2						0.6	1.5			
21	49.2	1.1	1	408.1			0.3						0.4	2.4			
22	52.0	0.8		840			0.5						0.1				
23	54.6	0.6		1060.1			2.8										
24	56.4	0.1		1186.3			0.8										
25	59.4	<0.1		916.1			0.2							1.2			
26	61.66	0		764													
27	64.23	0.6		2169.8			0.7										
28	70	0.1		1321			0.3							0.8		<0.1	
29	73.14	0		3252.9			1.2										
30	77.88	0		4362.4			0.8										
31	94.24	0.6		9413.5			3.2						<0.1	457		<0.1	
32	99.73	0.4		5300.8			1							2.9			
33	123.5	0.3		10502			1.6										

Table D.6. Non-stone cultural materials for Square 9F, Jagoliya.

Spit	Depth (cm)	Charcoal (g)	Ochre Stained Stone	Matrix (g)	Faecal Pellets (g)	Seeds (g)	Organics (g)	Bone (g)	Mussel Shell (g)	Land Snail (g)	Resin (g)	Beads	Burnt Earth (g)	Ochre (g)	Insect (g)	Termite Nest (g)
1	4.2	83		674	5.4	9.6	75.8	3.6	2.5	<0.1	0.7	1	1.6	0.8	2.7	57.5
2	5.0	9.1		48.2			10.3	<0.1	<0.1				0.3		0.4	2.6
4	6.3	13		271.2	0.3		16.1	0.1	0.3				0.5	0.1	0.1	2.3
5	9.4	18.3		137.9			21.8	0.2	0.3				0.1	0.2	0.6	5.8
6a	11.6	4.4		84.7	<0.1	0.2	6.4	0.1	<0.1				0.4	0.3	0.4	7
7	12.9	13.6		153.7	0.1	0.3	6.7	0.2	<0.1	<0.1			0.4	0.3	<0.1	5.4
8	16.8	34.6		240.2			11.8	0.5	<0.1				0.3	<0.1		73.3
9	18.2	18.9		107.5			8.3	<.1							0.5	5.9
10	21.0	16.2		138.1		0	10.4	<0.1					0.8	0.3	0.3	12.5
11	23.7	19.7		184.6			9						1.6	0.8	0.8	
12	26.7	20.4		196.9			25.2						0.4	1	0.5	0.7
13	29.0	12.5		138.7		0.2	3.5		<0.1				0.9	2.1	<0.1	5.6
14	32.2	15.3		260.7			13.8					1	2.2		<0.1	
15	35.1	10.1					22.3						1.4			0.3
16	38.0	4.4		409.2			4.5						5.1	0.7		
17	41.4	3.3		436.5			7						7.3	0.5	<0.1	<0.1
18	43.3	0.6		285.2			0.5						1	0.2	<0.1	
19	46.1	1.3		338.7			0.5						1.5	0.8		0.1
20	48.5	2.1		322.8			0.2						1.2		<0.1	
21	51.0	0.5	1.0	225.8		0	5.2						0.4			
22	52.7	<0.1		109.8			0.1						0.3			
23	55.7	0.2		753.8			0.3						1.7	0.6		
24	57.2	0.1		495.8			1.2									
25	59.4	0.1		815.6			1.1									
26	61.3	<0.1		594.6			<0.1									
27	66.5	0.1		1261.9			0.7							0.4		
28	68.5	<0.1		4442.4			1.6							<0.01		
29	70.4			2478.2			<0.1									
30	72.8			1972.9			0.4						0.6			
31	76.7		1.0	3680.8			2.2									
32	83.3	0.1		3942			0.5									
33	97.0	<0.1		7313.9			0.6									
34	106.2			4884.3			0									
35	116.7	0.1		3544.9			4.1									
36	123.3			2686			2.1									
37	124.8			734.3			0.2									

Table D.7. Stone artefact counts from Square 8E, Jagoliya.

Spit	Cumulative Depth (cm)	Cores	Bifacial Points	Unifacial Points	Lances	Retouched Flakes	Recycled Broken Flakes	Redirecting Flakes	Spalls	Stone Artefacts
1	3.8									28
2	4.5									3
3	4.9									8
4	6.6									14
5	7.0									10
6	8.4									19
7	11.4									57
8	13.7									23
9	15.8									31
10	18.2									40
11	21.3									37
12	23.5									51
13	24.3									17
14	26.1									43
15	28.2									53
16	31.6			1				1		142
17	35.0			1			1			141
18	37.0			5						138
19	39.0			2	2				4	187
20	42.2			4	2		1		1	206
21	45.3			1						209
22	46.1	1	1			1	2	1	1	174
23	48.9		1	1		1				115
24	51.2		2	1						119
25	53.6					1				79
26	56.1					1				55
27	58.0	1				2			2	42
28	62.9	2				1		1		33
29	66.6					1				4
30	70.3									2
31	75.1									0
32	80.0									0
33	85.1									4
34	95.0									1
35	100.8									0

Table D.8. Stone artefact counts for Square 8F, Jagoliya.

Spit	Depth (cm)	Cores	Bifacial Points	Unifacial Points	Lancets	Retouched Flakes	Burin	Redirecting	Spalls	Axe Flakes	Bipolar Core	Stone Artefacts
1	1											13
2	2.49											17
3	3.98											6
4	6.12			1								18
5	7.6											9
6	8.3											18
7	11.2									1		24
8	13.9											32
9	15.8											27
10	17.7									1		28
11	20.7											43
12	23.7											48
13	25.5											69
14	28.3			1								80
15	31.8									1	1	160
16	35		1	2	2							193
17	38.1		1	2	1		1					229
18	40.4			3	2				2	2		178
19	43.5		1	2		1				1	1	236
20	44.9		1		2							125
21	47.2		1		1					1		167
22	49.8		2	1	1							199
23	53.2		1									96
24	55				1							65
25	57.5	?										36
26	58.7								1			25
27	60.1					1		1				11
28	64	1				1						21
29	67.3											0
30	70.9											4
31	78.7											4
32	84.7											1
33	94.7											0
34	99.6											1

Table D.9. Stone artefact counts for Square 9E, Jagoliya.

Spit	Cumulative Depth (cm)	Core	Bifacial Points	Unifacial Points	Lancets	Tula	Retouched Flakes	Recycled Broken Flakes	Burin	Redirecting Flake	Spalls	Axe Flakes	Grindstone Topstone	Stone Artefacts
1	7.5			2	1		3							84
3	8.5													0
4	9.5													0
5	12.7													0
6a	12.7													0
6b														21
7	12.7													35
8	14.8						1							35
9	17.0						1							32
10	20.5			1			1							75
11	25.9													121
12	27.7													52
13	29.4													108
14	32.2			1										138
15	35.1			2										91
16	37.1		1	1	5		1				3			156
17	39.5		1	4	4		2				1	1		183
18	42.4		2	1							2		1	164
19	44.6		5	1	2				1		4			197
20	48.1		4	2										176
21	49.2		2			1	1						1	70
22	52.0	1	1		1									91
23	54.6						2							80
24	56.4	1			1									84
25	59.4		1				2	2						54
26	61.66	2					1							10
27	64.23						2			2				34
28	70	2					2							58
29	73.14													5
30	77.88													2
31	94.24						2							12
32	99.73													3
33	123.5													2

Table D.10. Stone artefact counts for Square 9F, Jagoliya.

Spit	Cumulative Depth (cm)	Cores	Bifacial Points	Unifacial Points	Lancets	Tula	Retouched Flakes	Burin	Redirecting Flakes	Spalls	Axe Flakes	Grindstone Flakes	Stone Artefacts
1	4.2												57
2	5.0												7
4	6.3				1								16
5	9.4												21
6a	11.6												17
7	12.9												23
8	16.8												59
9	18.2												38
10	21.0												50
11	23.7												67
12	26.7												71
13	29.0												72
14	32.2			1									117
15	35.1			1						1	1		136
16	38.0		3	5						2	1		174
17	41.4			3	1	1	4				1		207
18	43.3		2	2						1	1	1	124
19	46.1		1	2			1			2	1		244
20	48.5		2	1		1				3			176
21	51.0												129
22	52.7		2									1	33
23	55.7		1	1			3						131
24	57.2												41
25	59.4						2						62
26	61.3						1						40
27	66.5						1		2				23
28	68.5	1											26
29	70.4						1						14
30	72.8												3
31	76.7												2
32	83.3												0
33	97.0												0
34	106.2												1
35	116.7												0
36	123.3												0
37	124.8												0

Appendix E. Descriptions of excavated materials from Gordolya

Table E.1. Stratigraphic descriptions for Square N25, Gordolya.

Layer	Cumulative Depth (cm)	Colour	Texture	pH	Description
Ia	0-7	5YR 3/4 Dark reddish-brown	Sandy clay loam	8.5	Loose, scuffed surface with abundant organic matter.
Ib	7-15	5YR 4/3 Reddish-brown	Sandy clay loam	8.5	A loose fine sandy layer containing a hearth lens
Ic	15-35	5YR 3/4 Reddish-brown	Sandy clay loam	8.5	A loose fine sandy layer containing a hearth lens
II		5YR 4/3 Dark reddish-brown	Light sandy clay loam	8.5	Compact coarser-grained sandy layer
III	35-54	5YR 3/1 Very dark grey	Light sandy clay loam	8.5	Compact charcoal and ash-rich layer.
IVa	54-60	5YR 3/2 Dark reddish-brown	Light sandy clay loam	8.5	Compact coarser-grained sandy layer
IVb	60-70	Reddish-brown	Sandy loam	6.5	Sterile sand layer
V	70				Bedrock

Table E.2. Non-stone cultural materials from Square M24, Gordolya.

Spit	Cumulative Depth cm	Charcoal (g)	Bone (g)	Ochre (g)	Shell (g)	Other Organics (g)
1	2.7	76.4	25.9	0.1		100.3
2	3.9	73.2	7.1		0.9	51.5
3	7.0	63.3	3.6	1.0	0.8	18.7
4	9.7	74.8	4.3	0.1		1.1
5	12.6	76.0	6.6			
6	15.2	64.5	9			
7	21.2	46.1	12.4			
8	24.6	24.4	7.5			
9	27.0	18.5	24.9			
10	30.9	2.4	15.9	1.1	0.5	
11	35.1	71.1	41.1	0.5	0.5	
12	38.9	48.5	11.6			
13	43.5	85.9	27.1	0.1	1.2	
14	47.4	30.6	21.6			
15	50.2	17.9	16.3	1.9	0.5	
16	54.2	14.4	9.1	1.0	0.2	
17	57.0	6.5	3.6	3.0		
18	59.6	0.2	0.1			
19	62.7	0.1	0			

Table E.3. Non-stone cultural materials from Square M25, Gordolya.

Spit	Cumulative Depth (cm)	Charcoal (g)	Bone (g)	Ochre (g)	Shell (g)	Other Organics (g)
1	2.5	83.3	12.3			83.7
2	3.8	49.0	2.7			59.9
3	6.1	131.2	5.2		2.1	46.6
4	9.1	85.9	10.3	0.1	0.4	42.4
5	12.2	83.0	1.8			
6	16.3	149.0	3.7	1.5		
7	19.3	52.0	5.3	2.3	4.2	
8	22.1	15.2	4.9		0.5	
9	24.2	4.3	6.3		0.1	
10	28.7	7.3	11.2			
11	32.8	12.6	12.5	9.9		
12	35.9	8.2	8.6			
13	39.4	10.3	16.3			
14	43.0	12.7	18.2			
15	45.7	12.4	18.9	2.5	0.1	
16	50.3	7.1	13.3	6.2	0.1	
17	52.9	5.5	14.0		0.1	
18	55.5	2.2	2.1	1.9		
19	57.0	0.1	0.0			

Table E.4. Non-stone cultural materials from Square N24, Gordolya.

Spit	Cumulative Depth cm	Charcoal (g)	Bone (g)	Ochre (g)	Shell (g)	Other Organics (g)
1	3.7	46.7	4.4	0.8		36.4
2	4.5	11.1	0.8			6.2
3	7.9	25.1	2.7			6.2
4	9.7	16.2	0.2			
5	12.2	3.2				
6	15.0	37.3	2.3	0.1	0.1	
7	18.8	8.0	0.8			
8	22.2	7.0	1.2			
9	24.8	17.0	4.9			
10	28.0	95.0	34.7		2.0	
11	31.8	38.9	19.4			
12	34.4	15.3	3.8			
13	38.0	12.6	5.2	0.1		
14	41.1	0.7	4.0	0.3	0.1	
15	43.8	6.6	5.4		0.1	
16	47.6	0.3	2.1			
17	50.5	0.4	1.9	.1.1		
18	53.4	2.6	2.1			
19	56.3	0.7	0.2			
20	59.2	0.2	0.1			

Table E.5. Non-stone cultural materials from Square N25, Gordolya.

Spit	Cumulative Depth (cm)	Charcoal (g)	Bone (g)	Ochre (g)	Shell (g)	Other Organics (g)
1	1.5	102.3	7.6	2.1		36.7
2	2.7	40.2	3.0	113.0	0.1	35.8
3	5.3	63.8	5.5		0.6	137.9
4	8.2	33.8	2.3		0.1	5.6
5	11	47.2	1.5	5.9		
6	14	57.8	4.5	1.2	0.2	
7	18	43.4	18.7	0.2	3.0	
8	20	25.1	9.4		0.5	
9	22	34.6	16.8		2.5	
10	26	25.2	39.7		1.4	
11	30	19.3	32.4		0.1	
12	34	33.2	22.5		3.6	
13	37	38.0	27.9		0.3	
14	40	13.4	20.2	0.9		
15	43	17.2	18.4	0.4		
16	47	8.5	8.6	0.1		
17	50	6.1	3.6	0.6		
18	53	4.0	3.9	5.7		
19	55	1.4	3.3			
20	60	2.9	7.9	0.2		
21		0.9	2.0			
22	65	0.3	0.2			
23	67	0.2				

Table E.6. Stone artefact counts from Square M24, Gordolya.

Spit	Cumulative Depth (cm)	Unifacial Points	Lancets	Leilira	Retouched Flakes	Redirecting Flakes
1	2.7		2	1		
2	3.9		2			
3	7.0		1			1
4	9.7	2	1			
5	12.6		2		1	
6	15.2		1		1	
7	21.2					
8	24.6					
9	27.0					
10	30.9				2	
11	35.1					
12	38.9				2	1
13	43.5					
14	47.4					
15	50.2					
16	54.2					
17	57.0					
18	59.6					

Table E.7. Stone artefact counts for Square M25, Gordolya.

Spit	Cumulative Depth (cm)	Cores	Unifacial Points	Lancets	Retouched Flakes
1	2.5		1	1	
2	3.8				1
3	6.1		1	1	
4	9.1				
5	12.2				
6	16.3			2	
7	19.3				
8	22.1				
9	24.2				
10	28.7				
11	32.8				
12	35.9			1	
13	39.4	1			
14	43.0				
15	45.7				1
16	50.3				

Table E.8. Stone artefact counts for Square N24, Gordolya.

Spit	Depth cm	Bifacial Points	Unifacial Points	Lancets	Leilira	Retouched Flakes	Redirecting Flakes
1	3.7			1			
2	4.5			1			
3	7.9		1	2			
4	9.7						
5	12.2						
6	15.0						
7	18.8						
8	22.2						
9	24.8			1			
10	28.0			5	4		
11	31.8		3				
12	34.4			1		1	
13	38.0	2	1				
14	41.1	1					1
15	43.8						
16	47.6						
17	50.5						
18	53.4						
19	56.3						
20	59.2						

Table E.9. Stone artefact counts for Square N25, Gordolya.

Spit	Depth	Hammerstone	Cores	Bifacial Points	Unifacial Points	Lancets	Leilira	Tula	Retouched Flakes	Redirecting Flakes	Bipolar Core
1	1.5	1				1					
2	2.7					1					
3	5.3					2					
4	8.2										
5	11										
6	14					1	1				
7	18				1	2					
8	20							1	1		
9	22				2	1					
10	26				3						
11	30				1	2		1			1
12	34				2	1					1
13	37				1	3					
14	40					2					1
15	43			2		1					
16	47		1								
17	50										
18	53										
19	55									1	
20	60										
21	62								1		
22	65										
23	67										

Table E.10. Raw material counts for Square M24, Gordolya.

Spit	Depth cm	Unprovenanced Chert	Local Hydrothermal Chert	Hydrothermal Chalcedony	Antrim Plateau Quartzite	Red Banyan Chert	Jasper Gorge Quartzite	Basalt	Silcrete	Black Chert	Stone Artefacts (#)	Stone Artefacts (g)
1	2.7				8	1					9	69.3
2	3.9			2	16		2				20	21.7
3	7.0	1		1	8	2					12	21.2
4	9.7			1	5						6	49.8
5	12.6				7	1		1			9	34.6
6	15.2				1	1					2	13.7
7	21.2		1	3	9	2					15	10.0
8	24.6		1	2	11				2		16	10.2
9	27.0	1	4	4	19						28	37.6
10	30.9	1	2	7	27		1				38	57.7
11	35.1		5	15	69	5	3				97	31.8
12	38.9		1	12	44		1		1		59	43.5
13	43.5	3	10	20	106	2	7	2			150	71.4
14	47.4		5	21	88	5	1				120	73.5
15	50.2		10	11	60	8	5			1	95	32.2
16	54.2	2	4	5	34	5	2				52	10.0
17	57.0		1	1	21		3				26	1.1
18	59.6	1			2						3	0.4

Table E.11. Raw material counts for Square M25, Gordolya.

Spit	Depth cm	Glass	Montejinni Chalcedony	Local Hydrothermal Chert	Hydrothermal Chalcedony	Antrim Plateau Quartzite	Red Banyan Chert	Jasper Gorge Quartzite	Basalt	Black Chert	Stone Artefacts (#)	Stone Artefacts (g)
1	2.5					4	1				5	64.7
2	3.8					8					8	318.4
3	6.1		1		1	8	1	3	1	1	16	33.5
4	9.1	1			1	7					8	2.8
5	12.2			2	1	20		6	1		30	1.1
6	16.3				2	13		1			16	5.3
7	19.3				6	14		1			21	38.4
8	22.1				2	4		1			7	2.8
9	24.2				2	12	1	2			18	7.9
10	28.7			2	17	55	8	2			84	8.1
11	32.8			2	4	48	3	4	1	1	63	7.8
12	35.9			1	5	34	3				43	35.0
13	39.4			1	6	49	7				63	17.5
14	43.0			2	6	73	9	1			91	65.5
15	45.7			10	11	68	3	1			93	48.2
16	50.3			4	2	37	2				45	37.2
17	52.9										0	21.1
18	55.5										0	0.0
19	57.0										0	0.0

Table E.12. Raw material counts for Square N25, Gordolya.

Spit	Depth cm	Unprovenanced Chert	Montejinni Chalcedony	Local Hydrothermal Chert	Glass	Hydrothermal Chalcedony	Antrim Plateau Quartzite	Red Banyan Chert	Jasper Gorge Quartzite	Basalt	Silcrete	Stone Artefacts (#)	Stone Artefacts (g)
1	3.7					1	2					3	19.4
2	4.5						9					9	4.4
3	7.9				1	1	26	1				29	14.1
4	9.7	1					7		1			9	0.3
5	12.2					1	13		1			15	0.0
6	15.0				1	3	18	1	3			26	2.1
7	18.8					1	17	1	2			26	1.1
8	22.2	1				1	12		1	1		21	6.2
9	24.8						17	1	4		1	16	93.4
10	28.0			5		18	149	2	6	1		181	77.1
11	31.8	2		3		14	109	1	3	2	1	135	22.8
12	34.4	2		2		6	23		3			36	2.8
13	38.0			5		5	75	3	1		1	90	8.7
14	41.1			8		11	89	8	1			117	5.8
15	43.8			12		9	52	3	2	1		79	8.5
16	47.6	2	1	5		2	33		3	1		47	2.9
17	50.5			3		9	13					25	2.0
18	53.4											19	4.2
19	56.3											12	120.0
20	59.2											2	0.2

Table E.13. Raw material counts for Square N25, Gordolya.

Spit	Depth	Unprovenanced Chert	Glass	Local Hydrothermal Chert	Hydrothermal Chalcedony	Antrim Plateau Quartzite	Red Banyan Chert	Jasper Gorge Quartzite	Basalt	Silcrete	Quartz	Stone Artefacts (#)	Stone Artefacts (g)
1	1.5				2	11						13	88.9
2	2.7				1	7	1					9	7.4
3	5.3					5		2				7	7.9
4	8.2		1			14						15	4.3
5	11					8	1					9	1.1
6	14			4	3	50	2	1	1			61	84.0
7	18	1			5	51	1	1				59	60.1
8	20	2			6	23	1					32	49.3
9	22				3	24		1				28	22.1
10	26	1			8	24		3				36	74.2
11	30	1			11	27	3	7			1	50	74.5
12	34				10	29	2	3				44	36.7
13	37				10	48	1					59	60.4
14	40			2	7	68	3	1				81	33.3
15	43			1	15	168	11	1				196	19.4
16	47			2	5	103	3			4		117	47.7
17	50			3	9	67	4	2				85	7.7
18	53	1		2	3	42	2					50	16.0
19	55	7		1	8	35	2					53	16.9
20	60	4		5	2	52	3					66	12.3
21	65	1		1	2	10						14	6.5

www.ingramcontent.com/pod-product-compliance
Lightning Source LLC
Chambersburg PA
CBHW040453290326

41929CB00059B/3462